Multifaceted Assessment for Early Childhood Education

Multifaceted Assessment for Early Childhood Education

ROBERT J. WRIGHT

Widener University

Los Angeles | London | New Delhi
Singapore | Washington DC

For information:

SAGE Publications, Inc.
2455 Teller Road
Thousand Oaks,
California 91320
E-mail: order@sagepub.com

SAGE Publications Ltd.
1 Oliver's Yard
55 City Road
London EC1Y 1SP
United Kingdom

SAGE Publications India Pvt. Ltd.
B 1/I 1 Mohan Cooperative
Industrial Area
Mathura Road, New Delhi 110 044
India

SAGE Publications Asia-Pacific Pte. Ltd.
33 Pekin Street #02-01
Far East Square
Singapore 048763

Printed in the United States of America

Library of Congress Cataloging-in-Publication Data

Wright, Robert J.
Multifaceted assessment for early childhood education / Robert J. Wright.
p. cm.
Includes bibliographical references and index.
ISBN 978-1-4129-7015-0 (pbk.)
1. Early childhood education. 2. Educational evaluation. 3. Curriculum evaluation. 4. Educational tests and measurements. 5. Learning ability–Testing. I. Title.

LB1139.23.W75 2010
372.126'4—dc22 2009018018

This book is printed on acid-free paper.

09 10 11 12 13 10 9 8 7 6 5 4 3 2 1

Acquisitions Editor: Diane McDaniel
Associate Editor: Deya Saoud
Editorial Assistant: Ashley Conlon
Production Editor: Brittany Bauhaus
Copy Editor: Taryn Bigelow
Typesetter: C&M Digitals (P) Ltd.
Proofreader: Jeff Bryant
Indexer: Diggs Publication Services, Inc.
Cover Designer: Arup Giri
Marketing Manager: Christy Guilbault

Brief Contents

Detailed Contents

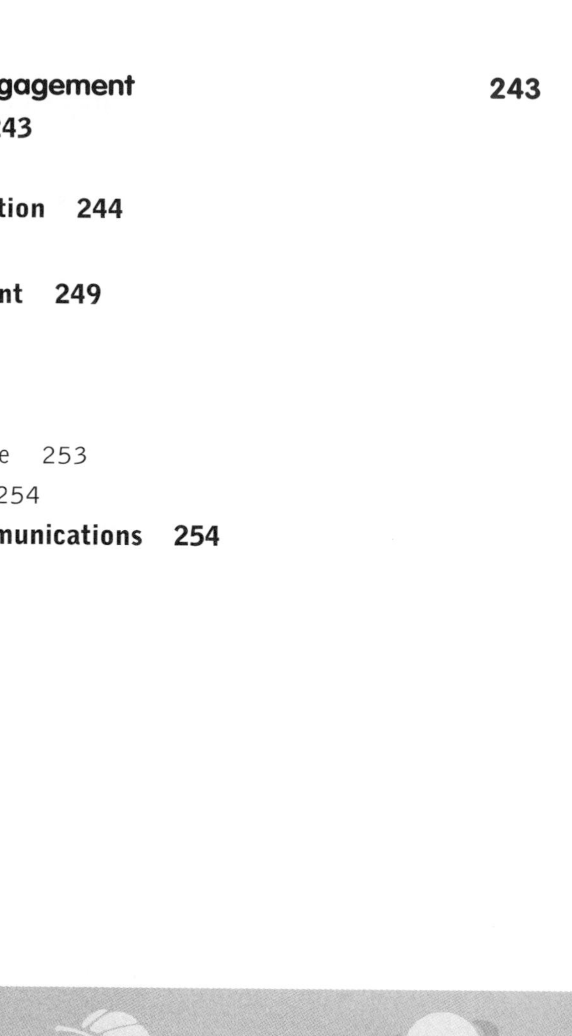

Preface

Mission and Goals

My goal in writing this book has been to provide students with an understandable and useful interpretation of the critical information related to the measurement and evaluation of young children. There has never been a time when it is more important for early childhood educators to have an understanding of educational assessment and measurement. Educational accountability has taken root in our nation, and the public is looking for "scientific" documentation of our successes. It is no longer prudent or even possible for teachers of young children to ignore this national zeitgeist. Child care staffs along with preschool and primary grade level teachers are being drawn into the need to prove the merit of their programs and the quality of their instruction.

A second irresistible trend encouraging ever more testing of young children is provided by legislation mandating the identification of children needing early intervention and special education. The process of providing a child and his or her family with early special education is based on standardized assessment instruments. These entitlement decisions require scientific data as the basis for each placement decision. Once an intervention program is started, children must be continually monitored for their development and educational growth. All of the steps in early special education are data dependent, and early childhood teachers must be conversant in test score interpretation.

President Barack H. Obama has made early childhood education a priority of his administration, and there is now increased public awareness of the important role early childhood education plays in our society. In February 2009 President Obama signed the American Recovery and Reinvestment Act giving Head Start and Early Start programs an additional $2 Billion to expand programs and hire staff. With increased support and interest has come increased pressure for accountability. At the time of the publication of this book, all 50 states provide free public kindergarten programs for 5-year-old children, and 37 states provide tax supported prekindergarten programs. The use of public funds for the support of early education programs brings with it the need for accountability. Central to all accountability efforts in early childhood education are educational and developmental measurements and assessments.

Teachers are under increased pressure to understand the principles of educational assessment and to incorporate formative assessments into their ongoing instructional activities. Administrators and child care center directors need a measurement literate teaching staff that can assist in accreditation activities and meeting state mandates for accountability and special education. Parents want teachers for their children who know how to diagnose educational problems and provide methods of overcoming learning difficulties. Federal and state mandates require teachers and schools to locate all children at risk for significant learning problems and initiate early intervention programs. Meeting these expectations requires early childhood teachers who understand principles of educational measurement and approaches to the assessment of young children.

Game Plan

In 1979, I started the Child Development Center for Widener University. This center has flourished and is now a central feature of the university's Center for Education. Over the years, I taught educational assessment and testing to a population of preservice teachers who were headed into careers as elementary and early childhood teachers. I have never felt that the available textbooks were targeted to the needs of my students.

This new textbook is the outcome of my quest for a readable and highly engaging book that does not compromise basic principles of educational assessment and measurement in early childhood education. It provides insight into how cognitive, developmental, and educational tests work, how to interpret their scores, and how to define the value of measurements made with them. This book provides coverage of the issues of testing special populations including English language learners, academically gifted children, and children from impoverished homes. This book goes on to provide chapter-length coverage of measurement issues involved in accreditation and meeting state mandates. This textbook also examines the impact on early childhood programs of the high-stakes testing mandate in third grade. It also provides insight into the identification and planning to meet the needs of children with special educational concerns. Finally, this book provides chapter coverage of communication techniques with parents and another chapter on engaging parents in school programs.

Beyond these traditional concerns, this book has been grounded in the real world of young children and preschool and primary education. This early childhood focus was accomplished in several ways. All chapters in the textbook provide "Case in Point" examples that describe the implications of measurement decisions on the lives of children and their teachers. Also, over 80% of the 600 references cited in this book are from either early childhood education literature or education-focused agencies.

This text provides an engaging, insightful, and highly readable introduction to the inner workings of educational assessment and measurement in early education settings. Traditional topics are presented in approachable and understandable ways. This book employs an issue-oriented approach to the analysis and interpretation of complex concerns. As an example, this book examines issues such as the score gap, and the problem of grade retention versus social promotion. Intriguing real-life examples are introduced in each chapter that were selected to demonstrate how technical principles actually impact upon the lives of children who are involved. This provides the text with a true early childhood focus and insight into what is happening in child care centers and the primary grades.

This book includes a discussion of ethical and unethical approaches used to improve scores on mandated assessments. It also addresses the relationship between factors such as the child's personological characteristics, familial structures, teacher background, instructional approaches, and the leadership style of the principal or leader with the outcome scores on mandated assessments.

Finally, the application of educational technology in testing and measurement is explored, and future trends for the applications of educational technology are noted and discussed.

Helpful Apparatus

I have included a number of learning aids throughout this textbook. They have been incorporated in an effort to improve the quality and depth of learning that occurs for the readers of this text. These include:

- **Section descriptions** running a page or two lead off each conceptual segment of the book. These section descriptors provide an overview and framework for the next few chapters.
- A statement of **Introduction and Themes** at the start of each chapter provides the reader with insight into the perspective that I have taken in researching and writing the chapter.

- The **learning goals** for each chapter follow the Introduction and Themes and are presented in a sequential list.

Taken together, these three elements provide the reader with a set of advance organizers designed to provide an awareness of what is being learned and a structure for understanding how to interpret the new material.

The book also includes the following pedagogical features:

- Each chapter includes several special features labeled **Case in Point**. Each Case in Point provides a real-life example or application of the material being presented in the text.
- Another motivational device in every chapter is a **cartoon** addressing an aspect of the chapter's narrative.
- Many URLs are included in the chapters of the book. These **Internet resources** provide students with access to an expanded library of information associated with the material in the book.
- Each chapter provides a list of **discussion questions** designed to initiate classroom discourse and motivate students to employ higher order cognitive processes when considering the material covered in the chapter.
- A detailed **glossary** of terminology including 340 technical words and terms is also part of this book.
- Over 600 **references,** including hundreds of URLs, support the material in the book.

A Word to Instructors

Early childhood assessment is a topic that is now germane for all new early childhood educators working in our schools and centers. For that reason, I advocate using this book with classes composed of early childhood teacher education students. The best populations of students for using this book are those who are upper division undergraduates or first-year graduate students earning their first teacher certification in early childhood education.

Congratulations for electing to teach this course, and best wishes for a successful semester.

A Word to the Student

I accept the fact that very few students who enroll in collegiate courses in educational assessment and measurement do so voluntarily. Yet, the study of early childhood assessments can be an engaging and truly empowering experience for teachers of young children.

From my perspective, there are four things about any college class or seminar that are central to its success. These four things are the students who take the course, the instructor who provides the class, the content of the discipline being studied, and the book and other resources that are available to the students.

To be a professor is to profess the knowledge base of a discipline and share new ideas about that field with others. But it is the students who are the reason colleges exist. Students are the life force inspiring each professor who enters a lecture hall or classroom to profess his or her discipline. The only things good college instructors ask to do their jobs are students who have an open mind to the discipline being studied and who are truly willing to learn.

I took my first class in educational measurement as a graduate student in 1968. In that summer course, a good teacher inspired me to earn my doctorate in educational psychology. Good teaching is always the key to success for every course.

Beyond the ability of an instructor to inspire and motivate students, the next most important component of a good learning experience is the topic itself. The continuing presence of mandated screening and large-scale assessment programs, and the need for early childhood education programs to be accredited, is not debatable. There can be no argument that these measurement issues will be with us for the foreseeable future. Having a solid foundation in the knowledge about educational measurement and assessments is therefore a matter of survival for those who earn their living teaching young children. Today, it is axiomatic that no prudent early childhood educator can take the topic of educational tests and measurement lightly.

I have written this book with these concerns in mind. The text provides grounding in all of the aspects of measurement that an early childhood educator must have as background. I have worked to write this book in a highly readable and engaging style. By reading and studying the material in this book, you will be better equipped to advocate for improved approaches in the assessment of learning and child development for the children for whom you have the awesome responsibility of teaching.

To the Profession

A diligent and documented search has been made to ensure that the copyright holders of all material included in this work have been contacted and approve of its use. Also, all cited reference materials have been checked for accuracy. The URLs listed in this book have been carefully examined for accuracy as well. If the reader finds errors have been made in some of these efforts, please contact me at widenerbob@hotmail.com.

—*Robert J. Wright*, PhD
Professor, Center for Education
Widener University

Ancillaries and Technology Accompaniments

The ancillary materials for the text include a password protected Instructor website that includes an extensive selection of useful tools that can be implemented in the classroom. These tools are comprised of teaching tips, sample syllabi, PowerPoint slides for each chapter, a comprehensive test bank that includes multiple choice, true/false, short answer, and essay questions for each chapter, and a variety of useful Web resources. Instructors can register to receive access to the site at **http://www.sagepub.com/wrightinstr/.**

Acknowledgments

No project of this magnitude can be completed by one person working in isolation. This textbook would not have been possible without the encouragement, editorial assistance, creativity, and the freely given help of my wife and partner, Jeanne.

In addition, I must provide a word of thanks to Ms. Molly Wolf, Education Collection Librarian at Widener University's Wolfgram Memorial Library; Gloria Floyd, my secretary; and Drs. Richard and Ann St. John, my technology support team, critics, and friends.

Kudos are also due for the team at Sage Publications including my editor, Diane McDaniel, PhD, and associate editor, Ms. Deya Saoud. Their belief in this project and support of my efforts have been invaluable. Also, I owe a special dept of gratitude to the editorial assistant working with this manuscript, Ms. Ashley Conlon. It was Ashley who coordinated this project bringing together the many reviews and permissions that are part of this book. I also wish to express my gratitude to the many editorial reviewers who worked to make this the best possible textbook. This group of faculty reviewers includes:

Regina Adesanya, *New Jersey City University*

Laura F. Boswell, *Marshall University*

Barbara Foulks Boyd, *Radford University*

Sai Jambunathan, *New Jersey City University*

Susan Johns, *Saint Joseph College*

Carol Kessler, *Cabrini College*

Hedda Meadan-Kaplansky, *Illinois State University*

Arminta Owens, *South Carolina State University*

Juliette Relihan, *Salve Regina University*

Beth Satterfield, *West Virginia University*

Kathryn Sharp, *The University of Memphis*

Saundra Shorter, *Fayetteville State University*

Patricia Steinhaus, *Chicago State University*

Candra Thornton, *University of North Carolina–Wilmington*

Janette Wetsel, *University of Central Oklahoma*

Part I

Background, Current Issues, and Interpretation of Assessments in Early Childhood

The first section describes the major authors of the 19th century who have developed the instructional approaches, content, and skills that should be taught to preschool youngsters. There is a description of the nature of kindergartens as envisioned by Froebel and the Children's Houses created by Maria Montessori. In America, the growth of urban settlement houses and the efforts of President Franklin D. Roosevelt to provide nursery schools is described and placed in the context of the era. Of special interest is the creation of Head Start and its impact. The relation of assessment to policy initiatives for early childhood education begun during the 1960s is also examined.

Another focus of the book's first section is the No Child Left Behind law and its impact on the education of children enrolled in preschools and primary school grades. Ethics and testing policies of major professional associations are presented and described. Also included is a discussion of the problem of assessing children who are not proficient in the English language. A model for an assessment program for children enrolled in preschool, kindergarten, and primary grades in public schools is also presented in this section.

All educational assessments and measures are not exactly indicative of what children can do or know. They are estimates. As estimates, there is a degree of error in each score. The amount of error in a set of test scores is an indicator of the reliability, consistency, or stability of the measure. Proper uses of test scores and selection of appropriate measures are associated with the validity of assessment procedures or tests.

History and Framework of Early Education and the Assessment of Young Children

1

There is no other outward offence that in the sight of God so heavily burdens the world, and deserves such heavy chastisement, as the neglect to educate children.

—Martin Luther

Introduction and Themes

Long lost, the concept of childhood was reborn during the Renaissance; however, it was not until the 19th century that contemporary ideas about the education of children under the age of 5 years were developed in Germany. In America, early childhood education and education for children with disabilities was marginalized until the 20th century.

Principles of social science were used by American researchers to establish a measurement-based understanding of child development and learning. This approach was built on a belief that genetics is the primary factor determining each child's lot in life. Racism and discrimination against children with disabilities were by-products of this concept of human development.

The collection of child development data at university-based clinics led to **developmental assessments** and screening tools. However, the application of the principles of educational measurement for the evaluation of early childhood programs, and for the assessment of the special needs of young children with disabilities, was not mandated until after 1965.

Federal and state laws and regulations now require children be screened for potential learning or developmental problems. Children found to potentially be at risk for problems must be provided a thorough assessment. An assessment includes a number of approaches used to collect information about the performance abilities and limitations of a child. These can include test data, performance data, and observational records.

The model for program accreditation of the National Association for the Education of Young Children (NAEYC), first developed in 1929, was updated in 2008, but only one early childhood program in seven seeks that accreditation. Since the 1990s, state education departments have been providing leadership in developing early childhood program evaluations and licensing standards.

Learning Objectives

By reading and studying this chapter, you should acquire the competency to:

- Describe the first modern early childhood education programs.
- Discuss problems involved in assessing bilingual prekindergarten children.
- Explain educational rights of children with disabilities.
- Present arguments for and against the work by Lewis M. Terman with mentally gifted children.
- Describe research findings from early childhood education impact studies.
- Discuss reasons behind the growth of state-sponsored child care and preschool programs.
- Explain reasons behind the rapid growth of private tutoring companies focused on cramming for preschool children.

First Early Childhood Programs

Europe in the 19th century gave birth to a modern approach to early childhood education. Educators had always assumed that before the age of 7 children were too immature to focus on academic learning. The notion of education with children as young as age 3 was unheard of. This 19th century development resulted in an early childhood program that would be familiar to today's teachers. Early childhood education was first proposed by a Swiss educator, Johann Heinrich Pestalozzi, and later by his student Friedrich Froebel (or Fröbel) from Thuringia, Germany (Froebel, 1948; Pestalozzi, 1973/1894).

Pestalozzi's program was built around the concept that children learn first through the senses and experience, then through language-dominated cognitive channels. His teaching methods were aligned with the natural needs and instincts of children. Pestalozzi used the word **"anschauung"** from Emanuel Kant to describe how children reach this level of knowing. Anschauung can only occur through actively exploring the environment and through play. Pestalozzi believed the child needed to actually use objects before he/she could learn the words describing them and their uses.

Froebel, an architect turned schoolmaster, came to realize that children needed a school experience prior to age 6. The child's garden or **kindergarten** was introduced by Froebel as a necessary step in the educational ladder prior to first grade. In kindergarten, children find the balance between learning new skills and behaviors expected by society. It is a safe place where young children have the freedom to grow following natural (inborn) patterns. Froebel posited that play should be central in the kindergarten day.

Froebel's Kindergarten

Central to Froebel's kindergarten curricula was an emphasis on the child learning from nature. Young children were taught to observe patterns and the natural geometry and symmetry of nature. The creative use of play, supported by a series of "gifts" (educational toys) and "occupations" (material for practice in skill development), was central in the curriculum. The gifts were designed to teach colors, shapes, numbers, extent, symmetry, lines, rings, points, and proportion. Occupations included teaching materials for helping children learn solids, surfaces, lines (weaving, embroidery, etc.), points (stringing beads), and reconstruction. Froebel's kindergarten curriculum developed analytical thinking through teaching the child to observe patterns and geometric forms of individual aspects of nature but equally to evaluate them as "a whole both in its organic unity and in its component parts" (Froebel, 1948, p. 553). Toy blocks made of maple were used to construct and reconstruct the world of things. Froebel's goal was to have children learn through their own actions, and arrive at the concept that there is an inner coherence to all things (McCarter, 1999).

Today, the use of **standardized tests** in American kindergartens has been described as a violation of the original rubric for a "child's garden" given to education by Froebel (Jeynes, 2006). Froebel's curriculum was highly symbolic, providing children with materials (gifts) that helped youngsters cope with their world through play. The imposition of tests and high-stakes assessments into this idealistic children's garden can metaphorically be compared to the serpent in Eden. The impact of Froebel's "gifts" to children far exceeds that produced by standardized educational tests. See Case in Point 1.1 for an example.

Case in Point 1.1

Impact of Froebel's Gift of Wooden Blocks

In 1876, a New England teacher and her 9-year-old son traveled to Philadelphia to visit the Centennial Exposition of the United States. That young mother, Anna Lloyd Wright, with her young son, Frank, paid their $.50 admission fee and visited all 37 of the national exposition halls during their week in Philadelphia.[1] Froebel's followers had a booth in the German Hall where his kindergarten materials and program were demonstrated alongside other German exhibitions including chemicals and firearms.

Anna and young Frank were totally taken by Froebel's materials. She purchased a set of the smooth maple blocks for Frank. These were to have a profound influence throughout the life of her son, America's great architect, Frank Lloyd Wright. Anna Wright went to the new toy store in Boston, Milton Bradley Inc., and told them about the wonderful educational toys from Germany. In 1943, an adult Frank Lloyd Wright wrote in his autobiography attesting to the influence of the Froebel blocks on his work (see Photo 1.1).

> The smooth shapely maple blocks with which to build, the sense of which never afterward leaves the fingers: *form* becoming *feeling*. The box had a mast to set up on it, on which to hang the maple cubes and spheres and triangles, revolving them to discover subordinate forms. (F. Wright, 1943, p. 13)

Photo 1.1 The Influence of the Building Blocks From Froebel's Kindergarten is Apparent in Frank Lloyd Wright's Architecture. (McCarter, 1999)

SOURCE: From U.S. Library of Congress, Prints and Photographs Division, "Built in America" Collection. Used with permission.

Child Study in Europe

For most of the 20th century in America, the approach to the study of children was empirical using a philosophically positivistic and true scientific model. This approach required **evaluation** of large numbers of children. Individuals were compared to the mass of data collected from large groups. Such comparisons were made to determine if the individual child was growing and developing appropriately. This approach is central to tenants of the scientific approach, and provides much that is useful. It provides means for doing diagnostic **assessments** and getting children the help they need.

An entirely different worldview regarding children developed concurrently in Europe. That approach was more **qualitative** and focused on the individual nature of each child. One aspect of this approach was the use of careful observation of how infants and young children interacted with their environments. Another involved asking children to explain phenomenon they had seen or experienced. The key to this approach involved asking questions and pursuing the cognition that led the child to his/her explanation (Piaget, 1955). Whether the answer was right or wrong was trivial, the focus was on why the child answered the way he/she did. The goal of this approach was to find the reasoning behind the answer. Piaget believed that the child brings a series of rudimentary cognitive systems into the world (genetic) that facilitates interactions with the world. This linkage was referred to as **genetic epistemology**.

Charles R. Darwin

While best known as a naturalist and biologist, Darwin was an early proponent of a qualitative approach to child study. In the 19th century, he published a detailed description of his own children. His descriptions of neonatal reflexology and infant behaviors are compelling and medically precise. In observing his wife preparing to nurse their baby, Charles Darwin noted, "a warm soft hand applied to the side of his face excited a wish to suck. This must be considered as a reflex or an instinctive action, for it is impossible to believe that experience and association with the touch of his mother's breast could so soon have come into play" (Darwin, 1877, pp. 285–286).

Photo 1.2 Dr. Maria Montessori With Children at a *Casa Dei Bambini*

SOURCE: Getty Images. Used with permission.

Maria Montessori

Darwin was 73 years old when he died in 1882. That same year Maria Montessori was an academically **gifted** 12-year-old whose family had just moved from Ancona Province (in eastern Italy) to Rome where she could get a good education. Breaking with all tradition, she entered medical college, and at 24 became Italy's first female physician. She earned the rank of full professor at the University of Rome, and the Italian government gave her the responsibility for a school populated by the poorest children in Rome (see Photo 1.2).

In her school, *Casa dei Bambini* (the Children's House), Montessori introduced new concepts in early education that are commonplace today. Gone were fixed student desks, replaced with small chairs and movable tables constructed for the comfort of children. Teachers were given carefully prepared classrooms filled with manipulable materials that taught children as they interacted with them. Children were granted much freedom to explore and learn from graduated towers of stacking blocks, counting beads, graduated measuring sticks, nesting boxes, and sandpaper letters (Montessori, 1949). All materials used in a Montessori classroom were carefully designed to teach a specific concept to the child who manipulated them.[2] The teacher's role was to demonstrate to the child how the materials were to be used, then to stand aside while the child did the work of learning.

Assessment and Montessori

The Montessori educational model is currently used throughout the world, and in as many as 5,000 preschool classrooms in the United States.[3] The materials are designed to be self-correcting. That is, they only work when placed in the right order or form. Montessori assessments are based on this property. Did the child understand and use the "Golden Beads" correctly, or was the "10-Tower" built to full height? The assessments are frequently carried out using a checklist that can be individualized.

Sample Items on a Montessori Checklist

Linear Counting: Indicate all answers as **Y** for yes or **N** for not yet.

The child can:

______ Verbally count 10 beads while placing them in a cup

______ Make four or more combinations of beads that add up to 10

______ Demonstrate that the number 11 is a 10-bead column plus one more

______ Demonstrate all combinations of numbers from 11 to 20

______ Count by units of 10 using bead columns from 20 to 100

______ Demonstrate combinations of all numbers from 10 to 100 (e.g., 56, 73, etc.)

Anyone can confirm how little the grading that results from examinations corresponds to the final useful work of people in life.

—Jean Piaget

Jean Piaget

Piaget provided the theoretical basis for understanding the success of the teaching approach introduced by Montessori. Piaget's writings describing how children develop their understanding of the world and their conceptualizations about the processes of mathematics, science, language, space, and time have influenced curriculum writers throughout the world. His writing even provides a framework for understanding how children develop a conceptualization of morality (Piaget, 1932, 1952, 1955, 1960; Piaget & Inhelder, 1956).

Through tens of thousands of hours of patient questioning and observation, Piaget collected the qualitative data needed to build a model for understanding how thinking processes mature and develop over time with children. Case in Point 1.2 provides an example of Piaget's method of using questions to explore the cognition of young children.

Case in Point 1.2

Interview of a Child by Jean Piaget

The following is part of the translated transcript from Piaget (1960, p. 335).

Piaget: Terry (age 6 yrs., 6 mos.), How do people get wood?
Terry: They make it with things.
Piaget: With what things?
Terry: With wood.
Piaget: And where does that wood come from?
Terry: From the forest.
Piaget: How does the wood get into the forest?
Terry: God helps men to make the wood and then they plant it in the ground.
Piaget: Where do they get this wood which they plant?
Terry: First of all they make wood, then they plant it in the ground.
Piaget: Are there sometimes new trees?
Terry: Yes.
Piaget: How are they made?
Terry: You sow things.
Piaget: What do they sow?
Terry: Things like seeds you get at the shops.
Piaget: How do you get seeds?
Terry: You must have round things.
Piaget: Where do you find them?
Terry: In the fields, you move away the grass and then you take the seeds on the ground.
Piaget: How did they get there?
Terry: They were lost while being sowed.
Piaget: Where did they come from when they were sowed?
Terry: The shopkeeper. He makes them from other seeds.
Piaget: What did the shopkeeper do to get the first seeds?
Terry: They were sent to him from the factory.

Piaget never created **norm groups** or published a standardized test, yet his model for understanding the child's intellect is central to how educators interpret children's cognitive processing.[4]

American Child Study Through Testing

Americans are a pragmatic folk. We always stand ready and able to take ideas and use them in bigger and better ways. In Europe at the start of the 20th century, the scientific method was applied to educational and psychological **measurement** for the first time. This occurred at about the same time the scientific study of children began in the United States. The American leaders of this field, G. Stanley Hall and James M. Cattell, were greatly influenced by the application of the scientific method in the social sciences, first developed in the 19th century in Germany. This American movement for the scientific study of children grew rapidly through the support of the Laura Spelman Rockefeller Foundation, which provided initial funding for academic departments and university clinics from coast to coast.[5]

A central tenant of the American **child study movement** of that era was the prime role played by human genetics in determining all individual characteristics and many human behaviors. This faith in the primacy of genetics included every aspect of the infant and growing child, including cognitive abilities. One reason for this is the impact the writings of Charles Darwin had on his younger cousin, Francis Galton. Sir Francis was a physician by training and wealthy through inheritance. This made it possible for him to pursue scholarship on his own terms. The focus of most of his life's work was human heredity. He was among the first to do systematic research into the nature of individual differences. While all aspects of the human were fair game for his studies, the intellect became the focus of much of his study and writings.

G. Stanley Hall

An American scholar, G. Stanley Hall, believed that each human has a vestige of past eras in the elaboration of our human species, which is expressed in the pattern of growth and personality development seen among children.[6] While the child's genetics was seen as providing a blueprint for the growth and development that would occur, Hall also believed that the human brain was "handmade." That is, he agreed with many European authors who saw experience as central to all cognitive development (Hall, 1904).

Lewis M. Terman

One student of G. Stanley Hall was Lewis M. Terman, who became the leading authority on testing in the country. He created the first practical test of mental ability, the Stanford-Binet Scale of Intelligence (Terman, 1916), and the first standardized **achievement test** battery, the Stanford Achievement Test first published in 1923 (R. Wright, 2008). Contemporary versions of both tests are still published today. One of Terman's graduate students, Arthur S. Otis, was the father of modern group-administered tests of intelligence. One bearing his name is still used in schools today.[7]

Terman also was the first psychologist to systematically identify and study the nature of academically gifted children (see Case in Point 1.3). He held a strong belief in the importance of having those who were most capable of becoming society's leaders be provided with an enriched education, a concept known as **meritocracy.**

Case in Point 1.3

Terman's Monumental Study of Gifted Children

The first large-scale study of gifted children was initiated by Lewis M. Terman at Stanford University in 1921 with a longitudinal study of over 1,500 California children. Each child had a measured IQ score of 140 or more (99th **percentile**). This longitudinal study lasted into the 21st century, providing data on the lives of white, middle-class children as they grew and matured, and aged.[8]

(Continued)

(Continued)

Terman's sample of children was 11 years old when his landmark study began. As a group, they were well adjusted, middle class, happy, and otherwise quite normal. Public schools of San Francisco and Los Angeles provided the sample in 1921. Children were all nominated by their teachers and were tested by one of Terman's evaluators (graduate students). The gifted sample included only two children who were African American, six Japanese American, and none who were of Hispanic or Native American origin (Leslie, 2000; Shurkin, 1992).

Most children in the sample were born in 1910 and lived through two world wars, the cold war, and many lived to see the liberation of Europe from communism. For the most part, they lived longer and had healthier lives than did their less gifted peers. As a group, they were successful in their chosen careers. About 46% of the male sample became professionals with graduate-level degrees, and another 41% were managers and business executives. Girls in the sample later became leaders in a number of fields including education (Shurkin, 1992). It is important to note that while these bright children grew to become successful adults, none of them produced a work of great genius. The implication is that the creative genius of Newton, Mozart, or Einstein involves something beyond the measurement of cognition on an IQ test.

Today, researchers at the University of California, Riverside, are still collecting data from the sample to study the processes of successful aging and eventual causes of death for this group of bright individuals.

Arnold Gesell

The second highly influential student of G. Stanley Hall was Arnold Gesell (see Photo 1.3). After earning his graduate degree from Clark University in 1906, Gesell spent a short time in Los Angeles where he taught at the State Normal School.[9] In 1911, he moved back across the country to Yale University where he established a laboratory for the study of child development. The data he gathered at the Yale Clinic of Child Development provided the yardstick used by most pediatricians and many worried parents to chart dimensions of child development.

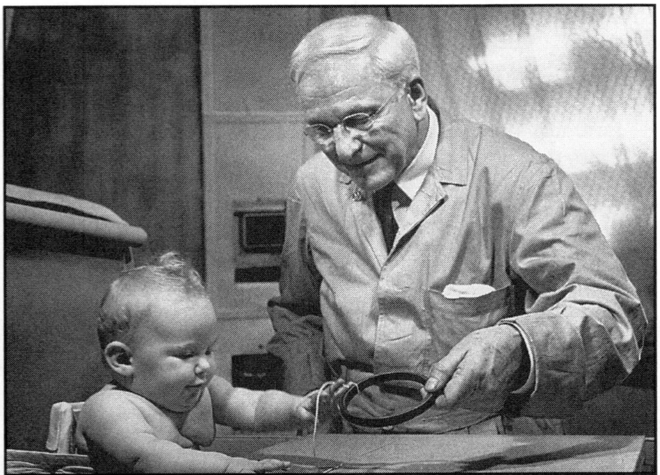

Photo 1.3 Professor Arnold Gesell at the Yale University Clinic

SOURCE: Getty images. Used with permission.

Gesell and his colleagues at Yale provided a sequence of milestones marking the growth of normal children over a range of dimensions. Gesell's sample was populated by children of middle and upper middle class families. Many of the children were offspring of Yale University's students and faculty. Virtually all of the children in the Yale sample were healthy, middle class, Anglo-white infants and youngsters. Gesell had the goal of finding and charting the ideal order and sequence that occurs in child development. These types of data were sought in order to chart the genetic plan for the progressive growth (sequential unfolding or flowering) of the human child. In this regard, Gesell never strayed far from what he was taught by G. Stanley Hall. For that reason, Gesell decided to concentrate on ideal examples of infants and children. All infants and children in his sample had to be well cared for, healthy, and from "good" homes.

His work was not without its critics. Lev Vygotsky (1998/1934), a leading child psychologist and psycholinguist of the Soviet Union, once described Gesell's approach as "delusional." He argued that the concept of an evolutionary basis for the growth and development of children is too stilted. He presented a model for a **dialectic** understanding of the processes, rather than a simple measurement-based model.[10] His argument was that development of children requires much more than a good set of genetic plans and time.[11] His position involved the full nature of the child across all aspects of the culture in which the youngster grows (Vygotsky, 1929).

Antecedents of Contemporary Problems in Measurement

Today, there are several pressing problems to be considered whenever young children are evaluated using a formal testing procedure. These problems are not new, and have been part of the American fabric since the colonial era. One of these issues is that of measuring children for whom English is not the primary language. The second concern is the assessment of children who have been identified as needing special educational assistance.

English Language Learners

From the colonial days, there has been a strong **nativist** movement in this country that has emphasized the need for all citizens to be English speakers (Franklin, 1751). A charge given to public schools was to be a melting pot in which many cultures and languages are balkanized and true Americans are created.

Language differences have also facilitated **cultural prejudice.** One basis for selecting certain schools to be studied by Lewis Terman in his research of gifted children was that there had to be few, if any, Mexican children enrolled (Shurkin, 1992). Today, we require that high-stakes tests published in English be taken by children who have not reached a level of English language proficiency required to even read the directions (see Chapter 2 for a discussion of the issues related to evaluating Hispanic children).

The problem many children have reflects the way families can live in communities where they never need to speak English (see Chapter 12 for a discussion of engaging Hispanic parents) (see Case in Point 1.4). Several German-speaking communities in Pennsylvania have avoided becoming bilingual in English for over 200 years. Today, 67% of the population of Miami, Florida, is not fluent in English (Booth, 1998). English is the preferred language in only 60% of the homes in New York City. The New York and Miami examples are typical of many large cities. Nationally, the 2000 U.S. Census reported that 82% of American households use English as the primary language. Spanish is the primary language in 11% of all homes (U.S. Census Bureau, 2003). The remaining 7% is made up of 47 other languages.

Case in Point 1.4

Roadblocks to Learning English

When families immigrate to the United States, they tend to live in communities of other people with similar life stories. For that reason, a child who is new to the country is frequently surrounded by children and adults who speak the child's first language. The community is likely to provide churches, stores, and medical practitioners who are also speakers of the child's first language. Television stations and radio channels also provide entertainment in the child's first language. This pattern means that the child may never experience emersion in an English language environment until he or she is in school. When the school day is over, the child returns to the family and the non-English-speaking community. This linguistic isolation continues for the 10-week summer break and can erase most of the English a child has learned at school.

The assessment of young children who are **English language learners** (**ELL**) can result in inappropriate placement recommendations (Lopez & Flores, 2005; Spinelli, 2008). This occurs because as children struggle to learn English they will lose aspects of their native language proficiency. At some point in time, their skills in both languages will be relatively weak. At this low point, children will not be functioning well in either language. Barry McLaughlin and his colleagues at George Washington University (1995) describe this period as a time of **semilingualism.** With young children, there will be shifts back and forth between the languages that accompany this stage of semilingualism (see Case in Point 1.5). Early childhood educators should be sensitive to this **code-switching** and be extra sensitive to the complexity of the developmental process taking place.

Case in Point 1.5

Multiple Language Learning

During a visit with a Dutch-speaking tennis star and his French-speaking wife, I was introduced to their preschool daughter Natalie. The family lived most of the year in the United States and several months in Europe. The girl was attempting to make linguistic sense of a world of three languages. She picked the words and grammar that best fitted her goal in speaking. One example was when she asked her mother, *"Mama, me donnent davantage* ice tea, *tevreden"* (Mama, give me more ice tea please). At another time she asked me if I had children her age as, *"Avez-vous kinderin mon âge?"*

There is no appropriate way to use a standard **curriculum probe** to assess the prereading skill level of a child with this type of language development in progress. Any measure of her reading skills would need to be carefully crafted to her special circumstance.

Non-Asian children for whom English is not the first language tend to have lower assessment scores in reading than native speakers of English.[12] Testing rules under federal guidelines provide for immigrant children who are **limited English proficient (LEP)** to have a one-year waiver from being tested for reading skills in the English language; but no waiver is given with the required science and math tests (see Chapter 2).

Testing language minority children using standardized measures in English will not yield valid scores. Yet, reading and language skills of children are central factors measured by all high-stakes tests. At this point, there is no clear model as to how to evaluate the learning of language minority children, nor is there a clear set of goals for such evaluations (Solano-Flores, 2008). Yet, we go ahead as if there were no differences in how and what language minority children learn in our classrooms as compared with their English-speaking peers.

An appropriate assessment of children learning English requires a multifaceted approach (McLaughlin, Blanchard, & Osanai, 1995). The considerations include the cultural context in which the child is being raised. This issue is one requiring the assessor to understand the verbal and nonverbal cues that the child uses. An assessment of a prekindergarten ELL child needs to involve parents and English-speaking family members who can assist the assessor in understanding the child's context for language learning. The best assessments for young ELL children are based on authentic oral language tasks. Assessments should be based on the child's demonstration of what he/she can actually do (see Chapter 4 for a discussion of these measures). The best approach for tracking the progress and language development of young ELL children is through the use of portfolio assessments (McLaughlin, et al., 1995).

Children With Disabilities

Normally, it is a time of celebration when a baby is born into a family. The birth of a seriously disabled child, however, can be overwhelming for unprepared parents. It can become a time of heartache and feelings of guilt. For that reason, it is not unusual for parents to experience the emotion of grief over what is perceived to be a loss of the child's future (see Chapter 11).

Other children with milder forms of disabilities may not be identified until the youngsters enter a child care program or preschool. All too often, children who are not identified for their first few years are members of lower socioeconomic groups, including children of parents who are learning the English language (see Chapter 2).

Before 1960, public school was rarely an option for children with disabilities (Osgood, 2005). Arnold Gesell never included **children with disabilities** in the normative data used to assess child development (Gesell, 1940). Schools were under no obligation to provide an appropriate education for children with disabilities until 1973. That year saw passage of the reauthorization of the Rehabilitation Act. Title V, **Section 504** of that act specifies what schools must do to meet educational requirements of children with special needs. The right to a thorough and efficient education was spelled out in 1975 with passage of the Education for All Handicapped Children Act (P.L. 94-142). These two federal acts brought testing and assessment mandates with them (see Chapter 11 for a detailed discussion of early childhood **special education**). A series of amendments to the Education for All Handicapped Children Act was passed in 1986, extending special education programs to all children with disabilities from birth through high school graduation or age 21 (P.L. 99-457). The federal government could not require states to start schools for children below kindergarten age, but did require states to address educational needs of young children to qualify for federal funds (Bowe, 2004). The URL for the Division for Early Childhood for exceptional children is http://www.dec-sped.org.

In Summary

The framework for the modern world of education and assessment practice in the United States was well established by the dawn of the 20th century. This development occurred through the growth of the social sciences in the United States and Great Britain. Both countries chose to follow a scientific approach to the management of education and to the assessment of children. A continental approach to understanding and assessing children's learning has focused on how the child interacts with the environment. It is an approach that is more qualitative and less empirical.

Industrialization and the Rise of American Public Schools

After the Civil War, one state after another followed the lead of Massachusetts and passed enabling legislation for local communities to tax real estate in order to build schools and organize school districts (S. Braun & Edwards, 1972, p. 90). States created normal schools and churned out a stream of young female teachers who filled the new schools. Before 1830, almost all teachers were male; however, by 1880 almost all primary teachers were female.

From 1860 to 1900, preschools were not seen as being part of the organization of school systems. At the close of the 19th century, cities experienced a flood of families who came to the United States from Ireland, Russia, Poland, and Germany. Most ended up in the poorest neighborhoods of the inner cities. With adults and older children of families employed all day trying to make a living, the care of young children was a major concern. One answer to this need came from the **settlement house** movement. These social welfare outreach centers were established to strengthen neighborhoods and improve the lives of individuals in the community. They were usually secular, supported by private philanthropy, and provided a range of social and educational services including day care for preschool children. Goals of these programs were family focused and developmental. No one bothered to discuss evaluations of programs or children. That lack of oversight was an advantage of having private support provided by wealthy benefactors. By 1900, there were over 100 settlement houses in inner cities and over 400 by 1918 (Blank, 1998). Over 200 of these agencies are still serving their communities today (see Case in Point 1.6).

Case in Point 1.6

Role of Settlement Houses

Most settlement houses have kept their traditional names and continue their work today. A good example is the Corona-Norco Settlement House in Corona, California. This settlement house is an agency that offers a range of programs to assist the local community including the daily operation of a food pantry and providing food baskets to the indigent on holidays and wrapped holiday presents for children. It provides rent assistance, utility assistance, emergency shelter, and provides clothing and school supplies for poor children, permitting them to attend public school.

In 2010, New York City had 37 settlement houses serving over 200,000 people a year. One of these settlement houses is the Jacob Riis Neighborhood Settlement House in western Queens. It provides direct services to 450 people a day.

American Early Childhood Education During the 20th Century

Roosevelt's WPA

The crash of the stock markets in October of 1929 was followed over the next few years by a great economic depression. The Depression resulted in the failure of banks, the closing of industrial plants, and the downsizing of governmental agencies. By 1934, the unemployment rate was 25%. In 1932, Franklin Delano Roosevelt was elected the 32nd president of the United States. His Democratic Party, given a majority in both houses of Congress, was able to push recovery programs through to law. The name applied to these initiatives was the **"New Deal."** One of the initiatives of the New Deal was the **Works Progress Administration (WPA).** In an effort to employ laid off schoolteachers, the WPA established nursery schools throughout the country employing thousands of teachers (S. Braun & Edwards, 1972) (see Photo 1.4 for a view of one of these WPA nurseries).

Photo 1.4 A WPA Nursery in Scottsdale, Georgia, in 1936. Several of the Children in this Photograph May Not Have Had Shoes to Wear.

SOURCE: From National Archives and Records Administration, Still Picture Branch. Used with permission.

These "emergency nursery schools" had a curriculum focused on the social–emotional development of children. Two other elements in the curriculum included the health and physical growth of children. The missing component of the curriculum was the cognitive domain. The primary concern at that time was the rapid establishment of nurseries, and little thought was put into developing an evaluation model for emergency nurseries.

The Nursery School Goes to War

In 1942, the Second World War was raging and Congress updated the Lanham Act of 1940 to include funding for day care programs in support of war industries. These nursery schools provided child care needed to permit women to be employed in war industries. There was little thought given to evaluation and **accountability** (Rose, 2003). They existed for a very well understood reason, were assumed to be a temporary wartime measure, and were generally left alone.

After the war, federally funded nursery programs were closed and women returned to their homes, leaving factories that had employed them to the men of their families. The job of early education for young children was once again "mother's job." Settlement houses, university laboratory schools, and a few private and church-based nurseries remained the primary source of care for children outside of the home for the next 20 years.[13]

War on Poverty and Head Start

During his state of the union address on January 12, 1965, President Lyndon B. Johnson announced a major change in the direction of federal policy with regard to education. This new direction involved the development

"Be good while mommy is helping win the war."

SOURCE: Cartoon by Merv Magus.

of a partnership between the federal government, states, and local school systems. President Johnson called for, and Congress passed, a series of laws designed to address the root causes of poverty in America. This legislative package was designed to create a **"Great Society,"** and the **"War on Poverty"** was one step in that direction (Johnson, 1966). Part of that War on Poverty involved the establishment of **Head Start.**

A national educational assessment ordered by Congress and published by social scientist James Coleman in 1966 demonstrated how poor and minority children do not have the same educational opportunity or achievement that middle class children have. Coleman's report provided justification for a federally funded early childhood educational program (Viadero, 2006).

Head Start Program

Head Start started as a part-time, eight-week-long summer program designed to sharpen academic skills and improve the socialization and emotional growth of children from impoverished homes before they began public school. It has grown into a full-day program covering two and a half years.

One difference between the WPA nurseries of the 1930s and the Head Start program is the organized research and accountability studies that are part of the latter (McGroder, 1990). The Westinghouse Learning Corporation wrote the first report of Head Start outcomes in 1969 (Zigler & Muenchow, 1994).

That report was not positive, showing that academic and social gains made in Head Start by impoverished preschoolers faded out by third grade.[14] Numerous reports on the impact of Head Start since the original Westinghouse Report have been much more positive. Samuel J. Meisels of the Erikson Institute has argued that there is always a potential for what he describes as the **"fadeout effect."** This occurs when children transition from enriching prekindergarten education programs, where they are prepared for the academic experience of schools, and enter the enervating environment of inferior elementary schools (Meisels, 2007).

Governmental Initiatives

America is the only western democracy that does not provide universal preschool education for all children (Kamerman, 2005; Stipek, 2005). The first time universal preschool was proposed in the country was in the form of the John Brademas's Comprehensive Child Development Act of 1971. That bill cleared both houses of Congress and was vetoed on ideological grounds by President Richard M. Nixon. His veto message noted that public preschools should not raise the specter of "Sovietization" (Beatty, 2004; Stein, 1972).

Sometimes the voters of a state take matters in their own hands and force reluctant political leaders to provide preschool education programs. See Case in Point 1.7 for an example.

Case in Point 1.7

Public Demand for Universal Preschool Programs

In 2002, Florida saw its voters pass by referendum a requirement for universal preschool education. This occurred after the state's conservative legislature refused to provide universal preschool education. Florida's voter-mandated program began in 2004–2005. The program the state provided was a voluntary half-day preschool program that worked on a very limited budget.[15] These limitations notwithstanding, state tests of first-term kindergarten students in 2006 found that the new kindergarten class had significantly better academic preparation for school than did kindergarten classes prior to the preschool law. It is interesting to speculate what the outcome would be if Florida provided a fully funded, full-time program for all 4-year-old children.

The Heritage Foundation, a conservative think tank, has recently argued against tax-supported, large-scale preschool programs.[16] Two issues for the Heritage Foundation and other conservative organizations (including the Manhattan Institute) are cost-effectiveness and big government meddling in a field (early childhood education) dominated by private enterprise (Goldsmith & Meyer, 2006; Olsen & Snell, 2006).

Impact of Early Childhood Education

Recently these concerns of conservative policy experts have been addressed, and the lasting value of preschool education has been established (Preschool Curriculum Evaluation Research Consortium, 2008; Schweinhart, Montie, Xiang, Barnett, Belfield, & Nores, 2005). In an **experimental study** including a **control group,** Lawrence Schweinhart and his colleagues at the Perry Preschool in Ypsilanti, Michigan, followed a group of children who had a two-year preschool experience involving the **HighScope approach.**[17] The experimental sample was compared to a true control group that did not attend preschool. Both groups (experimental and control) were children from urban African American families living in poverty. After 40 years, members of the experimental group were significantly more likely to have graduated from high school and be married homeowners. They had significantly less drug addiction and far fewer run-ins with the court system.

The overall impact of high-quality preschool programs also has a significant positive impact on the American economy (Hurst, 2004). For every dollar invested in preschool education, the return is about $13.00 (Jacobson, 2004). Approximately two thirds of this economic advantage is brought about by higher graduation rates for inner-city children and lower crime rates. The importance of child care programs and preschools is growing along with the population (Holzman, 2005). In 2007, there were more children born in America (4.32 million) than ever before (National Center for Health Statistics, 2008).

During his presidential campaign, Barack Obama pledged that federal efforts to support early education programs would be greatly increased (Dillon, 2008a). After eight years of no growth, the Early Head Start Program was given additional funding with a goal of seeing it quadruple in size. The Obama administration established a federal Early Learning Council to coordinate federal, state, and local policies for early education.

The National Governor's Association has also gone on record in support of universal preschools. Their recommendation is that each state establish learning goals and standards, and develop valid and reliable measures for publically funded preschools (National Governors Association, 2005). Rand Corporation concluded that only a handful of states lacked a subsidized preschool initiative.[18] Some were only open to children of the poor, and others were open to children with disabilities (Christina & Nicholson-Goodman, 2005). In 2006, Illinois made preschool education free to all families, income level notwithstanding (Grossman, 2006). New Jersey followed suit in 2007 with a universal free preschool program.

Private Preschool Admission Assessments for 3-Year-Olds

While various states are developing universal preschool programs, private preschool education is also flourishing. In large urban centers like New York City, there are preschools that have a "buzz" about them. Whatever the source of the cachet may be, the result has been an increased amount of pressure by upper middle class parents to gain admission for their children into these schools. In 2006, an increase in the population of toddlers had resulted in the most competitive year ever for admission into the top-ranked urban preschools (Saulny, 2006). Additionally, their popularity has made it possible for some preschools to increase their costs to a level not too different from the cost of attending an undergraduate college (Moyer, 2007). Tony preschools in Washington, D.C., Philadelphia, Boston, and New York now charge parents over $30,000 per year for tuition for their 3- and 4-year-old children. In these selective and expensive preschools, there are many more applicants than there are admission slots for children.

A consortium of preschools in New York City cooperates in a joint effort to test and screen 3-year-old children whose parents wish to have them attend one of the prestigious independent preschools. This admission testing in New York is repeated in many schools and communities throughout the United States. Since 1966, the Educational Records Bureau (ERB) has served as the testing agency for admission into the 138 preschools (lower schools) of the Independent Schools Admission Association of Greater New York. Naturally, parents have a vested interest in seeing their children admitted into the best possible school. These parents often hire tutors for their 3- and 4-year-old children (Borja, 2005; R. Gardner, 2005) (see Case in Point 1.8).

Case in Point 1.8

Entrepreneurial Opportunities in Early Education

The press for academic and cognitive achievement in early childhood can be seen in a decision by the Sylvan Learning System to tool up and provide 1,200 locations nationwide where parents can take 3- and 4-year-old children for tutoring (Paul, 2007). Centers owned by Sylvan developed a preschool reading curriculum based on the report of the National Reading Panel. That curriculum is a **phonics**-based approach to developing prereading skills. Those centers also employ flash cards, worksheets, and workbooks to reinforce learning. The tutorial program makes heavy use of online instruction at Sylvan learning centers with the child's tutor present to provide encouragement and answer questions.

Not to be outdone, Kaplan, Inc. reports having enrolled 16,000 preschool children in structured tutoring classes in 2005 (Kronholz, 2005). Another entrepreneur, Kumon North America, offers anyone the opportunity of owning and operating a tutoring center through a franchise operation. This Japanese-based company has a long history of offering tutorial schools in Japan and has recently gone worldwide with variations of the Japanese *juku* (cram school) for young children.

This pressure for admission into the elite preschools was documented on a DVD movie *Nursery University.* (Docurama Studio, 2009, a Mark H. Simon & Matthew Maker Production).

Parents in New York can find listings for ERB coaching services in phone directories and online. ERB coaches typically provide hour-long tutoring sessions, three or more days per week, for several months prior to the big test day. The cost of a private tutor in the child's home runs between $75.00 and $150.00 per session. Another strategy that has become common for these parents involves taking children to the office of one or more licensed psychologists for a cognitive assessment. It is usual in such circumstances to arrange to have a parent watch the child respond to the type of questions and tasks that the ERB employs to assess young children applicants.[19]

Summary

Modern concepts of early childhood education were born in the writings and educational practices first developed in Germany during the early years of the 18th century. The push to make preschool education more academic and to use high-stakes assessments with young children is a recent development that is not universally admired.

The culture of educational testing and developmental assessments was originally built on an assumption of a genetic basis for individual differences among children. The unabashed goal for educational leaders including Lewis Terman was the establishment of an American meritocracy. One result from that golden age of testing was the justification of cultural prejudice.

Early education programs started in settlement houses at the start of the 20th century. The Depression and war years saw great expansion of publicly supported nursery education. The 1960s and 1970s brought new social policies and federal laws designed to provide children with disabilities a level playing field, and the ability to partake in a school's educational offerings. Beginning at birth, public agencies must work to identify children who may have special needs and provide them and their families with services and support.

Children who are English language learners (ELL) represent another class of preschoolers that requires extra services. One major concern for early childhood teachers is finding appropriate techniques for assessing bilingual and other young ELL children. The assessment of English language learners is also a special concern for people administering large-scale tests with young children.

Discussion Questions

1. How is the kindergarten concept developed in the 19th century being changed by American educators today?
2. The American approach to assessing children is highly empirical and involves comparing individuals to group outcomes. Many European educators encouraged a child-centered and qualitative approach. Which is a better model for preschool children in the United States today? Explain your position.
3. What factors led President Roosevelt to involve the federal government in preschool education programs?
4. Why did federally sponsored WPA nursery schools not include a systematic evaluation of the programs?
5. President Nixon rejected an effort to establish universal child care (John Brademas's Comprehensive Child Development Act of 1971). From your knowledge of the history of that era, what are some reasons that would lead two successive American presidents (Lyndon Johnson and Richard Nixon) in such different directions?

Related Readings

Bowe, F. G. (2004). *Birth to eight: Early childhood special education* (3rd ed.). Clifton Park, NY: Delmar-Thomson Learning.

Fischer, C. S., Hour, M., Jankowski, M. S., Lucas, S. R., Swidler, A., & Voss, K. (1996). *Inequality by design: Cracking the bell curve myth*. Princeton, NJ: Princeton University Press.

Gesell, A. (1943). *The infant and child in the culture of today: The guidance of development in home and nursery school.* New York: Harper Brothers.

Notes

1. Frank was named Frank Lincoln Wright, but later changed his name to Frank Lloyd Wright to honor his mother.
2. The Montessori curriculum has recently been used with good success in assisted living centers to reduce cognitive decline among senior citizens (Leland, 2008).
3. At the turn of the 20th century, most of the leading experts on childhood (including the psychoanalysts Anna Freud, Eric H. Erikson, and Alfred Adler) spent time in Rome studying with Maria Montessori. After spending time in Rome with Maria Montessori, the Genevan theorist Jean Piaget established *La Maison des Petits* (the Children's House) in Switzerland. This became the center for his early research into the cognition of children.
4. In 1920–1921, a young Piaget spent a year working with Theodore Simon in Paris to translate and standardize the English intelligence tests created by Sir Cyril Burt of the University of London. After that year, he never revisited the idea of a group measure of intelligence.
5. The foundation was created by John D. Rockefeller in memory of his wife Laura in 1918 following her death. The Laura Spelman Rockefeller Foundation was focused on educational, race relations, health, and child welfare matters. It was folded into the Rockefeller Foundation in 1929 when the Rockefeller foundations were merged. At one point in his life, John Rockefeller was the wealthiest man in the history of the world with an estimated worth of $320 billion (inflation adjusted). In addition to the many child study clinics and laboratories, he was responsible for starting and endowing Spelman College, Rockefeller University, and the University of Chicago.
6. This was named the recapitalization theory, and it was simply expressed as "ontology recapitulates philology." In other words, the growth of children (ontology) goes through stages similar to the stages in the genetic evolution (philology) that led to *Homo sapiens*.
7. The Otis-Lennon School Ability Test, 8th ed. (OLSAT-8). Information about this assessment is available at https://harcourtassessment.com/haiweb/cultures/en-us/productdetail.htm?pid=OLSAT.
8. There is no doubt that Lewis Terman was a man of his times and a racist. In the manual for his first test of mental ability, he stated, "Their [i.e., children of minorities] dullness seems to be racial, or at least inherent in the family stocks from which they came. The fact that one meets this type with such extraordinary frequency among Indians, Mexicans, and Negroes suggests quite forcibly that the whole question of racial differences in mental traits will have to be taken up anew by experimental methods." He went on to predict that there would be enormous differences by race in measured levels of general intelligence (Terman, 1916, p. 91).
9. Today we know that normal school as the University of California, Los Angeles.
10. Vygotsky saw child development as a continuous process, internally regulated and powered by the formation of mental structures that were not previously present. To read a translation of the works of Vygotsky, see http://www.marxists.org/archive/vygotsky/works/1934/problem-age.htm.
11. As a psychologist working in the Soviet Union, Vygotsky had to follow the official orthodoxy espoused by the other scientists of the USSR. The Russian Academy of Science had adopted an anti-genetic explanation for evolution and the diversity of life. This was espoused by the biologist Trofim Denisovich Lysenko and published in *Biulleten' VASKhNIL*. This position in opposition to Mendelian genetics was endorsed by Joseph Stalin, the dictator of that era. As such it was assumed to be fact by all of Soviet science (Roll-Hansen, 2008).

12. Not all Asian Americans share the same heritage and culture. Therefore, it is inappropriate to make generalizations about the academic ability of Asian American children. On average, children whose families immigrated from Korea, China, and many Southeast Asian countries have the highest scores on standardized tests compared to all other groups of American children (Xie & Goyette, 1998). The test scores of Asian American children tend to be about equal or slightly lower than the scores of Anglo-white children.
13. This can be seen in the size of the membership in the National Association of Nursery Educators (NANE), which was less than 5,000 in 1950. By 2000, the National Association for the Education of Young Children (née, NANE) had a membership of over 100,000 (NAEYC, 2001). During these slow years (1945 to 1965) assessment and program evaluation were rarely issues as preschools struggled to survive.
14. The Westinghouse Report was an example of badly flawed research (Morris, 2006, p. 204). Another outcome of this report was a major cut in Head Start funding by the Nixon administration.
15. Research has shown that a full-day program is far superior for teaching early academic skills to young children (Lee, Burkam, Ready, Honigman, & Meisels, 2006).
16. Before World War II, the term day care was universally employed to describe the setting where children were cared for away from their families. More recently, the term child care has supplanted that term. The point can be made that the care of children can occur at any time of day or night. In a similar way, the term nursery school, common prior to World War II, is now described as preschool.
17. The HighScope approach requires that only fully certified teachers with a bachelor or master's degree be employed to teach, and that preschools provide five days of education in small classes a week. Preschools follow an academic and social skills curriculum. Only about 20% of the Head Start centers follow this approach to preschool education. More about the HighScope curriculum can be seen at http://www.highscope.org/Content.asp?ContentID=223.
18. States without programs for early education in 2008 included Alaska, Idaho, Indiana, Mississippi, Montana, New Hampshire, North Dakota, Rhode Island, South Dakota, Utah, and Wyoming.
19. For more information on preschool admissions in New York City, see https://www.ecaatest.org/ERBRegistration/ParentPortal/PDF/ERB-In-School-Brochure-2008.pdf or http://www.isaagny.org.

Issues and Current Practice for Assessing Young Children

2

Merely having a number associated with something makes it sound worthwhile, even if the number isn't all that valid.

—Robert J. Sternberg, Tufts University

Introduction and Themes

America has embraced educational testing as the cure to most problems in education. Perhaps this faith in testing reflects our belief that objective scores are somehow fair and just. Test scores are not the problem; it is how we interpret and use them that is of concern. Professional associations have taken clear positions regarding testing and assessment of children. The key provision for young children is that the testing must provide some clear benefit for the child.

A new emphasis on testing has become part of American education following the election of President George W. Bush in 2000. The No Child Left Behind Act (NCLB) (2002) had a series of mandates including one requiring that public schools show annual progress toward reaching the goal of universal achievement proficiency by the year 2014. This brought about significant changes in the organization and approach to teaching followed in kindergartens and the primary grades. Many of the original testing mandates were continued under President Barack H. Obama, including the publication of a school report card to the media each year.

Public schools under great pressure to show improved achievement test scores have resorted to curriculum and program modifications that emphasize academic drill in the basic skills. In kindergarten, even nap time and free playtime have been reduced.

Data show that the rate of children being asked to repeat the kindergarten year is increasing. In addition to more children "flunking" kindergarten, there are also data indicating that parents are voluntarily keeping their children away from first grade for an extra year.

Children for whom English is not the primary language present an assessment problem. The population of these children now represents the largest minority group in our schools, and evaluations of children with limited proficiency in the English language require special provisions.

There is a developmentally appropriate progression from preschool through third grade for the types of assessments that should be used to measure children's learning. Brief developmental and skill assessments can be completed with preschool children. By kindergarten and the first grade, tests and assessments should be designed to assist the public school teacher in tracking each child's growth and skill acquisition. Therefore, most classroom assessments should be formative and designed to help plan for instruction. Primary grades may include standardized achievement measures starting in the spring of first grade and/or during second grade. By third grade, classroom tests become part of the mix, and children will face a high-stakes **test battery**[1] mandated by the NCLB Act (see the discussion of formative assessments in Chapter 4).

Learning Objectives

By reading and studying this chapter, you should acquire the competency to:

- Describe the position on testing young children taken by the National Association for the Education of Young Children (NAEYC).
- Describe the impact of federal testing mandates on the education of young children in the United States.
- Plan an assessment program appropriate for preschool and primary grade children who have a limited proficiency in English.
- Describe the changing pattern of testing as conducted in schools from preschool through third grade.
- Discuss and describe the recent development of technology for the purpose of assessing young children.

America's Culture of Testing

In American education, there are four levels of assessment.[2] At one layer are classroom tests, quizzes, and the grading of homework and projects. These measurement activities are done to assist teachers in the instructional process. A second layer of measurement serves the guidance, selection, and admissions needs of our schools. The third layer of testing measures children and compares their achievement outcomes with the achievement of the broad population. The final layer has been imposed by federal and state mandates for the assessment of children's achievement of published standards for learning.

This multifaceted testing program is unlikely to change anytime soon. More than any other nation, America has developed an educational system wedded to testing. Perhaps this reflects our fascination with things that appear to be objective and fair (Strauss, 2006). As a people, Americans believe in "being fair," and giving everyone an "equal shot." What could be fairer than a test that everyone must take? In 1923, Sidney and Luella Pressey wrote the first American textbook on educational testing in which they argued that teachers should not be trusted to make impartial assessments of their students and should rely on the new standardized tests to provide honest grades.[3]

It can be argued that it is not the amount of testing done that is the problem; it is the type of testing. Research by Samuel Meisels has shown that formative assessments in the form of **curriculum-embedded performance assessments** during Grades 1 through 3 can greatly improve reading test scores on standardized test batteries (Meisels, Atkins-Burnett, Xue, Bickel, & Son, 2003). Meisels used the term **work sampling system**[4] to describe the embedded performance measuring system.

Professional Standards and Guidelines

Professional associations hold themselves to be keepers of the best traditions and practices of their fields, and assume that the general public will have confidence in their work and respect for their members. To ensure this continuing high regard of the public, the various professional associations publish guidelines for ethical behavior and the practice of their members. The professional associations with an interest in educational measurement have worked together to publish a combined document on testing ethics.[5]

Five Principles of Testing Ethics[6]

1. The first of these principles for the ethical practice of testing involves *communication* with those taking the test. The purpose of the test and areas to be measured should be fully understood by the test taker (or the parent/guardian) prior to the time of the test. The use of scores from the test should be explained and the test takers should be told how long their results will be on file. The administrator should provide special accommodations for test takers with disabilities.
2. The second area involves *confidentiality*. The test administrator must ensure that scores from individual students are disclosed only to people having a professional need for those data. Students' parents are included in the group who should have full access to the test score data. It is also critical that test materials are stored in a secure location and never released for review by others.
3. Third, the *interpretation* of scores should be carried out in a way that conforms with guidelines provided by the test publisher. The person interpreting scores should be trained and knowledgeable of the test and its scoring system. Parents and students should be informed of the scores and their interpretation in a developmentally appropriate way. In addition, scores should be reported using understandable language that parents can follow, avoiding educational jargon. This includes **"cut scores"** and minimal standards for success. Scoring errors should be corrected immediately and the correction noted through all of the student's records.
4. A fourth issue is the *use of test scores*. A single score on a test should never be used to determine the placement of a student. Interpretations should always be made in conjunction with other sources of information.
5. A final point involves the *development and selection* of tests. A test or assessment should only be used for a purpose for which it was designed and standardized. The test should provide a manual documenting that the measure is valid and reliable and explaining the tasks it is designed to accomplish. Also, the manual should provide evidence that there is no consistent bias (gender, ethnicity, socioeconomic status, etc.) influencing the scores. The test should also include clear directions for administration and scoring.

SOURCE: Joint Committee on Testing Practices, 2005.

Testing Young Children

The **National Association for the Education of Young Children** (NAEYC) has studied the question of testing young children and has taken a position that such testing should only be pursued if it is clearly beneficial for the child (see Case in Point 2.1 for an example of inappropriate testing of young children). The NAEYC believes that appropriate and beneficial purposes for testing young children fall into three categories (NAEYC, 2005a). The first reason to assess is to make sound decisions about learning, and to have information to plan the most efficacious instruction for each child. The second is to identify concerns that will need special programs of individual intervention. The final reason is to provide data to assist the early childhood program improve its instructional practices. The full set of guidelines is available from the NAEYC Web site at http://www.naeyc.org/about/positions/pdf/pscape.pdf.

Case in Point 2.1

High-Stakes Testing for 4-Year-Olds

Perhaps the most egregious violation of the principles for the ethical assessment of young children was carried out between 2003 and 2007 by the U.S. Department of Health and Human Services (USDHHS). In 2002, the George W. Bush administration introduced a high-stakes testing program for 4-year-old children called **"Good Start, Grow Smart."** This initiative added testing provisions for all **Head Start** early childhood programs. Provisions of this initiative included a requirement that a single empirical assessment be used for all 2,700 Head Start and Early Head Start centers (Bush, 2002). That assessment was developed and pilot tested in 2003, and universally used between 2004 and 2007 (see Photo 2.1). That national testing program assessed over 400,000 4-year-old children a year (Strauss, 2007). The assessment included measures of the child's expressive and **receptive language,** literacy, and **numeracy** (USDHHS, 2007a) (see Figure 2.1).

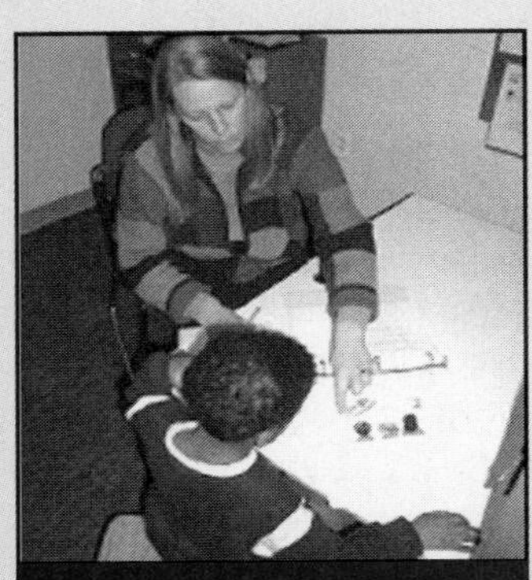

Photo 2.1 A Child Being Evaluated Using the Required Test in a Head Start Center

SOURCE: From Government Accountability Office, Document GAO-05-343 Head Start, Highlights. Used with permission.

In the summer of 2005, the Government Accountability Office (GAO) reported to Congress that the Head Start testing program should not be used in accountability studies as it was not validated for that task (GAO, 2005) (for a discussion of validity, see Chapter 3). Also, the measurement system did not assess many areas covered by the 1965 Head Start mandate.

Professional associations were also critical of the use of standardized testing programs with preschool children. The argument posed by Samuel Meisels and Sally Atkins-Burnett (2004) was that children are in a state of flux and rapid change at the age of 4. That lack of consistency creates an environment where it is not possible to do meaningful analytical testing.

The off-year elections of 2006 brought a new Congress that did not support the concept of high-stakes testing of Head Start children. The five-year reauthorization of Head Start signed into law in December 2007 did away with the mandate for using high-stakes tests. President Bush disapproved of the fact that the Head Start reauthorization bill of 2007 did away with the mandate for the individualized testing of children, but signed it into law because of the overwhelming bipartisan Congressional support that it received (Klein, 2007).

Figure 2.1 Sample Items From the Head Start Assessment

Example of NRS Letter Naming Instructions and Task

Here are some letters of the alphabet.

GESTURE WITH A CIRCULAR MOTION AT LETTERS AND SAY:

Point to all the letters that you know and tell me the name of each one. Go slowly and show me which letter you're naming.

INDICATE ONLY CORRECTLY NAMED LETTERS ON ANSWER SHEET.

WHEN CHILD STOPS NAMING LETTERS, SAY:

Look carefully at all of them. Do you know any more?

KEEP ASKING UNTIL CHILD DOESN'T KNOW ANY MORE.

Aa	Oo	Ss
Bb	Ee	Cc
Dd	Xx	

(Continued)

Figure 2.1 (Continued)

Example of Type of Vocabulary Instructions and Task Used in the NRS

Say: point to mowing.

Training Plate D

Example of NRS Early Math Skills Instructions and Task

Run your finger across the item and say:

If you gave a friend one of these books, how many books would you have left?

Correct: Two (Books)

SOURCE: From "Full National Implementation of the Head Start National Reporting System on Child Outcomes, Office of Management and Budget Clearance Package Supporting Statement and Data Collection Instruments," by the U.S. Dept. of Health and Human Services, Administration for Children and Families, Administration on Children, Youth, and Families, June 23, 2003.

No *Young* Child Left Behind

Federal mandates for high-stakes testing have had a far-reaching impact on young children. This impact reverberates throughout our culture and is felt by every public school student and parent. One result is that many children experience test anxiety and unreasonable fears related to being evaluated while they are preschoolers (Strauss, 2006).

Adequate Yearly Progress

This preschool testing emphasis reflects the requirements that all public and charter schools demonstrate that they are making **adequate yearly progress (AYP)**. This involves having each grade from third to eighth demonstrate that all groups of children are making progress toward meeting the goal of universal proficiency in reading and mathematics (see Photo 2.2).[7]

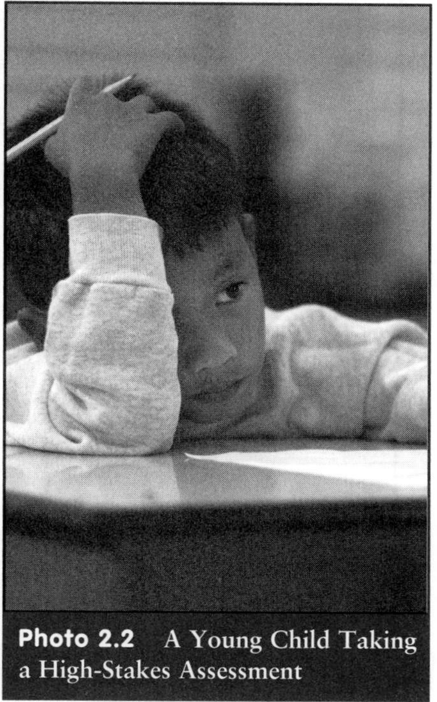

Photo 2.2 A Young Child Taking a High-Stakes Assessment

To demonstrate AYP, every public and charter school (parochial, private, and home schools are exempt) must show that the average achievement score from children in each of nine identified groups meets or exceeds the annual benchmark set by the state's education department. These nine groups are Anglo-white children, Asian American children, Hispanic children, non-Hispanic African American children, mixed race children, children from poverty, children with one or more disabilities, Native American children,[8] and children who are English language learners.[9]

Failure to demonstrate the school has met its AYP targets for only one year will result in the school being marked as not meeting standards on the required annual **"school report card."**[10] The label is almost always presented to the public by local media as "failing." The general public has no way to discern anything from such headlines beyond the fact that their expensive and heretofore highly regarded school system is a failure. Schools that have a three-year history of such "failure" must offer children the option of transferring to other higher-performing schools. If the "failures continue" the school must be reorganized or closed. Reorganization involves firing the principal and transferring or firing the teachers. In 2008, there were a total of 3,559 schools in the United States that had a five-year history of failing to meet the AYP standard and were in the process of being reorganized or closed (Hoff, 2008). That same year, 28% of all schools, a total of 29,873, failed to meet the AYP target.[11]

Rubber Rulers

One result of all this pressure has been the practice of most states to lower their test score standards (see Case in Point 2.2 for an example of how the stress of high-stakes tests is used to make money). This reduces the requirements for having children pass the state's tests. All too often, the **cut score** used to determine if a child is "proficient" is influenced by politics. The practice of lowering standards has been described as "measuring with **rubber rulers**" (Jehlen, 2007; Schumacker, 2005). Another result of this pressure is that at the local level teachers and hundreds of schools have been identified as having "cheated" on the state tests (Kaczor, 2008; Patrick & Eichel, 2006).

Case in Point 2.2

High-Stakes Testing in the Media

American culture, with its focus on each child as a potential revenue source, has not missed the stress felt by so many children and parents over high-stakes testing (S. Steinberg & Kincheloe, 2004). Popular media picked up on this angst produced by mandated assessments and used it as a source of entertainment. One example can be seen with children's literature that has begun to play on this theme with fictional books such as Judy Finchler's (2000) *Testing Miss Malarkey;* Pansie Hart Flood's (2004) *It's Test Day, Tiger Turcotte;* Edward Bloor's (2004) *Story Time;* even the fifth book of the wildly popular children's series by J. K. Rowling (2003), *Harry Potter and the Order of the Phoenix,* finds the hero under stress to achieve a passing score on an "Ordinary Wizarding Level" (OWL) examination. Hollywood has not missed this trend either. Disney released the movie *Recess: School's Out,* a story of a radical educational reformer who wants to cancel recess to have more time for students to work on better test scores (Suzuki & Swuz, 2001). Art imitates life, as this is occurring in our public schools today (Bodden, 2005).

Rewards and Prizes

Pressure has also been put on primary grade children to motivate them to score well on the state tests. Schools have worked with their local business communities to offer a range of prizes and rewards for good test scores (see Case in Point 2.3 for a large-scale example of monetary rewards). These have included free restaurant meals, savings bonds, and gift certificates (Belluck, 2006; Knight, 2005; Lou, 2007; Pakkala, 2006; Viadero, 2008b; Woods, 2007). Perhaps the most unusual reward program for children occurred in Florida. In some of the elementary schools of the City of Gainesville, the third grade students who performed best on the state assessment, the FCAT, got to stand in a chamber filled with swirling money and grab as many handfuls of $1 and $5 bills as they could in 15 seconds as their classmates looked on. This unusual project was cosponsored by a local bank (Finger, 2006).

Case in Point 2.3

Paying Children for Their Success

Mayor Michael Bloomberg of New York City introduced a reward plan open to schools in the poorest neighborhoods. The privately funded program paid children for good test scores. Only 90 of 200 potential schools accepted the offer because it also included bonuses for the teachers with the highest-scoring students.[12] Teachers were paid bonuses of $3,000 while many children earned $100 for good grades (Medina, 2008). In 2007, Mayor Bloomberg began paying families for keeping their children engaged in education. This included rewards for getting all family members a health checkup ($200). Families were also paid $500 for each child who was present in school 95% of the time (maximum absences = eight days/year) (Lucadamo, 2007).

Impact of Testing Mandates on Early Childhood Education Programs

The original notion of kindergartens as designed by Friedrich Froebel was that young children should spend their days in a low-key environment (see Chapter 1).

Today, kindergartens are being radically reshaped by the need of school systems to prepare children for high-stakes tests. This push for academically oriented kindergarten programs has also changed the focus of preschool education in America (Burrell, 2007).

"This place is my respite from an otherwise hectic world."

SOURCE: Cartoon by Merv Magus.

Schedule

One of the changes in preschools and kindergartens relates to the use of time. The length of the kindergarten day is getting longer with about 80% of school systems now using full-day kindergarten programs that average about 6.5 hours (Ackerman, Barnett, & Robin, 2005). In many of these kindergarten programs, children are provided with very little unstructured playtime (Jacobson, 2008a). This trend can be seen with the loss of the play kitchens and the traditional large box of wooden building blocks (Hemphill, 2006). David Elkind (2007) has reported that between 1985 and 2005 American children lost an average of 12 hours of free playtime a week outside of school. Thus, the loss of this vital part of child development is twofold, from within the school and also from without when the child is at home. There is neurological evidence that the need for play behavior is a genetically wired requirement, and that the need may be greater with children who are hyperactive (Bergen & Coscia, 2000; Henig, 2008).

Environment

Another sign of the change is the appearance of a circle of small chairs arranged in a semicircle around the teacher's chair. In this format, the teacher can provide several hours a day of scripted instruction in phonics and prereading skills. The new kindergarten also provides an hour or so developing numeracy and providing instruction in basic arithmetic (Gao, 2005; Shellenbarger, 2005). The National Association for Education of Young Children considers the extensive use of whole group instruction as a sign of an inferior preschool (NAEYC, 2001). Computer workstations are also part of new kindergartens, providing a place where children work alone in cubicles to reinforce what they have learned through the use of interactive game-formatted software. What is missing is the space dedicated to free play and imagination.

Playtime

The loss of free time to play in a play yard or with the educational and creative toys in the classroom does a disservice to children in terms of their cognitive growth and social development (Crain, 2003). Social skills are retarded by the lack of time designated for children to interact and learn to negotiate with peers. Social skills are developed during the process of learning to establish rules and playing cooperatively. Solitary and parallel play of young children cannot undergo this natural evolution when children are containerized all day and focused only on the teacher.

Cognitive development is enhanced when children can interact with the elements of their environment through play and simulations (Jones & Cooper, 2006; Piaget, 1962). Many preschools are stunting the social and emotional development of young children by cutting playtime and reducing time for pretend and fantasy activities (Fein, 1981). Being competent and masterful at games is a major developmental achievement for all children between ages 3 and 5 (Jones & Reynolds, 1992). From game competence comes the foundation of the child's self-esteem and social development.

Time to Rest

Another element missing in the schedule of many kindergarten programs is naptime. Small bedrolls, mats, and/or cots are gone, and the half hour needed to set up and take brief naps has been sacrificed to provide more time for instruction (Smith-Arrants, 2006). The need for sleep is an individual issue, but pediatricians have long recommended that preschoolers be given naps each day (K. Davis, Parker, & Montgomery, 2004).

The time gained by these changes (less playtime and naps) can add up to 6 hours a week to the time spent on scripted learning or practice drills. To date, there is no clear evidence that these revisions have a significant positive impact on the acquisition of academic skills.

Academic Redshirting

There have always been parents who delay starting their child's school career. Likewise, there are parents who work to get their child into public school as soon as legally possible. Recently, the former group has been growing. This is especially true in those cities and states using standardized tests to make promotion decisions for third graders.[13] This phenomenon is referred to as **academic redshirting,**[14] a term derived from college athletics (Gordon, 2007). The result is that the age differential between the youngest and oldest child in a typical kindergarten class is two or more years.

There are a number of reasons why parents elect to hold their child out of school for an extra year. Generally, parents see the extra year as giving their child an advantage over their younger peers. That advantage is evident in the child's size and strength, but parents also believe that the extra year in a preschool provides time for their child to become more socially competent and cognitively advanced. Nationally, about 9% of all children are redshirted, but in some suburban neighborhoods the number is closer to 50% (Katz, 2000; M. Keller, 2006; West, Meek, & Hurst, 2000). The practice is more common in communities where parents are relatively affluent. Boys are more likely to be held out an extra year, as are children who were born in the fall.

Admission into private elementary schools is also related to redshirting young children (Graue, Kroeger, & Brown, 2003). The most prestigious of these **lower schools** have high standards for admission that are easier for older preschoolers to meet. Also, private lower schools want children who are better able to fit into the academic culture of the school, and more mature youngsters are often a better fit.

Quantitative research into the question of redshirting has demonstrated a positive impact that diminishes over time. Redshirting has the largest positive effect on first grade test scores for children from impoverished homes (Datar, 2003). However, this positive effect begins to fade by second grade and is generally washed out before the end of eighth grade (Elder & Lubotsky, in press; H. Marshall, 2003).[15]

See Case in Point 2.4 for another parental strategy to avoid high-stakes tests.

Case in Point 2.4

The Home School Option

One strategy being adopted by parents of children at risk for failing a state assessment is home schooling. Fewer than half of the states have testing requirements for home-schooled children. States that do have a testing requirement often leave it up to the parent to select and administer the examination. To learn about home schooling and testing standards for the various states, see http://homeschooling.about.com/od/legal/Staying_Legal_Homeschool_Laws_and_Requirements.htm.

English Language Learners and High-Stakes Tests

American Nativism

America has received major populations of immigrants from around the world. This trend predates the founding of the nation. Since the arrival of the first colonists, these populations of new immigrants have been frequently met with hostility and fear. In the 1920s, the Ku Klux Klan targeted central and southern European immigrants along with other "undesirables" (F. Allen, 1931). Today, there are periodic calls for amending the American Constitution to make English the official language. The U.S. Senate voted upon a proposed language amendment as recently as 2006 (Hulse, 2006).[16]

Throughout this country's history, people have immigrated here from all corners of Europe and Asia. Also, as a nation we did an unthinkable evil and brought an enslaved population to North America from Africa. Today, we face a new wave of immigration of Spanish-speaking people from the Caribbean, and Central and South America. The same nativism first expressed in the colonial era, and which has followed every new wave of immigrants, is being voiced again about our growing Hispanic population (see Case in Point 2.5 for an historical example of **American nativism**).

Case in Point 2.5

History of American Nativism

By 1760, a third of the population of the Pennsylvania Colony were German-speaking immigrants. This aroused a nativist sentiment and fear among the English-speaking population, including the leading citizen of Pennsylvania, Benjamin Franklin. He suggested that the Germans should be rounded up and redistributed throughout the other 12 colonies. Once they were mixed into the English-speaking population, he felt they would become English-speaking members of the United Kingdom in America (Franklin, 1751). It was his goal that all colonists would be English speakers.

In reality, the Hispanic part of our population now represents the largest single minority group in America, and it is tracking to grow even larger over the foreseeable future (see Table 2.1). Before 2000, there were 35.2 million Hispanic children enrolled in the schools of the United States. That number had grown to 44.3 million by 2006, an increase of 26% in six years (Pew Hispanic Center, 2008).

Table 2.1 Statistical Portrait of the Hispanic School Enrollment in the United States in 2000 and 2006

	Nursery School Enrollment			
	2000	2006	Change, 2000–2006	Percentage of 2006 Nursery School Enrollment
Hispanic	670,425	857,371	186,946	17.5
Native born	629,884	826,000	196,116	16.9
Foreign born	40,541	31,371	–9,170	0.6
White alone, not Hispanic	3,150,786	2,890,402	–260,384	59.2
Black alone, not Hispanic	770,591	711,794	–58,797	14.6
Asian alone, not Hispanic	158,761	213,620	54,859	4.4
Other, not Hispanic	212,556	212,143	–413	4.3
Total	4,963,119	4,885,330	–77,789	100.0
	Kindergarten Through 12th Grade Enrollment			
	2000	2006	Change, 2000–2006	Percentage of 2006 K–12 Enrollment
Hispanic	8,317,636	9,983,165	1,665,529	19.1
Native born	6,888,050	8,574,116	1,686,066	16.4
Foreign born	1,429,586	1,409,049	–20,537	2.7
White alone, not Hispanic	32,391,693	30,482,912	–1,908,781	58.3
Black alone, not Hispanic	7,736,287	7,764,820	28,553	14.9
Asian alone, not Hispanic	1,759,910	1,998,043	238,133	3.8
Other, not Hispanic	1,996,398	2,039,563	43,165	3.9
Total	52,201,924	52,268,503	66,579	100.0

SOURCE: Pew Hispanic Center, 2006, Table 23. Available at http://pewhispanic.org/factsheets/factsheet.php?FactsheetID=35.

NOTE: School enrollment consists of both private and public schools.

The **distribution** of Hispanic families is not even across the 50 states. Ten states account for more than 80% of all Hispanic families. Table 2.2 provides data demonstrating this distribution.

Second Language Learning

The human ability to learn more than one language is unique (Mechelli et al., 2004). The age of the child learning a second language is a critical factor in the emerging literacy in the second language (**L2**). Typically, all children placed in an environment where they cannot communicate with either teachers or other students will refrain from speaking. Children in an alien language environment focus on listening and attempting to create the new language from what they see and hear around them (Cook, 2008). Younger children will spend a longer period of time being mute than will their adolescent siblings. Yet, preadolescent children will have less difficulty developing fluency in the new language. This reflects the greater plasticity of their developing neurology. The **language centers in the brain** lose **plasticity** with adolescence and learning a second language becomes more difficult (Lenneberg, 1967).

Most kindergartens and public schools require any child who has resided in the United States for the past 12 months to take mandated tests in English even though English is a complex language to master as a L2 (Hayden, 2008). The neurology of young children is still growing and developing, giving primary grade

Table 2.2 Distribution of Hispanics Across States, 2006

	Hispanic Population	Total Population	Percentage Hispanic
California	13,087,981	36,457,549	35.9
Texas	8,379,992	23,507,783	35.6
Florida	3,642,610	18,089,889	20.1
New York	3,139,787	19,305,183	16.3
Illinois	1,889,528	12,831,970	14.7
Arizona	1,796,643	6,166,318	29.1
New Jersey	1,360,784	8,724,560	15.6
Colorado	927,453	4,753,377	19.5
New Mexico	874,125	1,954,599	44.7
Georgia	695,521	9,363,941	7.4
Nevada	605,059	2,495,529	24.2
North Carolina	595,376	8,856,505	6.7
Washington	586,020	6,395,798	9.2
Pennsylvania	522,280	12,440,621	4.2
Massachusetts	509,219	6,437,193	7.9
Virginia	465,545	7,642,884	6.1
Michigan	398,935	10,095643	4.0
Connecticut	384,308	3,504,809	11.0
Oregon	378,444	3,700,758	10.2
Maryland	341,261	5,615,727	6.1
Indiana	301,681	6,313,520	4.8
Utah	294,116	2,550,063	11.5
Ohio	267,712	11,478,005	2.3
Wisconsin	261,827	5,555,506	4.7
Kansas	245,401	2,764,075	8.9
Ociahoma	243,371	3,579,212	6.8
Minnesota	200,290	5,167,101	3.9
Tennessee	187,761	6,038,803	3.1
Missourt	161,831	5,842,713	2.8
South Carolina	149,931	4,321,249	3.5
Idaho	144,846	1,466,465	9.9
Arkansas	144,394	2,810,872	5.1
Nebraska	133,646	1,768,331	7.6
Iowa	120,091	2,982,085	4.0
Rhode Island	119,512	1,067,610	11.2
Louisiana	118,968	4,287,768	2.8
Alabama	109,325	4,599,030	2.4
Hawaii	99,917	1,285,498	7.8
Kentucky	83,032	4,206,074	2.0
Delaware	55,572	853,476	6.5

(Continued)

SOURCE: Pew Hispanic Center, 2006, Table 12. Available at http://pewhispanic.org/files/factsheets/hispanics2006/Table-12.pdf.

Table 2.2 (Continued)

	Hispanic Population	Total Population	Percentage Hispanic
Mississippi	48,911	2,910,540	1.7
Dist. of Columbia	46,500	581,530	8.0
Alaska	37,142	670,053	5.5
Wyoming	36,728	515,004	7.1
New Hampshire	29,442	1,314,895	2.2
Montana	19,052	944,632	2.0
Maine	14,296	1,321,574	1.1
South Dakota	13,389	781,919	1.7
West Virginia	12,378	1,818,470	0.7
North Dakota	10,426	635,867	1.6
Vermont	6,616	623,908	1.1
TOTAL	44,298,975	299,398,485	14.8

children greater neurological plasticity and making learning a new language easier. Once a child reaches adolescence that plasticity is gone and with it the facility with new languages.[17] On average, a primary grader who is immersed in a total English-speaking school environment can achieve fluency at the **Basic Interpersonal Communication Skill (BICS)** level in one or two years (Dong, 2007; Roseberry-McKibbin & Brice, 2005). However, this same child will not achieve a fluency in English permitting context-reduced academic language known as **Cognitive Academic Language Proficiency (CALP)** for another three to five years (for a total of five to seven years of immersion). During this learning process, the child will experience a period of time when he or she is semilingual (McLaughlin, Blanchard, & Osanai, 1995). **Semilingualism** occurs when the child is not ready to speak English at the BICS level, and has lost some fluency in the native language. This transition phase can lead to a child being misdiagnosed as having a language disability.

Related to this is the problem that most young children who are native Spanish speakers tend to attend school in the same neighborhood. A study of the schools of California found that there is a natural segregation with most students who are ELL attending schools where the dominant population is made up of native Spanish speakers (Rumberger, Gándara, & Merino, 2006). Frequently, neighborhood schools are located in communities where the local culture assumes a distinctively Hispanic flavor. There are many communities in the United States where English is rarely spoken or heard. In such environments, the process of learning the English language will take longer than if the child is immersed into a total English language environment.

Assessing English Language Learners

The implication for early childhood educators is that special consideration must be given to the task of assessing language minority children. Professional associations of early childhood educators recommend that the parents of young English language learners (ELLs) be used as a source of information about the child before the assessment is conducted. English language learners should have their English language development periodically reevaluated, and the results should be shared with the parents (NAEYC, 2005b). Recommendations also include using a bilingual/bicultural teacher to conduct assessments. Bilingual teachers who administer assessments should be fluent in English and the child's native language. The assessor should be very familiar with the culture of the child including social norms and appropriate behaviors.

Model Testing Program for Young Children

All testing with young children should be done for the direct benefit of the child. One example of this is the early assessments needed to organize early interventions. The advantage of initiating interventions before the child reaches kindergarten cannot be understated (Wybranski, 1996). Major developmental problems can frequently be identified before the child is 3 years old. Other reasons for testing young children may include the ongoing monitoring of children receiving special assistance, and/or to meet the requirements of an **Individual Family Service Plan (IFSP)** or **Individual Educational Plan (IEP)** (see Chapter 11).

Testing for instructional planning and placement is also part of many preschools and kindergartens. This may involve using a commercially available developmental **screening assessment** (see Chapter 7), or involve using one of the developmental measures designed to provide the information periodically required by the Office for Special Education Programs, for example, the Indicators of Individual Growth and Development for Infants and Toddlers (IGDIs). More can be found about IGDIs at http://www.igdi.ku.edu/index.htm.

Collectively, these measures are **formative evaluations** or assessments. Formative measurements are designed to provide information to the teacher about how learning is progressing in **"real time."** By collecting information on how well a child is doing during instruction, it is possible to tweak the learning experiences to correct a misconception or provide the child with information that facilitates his/her learning (see Chapter 4).

Federal mandates emphasizing high-stakes testing of children has resulted in an increase in the use of **standardized achievement tests** in the primary grades (K–3). An obvious outcome has been a boom for the educational testing industry. Federal testing mandates have been described by a vice president of ETS as a "full employment act for test publishers" (Bracey, 2004).

Special Problems in Testing Young Children

There are many reasons young children are more difficult to test than children who are older. First, young children have short attention spans and are easily distracted by elements in the environment. Long assessment protocols must be broken into several shorter testing sessions and may require several days to complete. Additionally, preschool children are more active and need to be physically involved in the measurement tasks. Because young children have limited expressive language, they are more likely to gesture or point than they are to verbally express answers. Most young children are shy and may be reluctant to work with an unfamiliar adult. It is not unusual for the child who is less than 5 years old to need to be in visual or even physical contact with a parent during an evaluation.

For these reasons it is necessary for the evaluator to spend time prior to testing in a concerted effort to develop a working rapport with the child and his/her caregiver. Also, young children need constant **reinforcement** for their work. Preschoolers have less **emotional strength** and may cry when faced with difficult tasks. Also, testing should avoid the threatening feelings that a visit to a professional office can evoke. Children should be assessed in a familiar environment whenever possible

Preschool Testing Programs

All public and most private preschools will admit young children without a preliminary assessment. During the child's first month of preschool, he/she is likely to experience **informal screening** assessments, the outcomes of which are normally maintained in a **portfolio** (hard copy or digital).

Without a preadmission screening, there is an increased likelihood that children may end up attending preschools that are developmentally inappropriate. This may explain why the number of children being expelled from preschool has increased (della Cava, 2005). The distribution of young children who are expelled varies by type of program with faith-affiliated and for-profit prekindergartens expelling about 12% of entering children. Public preschools and Head Start programs expel only half as many children (Gilliam, 2005). Walter

Gilliam speculated that the difference might have a lot to do with the education and professionalism of teachers working for Head Start and for the public schools. He opposes the expulsion of young children from prekindergarten by arguing that children being expelled are the very ones who most need the preschool environment.

The old solution to the problem of preschool admission was to employ a developmental screening test. **Readiness** scores from a standardized measure were frequently employed as the gatekeeper in admissions. The policy of the NAEYC (2004) is that this is not an appropriate assessment function. The point made by NAEYC is that preschools and kindergarten programs should be ready to teach all age-appropriate children.

Kindergarten

Tendencies for an increasingly large group of parents to redshirt their young children notwithstanding, the majority of children enter kindergarten when they are 5 years old. Until recently, school **readiness tests** were employed du rigueur, during what has been described as **kindergarten roundups.** Parents have been counseled to hold children at home for an extra year if their youngsters tested poorly on the kindergarten's readiness test. As noted above, this policy of admitting children into public school kindergartens based on scores on a readiness test is one to which the professional associations are opposed (National Association of Early Childhood Specialists in State Departments of Education, 2000).

In order to plan for individual needs of each child, the teacher needs information about each child's status on a number of dimensions. Data collection for this is best carried out on an individual basis. One approach is to provide two days when kindergarten children and their parents can come to school. During this meeting, the child should spend time working one-on-one with the teacher while the parent(s) meet with the elementary school's counselor/social worker. To ensure the comfort of the child, the teacher and counselor should be in the same room a few strides apart. This will make it possible for the child to see his/her parents while working with the kindergarten teacher.

The role of the elementary school counselor is to interview parents about their child and the home environment. Figure 2.2 presents a sample form used to collect relevant data during the kindergarten enrollment meeting.[18] The interview should be carried out in a friendly atmosphere with every effort made to make parent(s) comfortable. The goal is to have parent(s) view the school as a partner in their efforts to raise a healthy happy child. Therefore, the interview should not be rushed. It should be planned to last for approximately 20 minutes.

The teacher should use this time to determine the child's special strengths and form opinions about the child's cognitive, language, and physical status. The youngster's temperament and basics of his/her personality can also be revealed during the interview.

Dynamic Indicators of Basic Educational Literacy (DIBELS) is a public domain battery of measures that can be employed as part of this kindergarten roundup to assess the child's prereading skills (Good et al., 2002).[19] DIBELS requires only a few minutes with each child. At the kindergarten level, the DIBELS assessment provides educators with measures of Initial Sound Fluency, Letter Naming Fluency, Phoneme Segmentation Fluency, and Nonsense Word Fluency (DIBELS can be scored with a handheld computer system as described in Chapter 9); however, scores from this measure are volatile and not consistently accurate/reliable (Brunsman, 2005).

The best system to evaluate a new kindergarten student should include items and tasks designed by the teacher based on the school's learning objectives for the coming year. This informal assessment should be dynamic, engaging the child with educational materials and equipment. The focus of this classroom measure is to identify what the child is ready to learn in kindergarten. It also should be structured to identify the child's physical capabilities and skills. Finally, teachers should also gain insight into the child's tempo and personality through the informal procedures (see Figure 2.3 for possible areas for pre-enrollment assessment).

During the kindergarten year, most of the evaluations of student growth and skill development are informal. Informal evaluations involve observational data as well as checklists and work samples. These data are best organized in a portfolio that can be used to make summative statements providing information for parents. (Portfolio assessment is described in Chapter 4.)

Figure 2.2 Sample Kindergarten Enrollment Questionnaire

Today's Date ___/___/_______
Date of your Child's Birth ___/___/_______
Child's Name ____________________
Nickname ____________________
Parents or Guardians of Record ____________________
Is the child's custody shared? (__) Y (__) N With whom? ____________________
Other adults at home or frequent visitors (e.g., grandparents) (__) Y (__) N
If yes, who are these adults? ____________________
Child's Address ____________________ State ____ Zip _______
Phone Number (Home) (___)- ____________ (Cell) (___)- ____________ (Work) (___)- ____________
E-mail address ____________________
Language(s) spoken at home ____________________
Can the child speak a language other than English? (__) Y (__) N
Which language? ____________________
Have you and your child moved recently? (__) Y (__) N
If yes, please describe ____________________
____
What special days and holidays do you and your child celebrate?
____
Are there other children living at home (__) Y (__) N
Names, gender, age, and grade (if in school)
____
____
What child care or preschool experience has your child had?
Provider ____________________
Dates from _________ to _________
Describe your child's sleeping cycle (bedtime, wake time). Does he or she nap?
____
Nap Time ____________________
What foods does your child refuse? ____________________
What are your child's favorite foods? ____________________
How does your child respond when you are separated from him or her? ____________________
How does your child respond around new adults? ____________________
How does your child interact with other children? (bully, leader, shy, etc.) ____________________
Child's favorite book? ____________________
Favorite TV show ____________________
Favorite computer game ____________________
Favorite video/movie ____________________
Is there a possible significant change expected in child's life this year (e.g., birth, divorce/separation, serious illness, or incarceration)? ____________________
____

Figure 2.3 Topics for Observation During a Child's Enrollment Assessment

Temperament traits:

* Activity level
* Outgoing vs. shy
* Good cheer vs. anger
* Attention span
* Talks with adults and children
* Aggression toward others
* Plays cooperatively
* Withdrawn vs. engaged
* Reflective vs. impulsive

Physical Traits:

* Can run, hop, & jump
* Can use stairs step over step
* Can use scissors & crayons
* Can stack a tower of blocks
* Can string beads on a lacing

Cognitive traits:

* Counting skills
* Holds book correctly
* Follows directions
* Knows own address and phone number
* Can recognize and name letters
* Answers simple information questions
* Can name seven colors
* Speaks in grammatical sentences
* Knows basic geometric shapes

Social Characteristics:

* Addresses teacher by name
* Exhibits prosocial behaviors (e.g., empathy)
* Self-assured and confident vs. anxious
* Shares with others vs. self-centered
* Initiates contact with others

Grades 1 and 2

Mandated high-stakes tests scheduled in third grade color many of the educational activities during these first school years. When children begin first grade, the primary classroom assessments by teachers are formative. These tests provide information about each child and his/her learning. This makes it possible for the teacher to reteach when needed and keep track of how well each child is doing.

Second grade is a time when children should experience both summative quizzes as well as frequent formative assessments by the teacher. By introducing brief quizzes at this grade level, children can become familiar with what will be expected of them in the next few years. Classroom testing should be designed to match both the curriculum and the learning standards the school has adopted. This makes it possible to explain each child's progress to his or her parents in terms of the expectations that are in place for all children.

In both first and second grades, symbolic awards such as stickers are more easily interpreted than are letter grades on a quiz or homework. By second grade, all children should have daily homework designed to provide practice with new concepts introduced in class (Cooper, Robinson, & Patall, 2006). Teachers have an obligation to check that work. Homework can provide important informative data about how well a concept or skill has been learned. Because of this diagnostic role, parents should be informed early in the year about the homework policy, and how it should be the child's work, not the parent's.

Grade 3

The assessment of children in public school third grades is dominated by the mandated assessment tests. During the school year, children should be taught basic test-taking strategies and take occasional tests designed by the teacher as unit tests, but which follow the standard format used by the state assessment (Crocker, 2003). Care should also be taken to verify that skills and areas of new knowledge specified by the state's standards have been well taught and practiced on classroom tests.

American children are in school for a total of about 1,000 hours of instruction each year (see Chapter 12 for a discussion of the educational role played by parents). Most of the time, over 7,000 hours each year, the child's education and development are out of the hands of teachers. This is a good point to make during Back to School Night. Children who do best on these third-grade tests have parents who are engaged with the school. They attend activities, communicate with teachers, and are rarely surprised by what they hear from the school. Generally, children who score well on assessments have limits placed on television and computer gaming time. Reading is a family activity for children who test well. Dina Borzekowski and Thomas Robinson (2005) found that third-grade children who have television in their bedrooms have significantly lower mathematics achievement test scores than a matched group of children who do not. This study also reported that language arts scores of children who lived in homes with a home computer were better than those children who did not have a home computer. Between 15% and 40% of the variation in the assessment test scores of children are controlled by these few variables (Holbrook & Wright, 2004; NAEP, 2004).

Technology and Testing in Early Childhood

The process of assessing young children in preschools and kindergartens is normally carried out by one adult (teacher or aide) working with one child. The format involves a clipboard and a paper record form used by the adult to collect and record the child's responses. Today, that method is fast disappearing from the preschool and in a few years will be another quaint remembrance about how schools used to be. University demonstration schools or school of education laboratory preschools are doing much of the innovation in this movement toward the use of technology for early childhood assessment.

Handheld Computers

The new approach to data collecting and recording with young children involves the use of a personal digital assistant (PDA)[20] supported with Bluetooth software. The first step involves having the teacher load the PDA with forms used to keep track of each child's answers on an assessment. The teacher can then enter the child's answers into the handheld device, and with the press of a button transfer those assessment data into a notebook computer located in an office in the same Wi-Fi hotspot environment.

The use of PDAs in association with a laptop or notebook computer by classroom teachers makes it possible to chart and track individual student learning patterns. The assessments of individual children can occur on the fly, and the data is charted and ready for the teacher's review instantly.

Summary

The modern era for testing children in this country began at the turn of the 20th century. Professional associations including those for early childhood educators have established ethical guidelines for the use of assessments and tests.

Federal mandates have had a major impact on education programs from preschool through the third grade. Currently, high-stakes testing of third graders can lead to grade retention in seven states and many large cities. Low average scores can result in schools being reorganized.

The angst brought about by testing mandates has been the impetus behind an overhaul of the curriculum and programs of many preschools. More time is now being spent on large group activities and less on free play. Another change involves schedules followed in early childhood education. Many kindergartens have moved to eliminate naptime and extend to a longer school day of 6 or more hours.

Parent concern with the need for good test scores can be seen in the increasing tendency for middle class parents to keep their children from enrolling in kindergarten until they are 6 years old. This tendency is especially obvious with the "boys of the 'burbs."

In general, classroom-testing programs for preschoolers move from formative observations and checklists to the use of standardized curriculum-based measures. The evaluation systems used in elementary schools are also moving in the direction of preparing children for high-stakes testing.

Testing technology is also changing the high-stakes tests being given to third graders as part of the federal mandates. In 2004, a total of 17 states were offering to administer some or all of the mandated assessment tests online over the Internet. This migration of assessment activities to the Internet has taken the name of e-assessments.

Discussion Questions

1. Many states have assumed early education responsibility. How should these state-sponsored programs be evaluated and made accountable for public funds that operate them?
2. Describe the indirect impact of the AYP requirements on preschool education in the United States.
3. Are American kindergartens making progress toward or away from the ideal set by Friedrich Froebel in 1840? Explain your position.
4. What steps should be taken to conduct a screening test or full assessment of a child who is an English language learner?
5. Survey a local preschool (e.g., university laboratory school) and determine the status of assessment technology being used in that school. Describe your findings.

Related Readings

Baker, J. M. (2005). *Achievement testing in U.S. elementary and secondary schools*. New York: Peter Lang.
Elkind, D. (2007). *The power of play: Learning what comes naturally*. Philadelphia: Da Capo.
Jones, E., & Cooper, R. M. (2006). *Playing to get smart*. New York: Teachers College Press.
Meier, D., & Wood, G. (Eds.). (2004). *Many children left behind: How the No Child Left Behind Act is damaging our children and our schools*. Boston: Beacon.

Notes

1. A battery describes a measurement tool that has two or more components.
2. Assessment refers to the measurement process (verb), or a measurement device (noun), for measuring one or more variables related to the current condition, ability, status, or knowledge of an individual. Assessments may include observations, interviews, tests, and various other forms of measurement.

3. N.B. Presseys' book reflects the sexist attitudes of American higher education in the 1920s. The authors assume elementary teachers are a bunch of moody women who have problems being fair with male students. This text was the first book ever written on the topic of classroom testing in the United States and may have influenced thousands of teachers of that era. Here is a sample: " . . . the mark assigned by the teacher is also dependent upon her standards as to what should be required of a class, her judgment as to the comparative importance of various points, and her conception as to the worth of various types of answers. In spite of the best of intentions the mark may be influenced somewhat by her mood at the time, and perhaps toward the boy in question. In contrast the score which a boy obtains on a modern 'test' is always fair and impartial, and uninfluenced by the special factors just mentioned; the score is thoroughly objective" (Pressey & Pressey, 1923, p. 15).
4. The work sampling system consists of developmental guidelines and checklists, portfolios, and summary reports. The system also involves parents and students in the assessment process and provides clear documentation of the progress each child makes. At its heart, it is a curriculum-based assessment designed to document what the child can do at a moment in time.
5. This document represents the efforts of the American Counseling Association (ACA), the American Educational Research Association (AERA), the American Psychological Association (APA), the American Speech-Language-Hearing Association (ASHA), the National Association of School Psychologists (NASP), the National Association of Test Directors (NATD), and the National Council on Measurement in Education (NCME).
6. The ethical principles for classroom-level testing by teachers are similar to those for large-scale assessment tests.
7. An additional test must also be given between the 10th and 12th grades.
8. The federal government and many states have programs to save and encourage Native American languages. There are hundreds of these languages from Algonquian spoken in northern Minnesota to the Zuni language of New Mexico. To see more on these languages, see http://www.native-languages.org/languages.htm#alpha.
9. A number of these categories can overlap. This makes it possible for a school administrator to move children between categories to improve the average scores of the various subgroups within the school. To protect the privacy of children, categories populated by a small number of test takers (e.g., less than 50) are not reported, thus making it possible to hide a small group of low-scoring children from scrutiny by state audits and the media.
10. The publication of an annual school report card for each public and charter school and each school district was a mandate of the original No Child Left Behind Act. This report card was reprinted by local newspapers and discussed on television and radio shows.
11. In 2008, Claudia Wallis presented evidence that within the U.S. Department of Education the NCLB Act had a covert goal of damaging the American public's attitude toward public schools with the sub-rosa goal of encouraging a program of "school choice" and "vouchers" (Wallis, 2008). A similar point was suggested by Robert Lynn, former president of the National Council on Measurement in Education (Hoff, 2008).
12. The American Federation of Teachers opposed the bonus provision as established by Mayor Bloomberg.
13. The states are Delaware, Florida, Georgia, Louisiana, North Carolina, Texas, and Wisconsin, and the several large city school systems include Baltimore, Philadelphia, and New York City.
14. The term is derived from athletics in higher education. A college student is redshirted when he or she is held back one year from playing a sport. This is done to make it possible for the student-athlete to have a full four years (NCAA maximum) of sport eligibility. The student's eligibility would begin in the sophomore year instead of the freshman year and continue through the first year of postgraduate education. One reason this is done is to let another senior year athlete graduate and thereby open up a spot on the team for the new (redshirted) student during the next year. When these special athletes attend a sport practice session, they wear a red shirt so they can be spotted and not hurt by overzealous teammates.
15. This "fading of the effect" may reflect on the quality of the elementary school program the redshirted child enters. See Chapter 1 and Samuel Meisels (2007) for discussion of this issue.
16. The measure lost 63 to 34 with most of the Republican members of the Senate voting to support it, and the Democratic Senate leader, Harry Reid, calling the proposed amendment racist.

17. It takes adolescent and adult native Spanish speakers between 500 and 600 clock hours of classroom instruction to learn to speak English as an L2 (American Council for the Teaching of Foreign Languages, 1985).
18. If the parents do not speak English, a translator should be provided at all meetings. Schools should be prepared to pay for that service. In some schools, the translation task is provided by local clergy, retired high school language teachers, or other bilingual staff members.
19. DIBELS was designed to be an assessment of prereading and basic literacy. It is not a complete assessment of early skills in that it does not provide measures of numeracy, conceptual development, understanding, fine and gross motor skills, or socialization.
20. A personal digital assistant is a small electronic device that combines the capabilities of a cellular telephone and computer. Modern PDAs are equipped with the ability to access the Internet while being able to perform other communication and record-keeping tasks.

Understanding Early Childhood Assessment Scores

3

One test of the correctness of educational procedure is the happiness of the child.

—Maria Montessori

Introduction and Themes

High-stakes assessments are now part of early education programs. This is a logical development that follows the use of public funding to support early education.

All assessments consist of variables measured at one of four levels of precision. Scores from any measure are not perfect, and contain error. Test reliability provides insight into the amount of error in a test's score data. The magnitude of **true score** differences between children can be estimated from the reliability (stability and consistency) of the measure. Usefulness and **appropriateness** define a measure's validity.

Comparing the performance of a child to the average performance of other children the same age is how test and assessment scores are derived. That comparison group provides the database needed to assign standard scores showing how well the child performed compared to others. The comparison group is called the norm group and is one element in evaluating test quality. Other concerns include the test's possible bias and its standard error of measurement.

Those who have the responsibility of selecting a published assessment have independent analyses of various tests available. Perhaps the Buros Institute for Mental Measurements provides the most useful independent reviews.

Learning Objectives

By reading and studying this chapter, you should acquire the competency to:

- Explain the four levels of precision associated with data collected about young children.
- Describe the appropriate method for finding the central tendency for variables with different levels of precision.
- Be able to explain the concept of skewness and use it appropriately when describing data.
- Explain the relationship between the normal curve and standard deviation.

- Interpret and explain to others the concept of standards-based scores on early childhood assessments.
- Explain the relationship of reliability and validity when evaluating a standardized measure of early childhood education.
- Interpret data provided in technical manuals about norm groups and steps taken by test publishers to eliminate bias.
- Describe the general principles of a sensitivity review and a differential item functioning analysis.
- Use appropriate information sources to locate technical reviews of published tests.

Precision of Measurement Scales

Early childhood educators have never been supporters of the use of large-scale assessment tests with young children (Meisels, 2000). Before 1990, testing of young children was done to ensure the welfare of children and to better design an appropriate curriculum to meet their needs. Since 1990, the rules have changed. Now we have added assessments to the early childhood environment designed to provide accountability data. It is essential that early childhood educators learn to understand and interpret scores from standardized assessments.

There are thousands of characteristics about children that we can name and describe. Characteristics such as vocabulary, inseam length, muscle tone, counting skill, and weight can all be measured because they vary in some observable way. That marks these characteristics as **variables.** Central to this idea is the observation that variables can vary in some dimension or value.

Nominal Scale

Each variable also varies in the **precision of the scale** used to measure it.[1] At one level, variables can be identified that exist without any meaningful basis in numbers. These variables exist as names only and are therefore called nominal and make up a **nominal scale.** An example of a nominal variable is the religion a toddler's parents are raising their child to follow. This variable, religion, could be reported as being Roman Catholic, Baptist, Humanistic/Agnostic, Reformed Jewish, Church of England, Shinto, Sunni Muslem, and so on. An administrator could tally the registration information to find how many children are enrolled from different religions; however, the categories are not arithmetic (Stevens, 1946).

Ordinal Scale

The next level of precision includes variables that exist in a logical order. However, these variables lack a real number system with equal-sized steps. At a child care center, the director is the top-level employee. Next, is the assistant director, then lead teachers, teachers, assistant teachers, and finally teacher's aides. Because the job ranks for the instructional staff of an early childhood center can be arranged in a meaningful sequence they make up an **ordinal scale,** or ordered sequence. Once again, arithmetic does not apply to such scales. The application of arithmetic to any scale requires all steps be the same size. There are many ordered scales used with young children. For example, most behavioral rating scales are ordinal measures.

Interval Scale

The next **level of precision** involves an ordered scale designed to have steps of equal size. Interval measures are statistically defined by the **normal curve, or bell curve.** Because the intervals between the steps are of equal size, the scale is called an **interval scale.** Scores from most published standardized tests and assessments are interval scales. These include most developmental assessments, intelligence tests, basic educational achievement tests, educational or kindergarten readiness tests, and measures of prereading skills. Because interval scales have equal unit sizes, they can be subjected to arithmetic operations. This includes finding the **mean** (average) and calculating the spread of individual scores (**variance** and **standard deviation**). These measures are based on a statistical model (the bell curve) that prevents finding a true zero point or defined ceiling point.

Ratio Scale

The precision of physical measurements is only limited by the quality of the measuring devices. Ratio-scaled variables have true zero and ceiling points, and are not based on the bell curve.[2] **Ratio scales** include physical properties such as height, weight, speed in running 40 meters (measured in seconds), systolic blood pressure, the amount of money in a child's piggy bank, oral cavity body temperature, and serum platelet count. As is true for interval scales, data from measurements based on ratio scales are appropriate for all arithmetic operations and procedures.

NOIR

To better remember these scales, the French word *noir,* meaning the color black, provides a handy acronym. When arranged from least to most precise, the types of measurement scales are the following: Nominal, Ordinal, Interval, and Ratio, or NOIR (see Table 3.1).

Table 3.1 Examples of the Four Types of Measures

Nominal	Ordinal	Interval	Ratio
Social Security No.	Medical pain scales	Fahrenheit scale	Kelvin scale
Handedness	Movie ratings	IQ scores	Dollars in the bank
Least liked food	Opinion surveys	NCLB test scores	Vote count
Best toy	Horse race results	Developmental scores	Birth weight
Gender	Social class	SAT and GRE scores	Chronological age
Breed of dog	Restaurant ratings	Personality profile	Blood pressure

Averages

When data are described to others, they are normally in summary form. Commonly employed summary statistics include the average.[3] In science, there are three forms of average collectively called measures of central tendency.

Mode

The easiest of all of the types of average to find is the **mode**. This can be found for any type of data set—nominal, ordinal, interval, or ratio. Simply, it is the score or category reported for the greatest number of children. This is the only type of average that can be found with **nominal data**. The mode only requires that all cases included in a category be counted. For example, "It was recently reported that at an ecumenical breakfast there were more Baptists in attendance than any other denomination." This statement presents the mode (Baptists) in a data set (those at breakfast) measured as nominal data (denominations) (R. Wright, 2008, p. 91).

Mean

The first step needed to find the mean of a data set (e.g., a collection of scores from a spelling test given to third graders) is the simple addition of the spelling test scores. That summation should be divided by the number of tests taken. The result is the mean (average). The mean is the arithmetical middle of a group of scores. Because finding the mean requires that data be added and divided, it is not possible to find the mean of nominal or ordinal data. The mean can only be found for **interval and ratio data.**

Median

Another type of average appropriate for ordinal, interval, and ratio data is known as the **median.** This approach to finding central tendency is defined as being the middle of a data set by count. To find the median of any ordinal, interval, or ratio data set, it is only necessary to stack the scored pages in a pile from lowest to highest. Then simply count to the middle value. The middle value or score becomes the median. Half of all scores are above the median and half are below it. For example, the median rank of the children in a Cub Scout pack can be found by ordering the boys of the pack by rank from Bobcat, Wolf, Bear, Webelos, and finally the Compass Point Award and transition into the Boy Scouts of America. The median or middle rank with half of all pack members above and half below is a way to express an average of the ordinal data of Cub Scout rank for the pack. The median, with half of the cases above it and half below it, is also the definition the 50th percentile.

Table 3.2 presents simulated scores from three early achievement measures with a class of 11 children. The scores are similar to those from the Wechsler Individual Achievement test, 3rd ed. WIAT-III. It can be seen that the children's scores are normally distributed in reading and listening. The means and medians of

Table 3.2 Simulated Achievement Test Scores With Measures of Central Tendency

Student	WIAT Basic Reading	WIAT Math Reasoning	WIAT Listening Comprehension
Annie	105	110	100
Bobby	115	120	110
Carol	90	95	100
Donny	85	70	79
Liz	100	108	102
Frankie	125	115	109
Gracie	105	100	99
Harry	88	70	90
Iris	113	100	125
Joann	94	120	97
Kevin	80	70	88
Mean	100	98	100
Median	100	100	100
Mode	105	70	100
Standard Deviation	14	20	12

these two tests are equal and the modes are in the center of the data. The math subtest is **skewed** (see next section). The median and mean are not equal, and the mode is very different from the median. The three low scores of 70 on the math test are the cause of this skew.

Skew and the Normal Distribution

The U.S. Census Bureau reported in 2007 that the *mean* family income was $60,528, which was $17,210 more than the *median* family income that same year (U.S. Census Bureau, 2007b). The reason for this disparity is the great amount of wealth held at the top income levels by a small percentage of the population. In a sense, a small number of very wealthy families pull the mean income level for all families upward, and make all other American families look more prosperous. This statistical phenomenon of having a few very high scores, or conversely a few very low scores, pulling the mean in one direction is called skewness (see Table 3.3 and Figure 3.1).

Table 3.3 Raw Scores from a Hypothetical Spelling Test

Student	Score	Student	Score
Adam	19	Nick	17
Betty	15	Oceana	3
Craig	9	Paul	19
Diane	20	Quincy	20
Evan	18	Rob	19
Flo	5	Sarah	20
George	17	Tom	17
Helen	16	Ulyssa	18
Ike	2	Vince	16
Kathy	4	**Mean**	**14.4**
Lewis	20	**Standard Deviation**	**6.15**
Mary	14	**Median**	**17**

The income level of American families is a ratio scale variable when expressed in dollars. It is possible to find the mean family income by calculating the arithmetical average. But, it is also possible to find the median income. The median family income represents the family income with half of all families below it and half above (see Table 3.4). The great amount of skewness in family income data has led the U.S. Census Bureau to present the median family income, not the mean family income, in its reports.

There are numerous other cases where unusual scores can make the mean and the median very different. For example, if young ELL children are tested along with their native Anglo-white peers for reading achievement, score skewness may occur. The ELL students may have low scores resulting in the mean being lower than the median. This type of skew, called a **negative skew,** occurs when a small group of children score at an unusually low level on a test or assessment. In similar fashion, a group of students scoring at an exceptionally high level can cause the mean to be above the median and result in a **positive skew** in the data.

Figure 3.1 Histogram Created From Raw Scores in a Hypothetical Spelling Test

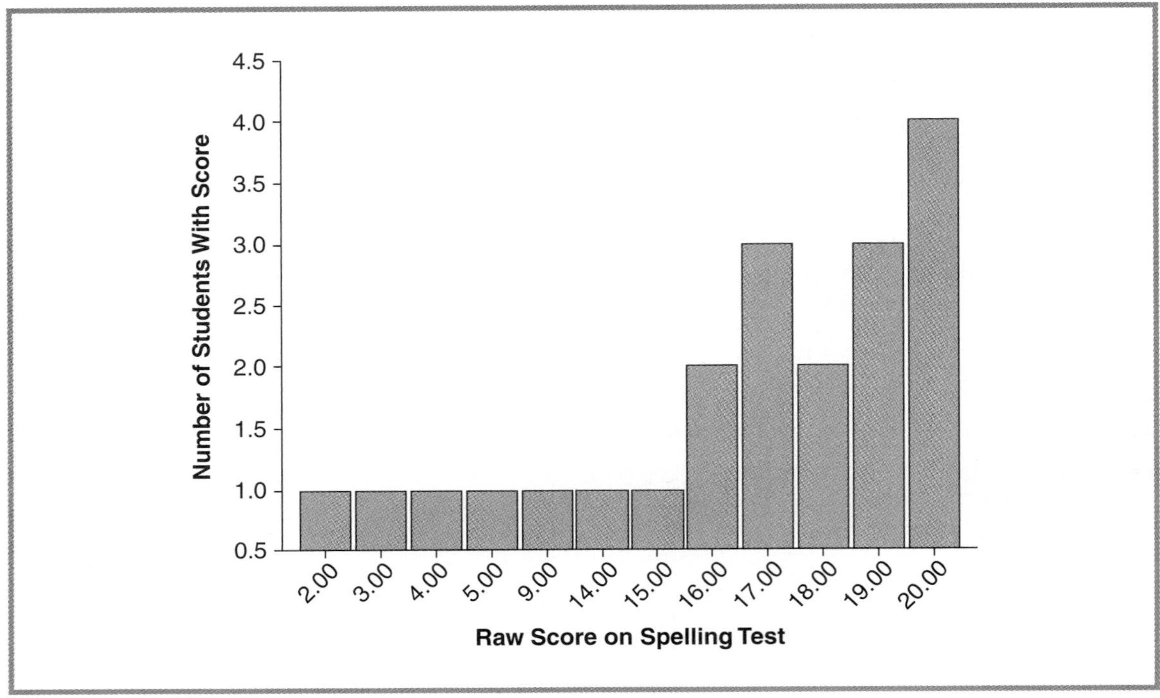

Table 3.4 Median Household Income for the 50 States and Washington, D.C.

State	Rank	Median Household Income (2006 dollars)
New Jersey	1	66,752
Maryland	2	63,082
Hawaii	3	61,005
Connecticut	4	60,551
New Hampshire	5	60,411
Alaska	6	57,071
Massachusetts	7	56,592
Minnesota	8	56,102
Utah	9	55,619
Virginia	10	55,368
California	11	54,385
Colorado	12	53,900
Washington	13	53,515
Delaware	14	52,676

State	Rank	Median Household Income (2006 dollars)
Rhode Island	15	52,421
Vermont	16	52,174
Nevada	17	51,036
Illinois	18	49,328
Wisconsin	19	48,903
Nebraska	20	48,820
New York	21	48,472
Georgia	22	48,388
Pennsylvania	23	48,148
Iowa	24	48,075
Michigan	25	48,043
United States National Median ($48,023)		
District of Columbia	26	47,473
Arizona	27	46,693
Wyoming	28	46,613
Oregon	29	46,349
Idaho	30	45,919
Ohio	31	45,776
Maine	32	45,503
Florida	33	45,038
South Dakota	34	44,996
Indiana	35	44,618
Missouri	36	44,487
Kansas	37	44,478
Texas	38	43,044
North Dakota	39	42,311
North Carolina	40	41,616
Tennessee	41	40,696
South Carolina	42	40,583
New Mexico	43	40,126
Montana	44	39,821
Oklahoma	45	38,859
Kentucky	46	38,694
Alabama	47	38,160
West Virginia	48	38,029
Louisiana	49	37,472
Arkansas	50	37,458
Mississippi	51	34,343

SOURCE: U.S. Census Bureau, 2007b.

Normal Distribution

The words **"normal distribution"** are applied to large samples of either ratio or interval data that assume a distribution shaped like a bell.[4] To be a normal distribution, it must have most scores in the center, be symmetric, and have the mean and the median equal, or nearly equal, to each other. Another characteristic of a normal distribution of scores is that it has only one mode in the center of the distribution of scores arranged from low to high.

What makes this characteristic curve so important is that it occurs throughout nature. The length of individual blades of grass growing on an isolated mountain meadow can be plotted as a bell-shaped (normal) curve. This is also true of the weight of schnauzers, the height of giraffes living on an African savanna, and the measured IQ of middle class children in third grade. This consistency is at the heart of many test and assessment scoring systems (see Figure 3.2 for a depiction of the curve and normal distribution pattern for data).

Figure 3.2 A Normal Curve of Scores (Bell Shaped) With Standard Deviation Marks, Percentiles, Stanines, and Nce Deciles Indicated

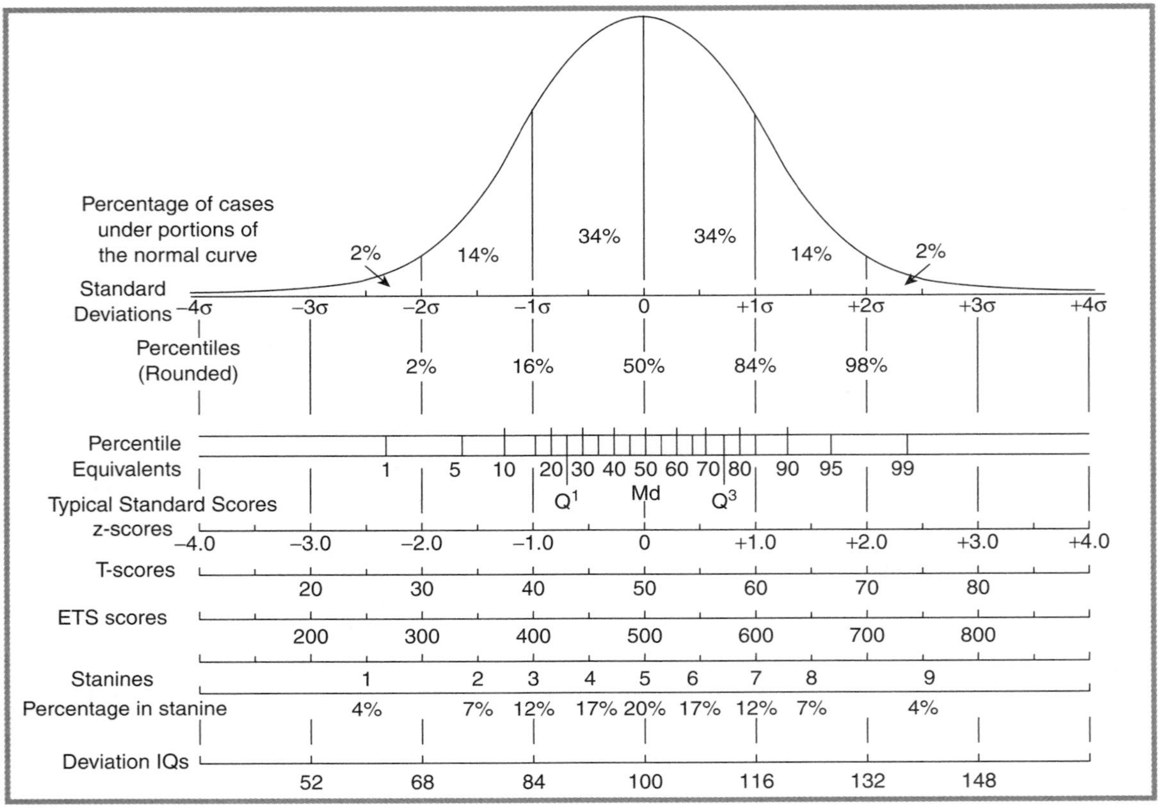

Percentage of cases under portions of the normal curve: 2% 14% 34% 34% 14% 2%

Standard Deviations: −4σ −3σ −2σ −1σ 0 +1σ +2σ +3σ +4σ

Percentiles (Rounded): 2% 16% 50% 84% 98%

Percentile Equivalents: 1 5 10 20 30 40 50 60 70 80 90 95 99

Q1 Md Q3

Typical Standard Scores

z-scores: −4.0 −3.0 −2.0 −1.0 0 +1.0 +2.0 +3.0 +4.0

T-scores: 20 30 40 50 60 70 80

ETS scores: 200 300 400 500 600 700 800

Stanines: 1 2 3 4 5 6 7 8 9

Percentage in stanine: 4% 7% 12% 17% 20% 17% 12% 7% 4%

Deviation IQs: 52 68 84 100 116 132 148

Score Spread and Variation

While there is a tendency for scores from assessments and tests to cluster near the median of normally distributed scores, 32% will spread farther away from the center. When a distribution is normal, about 68% of all scores are found near the mean.[5] Because the normal distribution is symmetric, 34% will be near each side of the mean for a total of 68%. This pattern of **variability** is constant with all normal data. This distribution of scores is mathematically expressed as the first standard deviation of the data. Thus, every normally distributed measure will have 34% of its scores pooled between the mean and one standard deviation above it. Likewise, another 34% will be found between the mean and one standard deviation below it. Every measure will have a different standard deviation value, but they will still have the same characteristic. That characteristic is that 68% of the scores will fall within ±1.00 standard deviation of the mean.

With normal data, two standard deviations cover 47.5% of all scores distributed from the mean to a point two standard deviations away. Therefore, if we look at how many scores are found within ±2.00 standard deviations of the mean, it will total about 95% of all cases (47.5% above and 47.5% below the mean). Only 2.5% of all children's scores will be above +2.00 standard deviations over the mean. Likewise, only 2.5% of all children's scores will be below –2.00 standard deviations from the mean (when the data are normal).

Because the median of normal data is also the 50th percentile (half above and half below), we can figure that the point equal to a score that is one standard deviation over the mean is approximately the 84th percentile. That is found by adding the 34% of the cases that are over the mean (+1.00 standard deviation) to the 50% of the cases that are below the median. Thus, 50% below the mean and 34% of the cases above the mean equal a point where 84% of the children will have done less well. At two standard deviations above the mean, the total percentile becomes even higher. Now the 50% below the mean are added to the 47.5% always found from the mean to +2.00 standard deviations over the mean. The result is the finding that a score equal to +2.00 standard deviations over the mean defines the 97.5th percentile.

Going in the other direction, a child's score found to be one standard deviation lower than the median (–1.00 standard deviation) will be at a point equal to about the 16th percentile. That is found by subtracting the 34% of the population that lie between the mean and a standard deviation below it from the 50% represented by the median. Likewise, two standard deviations below the median will mark the 2.5 percentile point. In other words, only 2.5% of all children will score at or below –2.00 standard deviations below the median (and mean) on an assessment (see Figure 3.3 for more detail about the distribution of scores).

The truth is, an experienced educator can identify a child functioning two standard deviations below the mean without using a test. A developmental or cognitive disability that large is easy to spot. The use of an assessment instrument reporting the child's comparative outcomes through the use of a standard scoring system provides the documentation required to get the child and his/her family the extra help they need. It also provides a method for tracking the progress and development of the child (see Table 3.5 for the relationship of percentiles to standard deviation score points in a normal distribution of scores).

Standard Scores

Scores that correspond to the number of questions or tasks correctly completed by a child on an assessment are referred to as the child's **raw score.** The raw score is simply the number of questions or tasks that the child actually got correct. In order to interpret this number, the publishers employ a number of standardized scoring systems. Each of these systems is based on a model that compares the raw score of a child to a normal distribution of scores earned by others who have previously taken the assessment and who are at the same age or grade level. The term **standard score** implies that the standard deviation of the comparison group is used to provide the child's score on the assessment.

Figure 3.3 Depictions of Areas of the Distribution of Scores Under the Normal Curve

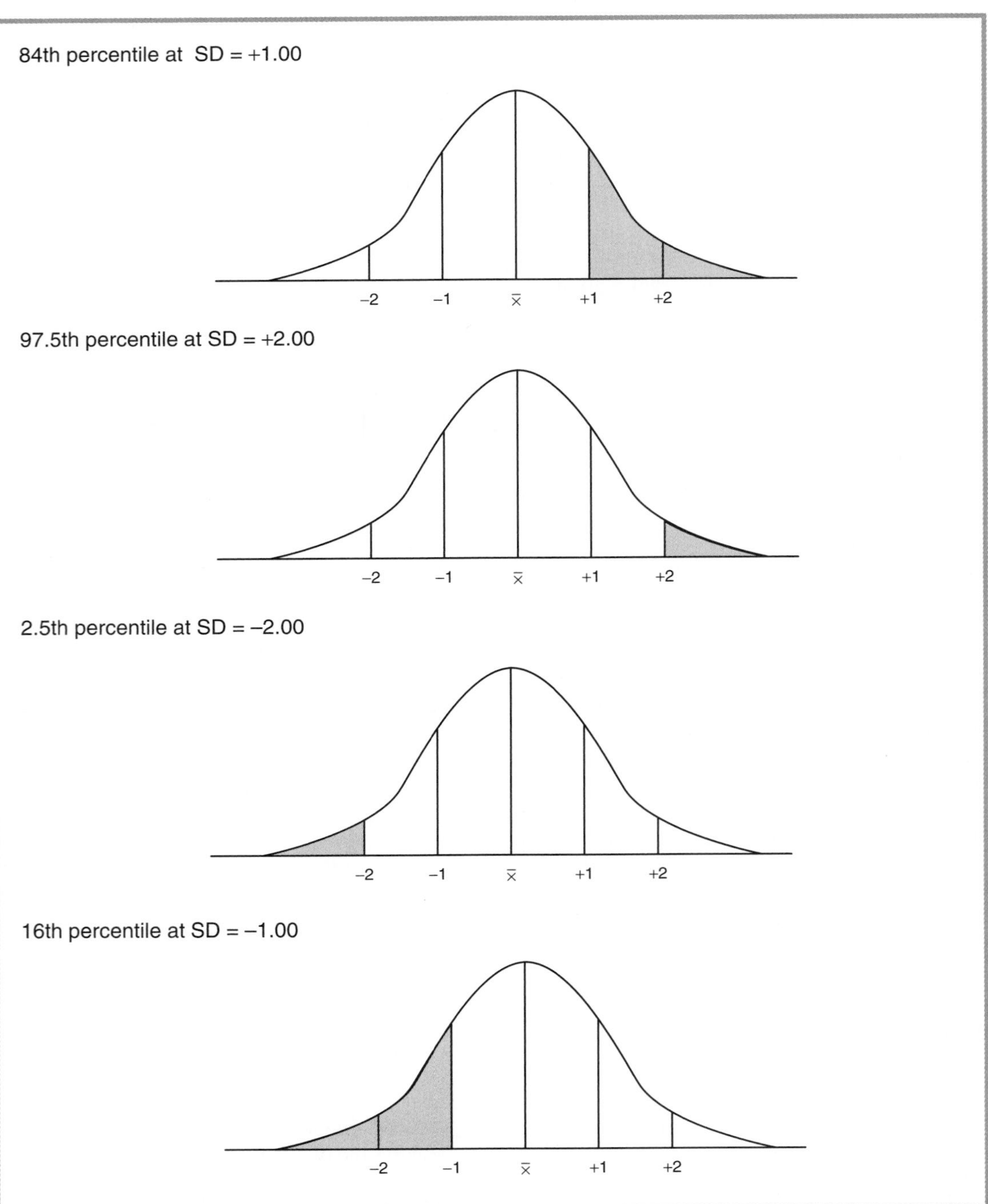

SOURCE: From Kanji, G. K. (1999). *100 statistical tests, 3rd ed.*, pp. 159–160. Reprinted with permission from Sage.

Table 3.5 Approximate Standard Deviations for Normally Distributed Data

Percentile Equivalent	Standard Deviations Above (+) and Below (–) the Mean
More than 99	+2.33
97.5	1.96
95	1.65
90	1.28
85	1.04
80	0.84
75	0.68
70	0.53
65	0.39
60	0.25
55	0.13
50 Median	0.00
45	–0.13
40	–0.25
35	–0.39
30	–0.53
25	–0.68
20	–0.84
15	–1.04
10	–1.28
5	–1.65
2.5	–1.96
Less than 1.0	–2.33

SOURCE: From Kanji, G. K. (1999). *100 statistical tests*, 3rd ed., Table 1a. Reprinted with permission from Sage.

Normal Curve Equivalent Score

One type of standard score is the **normal curve equivalent** (NCE) score. When any set of raw scores is transformed into NCE scores, the distribution will have a mean of 50 and a standard deviation of 21. NCE scores are scaled from a low of 1 to a high of 99. This gives the NCE score an appearance similar to a percentile. The advantage of NCE scores is that they can be averaged and compared.[6]

Stanines

Another commonly reported standard score is the **stanine.** There are nine stanine levels used to divide a normal distribution. The middle level is a standard deviation level of 5, while the lowest level is 1 and the greatest is 9. Middle-range scores are considered those at stanines 4–5–6. The highest group is made up of stanines 7–8–9; and, the lowest scores are in stanines 1–2–3.

Examples of the use of standard scores abound in the lives of young children. If a child in Head Start who is 48 months old is tested using the Wechsler Preschool and Primary Scale of Intelligence, 3rd ed. (WPPSI-III), the three central scores reported are standard scores called Verbal IQ, Performance IQ, and Full Scale IQ. The mean standard score (IQ) for each of the three scores is 100, and the standard deviation of each is 15. The child's raw scores from the WPPSI-III are compared to the outcome from a national sample of 200 (100 boys and 100 girls) 4-year-olds. From this comparison group, it is possible to find how well the child compares to others his/her age. A Full Scale IQ of 115 is the 84th percentile (one standard deviation [15 points] above the mean of 100). An IQ of 130 is two standard deviations above the mean of 100 and equal to the 97.5th percentile (Sattler & Dumont, 2004). To better understand all of the symbols and terms applied to test scores, see Table 3.6.

Table 3.6 Statistical Symbols at a Glance

Statistical Term	Symbol/Abbreviation	Meaning
1. Central tendency		A term that may be the mean, median, or mode
Average		A term that may be the mean, median, or mode
Mean	$\bar{X}$ or μ (the Greek letter mu)	Arithmetic center
Median	*Mdn* (No universal symbol, occasionally shown as *Mdn*)	Found as the center of data by counting individuals
Mode	*M* (No universal symbol, occasionally shown as *M*)	Arithmetic center of a set of data
2. Variability		The amount of scores in a data set spread out from the mean
Standard Deviation	*s* or *SD* σ	Measure of the spread of scores around the mean
Variance	s^2 or SD^2 σ^2 (the Greek letter sigma)	Standard deviation squared
3. Standard Scores		Any score transformed to conform to the normal curve
Stanine		Nine divisions of a distribution each ½ of a *SD* in size
Deviation IQ	DIQ	Mental ability with a $\bar{X}$ of 100 and a *SD* of 15
ETS Scores (SAT or GRE)		Subtests with a $\bar{X}$ of 500 and a *SD* of 100

Statistical Term	Symbol/Abbreviation	Meaning
4. Correlation		A mathematical expression of **covariance** between two variables
Pearson Coefficient	r	This can be employed as a measure of **reliability** measuring **stability** and stability over time (**test-retest reliability**). Minimum is zero, maximum is ±1.00
Spearman Coefficient	r_s	This can be employed as a measure of reliability measuring stability. Minimum is zero, maximum is ±1.00
5. Reliability		A form of **correlation** that also includes three additional coefficients. An expression of either the **internal consistency** of a test's items or an expression of the stability of test scores over time
Cronbach alpha	α	Measure of internal consistency with a minimum of zero and a maximum of +1.00
Kuder-Richardson 20	K-R 20	Measure of internal consistency with a minimum of zero and maximum of +1.00
Coefficient kappa	κ	Reliability measure for criterion-type measures with a minimum of zero and a maximum of +1.00
Split-Half Reliability	$r_{½}$	Can be employed as a measure of reliability measuring stability with a minimum of zero and maximum of +1.00
Spearman-Brown	r_{SB}	Measure of internal consistency with a minimum of zero and maximum of +1.00
Standard Error of Measurement	*SEM*	Value of one standard deviation of possible true scores measurement surrounding an obtained score. Inversely linked tests of reliability

Standards-Based Assessments in Early Childhood Education

The march toward establishing **standards-for-learning** and designing achievement tests for those standards started in 1994 with the passage of the centerpiece education legislation of the Bill Clinton White House, the Improving America's Schools Act (the Elementary and Secondary Education Act of 1994). The use of published standards-based assessments to measure primary grade and early childhood learning standards has become de rigueur. Test publishers have targeted the standards-for-learning approved by the various states to craft these tests for young children. Thus, schools can have an idea of which children are at risk for not being proficient on the high-stakes test before third grade. See Case in Point 3.1 for one outcome of this sorting.

Case in Point 3.1

Resource Allocation for High-Stakes Tests

One major problem with the testing mandates and sanctions is the excessive amount of stress placed on educators. One sad result has been a program of educational triage that occurs when children in the primary grades test low on standardized tests. Some schools focus most of their limited resources on helping children close to passing the assessment. These children have been described as being "on the bubble" for being proficient. The assumption is **bubble youngsters** get intensive help while the lowest of the low scoring at the bottom of the distribution are ignored. Children judged to be beyond the school's ability to help are provided with the equivalent of a palliative level of support. In other words, by second grade children are divided into three groups: those that are safe, those that can be helped with extra effort, and those that are beyond the resources of the school to ever help (Booher-Jennings, 2005).

There is evidence that quality prekindergarten and full-day kindergarten programs can reduce, and possibly close, the achievement gap between groups of children entering first grade (Lee, Burkam, Ready, Honigman, & Meisels, 2006). It was not until 2007 that all 50 states finally mandated the provision of public school kindergarten programs, and 39% are still only half-day programs (Paulson, 2007). See Case in Point 3.2 for another approach to funding full-day kindergarten programs.

Case in Point 3.2

Kindergarten Cost

A reason that kindergartens are not run on a full-day model is financial. Cash-strapped school districts have begun to charge parents who wish to have their children enrolled in full-day kindergartens. In 2008, the Corvallis School District (Oregon) charged parents a fee of $290 per month ($2,900/year) to enroll a child in an optional full-day kindergarten class (Jacobson, 2008b). In Oregon, only 17 of the state's 78 school districts offering full-time kindergarten charge such an enrollment fee. One question regarding this practice is the obvious disparity between children whose parents can afford the kindergarten fees and children whose parents cannot.

High-Quality Assessments

Whenever a child is evaluated, there are two unconditional requirements for the process. First, the measurement must be consistent. Similar measurement results will happen again when the child is reevaluated. This property is reliability.

The second required characteristic is **validity.** Valid measurements meet three requirements. First, valid measurements are focused on what they are purported to assess. Second, they align with other measures of the child. Finally, they are developmentally appropriate, properly employed, and correctly interpreted. The first two validity issues relate to how the measurement is designed and standardized. The third factor relates to the education and ability of the person giving the test.

Reliability

A measurement that is not reliable produces random results. Perfect reliability results in the same value or score for the child each time it is administered. Thus, highly reliable scores or assessment results are stable and consistent. However, the only measures of children approaching perfect reliability are of physical characteristics, for example, height. This reflects the high degree of accuracy physical measurement tools can achieve (see Case in Point 3.3 for a reliability example from everyday life).

Case in Point 3.3

Reliability of Athletic Activity Scores

Any person who participates in an individual sport (e.g., bowling, archery, golf, or running) has a fairly good idea of how well they will do during an outing. However, if the person keeps a diary/record of results, the reliability of the endeavors can be seen. If a member of a bowling team has an average score of 165 and a handicap of 11 pins (90% of the 220 rule), she could vary above and below her average on any day. On a really good day, she may become a hero to her teammates by rolling a 190 during a league match. But if that same bowler rolls a 140, she will become the bowling team's goat. This range of scores shows how a bowling average and handicap are only moderately reliable. To learn about bowling handicaps, see http://ezinearticles.com/?Handicap-Amateur-Bowling-Tournament—-How-To-Figure-Your-Handicap&id=786148.

Multiple facets of development, cognitive learning, and social–emotional growth of children are also measurable. Some have low levels of reliability ($\alpha \leq 0.30$). Low reliability can occur when a variable being measured is not easily defined, for example, **creativity.** Measuring well-defined variables can result in high **reliability coefficients,** for example, prereading achievement and numerosity measures can result in good reliability ($\alpha \leq 0.80$).

Correlation

Reliability is measured using statistical correlation. The **Pearson correlation coefficient** has a maximum of ±1.00 (e.g., $r = +1.00$) indicating two measures are the same, and a minimum of 0.00 indicating two measures have nothing in common. A correlation of –1.00 implies that if one measure is high, the other will be low. Positive correlations exist between the scores on different DIBELS probes ($r = 0.70$).

Pearson correlations are reported with interval and ratio data: **Spearman correlations** with ordinal measures. Spearman's coefficient, formerly expressed with the Greek letter rho (ρ) is now referred to as r_s.[7]

Stability[8]

This form of reliability requires a time interval between the first and second administrations of two measures. Most measures used in early childhood education have stability values or reliability coefficients of about $r = 0.70$ to 0.95. This potential for variation in scores over time is quite natural, and is one basis for making value judgments about a test's usefulness.

The quality of a measure can be found in a simple two-step process. Step one, multiply the reliability coefficient by itself, step two multiply the result by 100. The product is the percentage of variation between test scores caused by actual differences among children. It is vital to make sure that all measurements used to make important decisions about children are reliable ($r \geq 0.80$).

Examples:

If a reliability coefficient is $r = 0.80$, then

$$0.80 \times 0.80 = 0.64$$

Next,

$$0.64 \times 100 = 64$$

Thus, if a measure has a reliability of 0.80, we know that about 64% of the amount of differences among children's scores is caused by true differences on the test (the remaining 36% is **measurement error**).

In another example, only 49% of the individual differences identified by scores on a test with a reliability of 0.70 are true differences. The other 51% of the amount of differences or score variation is some form of measurement error. That error may reflect the individuality of the child, the skill of the examiner, or the quality of the assessment.

A stability problem for early childhood measurements is the relentless developmental course being followed by the growing child. This brings about a constant state of change that works against the stability/reliability of assessment scores.

Internal Consistency Reliability

Dividing the measure into two halves and calculating reliability using the results from each half as though the halves were two complete assessments can also establish reliability called **split-half reliability** ($r_{½}$). It is one of four major types of reliability measures described as being of internal consistency. The other three measures of **internal consistency reliability** are the **Spearman-Brown prophesy** coefficient (r_{SB}), the **Kuder-Richardson 20** coefficient (K-R 20), and the **Cronbach alpha** coefficient (α).

The fact that these are measures of internal consistency implies they are found by administering an assessment to one group of children only once. If an assessment has several subtests (e.g., listening skills, numeracy, and phonemic awareness) a total coefficient is not appropriate, and internal consistency should be found independently for each part.

Standard Error of Measurement

While reliability coefficients provide a good method for selecting the most stable and consistent measures, another statistic, the **standard error of measurement** *(SEM)* provides a handy guide to the meaning or value of any child's score. *SEM* is the standard deviation of measurement error found in scores. A measure reporting very high reliability will have a small standard error of measurement. If the *SEM* is relatively large, the reliability (stability) of the assessment is low. For example, the Wechsler Preschool and Primary Scale of Intelligence, 3rd ed. (WPPSI-III), has an internal consistency (Cronbach α) of 0.96. This is a very high coefficient of reliability, and the IQ (verbal) has a mean of 100 and a standard deviation of 15 (Madle & Meikamp, 2005).

The standard error of measurement for verbal IQ for 6-year-old children on the test is *SEM* = 3.00. Thus, if a school psychologist gave the WPPSI-III to a 6-year-old child and found a verbal IQ of 110, we would know that there is a 68% chance that the child's true verbal IQ is between 107 and 113—that is, the child's score of 110 plus or minus the *SEM* of 3. Likewise, we can assume that the child's true verbal IQ has a 95% likelihood of falling between 104 and 116. This value is the original IQ score of 110±2 *SEM* or 6 points (see Case in Point 3.4 for a more quotidian example of measurement error).

Case in Point 3.4

Standard Error of Measurement in the Bathroom

The concept of a standard error of measurement is well understood by people who have attempted to lose weight. We all understand that our body weight changes throughout the day, and is lowest in the morning before breakfast. But, even getting our personal weight at the same time each morning will include an amount of measurement error. Most home scales have "good spots" where if you stand just right you can get a lower reading than other "bad spots" on the scale. This can result in a range of weight scores if you get on and off the bathroom scale several times. The fact that each is slightly different is measurement error.

When younger children (3-year-olds) are assessed using the Battelle Developmental Inventory, 2nd ed. (BDI-2), the reliability is about 0.80 for the different assessment domains, and the *SEM* for the domains is about 5.00 (Athanasiou, 2007). To be very confident about a child's score, the range of possible outcomes would be 10 points above and below the child's measured score. This range is found by multiplying the *SEM* by 2 to provide a band within which the true score of the child is likely (95% of the time) to be found.

Validity

No assessment or measure can be valid if it is not reliable. It is necessary for a test to provide consistent outcomes before validity is possible. One concern with the validity of a measure is that it actually measures what its users intend. There are other dimensions an assessment may inadvertently be measuring instead of those targeted. It may measure the child's ability to interpret the teacher's directions, or his/her ability to focus and attend to the tasks being measured.

In designing measurements for young children, test makers should develop questions and tasks aligned with the state's standards-for-learning. It may also involve an analysis of the curriculums taught at the various age levels. The establishment of validity can involve **content** and **construct validity.** Content validity matches a measurement's items with the curriculum's content, while construct validity is established by demonstrating the measure provides an accurate picture of the construct being assessed. Constructs such as aggression, infant temperament, shyness, and creativity are among the areas that have had assessments developed for them.

All measures must also be developmentally appropriate for the child. This quality is known as **developmental validity.**

A concern for test developers is the validity of the measurement for the job it is to perform. The Government Accountability Office (GAO) reported that the use of the National Reporting System (NRS) for assessing Head Start centers was invalid because the measurement was not validated for that use (GAO, 2005). Likewise, measures should be culturally appropriate for children who are being assessed. Even when a test is appropriate for one population of children, it may be invalid for another.

Comparison Groups and Outcome Scores

When an early childhood teacher creates a brief assessment for finding how well children have learned a concept, it is unlikely he/she would use data to make comparisons between children. Primary grade teachers are more concerned with how well children are progressing in learning new concepts and skills, and less concerned with relative progress of children compared to others. As a point of comparison, standardized assessments and published measures require the use of comparison groups.

Norm Groups

"I am surveying what the children want for school lunches. So far my sample likes pizza, cheese-puffs, soda, and ice cream."

SOURCE: Cartoon by Merv Magus.

Published measures rely on a comparison group known as the **normative group**, or more simply, **norm group.** When a publisher markets a new assessment, it should provide a **technical manual** containing reliability and validity information. It should also describe the norm group used to provide the point of comparison for interpreting each child's outcome. The norm group should reflect all children of the country. It should be large enough that when divided into age groups there are still representative numbers of children making up the norm for each age level. These norm groups should reflect all races, both genders, and the various economic levels of families.

Another consideration when evaluating the norm group is the era of the **cohort** of children included in the comparison sample. Many measures base children's scores on old comparison groups of children. This happens when the test is not revised for 10 or 20 years. Norm group standardizations usually occur starting a year or two before the publication of the measure. Test users must decide if the norm comparison group is appropriate for use with current children.

Examples of Interpreting Norm Group Information in a Technical Presentation

1. The Developmental Indicators for the Assessment of Learning, 3rd ed. (DIAL-III), is designed to assess children between the ages of 3 and 6 years, 11 months. The DIAL-III was normed in 1995 to match the criteria of the U.S. Census Bureau. It includes 1,560 children, with an equal number of boys and girls, and is balanced for race and ethnicity, and parental education. Children in the norm group were drawn from 36 states and Washington, D.C. (Cizek & Fairbank, 2001).

2. The Stanford-Binet Intelligence Scales for Early Childhood, 5th ed. (Early-SB-5), is designed as a measure of cognitive ability for children between the ages of 2 years, 7 months, and 7 years, 3 months. It is scored based on a norm group of 1,660 children that was established in 2002. The normative group was selected to match the U.S. Census profile of American children. All ethnic groups are proportionally included and the group is gender, socioeconomic status (SES), and geographically balanced. A total of 400 trained examiners (100 working in each of the U.S. Census regions) were used to collect the normative data (Sink, Eppler, & Vacca, 2007). The SB-5 also tested 350 intellectually gifted children to provide a validation of the assessment. Another identified group of children with intellectual disabilities was also tested for the same purpose.

While both measures are being used to assess preschool and early primary grade children, it is clear that the Early-SB-5 has a more up-to-date norm group when compared with the Developmental Indicators for the Assessment of Learning, 3rd ed. (DIAL-III).[9]

Standards-Based Scoring

Required high-stakes assessments for all public school children include several types of scoring systems. At one level, these tests provide **norm-referenced scores.** These scores show how a child did on the assessment compared with other children. Commercially published achievement tests such as the Terra Nova II also provide percentile scores but also include a **standard score.** This dual score format is used by most states for their mandated assessment batteries.

Another form of standard score is the **Lexile measure.** This is a standard score based on a framework that represents the difficulty of comprehending literature. It also can be matched to the required reading level for comprehending millions of books and references in school libraries. This scoring system makes it possible to match children's skill levels to the reading material presented to them. More about the Lexile system is provided at http://www.lexile.com/PDF/Lexile-Reading-Measurement-and-Success-0504.pdf.

Proficiency Levels

A second set of scores provides a statement about each child's level of proficiency. To interpret a student's raw scores as ordinal labels such as below proficient,[10] **proficient,** and **highly proficient,** a set of cut scores must first be established. Committees called **Angoff committees** determine cut scores and set the criterion used to make proficiency decisions.[11] For this reason, the required tests of most states provide both normative (percentile) and **criterion-referenced** (proficiency) scores.

The relationship between the criterion scores (**proficiency levels**) and raw scores can be seen in Figure 3.4, a sample report for parents about the Texas Assessment of Knowledge and Skills (TAKS) at third grade.

Figure 3.4 A Sample Test Report for Parents of a Third Grade Child on the Texas Assessment of Knowledge and Skills for Reading

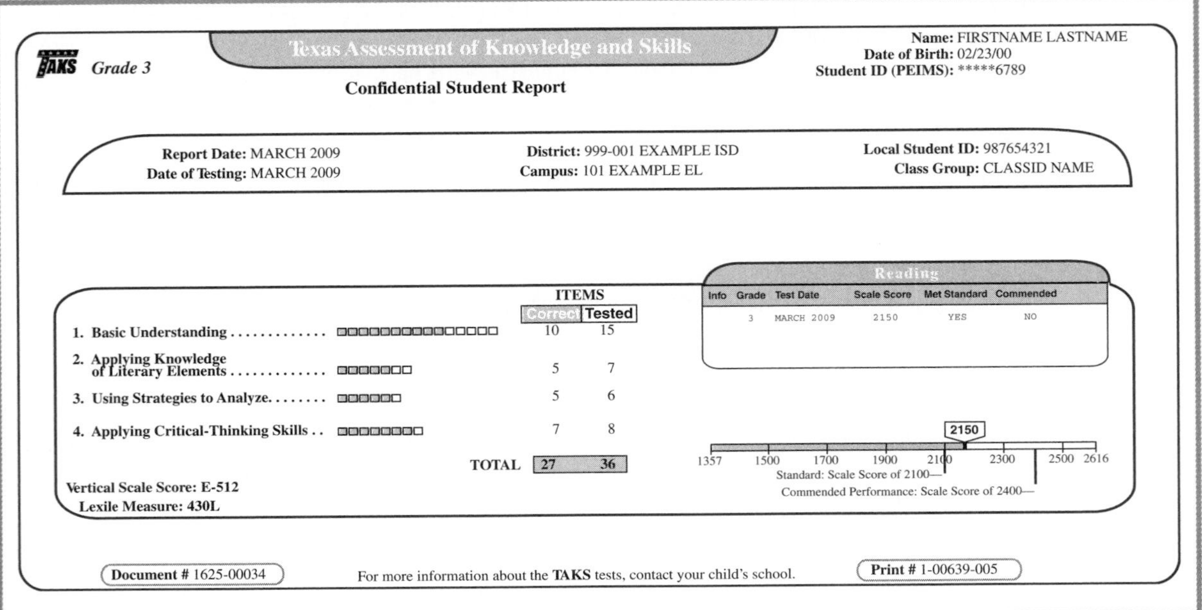

TAKS Grade 3

Texas Assessment of Knowledge and Skills

Confidential Student Report

Name: FIRSTNAME LASTNAME
Date of Birth: 02/23/00
Student ID (PEIMS): *****6789

Report Date: MARCH 2009
Date of Testing: MARCH 2009

District: 999-001 EXAMPLE ISD
Campus: 101 EXAMPLE EL

Local Student ID: 987654321
Class Group: CLASSID NAME

	ITEMS Correct	ITEMS Tested
1. Basic Understanding	10	15
2. Applying Knowledge of Literary Elements	5	7
3. Using Strategies to Analyze	5	6
4. Applying Critical-Thinking Skills	7	8
TOTAL	27	36

Vertical Scale Score: E-512
Lexile Measure: 430L

Reading

Info	Grade	Test Date	Scale Score	Met Standard	Commended
	3	MARCH 2009	2150	YES	NO

2150

1357 1500 1700 1900 2100 2300 2500 2616

Standard: Scale Score of 2100—

Commended Performance: Scale Score of 2400—

Document # 1625-00034

For more information about the **TAKS** tests, contact your child's school.

Print # 1-00639-005

NOTE: This sample from Texas indicates the third grader passed (is proficient) in reading and has a scaled score of 2159. At third grade, the TAKS reading subtest total standard score has a mean of 2303 and a standard deviation of 185. This child in the report scored 2159, which is 144 points below the statewide mean. Dividing this value by the standard deviation of the test ($SD = 185$, as reported by the Texas Education Agency [2009]) results in learning that the child scored 0.78 standard deviations below the mean. Texas's state standard for proficiency is a standard score of 2100. Thus, even though the child scored below average, he or she still scores as being proficient.

SOURCE: Texas Education Agency. Available at http://ritter.tea.state.tx.us/student.assessment/resources/guides/parent_csr/2009/TK09_parent_brochure_mar_g03R.pdf.

Criterion Measures

There are many tests scored exclusively as criterion tests. One good example of this is a state licensing examination required for a teacher's certificate. The written test is scored as either pass (become certified) or fail to earn a teacher's license. State-level Angoff committees set the cut scores.

The reliability of criterion assessments can be found using the statistic coefficient kappa. This reliability statistic is designed to cope with the highly skewed data that normally occur with criterion tests. Teacher's written licensing examinations provide an example of skewed data. The goal of most states is to have a pool of potential classroom teachers available each year. Thus, states set the minimum cut score for passing low enough that the majority of test takers pass. Thus, pass–fail tests will not have a normal distribution of outcomes, and about 85% of all test takers pass.[12]

Bias and Fairness

There are noticeable differences in the prereading and arithmetic scores of children in kindergarten on achievement measures when they come from different racial and ethnic groups (Sadker & Zittleman, 2004). Differences reflect different values, beliefs, and experiences of parents from diverse groups. The socioeconomic background of the child's family, his/her health status, and the use of language in the child's home are all keyed to these differences.

These background conditions are described as being related to the **fairness** of the assessment or test. Children from different homes will always enter early childhood programs and school with different academic skills and preparation levels. This disparity makes it difficult to construct a truly **fair test.** One goal of President Lyndon B. Johnson's War on Poverty (1965) was the elimination of the disparity of educational readiness between children from impoverished backgrounds and children from more fortunate backgrounds. His introduction of Head Start was then, as it is now, one powerful force working to make American education fairer.

If a measure has test items that give an advantage to children of one identifiable group, but not another, those items are potentially biased. **Bias** can result in some children being underestimated, and others being accurately assessed or even overestimated (see Case in Point 3.5 for more about "test bias"). One line of defense against the possibility of bias is a two-step process most test publishers undertake. At one level, a committee of experts representing both genders and various groups examine each question or task protocol and use their backgrounds to look for potential bias. This process is known as a **sensitivity review.** The second approach is a statistical one that is called a test of **differential item functioning (DIF).** The DIF process involves giving items from an assessment or measurement to children from different groups (gender, race, or SES) who represent the full range of ability.

Case in Point 3.5

Statistical Bias in Test Scores

The basis for statistical "test bias" lies in the use of a test or other measure in a comparison with an earlier test. If the score that is found when a preschool child is tested is compared with that preschooler's success later in public school, we can anticipate a degree of congruity to occur. Thus, high scores on a preschool measure should presage good achievement test scores in first grade.

Occasionally, tests will show that girls tend to score better than boys on some preschool and kindergarten tests. If that difference does not occur later when children are tested in first grade, the test given in preschool could be described as having a statistical bias favoring girls. This is not because the girls scored better as kindergarteners, but because the difference did not hold up later.

The results of each identified group are charted and the charts are compared looking for possible bias. An unbiased test item will be easy for all subgroups that share the same high ability level. Likewise an unbiased item will be difficult for less able students of each sample group. A biased item will be consistently easier for one group and more difficult for another. This will occur at all levels of ability.

Independent Sources of Information About Assessments and Measures

Beginning in 1930, Professor Oscar K. Buros of the University of Nebraska started a collection of every published test used in America. This collection was supplemented with the publication of test reviews beginning in 1934. Each new published test, and each new edition of a previously published measure, is independently reviewed by two experts. The Buros Institute of Mental Measurements then publishes those reviews every few years in the *Mental Measurements Yearbook* and online (fee based) at http://buros.unl.edu/buros/jsp/search.jsp.

A second source of independent information is the collection of all published measures and research instruments maintained by ETS. That library of over 25,000 items is also accessible online at http://www.ets.org/portal/site/ets/menuitem.1488512ecfd5b8849a77b13bc3921509/?vgnextoid=ed462d3631df4010VgnVCM10000022f95190RCRD&vgnextchannel=85af197a484f4010VgnVCM10000022f95190RCRD.

Summary

There are numerous aspects to the growth and development of young children. Thousands of different measures of these dimensions have been developed and published. Variables measured with youngsters can be expressed in four levels of precision. Physical measurements such as the child's body mass index are ratio scales while intelligence is expressed as an interval scale. Ordinal scales abound and describe many behavioral checklists. Nominal scales are measures that are simple categorical names.

Shorthand for describing data is central tendency (average). Central tendency statistics include the mode (most common), the median (the 50th percentile), and the mean (the arithmetic center). Naturally occurring data tend to cluster near the median, and spread out from there. This symmetric pattern results in a characteristically bell-shaped (normal) curve with large groups of data. The spread of scores from the median/mean is measured in standard deviation units that define a specific proportion of data. Scoring systems used by most test publishers employ standard scores determined by using standard deviation units. If the data lack symmetry, and there are too many extreme scores, the mean and the median separate, and the data are described as skewed.

When measurements take on a high-stakes role, they should be both highly reliable (stable and consistent) and valid (appropriate and on target) systems. One application of reliability coefficients is in the form of standard error of measurement. The more reliable the measure, the smaller will be its standard error of measurement.

Measurements should be free of bias (hidden advantages for some) and fair (all start at the same point) if they are to be used in a high-stakes environment. They should also have a representative norm group that is up-to-date.

Discussion Questions

1. What type of measurement scale describes the reading groups that are part of some primary grade level classrooms?
2. Old-fashioned letter grades (e.g., A, B, C, etc.) are what type of measurement scale?
3. What are the implications for using a test for kindergarten admission that has a relatively high standard error of measurement?
4. Would an IQ test such as the Stanford-Binet Intelligence Scales for Early Childhood, 5th ed., be a valid measure to use in deciding kindergarten readiness?
5. Use the online system provided by the university's library to look up the evaluation of an early childhood assessment measure described in this book or that is used at the school you have contact with. Read the reviews and describe your findings.
6. Can a test be unbiased and unfair at the same time? Explain your reasoning.

Related Readings

Mertler, C. A. (2007). *Interpreting standardized test scores.* Thousand Oaks, CA: Sage.

Salkind, N. J. (2005). *Tests and measurements for people who think they hate tests and measurements.* Thousand Oaks, CA: Sage.

Salkind, N. J. (2008). *Statistics for people who think they hate statistics* (3rd ed). Thousand Oaks, CA: Sage.

Wright, R. J. (2008). *Educational assessment: Tests and measurements in the age of accountability.* Thousand Oaks, CA: Sage.

Notes

1. Precision has a very different meaning to an engineer. The meaning of the word in the physical sciences is similar to what educational psychologists describe as measurement reliability.
2. Yet, statistical principles associated with the normal curve, that is the bell curve, can be applied to these ratio scales. This is done to provide statistical analysis including analyses needed for hypotheses testing (Warner, 2008).
3. The word "average" in vernacular English is normally considered as being what a testing expert would call the mean, or arithmetic center, of the set of scores.
4. In 1718, a friend of Sir Isaac Newton, the Huguenot refugee Abraham de Moivre, identified the mathematics defining the normal distribution. In 1809, his formula was employed by Carl Friedrich Gauss to describe errors occurring during astronomical observations, and has been called ever since, the Gaussian normal distribution. American students refer to it by its characteristic shape, the "bell curve."
5. Descriptions of variability referring to mean also imply the median, as they are the same value in normal data.
6. Percentiles are transformations of data that are ordinal. As ordinals, they cannot be averaged or used in arithmetic-based statistical analyses.
7. Correlation of nominal data involves probability statistics and is beyond the scope of this book. To learn more about this issue, see the textbook by Warner (2008).
8. The stability of a test is one type of reliability. It is measured by using a correlation coefficient (Pearson or Spearman) between the scores or results from two administrations of the same evaluation to the same group of children.
9. Information about the norm groups, reliability, and validity of a standardized test should be provided in a manual published by the test developer.
10. Children that score below proficient on the mandated statewide assessments (see Chapter 2) can be the reason that a public school gets a failing report card and put the school in danger of being reorganized or closed. The NCLB Act has a provision for the children with the most serious levels of disability. The federal mandate will allow only 3% of all children be tested with a developmentally appropriate measure. Developmentally appropriate tests are designed around what a child can actually do, not what the average child of a particular age can do. Use of such measures provides a measure of skill growth for a child with disabilities.
11. An Angoff committee consists of between 50 and 100 educators and testing experts, brought together by a state education department, who study the questions available to measure each learning standard. The committee decides how many items must be passed to reach the various criterion levels (cut scores).
12. For a university to be approved by the National Council for Accreditation of Teacher Education, it must have a minimum of 80% of its graduates pass the required state examination.

Part II

Formative and Summative Assessments and Tests

This section provides an introduction to the development and use of formative measures by early childhood teachers. The use of performance assessments and the- development of both analytical and holistic rubrics are presented. This section also provides suggestions and ideas for portfolio assessments.

The appropriate use and development of summative assessments is also described in this section. This includes a description of levels of cognition needed by young children to answer questions posed by classroom teachers. Mandated assessments and standardized instruments for measuring achievement among primary grade children are also examined. This includes a discussion of assumptions made by test developers, and addresses accommodations for measuring children with special needs.

Mandated assessments from the No Child Left Behind Act are also described along with problems in interpreting their meaning. This section also describes factors that can influence scores on assessments.

Teacher-constructed scales are also described in this section. These scales include checklists, semantic scales, hierarchical scales, and the use of discrete visual analog measures in the classroom. This discussion includes the question of scale fidelity and reliability.

Informal Evaluations of Young Children

4

When I approach a child, he inspires in me two sentiments; tenderness for what he is, and respect for what he may become.

—Louis Pasteur

Introduction and Themes

When children play "pretend school" and create a classroom in their playroom or basement, the ersatz teacher's roll book and "student marks" become a central theme. Be that as it may, when an adult becomes a teacher the tedium of assessment and data recording soon tarnishes the luster this part of teaching once held. As educators, however, we know educational assessments are essential to the process (T. Linn & Miller, 2005).

Preschool teachers view the collection of information about children as an ongoing process involving the child's family. Some of these data are designed to document what each child has learned and what skills were acquired following instruction. These data summarize the status of each child's learning and/or growth. The term applied to these types of data is summative.

Formative assessments provide teachers with data that inform the teaching–learning process. Formative assessments are used while teaching is ongoing; therefore, formative assessment information is essential for monitoring and improving learning. A related application of formative assessments supports differentiated instruction in the early childhood classroom.

Educators can employ alternative assessment models along with standard assessments. These alternative assessments can provide information for both formative and summative evaluations. Alternative assessments include performance assessments, authentic assessments, and portfolio assessments.

Performance-based assessments provide rich information about young children. They can focus on single or multiple assessment dimensions of the child. A variation of performance evaluation is known as authentic assessment, which is conducted using real world materials and/or natural settings.

Evaluations based on performance assessments are best carried out using a rubric. They can be designed analytically providing ordinal scores summarizing the quality of each child's work. Early childhood teachers can improve the reliability and validity of performance assessments by using multidimensional rubrics.

Portfolio evaluations (summative) are a logical process that has developed from organizational tools. Questions regarding data inclusion in children's **evaluative portfolios** need to be discussed in terms of goals and philosophies of the teachers. Careful planning and training can improve the reliability and validity of portfolio assessments.

Other data sources about young children are qualitative and unstructured. Much can be learned about young children by careful observations in free play settings. Another frequently overlooked source of data about young children is the initial enrollment report form. Other good sources of information are interview questions with parents, and observations of parents and child together.

Learning Objectives

By reading and studying this chapter, you should acquire the competency to:

- Explain the distinction between summative and formative assessments.
- Discuss why formative assessment is important for quality early education.
- Describe using children's play as an evaluative tool.
- Write an anecdotal record to describe a behavioral incident.
- Explain several roles for holistic and analytical rubrics in assessment.
- Create an analytical rubric for evaluating learning.
- Explain the use of portfolios in early childhood education.
- Discuss how technology is changing early childhood assessment.

Informal Evaluations and Assessments[1]

The evaluation of children is integral to teaching. While many assessments are scripted and highly structured, informal assessments and their component measures are part of day-to-day education. Informal assessments support student learning and keep children engaged in the learning process. Informal assessments should follow a cycle that starts with observations (see Figure 4.1):

1. Observing the behaviors and learning of children
2. Noting and documenting relevant observations
3. Examining evidence and reflecting on each child's needs and strengths
4. Organizing instruction to meet needs observed and documented in Step 2
5. Implementing the plan and providing needed instruction
6. Evaluating the effectiveness of the executed plan, and starting again

When the cook tastes the soup, that's formative assessment; when the customer tastes the soup, that's summative assessment.

—Grant P. Wiggins

Summative Assessments

Most of the general public thinks of assessment only in terms of large-scale published tests and the high-stakes measures required by state edicts. High-stakes tests are but one form of educational measurement in public schools. Teachers also evaluate and make inferences as to what each child can actually do.

Summative assessments follow instruction and summarize what happened up to a particular point in time. Data provided by summative assessments can be used to report a child's progress to parents or to

Figure 4.1 Observation, Instruction, and Evaluation Cycle

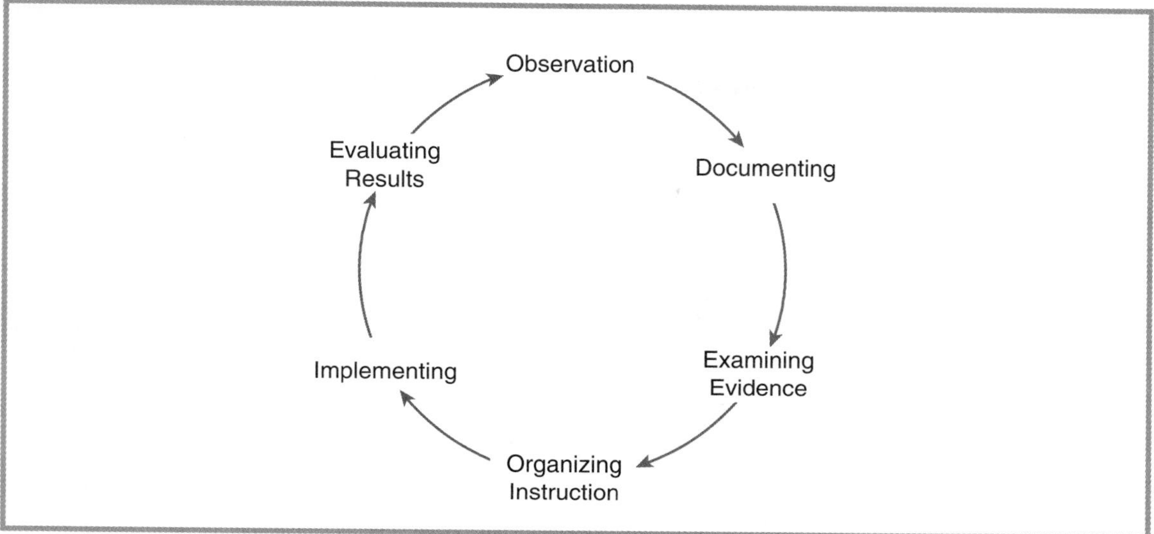

develop an educational plan for children. Summative assessments provide much of the information needed to make **entitlement decisions.**[2] They may include qualitative measures such as portfolio assessments and performance assessments; or they may be purely observational in nature.

In today's high-stakes world of assessment in primary grades, summative measures provide data required to make adequate yearly progress (AYP) decisions (see Chapter 2). High-stakes summative tests are usually given in the spring; thus, teachers may not receive score reports until the school is closed for summer break. The disconnect between child and outcome score is a reason why state mandated high-stakes tests offer little for classroom teachers. When teachers are informed how well particular children have done, a new class of students is starting the next school year.

Formative Assessments

At the heart of good teaching are formative assessments. Formative assessments inform teachers how learning is progressing. They provide teachers with insight into what cognitive systems are used by the child to learn new material (DiRanna et al., 2008). Formative assessments can include both formal assessment protocols or be highly informal measures. The classroom teacher makes up some of the best formative assessments on the spot. Formative measures are brief checkups that provide insight into how well children are learning.

Goal of Formative Assessments

The goal of all formative assessments is to make the teacher better at his/her job (C. A. Tomlinson, 2008). This happens when the early childhood teacher uses the formative assessment information to make needed modifications in his or her instructional activities. This tweaking process may be a simple reteaching of the topic, or a demonstration of what is being learned. It provides insight into each child's learning status while instruction is progressing.

Timing

A distinction between formative and summative assessments lies in the timing of their use. Summative assessments follow instructional programs whereas formative assessments are ongoing and integrated into the instructional process.

For formative assessments to improve the quality of teaching, they must delineate student conceptualizations and understandings. The teacher must then decide how to use that information. It can be used to reteach what the child has not understood; or it can be used to praise the student for being on the right track (see Table 4.1 for a summary of the characteristics that distinguish the types of assessments).

Table 4.1 Three Types of Measures

	Summative (Teacher Made)	Summative (High Stakes)	Formative
Frequency	Several times a month	Once a year	Ongoing each day
Timing	Following an instructional program	In the spring	Throughout the day
Format	Unit tests and quizzes	Standardized and decontextualized	Informal observations, worksheets, projects, oral questions
Purpose	Making informed decisions and judging success of each child after instruction	Evaluating programs, teachers, and children	Monitoring instruction and informing and tweaking the process

Performance Evaluations

Every assessment requires a type of performance by children. Performance assessments may be designed by the teacher or drawn from standardized assessments. They may include spontaneous creative products from children.

Teacher-administered performance assessments measure the skills and knowledge as well as the judgment and insights exhibited by children. Performance assessments can require children to demonstrate critical thinking and various levels of problem solving. Teachers employing a performance assessment model are as concerned with the process used to solve problems as with the actual outcome.

Three Phases

The performance assessment process has three phases. First, the teacher must frame the problem or task for the child. Next, that framework must be explained and the child motivated to complete the task or project. Finally, the teacher must be able to observe what the child can do without help, and then again with help as needed. The whole assessment must then be recorded and written up or otherwise filed for future comparisons or evaluations (see Figure 4.2 for an example of a brief formative assessment).

Figure 4.2 A Simple Performance Assessment for a 4-Year-Old Child

1. Engage the child with a stack of plastic poker chips. Demonstrate by laying 10 of the chips on the table without ordering them in any way.
2. Ask the child to give you 4 of the chips. Then ask the child how many chips are left for the child to play with.
3. Assist the child in counting as necessary.
4. Record the child's behaviors and answers to this counting task.

Another performance data source is drawn from spontaneously produced products. Kindergartens and child care centers should provide space and materials where children are free to draw or print letters and write.[3]

Creative products of children can be very informative. An effort should be made by every teacher to collect several examples of each child's work each month. Those products should be filed with the date of their production, and a transcript of any story the child told about the pictures. See Case in Point 4.1 for an example of the work of Jean Piaget on the nature of young children's cognition.

Case in Point 4.1

Examples of Piagetian Measurements

A rich source of performance assessment items can be found in research questions developed by Jean Piaget. Dimensions covered by Piaget in his work include many aspects of young children. These include questions related to the child's developing understanding of morality, time and space, collections and subgroups, continuous quantity, number, geometry, causation, visual perspective, three-dimensional space, and the personal understanding of the self (Piaget, 1932, 1952, 1955, 1960, 1962, 1965, 1967; Piaget & Inhelder, 1956; Piaget, Inhelder, & Szeminska, 1960).

A number of examples based on Piaget's writing have turned up on the Internet. These performance tasks can provide teachers with insight into the developing cognitive processes of young children. The following URLs connect with video examples of conducting Piagetian assessments:

http://www.youtube.com/watch?v=MpREJIrpgv8
http://www.youtube.com/watch?v=YJyuy4B2aKU&NR=1
http://www.youtube.com/watch?v=tYtNk0BotRE&feature=related
http://www.youtube.com/watch?v=uozcxn9tVzs

Authentic Assessments

Authentic assessments are a special case of performance assessments.[4] These assessments involve objects and/or measurement tasks taken from the real world. This approach to assessment can be compared with **decontextualized** standardized assessments that are not grounded on elements in the child's world (Torulf, 2008).

Well-designed authentic assessments engage the young child with interesting and motivating activities. Literacy recognition tasks can provide an authentic assessment experience, for example, a literacy assessment including questions based on books a child has in his/her home collection. Another approach to authentic assessment involves counting, sorting, and seriating tasks. These assessments can involve materials taken from a kitchen or garage (e.g., spoons, muffin tins, lug nuts, etc.). The use of authentic assessments can replace workbook picture coloring with problems that resonate with reality.

By second grade, children can have authentic language arts assessment tasks, for example, writing a letter to our troops overseas. These tasks can be highly motivational and truly authentic to the child. Mathematics can be authentically assessed by having children use play money to simulate a store selling school supplies.

Evaluation of Performance Assessments

Rubrics provide one method for assessing a child's performance (Ainsworth & Viegut, 2006). The levels of quality are indicated on a **rubric** as an ordinal number representing a qualitative judgment. The use of rubrics can be very flexible.

A rubric-based assessment can consist of a series of number lines. For example:

Drawing by Kindergarteners

Scribbling & random drawing	Use of lines & shapes	Draws simple objects	Draws pictures with action	Draws pictures with action & much detail
______1	______2	______3	______4	______5

A rubric can also be formatted as a table:

Kindergarten Writing (Check appropriate level)

Level 1 Child scribbles (no coherent letters evident). ______

Level 2 Child produces random letters. ______

Level 3 Child randomly writes recognizable words. ______

Level 4 Child writes a recognizable thought. ______

Level 5 Child writes a statement with beginning, middle, and end. ______

Level 6 Child writes entire sentences with effort to control spelling. ______

Rubrics provide **benchmarks** for optimal performance based on standards for learning; they also provide a series of **qualifying terms** describing various levels of quality for each possible level of performance. The qualifying terms are abbreviated by using a number representing the ordinal level. Most rubrics have between three and six levels of qualifying terms. It is possible to present the child with the same task several times during the school year and chart his/her progress by using the rubric. The great advantage in performance assessments is they demonstrate something the child can actually do and how well it is done.

Rubric Writing

There are five elements in a rubric. One is the title and/or descriptor of the rubric. The second is a benchmark statement of the instructional expectations being assessed.

The third element includes qualifying terms. There are a broad range of possible terms that can be used for this, for example, Exemplary, Mastery, Approaching, Emerging, and No Evidence. These qualifying terms should be clearly differentiated from each other, and form an obvious hierarchy. Other systems can include:

1. Standard greatly exceeded

   Minimum standard exceeded

   Minimum standard met

   Does not meet minimum standard

2. Excellent work

   Good work

   Needs more developmental effort

   Incoherent and confused

3. Master craftsman

   Journeyman

   Beginner/novice

   Apprentice

4. Highly proficient

   Proficient

   Below proficient

   Significantly below proficient

5. Extending learning

   Achieved learning

   Developing the learning

   No learning accomplished

The fourth element provides definitions and/or examples for each qualifying term. Each qualifying term may be linked to better-elaborated sets of descriptions. The following example from the Santa Barbara School District (CA), is adapted from the district's rubric for assessing letter-writing skills of second grade children:

Goal: Personal Letter Writing

- Benchmark: All parts (date, salutation, body, closing, and signature) are accurately used.

Level 4 Mastery

The writing:

- Clearly focuses on topic and addresses all parts of the writing task.
- Maintains clear and coherent sentences and paragraphs developing a central idea.
- Uses some concrete-sensory details.
- Consistently uses complete sentences.
- Contains few, if any, errors in the conventions of the English language (grammar, punctuation, capitalization, spelling).

Level 3 Approaching Mastery

The writing:

- Focuses on topic and addresses the writing task.
- Maintains coherent sentences and paragraphs that develop a central idea.
- Uses some concrete-sensory details.
- Consistently uses complete sentences.
- Contains some errors in the conventions of the English language (grammar, punctuation, capitalization, spelling).

Level 2 Emerging

The writing:

- Inconsistent focus on topic and addresses only parts of the writing task.
- Demonstrates little organizational structure.
- Includes some appropriate details.
- Contains some complete sentences.
- Contains several errors in the conventions of the English language (grammar, punctuation, capitalization, spelling). These errors may interfere with the reader's understanding of the writing.

Level 1 *Beginner*

The writing:

- Lacks focus on topic and addresses only one part of the writing task.
- Demonstrates no organizational structure.
- Lacks appropriate details.
- Contains few complete sentences.
- Contains serious errors in the conventions of the English language (grammar, punctuation, capitalization, spelling). These errors interfere with the reader's understanding of the writing.

To see more of this school system's standards and rubrics visit: http://www.sbsd.k12.ca.us/District/Curriculum/AnchorPapers/ScoringRubrics/Grade2Rubric.pdf.

The following example is drawn from inservice materials for primary teachers in the City of Chicago that used a **scoring rubric** with four levels (Low = 0, High = 3) to assess writing skills:

Analytical Rubric Used in the Chicago Public Schools

Second grade, writing from an **oral prompt**. The oral prompt is underlined.
The writing by three children in the second grade is assessed using a 4-point rubric covering four domains of writing skill:

(F) Focus

(S) Support

(O) Organization

(C) Use of writing conventions

The prompt: I wish it would snow.

(Child One)
I wish it would snow because I cude have a snowball fight. I wish it would snow because I wlud Make a snowman because I like to Make it. I like to ics sking I want to Play hikey. I like to Make snowanjls.

(F) 3 (S) 2 (O) 1 (C) 3

(Child Two)
I make money. I would go to Michaigain and ice skate. I would make two snow man and a women. I would help my brother make snow angles. Sometimes we stay in Chicago and sometimes we go some where for christmas. We go to cruch and than we go home and open our prizes. Last year my cats go a new food feeder. Christmas night watching movies. I Love christmas.

(F) 2 (S) 2 (O) 2 (C) 2

(Child Three)
I can make Angele picers and I could go snow Bording. And I can pretend with The snow that I have berd and a snow ball fight and I can make a snowman. I can get Toys and play like The snow is Lava or I can dive in the snow. We can Take Pictrs of us playing in the snow.

(F) 3 (S) 2 (O) 2 (C) 2

To learn more about rubrics for writing, visit the Web page from the California Department of Education: http://www.sdcoe.k12.ca.us/score/actbank/srubrics.htm

Holistic Rubrics

Holistic rubrics include benchmarks and qualifying terms describing various levels of performance simultaneously over several skills. The holistic rubric is widely employed for grading writing and for other complex assessments. Holistic rubrics facilitate teachers quickly grading an impossible number of student writing samples. For example, the Arkansas Department of Education administers a statewide assessment of writing for public school children starting in Grade 3 that is scored by teachers evaluating over 60 tests/hour. While widely employed for large-scale assessments, holistic rubrics are used at all grade and developmental levels (see http://arkansased.org/testing/pdf/rib_gr3_spr07.pdf).

Analytical Rubrics

Rubrics that are part of an assessment of a complex learning or skill can be layered. Each layer is focused on one dimension. For example, an analytical assessment of a written essay answer by a third grader could provide three areas for assessment, each with five qualifying descriptors (see Figure 4.3).

The dimensional scores from an **analytical rubric** can be combined into a single value, or recorded separately and used to track progress during the year.

Figure 4.3 Analytical Rubric

A. Mechanics (grammar, spelling, and punctuation)
   5. Free of grammar, spelling, or punctuation errors
   4. Less than 4 errors in mechanics
   3. 4 or 5 errors in mechanics
   2. Difficult to read because of numerous mechanical errors
   1. Unreadable mass of errors

B. Organization and Readability
   5. Easy to follow, logically organized, holding reader's interest
   4. Has gaps in logic but can be easily understood
   3. Makes illogical leaps, hard to follow
   2. Disorganized, very hard to follow
   1. Off target jumble of words

C. Facts and Details
   5. More than expected and factually accurate
   4. Good basic response to the question
   3. Marginal with some correct elements
   2. No real understanding of the issue
   1. No answer attempted

Checklists Versus Rubrics

In early childhood classrooms, there is a tendency to blend meanings between rubrics and checklists. These are two unique measurement tools. A checklist provides a statement of what a child can do, which is answered by a simple check mark. It has no benchmarks set up as an ordinal scale. For example, a questionnaire item and rubric for assessing the same educational goal are presented in Figure 4.4.

Scaling

At each level, rubrics are scored using an ascending ordinal scale. These scores imply the child has achieved all the lower steps. If a child is scored at Level 3 (from Figure 4.4), we know he/she has met Levels 1 and 2. This format is called a **Guttman scale**. This facilitates the use of advanced statistics to demonstrate the reliability of any rubric.

Figure 4.4 Checklist Versus Rubric

The following could be an item on a kindergarten language arts skills **checklist:**

The child can recognize his/her name in block print form. ( ) Yes ( ) No

A **rubric** for a similar issue:

Title: At what level is the child able to represent him/herself in writing?

Benchmark: The child should recognize his/her name when it is block printed on an oak-tag strip or kindergarten ruled paper.

Qualifying terms		*Qualifying level descriptor*
Exemplary	(5) ___	Writes his/her name using block-print and recognizes it on an array of other names
Mastery	(4) ___	Writes his/her name using block-print without recognizing it among others
Approaching	(3) ___	Recognizes his/her name on an array of block-printed names
Emerging	(2) ___	Recognizes his/her name in block print form on his/her desk
No Evidence	(1) ___	The child cannot recognize his/her own name

A rubric for a similar issue:

Title: At what level is the child able to represent him/herself in writing?

Benchmark: The child should recognize his/her name when it is block printed on an oak-tag strip or kindergarten ruled paper.

Qualifying terms		*Qualifying level descriptor*
Exemplary	(5) ___	Writes his/her name using block print and recognizes it in an array of other names
Mastery	(4) ___	Writes his/her name using block print without recognizing it among others
Approaching	(3) ___	Recognizes his/her name in an array of block-printed names
Emerging	(2) ___	Recognizes his/her name in block-print form on his/her desk
No Evidence	(1) ___	The child cannot recognize his/her own name

Special Education

Rubrics are designed to be reliable measurement tools. On performance assessments, all children should complete the same task and be evaluated with the same rubric, including children with special needs. The exception to this rule involves appropriate accommodations spelled out in an Individual Family Service Plan (IFSP) or Individual Educational Plan (IEP) (see Chapter 11) (Glickman-Bond & Rose, 2006).

Differentiated Instruction

Rubrics are used in differentiated instruction. **Differentiated instruction** assumes that all children have different learning profiles. The teacher's job involves knowing the learning profile of each student and matching him/her with appropriate learning activities. A differentiated curriculum offers children an array of options for the learning process. Differentiated instruction also facilitates meeting the learning needs of children with special needs as well as providing opportunities for gifted children to accelerate their learning.

A common set of core rubrics based on learning standards are essential in gifted education. Before a child can be accelerated he/she must first demonstrate having achieved the required learning standard. For example, if a child has mastered arithmetic addition and subtraction and demonstrated those skills on a measure graded by using a rubric, then he/she can be offered the opportunity to learn multiplication.

Problems With Rubrics

One problem with rubrics is they are difficult to create. Writing meaningful benchmark descriptions requires teachers to first have a great deal of experience teaching the topic so they know how children progress in their learning, and what developmental steps are expected.

There is a need for extensive training to ensure high interrater concordance when two or more teachers are to use a rubric to evaluate a performance assessment. There is a tendency for some raters to focus on extraneous factors of the performance and ignore the objective of the evaluation. The degree to which two teachers agree on a set of rubric-based scores from a class can be found using Spearman correlation. The result of a correlation analysis between the rubric scores assigned by two independent teachers is known as the **interrater reliability coefficient.**

Reliability of Performance Evaluations

Research into the reliability of alternative assessment systems including portfolio assessments has yielded mixed results (Bateson, 1994). Having more than one independent reader assess each child can enhance reliability of performance measures and rubrics.

There is a tendency for **"rater drift"** to occur when a person evaluates a number of children. Rater drift caused by fatigue/boredom results in higher scores for children being evaluated toward the end of a group. Multiple raters should exhibit a high degree of agreement in the scores they assign ($p \geq 0.70$). If there is a difference of more than a point, scoring should stop and scorers work together to improve consistency. Tweaking the rubric may also help improve scorer agreement.

Portfolio Assessments

In early education settings (PK–3), portfolios are a normal feature of the evaluation process. Portfolios are much more than a manila folder stuffed with an assortment of mementos from a child; they are purposeful compendiums (not omnium-gatherums) of data documenting a child's growth in skills, knowledge, and new understandings over time.[5] It also describes the child's abilities and work habits (Collins & Dana, 1993). It should be periodically reviewed with the child so he/she can see his/her own progress and help shape future development.

Evaluative Portfolio

Each child's portfolio provides the bridge between the teacher's instructional efforts and the young child's educational attainment. That linkage implies portfolios can be used to evaluate student achievement in various curriculum areas.

Well-conceived rubrics employed by well-trained evaluators can provide highly reliable portfolio evaluations (Gadbury-Amyot et al., 2003). The goal of using the portfolio's documents and artifacts in an assessment of the child's learning and development supersedes all individual evaluations contained in the portfolio. In other words, the whole is more than the sum of its parts.

"How do you like my portfolio?"

SOURCE: Carton by Merv Magus.

Portfolio Reliability

Heretofore, portfolio assessments have been seen as unreliable and not appropriate evaluation tools. An analysis by Mark Reckase (1995) determined that portfolio assessments can have good reliability ($r \geq 0.75$).[6] Well-trained evaluators enhance portfolio-scoring reliability. Programs for training portfolio evaluators should include practice with the benchmarks and qualifying levels using the scoring rubric.

Good reliability requires portfolios be evaluated, element by element, using analytical rubrics not holistic rubrics. **Holistic assessments** are too idiosyncratic and tend to produce lower levels of reliability. The final evaluation of a child based on his/her portfolio is determined from the summation of all the analytical elements, and can have a much higher reliability (Reckase, 1995). To get a better sense of what to evaluate, see Figure 4.5.

Portfolios used for evaluation should contain elements (documents and artifacts) linked to the approved learning standards. Evaluative portfolios should always be grounded in the instructional objectives of the preschool or primary grade elementary school (Doherty, 2004).

Figure 4.5 Elements Included in a Kindergarten Portfolio

Portfolios can take many forms including oak-tag folder, accordion folio file, scrapbook, or digital database. One school used new pizza delivery boxes with each child's name on the box's side. Portfolios should provide samples of an individual child's best work in prespecified areas. The specified areas include those considered by teachers as central. Materials should be dated when selected for storage in the portfolio.

1. Enrollment data about the child (e.g., birthday, age, siblings, family structure, etc.)
2. Work samples (artifacts). Organize these data by learning area:
   Worksheets that have evaluative information
   Art samples and freely drawn illustrations
   Writing samples
   Video of child doing cognitive tasks
3. Standardized measures including checklists
4. Observations, **anecdotal records,** and teacher-made checklists
5. Transcripts or video of the child's creative storytelling
6. Products, photos, and objects selected by the child (Kingore, 2008)

SOURCE: From Kingore, B., 2008.

Getting Started

Individual teachers are likely to have different ideas regarding items for inclusion in portfolios. A first step in changing a school's culture and introducing portfolios is the provision of adequate meeting time to develop a faculty consensus about portfolios. Naturally, reaching an agreement among faculty requires flexibility. Many teachers may wish to add extra materials to the portfolios including meaningful artifacts beyond the established standards.

The faculty must also decide whether the work that is collected in student portfolios should be **"typical products"** or **"best products."** In order to maximize the reliability of a portfolio evaluation, all included work should represent the best products from the child. Portfolios can be maintained for the entire year while still being segmented to permit evaluations at several points (report card periods) in the school year.

By the close of the academic year, students' best products will be qualitatively different from the "best products" when the school year began. This pattern of growth should be shared with parents during the final conference.

Faculty must also decide what materials in portfolios should be retained for next year's teacher. Most preschool programs retain only a minimal amount of material from each year to serve as a new baseline in the fall. When the child moves into public school, his/her parents should be given the final portfolio to share with the next teacher in the new school.

Technology and the New Age of Portfolios

The need to store hard copies of artifacts in portfolios is being replaced by efficient new digital systems (Montgomery & Wiley, 2008). These new digital files (e-files) can be edited with ease and given to parents on a CD–ROM or even electronically transferred. Within an e-file portfolio, all the typical artifacts can be stored and updated daily. It is also easy to organize by setting up a table of contents (subfile directory) and a collection of subfiles. Artifacts can go home with the child to adorn the family's refrigerator door after digital copies are scanned into the child's e-file portfolio.

If we wish to understand our child, we need to understand his play.

—Montaigne

Play-Based Assessment

A widely used method for collecting information about children involves **play-based assessment.** The impact of play on development is evident in dimensions including early socialization, cognition, creative development, and the acquisition of physical and motor skills (Bettelheim, 1987; Linder, 1993). All adults can remember the pure joy felt as children when we were totally immersed into our fantasy life through play. Play-based assessments can be carried out by highly trained teams following a formal protocol, or conducted by a well-prepared preschool teacher. For an example of the prelogical thinking of 4-year-olds, see Case in Point 4.2.

Case in Point 4.2

Preschool Children's Understanding of Cause-and-Effect

A preschool had a large glass aquarium with two dozen fish in September. By the spring, only six survivors were left in the school's aquarium. On the playground, a teacher's aide heard one child telling another 4-year-old, "I think the teachers are eating the fish." This bit of **observational data** later became the inspiration for the development of a unit on the care of pets.

Play-based assessments, like all assessments, should be built around a set of goals. Assessment goals may include gaining insight into various dimensions of the child's development including cognitive, communication/language, social/emotional, and motor.

Once an assessment domain is selected, the teacher should organize the equipment (developmentally appropriate) and setting (free of distractions) being used. If the assessment involves language skills, play equipment may be lettered blocks or tiles from the game Scrabble. Materials to assess numerosity may include poker chips or small counting sticks. The child being tested should have ample time for free play with the assessment toys. Play assessment includes a specific series (protocol) of questions for the child and a written or video record of these answers should be made.

Related to play assessments are observations a teacher can conduct of the child playing. These observations of the child at play can provide much understanding of how he/she interacts with peers. It can also provide insight into the child's fantasy life and/or socialization. For example, careful observation of children playing can reveal which child is becoming a leader. Young leaders are the rule givers in organizing group games.[7]

Understanding the child at play comes from careful and nuanced observations of the ongoing scene in the child's environment. Naturalistic playground observations conducted "in the field," when subjected to careful reflection (see Steps 2 and 3 in Figure 4.1), can reveal much about a child.

Home and Family Data Sources

There are unobtrusive and informal sources of information that educators have available for learning more about children.

Community Sources

Early childhood centers should subscribe to local (community) newspapers. Newspapers are where many of the problems that a family may be experiencing are aired. Issues of marriage and divorce are listed in local newspapers, as are police call outs. Police call outs document domestic disturbances and DUI arrests. This may seem trivial, but the question of which parent should pick up the child and which parent may be an impaired driver must be considered. Items clipped from the paper need to be verified by asking the parent. Child care centers are not immune from violence and children must never be put at risk. (Bad things do happen in child care centers, see http://www.nbc-2.com/articles/readarticle.asp?articleid=17102&z=3&p).

Written Communications

A source of information about children includes the e-mail and handwritten notes sent to school. Parents under stress often write more than they intend in their parent-to-teacher communications. All e-mails and handwritten notes should be read, responded to, and saved for a year.

Enrollment Data

Preschools need to review the information they collect when children are enrolled. The Family Educational Rights and Privacy Act limits use of these data (see Figure 4.6). But, the enrollment instrument data can be an important source for insight about a child.

Parental Observations and Interviews

Sometimes the shortest distance to a goal is a straight line. Parents occasionally stop the preschool teachers while collecting their youngster and his/her equipment. This presents a good moment to just ask the parent for a needed bit of information (see Chapter 12). These "on the run" interviews are not conferences and can

Figure 4.6 Information to Collect When a Child Is Enrolled

Data on this form should include:

Family/Home Information

- Name, birth date, address, previous school history
- Names and marital status of the child's guardians
- Employer and contact information for parents or guardians
- Names, ages, and school contacts for siblings and nonrelated children at home
- Custody and visitation rights of all interested parties. All related court orders should be reviewed by the center/school's administrator
- Child's pediatrician contact information
- Child's insurance information
- Other adults (related and unrelated) living in the house with the child and their age and contact information
- Other caregivers (current and former) for the child

Developmental Information

- Child's health (allergies, hospitalizations, frequency of illnesses)
- Vaccination history and plans
- Chronic illnesses
- Special instructions if child becomes ill or injured

Eating Behavior

- Favorite foods
- Refused foods
- Digestive or other food-based problem
- Dietary concern or special dietary needs

Toileting

- Toileting behavior including assistance required when toileting
- Frequency of accidents
- Child's response to accidents

Sleeping

- What is the child's bedtime, and time to awaken?
- What special toy (or blanket, etc.) does your child sleep with?
- What is your child's nap schedule?

Interests

- How long will a new toy hold your child's attention?
- What is your child's favorite outdoor activity?
- Favorite indoor activity
- Hours per day he/she spends watching TV
- Does child like to be read to, length of attention span?

Socialization

- Hours per week, and setting, spent with other young children
- Child's interaction style (check all that apply) ( ) Friendly ( ) Shy ( ) Aggressive
- Is the child independent or does he/she work best with a familiar adult
- Child's most significant fears
- Child's willingness (or preference) to play alone

SOURCE: Points adapted from the enrollment form of the Child Development Center, Center for Education, Widener University, 2009.

never replace the need for the teachers to schedule two or three individual conferences with parents during the year.

A sensitive teacher can observe the parent(s) and child together during transitional times (on arrival or when packing up to go home). All families are psychosocial systems that create roles for each member to play. Family units are dynamic entities, more than the sum of their individual members. Teachers can observe communication styles, rules for child behavior, and parental expectations. Tolerance levels of parents can be observed along with the type of language used with the child (J. Allen, 1985). The child's reactions to his/her parents tell much about what happens at home.

Classroom Observation as a Data Source

A tool in the kit of all successful teachers is the ability to make careful observations and cogent interpretations of behavior. Observations and their interpretations can be reliable or potentially flawed sources of information. To improve the reliability of unstructured observations, a teacher should have a clear idea of what is being observed and why. For example, an aggressive child's interactions with others can be the theme that guides observations. Teacher observations can be made over a range of cognitive, motor, and social–emotional behaviors.

Teachers should always be aware of their own biases and prejudices. These reflect personal values, religious beliefs, and/or social class of the teacher. Before interpreting observations, a teacher should examine him/herself for biasing notions about the child.

Another task for the observer is being unobtrusive so as not to change the child's behavior by simply being present. Being a good observer involves appearing uninterested in the child's activity, while actually being fully focused on it.

Time Sampling

One systematic observational technique involves **time sampling.** This is one of three systems for organizing observations, the other two being **interval sampling** and **frequency sampling** (Repp, Roberts, Slack, Repp, & Berkler, 1976). Time sampling involves using an observational checklist and a time counter.[8] First, the timer is set to a useful observation interval (e.g., 60 seconds). The observation is made, and recorded on the checklist at the prescribed time interval (see example of an observational form in Figure 4.7). Observations continue for the duration of the observation session. Sessions should occur at different times during the school day.

Interval Sampling

This method is employed to observe a simple target behavior (e.g., in seat behavior versus out of seat behavior). During specified time frames the actual amount of time spent on one or the other condition is recorded and tabulated. Frequency sampling has the observer count how many unique incidences of a particular behavior occur over a time frame.

Event Sampling

The second observational approach is **event sampling.** This involves periodic observations during a limited time frame (e.g., recess) and determining in which activities the subject participates. The best method involves making a digital video of the activity, then conducting the observations later by using checklists for one or more children being observed. See Case in Point 4.3 for a model of event sampling in classroom research.

Figure 4.7 Observational Record During Circle Time

Directions: Make one observation every 15 seconds and record your observation in one of the following categories. Use stroke marks to indicate each observation. The observations should be made of one child for a minimum of 10 minutes.

		Subtotal
Sits quietly appearing to attend	______________________	_____
Participating appropriately	______________________	_____
Fidgeting and/or squirming	______________________	_____
Distracted and not attending	______________________	_____
Seeking attention from others	______________________	_____
Interrupting teacher	______________________	_____
Other behavior, inappropriate	______________________	_____

Case in Point 4.3

Timing for Observational Data Collection

One of the data sources for a study I conducted required the collection of observational data using a checklist of teachers' behaviors. The event sampling system required that every 10 seconds an observation be made and recorded on a checklist. To accomplish this, I selected a tune with a 10-second-long refrain. During the observational period (20 minutes a session, 3 sessions per teacher, for 10 teachers), I heard that song playing in my head, and made an observation each time it started. Today, over 30 years later I still can't listen to that piece of music (R. Wright, 1975).

To do this observational research today, I would employ an iPod with an interval counter loaded on the digital record. That would tell me exactly when to make the next observation. Or better yet, I could record the classes using digital video cameras and do the behavioral counting at my leisure.

Anecdotal Data Collection

Another type of observational data comes from a written record of an ongoing activity. The technique, known as **anecdotal data collection,** uses the observer like a digital video recording device.[9] The goal is to make an accurate record of an unusual or example incident involving a child. It requires that the observer be just that—an observer, not a participant in the action.

The anecdotal record may be time stamped to inform readers of the duration of what was observed. Naturally, anecdotal records and time-stamped records do not contain any conjecture (e.g., seemed pleased with herself) or opinionated comments (e.g., made an inappropriate gesture). These interpretative comments should be written later on a commentary that accompanies the anecdotal record or time-stamped record.

Sample Anecdotal Record

Subject:	Heather J. (HJ)
Location:	Art corner
Start time:	1:35 pm
Date:	Monday, April 12, 2010

HJ and two other girls were in the art corner using crayons with large news print paper (24 in. by 36 in.) spread over a table. While drawing Easter eggs, Heather spoke to the two and related a story about a trip she was on during the kindergarten's spring break. Her family vacationed together in Disney World. She told her companions that her family was "Christians so we went to Disney World at Easter time. At Easter, others had to stay away, and only Christians could be there."

Commentary:

This conversation presented a teachable concept. Later, the teacher asked HJ about her trip and was told the same story. The teacher explained that all children and their families are welcome to go to theme parks like Disney World all year long. There is no special time for any religion to be there.

The realm of anecdotal record keeping is very broad, and each day provides many observational opportunities. Anecdotal records capture a critical incidence or illustrative story. One rule of thumb is that to be meaningful, anecdotes should provide insight into a characteristic of the child in question and should describe one occurrence. Opportunity for making an anecdotal record can occur when the child interacts with peers during unstructured playtime. It is good to conduct an observation when the child is beginning the school day, and whenever there is a change of activities or tempo in the classroom. Observations should be written down immediately following the observation, or better yet during the actual occurrence.

Sample Time-Stamped Anecdote From a Kindergarten Observation

Subject:	Richard P. (RP)
Location:	School playground
Start time:	10:05 am
Date:	Monday, November 1, 2010

10:05	RP runs from the mid-hall door onto playground.
10:07	RP is the first to find the 12 in. rubber ball and he takes it into his custody
10:08	RP begins bouncing the ball and running with it
10:10	Three other boys approach RP to use the ball for a game
10:11	RP raises his voice and refuses to stop holding the ball and using it alone
10:12	Ms. Padula, recess attendant, stands between RP and the group of other children
10:13	Ms. Padula expresses to RP that "the ball is there for all to enjoy and use and he should share it with others"
10:13	RP throws the ball over the play yard fence and onto Chestnut St.
10:14	Ms. Padula asked RP to follow her back into the classroom
10:14	RP runs away and tries to exit the play yard
10:16	RP is quickly overtaken by Ms. Blackburn, the teacher of record for the recess period
10:19	RP crying and struggling to free himself from the hug that Ms. Blackburn uses
10:24	RP introduced to the climbing frame area
10:27	RP playing alone on the climbing frame

A separate page of commentary should follow the anecdotal record providing the teacher a place for his/her thoughts and interpretation about what happened. For example, as November 1 is the day after Halloween there may be a link between behavior and an alteration in RP's eating habits. It is also possible that he did not get his usual night's sleep and was tired when it was time for kindergarten. As these were not directly observed, they are not part of the anecdotal record.

Ethics and Observational Data

Observational data collected about a child may be maintained in the child's portfolio and only shared with the child's parents and educators who have a valid reason to see it. Even the written observations made by student teachers and preservice teachers as part of an education course are to be considered confidential and the child's name redacted from any report or paper.

Family Educational Rights and Privacy Act (FERPA) (1974)

All early childhood educators should be familiar with the rights that children and parents have in educational settings. These rights were spelled out in 1974 in an amendment added to the Freedom of Information Act by Senator James **Buckley** (R-NY). The rights of children under this act include two dimensions of privacy. At one level are limitations as to what type of information can be collected and maintained. The second involves the limitations as to who can access that information.

FERPA provides parents with the right to access their child's educational records and to have those records presented and explained in a language that they understand. This requires schools honor parental requests to have their child's educational records explained without confusing technical jargon. Parents have the right to add explanatory material to their child's record. At the request of a parent, schools are obligated to provide the test materials and the recording sheets used to collect data. That access does not require that parents be given a copy of the test booklets, just permitted to review the material.[10]

Educators are not permitted to collect data on topics considered unrelated to the child's education including parent information about sexual practices, political affiliations, mental disease or disorders, illegal and self-incriminating behavior, privileged communications (lawyers), income, and religious practice.

FERPA also limits who can have access to a child's records. As a rule of thumb, only those education personnel with a legitimate need to see the records should have access. One exception to this is the access that legitimate educational researchers can have to educational data.

When information about a child is released to another agency, the parents must give their signed consent. That signed and dated form must be kept with the child's permanent record. Figure 4.8 shows a sample release form.

Figure 4.8 Sample Release Form for School Records

Request Date ___/___/______

Date Records Sent ___/___/______

I hereby authorize the ***University Child Development Center*** to immediately release the records of:

____

Last, First, Middle Initial

Records to be released include:

____

____

____

These records should be sent to:

____

____

Parent Signature ______________________________

Date ___/___/______

Name of Employee Sending Records ____________________ Initial ______

Summary

Information about a child summarizing how well he/she has learned is a summative evaluation. Formative evaluations are designed to provide teachers and child care workers with information about each child's learning process. Skilled teachers use both forms of assessment to carefully plan their instructional programs. This makes it possible for teachers to provide young children with differentiated instructional programs.

One source of information about young children is collected using observational systems. For example, writing an anecdotal record describing the ongoing behavior of a child can facilitate observations. One activity that can provide a lot of information about a child is observing him/her at play in an environment with other children. Play can also be used as the vehicle for assessing a child in an area of cognitive or social learning.

Performance assessments are central to most early childhood measurements. Performance demonstrates to teachers what a child can actually do. The evaluation of performance assessments can be done by employing a rubric describing the ordinal sequence of possible levels of accomplishment shown by the child.

Early childhood educators typically compile a portfolio of each child's work to document the growth and learning taking place over time. Portfolios can provide the basis for the rubric-based evaluation of young children.

Discussion Questions

1. Visit the university's writing center and ask to see the rubric used to help undergraduate students with their writing. Evaluate this document and bring any suggestions for its improvement to class. (As an alternative, use the Internet to visit other college's writing centers. Evaluate their rubric for writing and prepare a report for class.) What are the strengths and weaknesses of the documents you found?

2. With advance permission, observe a playground where young children are free to play. Observe one child for 10 to 15 minutes and write an anecdotal record of what you observed. Evaluate your experience and explain what you did well. What aspect of your performance of the task can be improved?

3. How can teachers assure parents that **anecdotal observations** are free from the personal values and judgments of the teacher, and represent a simple record of what happened?

4. Design a rubric that can be used to assess a second grade student's level of mathematical understanding for the concept of additivity. Share your rubric with another student and ask for an evaluation of its strengths. How can it be improved?

5. Develop a rubric that could be used to evaluate the statement of "teaching philosophy" from the professional portfolio of a senior year education student who has not yet had a student teaching semester. Share your rubric with another student and ask for an evaluation of its strengths. How can it be improved?

Related Reading

Gober, S. Y. (2002). *Six simple ways to assess young children.* Albany, NY: Delmar.

Johnson, R. S., Mims-Cox, J. S., & Doyle-Nichols, A. (2006). *Developing portfolios in education: A guide to reflection, inquiry, and assessment.* Thousand Oaks, CA: Sage.

Kingore, B. (2008). *Developing portfolios for authentic assessment, preK–3: Guiding potential in young learners.* Thousand Oaks, CA: Corwin Press.

Montgomery, K. K., & Wiley, D. A. (2008). *Building e-portfolios using PowerPoint: A guide for educators* (2nd ed.). Thousand Oaks, CA: Sage.

Notes

1. Assessments are measurements of one or more variables related to the current condition, ability, status, or knowledge of a child. An evaluation uses several formal and/or informal assessments to provide a picture of what the child's status is across a number of dimensions. Evaluations require the evaluator to make an informed interpretation of the assessment data. Periodic evaluations are also used to monitor the changes that have occurred with the child over a period of time.
2. This is a decision made by a team of educational professionals about a child's need and eligibility for support services and additional help beyond what is provided to other children (e.g., special education).
3. Crayons and markers that are friendly to young children, and a large box of clean newsprint, are all that is needed to create a writing/drawing center.
4. All authentic assessments are performance assessments, but not all performance assessments are authentic assessments.
5. If the child's portfolio is to be holistically evaluated, it should represent only one dimension of the early childhood curriculum.
6. See Chapter 3 for a full description of the meaning of reliability coefficients.
7. The ability to understand and apply rules is a cognitive mile marker indicating significant cognitive development (Piaget, 1932). Children who understand games and their rules quickly marginalize those who do not.
8. The time counter can be the observer's wristwatch, a stopwatch, or simply an internalized silent count by the observer.
9. New child care centers and those that are part of universities frequently have digital video cameras in each classroom. This technological advance makes it easier for teachers to make and later write up observations. These recordings can be provided to the parents during a conference.
10. This law impacts every level of education. Even the ETS will send college-bound students copies of their SAT questions and answers. The fee for this service was $43 in 2008.

Teacher-Constructed Scales and Checklists

5

USA Today has come out with a new survey—apparently three out of four people make up 75% of the population.

—*David Letterman*

Introduction and Themes

Rating scales and checklists pervade our lives. It seems that just about everyone who provides us with goods or services wants to know how satisfied we are. There are two general forms for rating scales: semantic scales and hierarchical scales. The former include Likert-type scales and semantic differential scales. Hierarchical scales include frequency measures, intensity scales, and discrete visual analog scales.

While rating scales are designed as multilevel measurements of activities, products, or outcomes, checklists are designed to require binomial responses (e.g., Yes vs. No). Checklists can be used to ensure that complex systems are completed in the correct sequence, to ensure safety, or to focus attention on tasks during a formal observation.

The use of multiple raters is the best approach to use when trying to improve the reliability of a judgmental rating system. Other issues in the reliability of checklists and rating scales concern (1) following all observational and scoring directions, and (2) having all raters share a common understanding of the process and score points.

The validity of rating scales and checklists can be based on analyses of the linkage of the measure to the content of the curriculum or program. When these scales are used to measure learning outcomes, it is important that each of the items is linked to the published learning standards.

Learning Objectives

By reading and studying this chapter, you should acquire the competency to:

- Explain why early childhood educators would develop and use checklists and rating scales.
- Explain the difference between hierarchical and semantic scales.
- Design and write a Likert-type scale to measure staff attitudes on a school issue.
- Design and write a semantic differential scale to measure parent attitudes toward a new school policy.
- Explain what can be done to improve the reliability of rating scales.

- List and explain each step to be followed in the development of a checklist.
- Discuss how the reliability of checklists can be improved.
- Explain the concept of a curriculum map.
- Discuss how a curriculum map is linked to the development of checklists and rating scales in early childhood education.

Identification of Goals for Assessment

When teachers plan for a new academic year, they must consider ways to measure progress children are making toward meeting the school's academic expectations. Some skills specified by the curriculum for children to acquire may not fit a standard assessment format. Two measurement formats that can be developed for these assessments are **checklists** and **rating scales.**

Applications

Checklists and rating scales are used beyond school to measure complex adult behaviors including Olympic sports (figure skating, diving, and dressage), advanced flying skills of instrument pilots, and the developing teaching skills of student teachers. In preschools, these instruments are used to measure what is difficult to assess by other means. They can be used to assess children's socialization, the possibility of learning and attention problems, and emotional development.

Construction

Prior to the construction, the teacher must decide on the goal for data collection. The goal and the nature of the task, activity, or product determine the type of instrument that is needed. Two rules in building an instrument are to keep it simple and keep it clear.

The first step in the development of most scales is a detailed analysis of the behavior being evaluated. Items are then written to match the component parts of the behavior. Next, the teacher should decide on a logical sequence for the items to appear on the new instrument, and then write the actual items. A decision should be made about providing space for taking **marginal notes** on the form. Marginal notes record behavioral observations not covered on the form, but descriptive of the child's approach or thinking.

Formats for Construction

Checklists tend be tallies and/or simple counts, or a record of dichotomous (binary) outcomes (Yes vs. No). Checklists play a role in diagnosing children with special needs and in assessing the developmental status of children.

The ordered nature of a rating scale implies that the items measure the degree something is happening or the relative value of a product. Rating scales can provide **respondents** with a number-line format. When the rating scale is a simple count or description (**demographic variable**), one item may be all that is needed. For example, the following items are asking demographic questions and only need to be asked once:

- Child's birth date ___/___/___
- Child's gender ___(boy) ___(girl)
- Number of siblings living at home ______

Designing Attitudinal Measurements

Measurement of more complex areas, for example, attitude or opinion, requires instruments to have 10 or more items asking about different aspects of the same topic. Each of these items should be focused on the same issue. An example of this type of measurement is presented in Figure 5.1.

Figure 5.1 Measure of Childhood Popularity

Which best describes your child's popularity?	Always True	Sometimes	Rarely or Never
1. My home is always filled with neighborhood kids playing with my child.	( )	( )	( )
2. My child is a kid magnet.	( )	( )	( )
3. Every kid wants to attend birthday parties for my child.	( )	( )	( )
4. Other children look up to my child.	( )	( )	( )
5. My child receives a number of presents from other children.	( )	( )	( )
6. My child seems to be a leader.	( )	( )	( )
7. Everyone wants to sit near my child on the school bus.	( )	( )	( )
8. My child is picked to be captain of sports teams.	( )	( )	( )
9. Teachers describe my child as popular.	( )	( )	( )
10. Children will walk blocks to ride the the school bus from my child's stop.	( )	( )	( )

Checklists and rating scales often appear on the same measure and take the form of a **questionnaire** or **opinionnaire.** These instruments appear in both our professional and private lives (see an example in Case in Point 5.1). Whenever you visit your physician, eat at a restaurant, buy a book online, or have your car dealer repair your vehicle, you are likely to be asked to complete a questionnaire. Likewise, teachers of young children can design useful instruments.

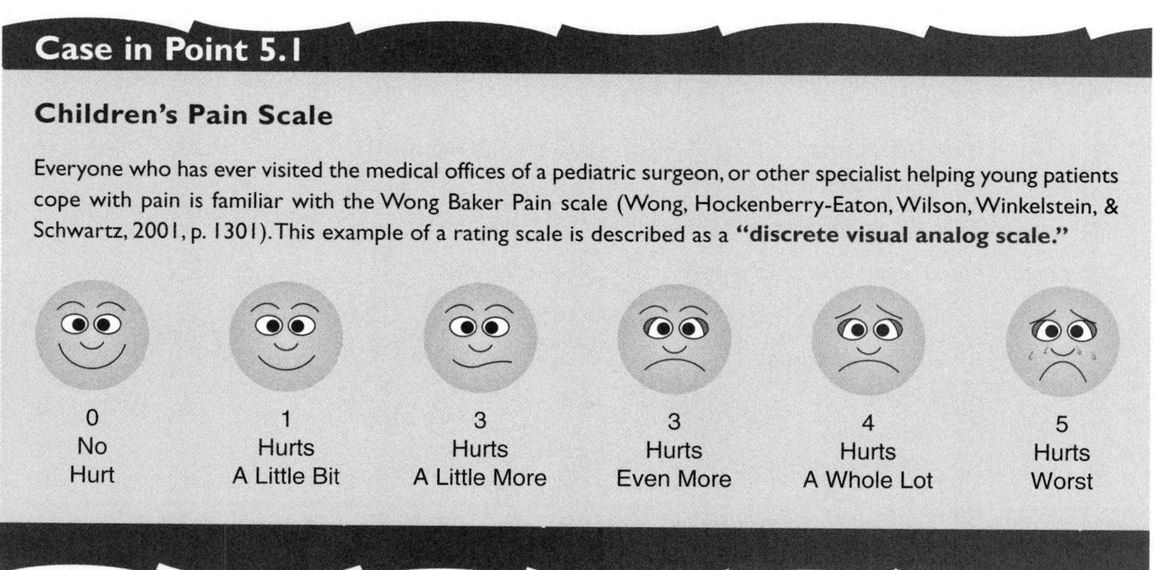

Case in Point 5.1

Children's Pain Scale

Everyone who has ever visited the medical offices of a pediatric surgeon, or other specialist helping young patients cope with pain is familiar with the Wong Baker Pain scale (Wong, Hockenberry-Eaton, Wilson, Winkelstein, & Schwartz, 2001, p. 1301). This example of a rating scale is described as a **"discrete visual analog scale."**

Rating Scales

These instruments are evaluative, providing an ordinal ranking useful for assessing a wide range of things including learning products and/or behaviors. There are three classes of rating scales used by educators: semantic/hierarchical scales, frequency scales, and discrete visual analog scales.

Semantic and Hierarchical Scales

Semantic scales include **Likert-type scales** and **semantic differential scales; hierarchical scales** include **intensity scales** and rubric-based evaluations. Report cards represent a specialized type of rating scale (see Chapter 10).

Likert-Type Scales

Rensis Likert originally developed social science's (including education) most commonly employed semantic scale in 1932. The Likert scale (pronounced as LICK-ert) has been used to measure opinions, attitudes, and feelings for the past 80 years.

Construction of a Likert-type scale begins with a measurement goal (Colton & Covert, 2007). The next step is writing several simple declarative sentences about the topic. These sentences should contain only one central idea, avoid jargon, and have a single meaning for the respondents (Figure 5.2 provides examples).

Figure 5.2 Two Questions That Employ Likert's Actual Format From his Doctoral Dissertation at Columbia University[a]

The first item for a parent survey:

To maintain good nutrition for all center children teachers should exclude all class treats from home, including those for birthday parties and holidays.

___SA ___Ap ___Undecided ___Ds ___SD

Note: SA = Strongly approve
Ap = Approve
Ds = Disapprove
SD = Strongly disapprove

The second item is related to an individual child:

When storing equipment the child is well organized and careful.

___SA ___Ag ___Undecided ___Ds ___SD

Note: SA = Strongly agree
Ag = Agree
Ds = Disagree
SD = Strongly disagree

a. These declarative sentences were designed for early education.

For example, if a questionnaire for parents included the sentence, "*Standardized assessments in early childhood education should be replaced by authentic assessments,*" this would not be acceptable because it contains ill-defined jargon. The following would also be inappropriate as it contains two foci for simultaneous consideration: "*Kindergarten buses should have onboard GPS trackers and seat belts for all passengers.*" This statement should be divided into two different items, one about onboard GPS and the other about seat belts. An appropriate statement for a Likert-type item is, "*A free summer camp program should be provided for all preschoolers.*"

Once the declarative statements have been created, the next step involves developing between 3 and 7 statements expressing a degree of agreement with the declarative statements (Pemberton, 1933). Likert scale items should never stand alone, but should be combined with others dealing with the same topic (Uebersax, 2006). When an odd number of choices are provided, the central choice is usually neutral. The following is a typical Likert-type survey item including a neutral point:

Scores on the state test in third grade should only be one factor among many when deciding if a child will be promoted to fourth grade.

___A) I agree.

___B) I agree moderately.

___C) I am not sure and have no clear opinion.

___D) I disagree moderately.

___E) I disagree.

In this example, alternative answers are complete sentences. This is not the usual, as the choices are normally: "Strongly Disagree, Disagree, Neither Agree nor Disagree, Agree, Strongly Agree." The advantage of the shortened format is ease of reading.

A frequently overlooked issue is the middle point. Is "neither agree nor disagree" an ordinal score point between "disagree" and "agree"? Or is it a score indicating that the respondent has no opinion? Perhaps it is best to always score the middle position as having no opinion and not assigning it an ordinal score.

Wording of Likert-type scales. Another concern is the adjective "strongly" when used to modify the verbs "disagree" and "agree." This is not appropriate because the verbs agree and disagree are members of a class of absolute verbs that include others such as pregnant, broke, and dead. As such, there is no appropriate modifier. The adjective moderately indicates a sense of vacillation and a lack of solidarity with the notion. Consider the example of a "moderately dead body." Yet, this nicety of the English language is usually overlooked in the interest of creating a scale.

Number of options on a Likert-type scale: The number of answer choices is related to the reliability. When Likert scale questions have 7-answer options, there is a small improvement in reliability over the 5-answer option. When the number of options is increased beyond 7 or under 5, the reliability of the question actually decreases (Dawes, 2008). The problem with a 7-option scale is in selection of descriptors. For example, consider the following 7-option item:

All newly certified early childhood teachers should have extensive preservice academic preparation in special education.

___A) Agree

___B) Moderate agreement

___C) Slight agreement

___D) Neither agree nor disagree

___E) Slight disagreement

___F) Moderate disagreement

___G) Disagree

In this example, the problem is in selecting adverbs that represent clearly different levels on an ordinal scale (i.e., moderate vs. slight). Others, such as somewhat versus slightly, do not provide as crisp a distinction. Some authors have suggested using 3-point Likert-type scales with young children (R. Linn & Gronlund, 2000). The problem with this strategy is the significant loss of reliability that occurs with only three choices (Murphy & Likert, 1938).

Other combinations of agreement terms are useful for meeting other measurement needs. For example, a judgment question can be asked using a variation on the Likert-type format:

What do you feel would be the impact on faculty morale if a merit pay program is started in your preschool?

___A) Powerful positive impact

___B) Minor positive impact

___C) No impact either way

___D) Minor negative impact

___E) Powerful negative impact

When a Likert-type scale has an even number of options there is no neutral position. It is likely that the question's author wants to force the respondent to take a position. For example, this is a 6-option item assessing teaching:

The professor for this course seems very well prepared to teach this subject.

___A) Agree

___B) Moderate agreement

___C) Slight agreement

___D) Slight disagreement

___E) Moderate disagreement

___F) Disagree

Semantic Differential Scales

Another format for writing questions about opinions of people on a topic is the semantic differential (SD). The SD is a flexible technique for collecting opinion and attitude data. Subjects answer an opinion question along a straight line of points between two polar opposing adjectives. It requires the teacher (test developer) create a series of questioning statements about an issue. Next is the selection of opposing adjectives related to the topic being studied. A straight line is then drawn between the two adjectives, and the respondent is asked to check a position along the line showing the respondent's attitude or feeling about the topic.

The following is an example of a semantic differential scale using five related questions on the same topic:

Indicate your opinion below by marking "√" on the lines between the two extreme adjectives.

How do you feel about using a high-stakes tests in third grade as the final authority in deciding which children will be promoted to fourth grade?

Unethical	______________________________	*Highly Ethical*
Unnecessarily punitive	______________________________	*Justified*
Demoralizing	______________________________	*Encouraging*
Pernicious	______________________________	*Positive*
Repulsed	______________________________	*Hopeful*

This example of a semantic differential scale can be assessed using a ruler. The opinion of a respondent to each of the five items can be read as the distance away from the negative adjective in centimeters. The mean distance can be determined, and used as an expression of the strength of a respondent's attitude. This approach to measurement means that the average from a semantic differential scale is scored as an interval scale (see Chapter 3).

This measurement can also be designed for easier evaluation by placing tic marks or numbers along the line used to express the level of opinion. For example:

Indicate your opinion below by marking "√" on the lines between the two extreme adjectives.

The child care center is considering a new rule to forbid parents from bringing a firearm onto the preschool's campus. Please show your attitude on this newly proposed policy.

Disappointed	___ ___ ___ ___ ___ ___ ___ ___ ___ ___	Overjoyed
Frightened	___ ___ ___ ___ ___ ___ ___ ___ ___ ___	Comfortable
Defeated	___ ___ ___ ___ ___ ___ ___ ___ ___ ___	Confident
Frustrated	___ ___ ___ ___ ___ ___ ___ ___ ___ ___	Thrilled
Bewildered	___ ___ ___ ___ ___ ___ ___ ___ ___ ___	Sure

The number of bipolar adjective pairs used to assess a topic or issue is related to the overall reliability of a combined score. The optimal number of bipolar adjective pairs on a scale has been empirically shown to be 10 (Heise, 1970).[1]

Factor structure. Research into the use of semantic differential scales has shown that they are usually influenced by three **factors** in the attitude and opinions held by respondents. These dimensions of attitude are good versus bad, fast versus slow, and powerful versus powerless (Heise, 1970). This **factor structure** is generally referred to in a shortened form as evaluation, potency, and activity, or EPA. In the development of an SD scale, if the educator keeps these three factors in mind, a relatively stable survey is possible. Asking several semantic differential questions representing each of these three factors can effectively assess a measurement topic.

Hierarchical Scales

Hierarchical scales provide ratings arranged in an ordinal sequence. Hierarchical questions provide a sequence of levels.[2] Each level implies that the lower levels have already been met. For example, a child learning to ride a two-wheel bicycle first uses "training wheels." Later, comes the ability to ride a two-wheeled bike with the assistance of a parent to help provide balance. Finally, comes independent riding on flat surfaces, and the final step is independent riding on and off roads. Being able to do the last step in the hierarchy implies all other steps were accomplished.

Rubrics

In Chapter 4, there was a discussion of the development and use of rubrics. This topic is again introduced because rubrics are hierarchical rating scales.

Intensity Scales

This hierarchical scale is widely employed in the earth sciences in the form of the Stafford-Simpson scale, Beaufort scale, Mohs scale, and Richter scale. These scales replace the level of agreement statements from a Likert-type scale with expressions of intensity, for example, "How powerful is a tropical storm?" or "How hard is a stone?"

Structure of intensity scales. Intensity scales can explore the strength of feelings of children. Intensity scales are arranged sequentially so that every choice includes those before it in the sequence. For example, in measuring a child's feelings about being required to share with other children an adjective sequence could include the low anchor, *furious.* The next three levels in the scaled sequence could include *very upset, annoyed,* and the high anchor point, *pleased.*

The item should first present a question about some situation. The identification of evaluation terms comes next. This list should be brief and understandable to the child. Terms could be an ordered series of emotional descriptions familiar to the child. Children in primary grades can be asked and simultaneously shown the words. Prereaders should have the assessment administrator just say the words. The following is an example of this type of measure:

How do you feel when Mommy tells you "It is time to go to kindergarten"?

____ Wonderful, best thing of all

____ Good/Cheerful

____ Upset

____ Bad/Unhappy

How does playing in the playground with other children make you feel?

____ Happy

____ It's OK

____ Nervous & Shy

____ Unhappy

Frequency Scales

Hierarchical scales can assess the frequency of a behavior or activity within a defined time frame. These scales are referred to as frequency scales. There are three parts to developing a **frequency scale.** The first component is a clear definition of the activity being studied; next is a time frame. The final part of the scale is the selection of frequency points.

Constricting of the answer range is a common error. It can be avoided by knowing the likely range of possibilities. If most respondents give the same answer, the item will have a very constricted range and little can be learned.

For example, the following is an annotated sample item:

Statement of behavior for study and time frame	*In an average month how frequently does your child experience a bladder or bowel accident?*
Mark your choice with an "X"	
Levels of frequency	_____ Never _____ One to three _____ Four to seven _____ Eight or more

Second example:

Through your observations of the child, what is the proportion of time (when he/she is at free play) that is spent in cooperative or group play?

_____ 0 to 10%
_____ 11 to 25%
_____ 26 to 75%
_____ 76% or more

Discrete Visual Analog Scales

The combination of a hierarchical scale and visual cues provides a measurement tool that is user-friendly for children. The Wong Pain scale shown above is an example of this type of measurement. This format makes it possible for children to evaluate themselves and the products of their work.

Like other scale formats, the first task is to decide on the measurement's goals. Introspection and reflection are not normal parts of young children's cognition. For that reason, evaluative questions posed to young children are best written as observable behaviors. Despite the reduction in reliability that will result from using an abbreviated format, answer choices should be limited to two or three for children below the age of 6 years.

For example, Figure presents depictions of various preschool activities and an array of three emoticons that can be used by children to indicate their feelings. This instrument measures which activities young children most and least enjoy. The preschool teacher would show this array, one frame at a time, and ask a young child to point to the face that shows how he/she feels during that activity. An experienced teacher can then ask probing questions for each "sad face" selected.

Reliability of Rating Scales

There is an obligation on the part of the person using a rating scale to ensure that it is reliable. One way to improve rating scale reliability is to increase the number of items assessing the same activity or product. There is a monotonic relationship between the number of questions on a measurement device and its reliability (Gulliksen, 1950).

A discrete visual analogy scale for measuring opinion among young children related to different activities in a preschool setting

SOURCE: Drawings by Merv Magus.

Another factor in improving reliability involves its directions. A strict adherence to the directions for the scale's use is essential. If two or more teachers are to assess children using a rating scale it is important that they are familiar with the scoring expectations and administration rules. This is not a time for a rater to take a creative approach.

Valance

The first step in any analysis of checklists or rating scale data involves assuring that most questions have a positive **valance.** Occasionally, scale developer's items have a negative valance.[3] In other words, an item may read as a positive: *The child is usually focused on the class activity,* or as a negative: *The child rarely is focused on the class activity.* In the former case, the value of 4 can be assigned to "highly agree" and 3 to "somewhat agree." The middle (neutral) position is not scored, while the value of 2 goes to the answer of "somewhat disagree." The value of 1 is used for those who "disagree." When a Likert-type item has a negative valance, the numeric values are reversed. Thus, a statement of high agreement earns a value of 1, and a strong disagreement is assigned the value of 4.

Measurement Level

Likert-type items are scored as ordinal values. By combining Likert item results from 10 or more people, the data become more stable and more "numberlike" in character (Heise, 1970). This form of a collective ordinal value is described as **ordinal type II** data. In that way, it is possible to average the answers of a number of respondents on a subject. University faculties are familiar with this process at the end of the semester when students complete a Likert-type scale describing the quality of teaching they experienced. Among the uses of Likert-type scales in early childhood education is the development of staff and/or parent surveys. This is often an important step prior to the implementation of new policies.

Alpha Coefficient

When a semantic scale is designed to measure only one dimension, its questions can be evaluated using measures of internal consistency reliability (see Chapter 3). Perhaps the most widely employed of these is the statistic Cronbach's alpha. The optimum value of an **alpha coefficient** is 1.00. This indicates that everyone was in total agreement on each item on the semantic scale. The minimum value is 0.00. This indicates that the Likert scale is not reliable, and that none of the evaluations made on the measure are related to any other question on the Likert scale. A reliable measure will have an alpha coefficient of $\alpha \geq 0.70$.

Interrater Reliability

For most rating scales, the best approach for determining reliability is to find the interrater reliability (Uebersax, 2008). This requires that two or more people independently evaluate the same behavior or project with a rating scale (see Chapter 4). Whenever a rating is made of a child's behaviors or products, it is better if two teachers independently evaluate the child. Independent rating scores can be combined into a total score. In the case of a wide differentiation between raters, a meeting to discuss scoring criteria is indicated.

When two or more teachers rate a number of children using the same instrument, it is possible to determine the statistical coefficient of interrater reliability. With two evaluators, the process is carried out as a simple correlation. When a team of evaluators is involved, then a model developed for the evaluation of Olympic sports can be used. By this system, the lowest and highest scores are removed and the others are averaged into a mean score for the performance.[4]

"Does your 'naughty vs. nice' checklist have high reliability?"

SOURCE: Cartoon by Merv Magus.

Checklists

Rating scales are designed to be evaluative, providing raters with several levels of behavior to select among. Checklists are not as complex and typically are answered as a dichotomous (Yes vs. No) choice, or as a simple count. There are many good reasons for a teacher to develop checklists for classroom use. One of the most obvious is to serve as a memory aid. The safety of children can depend on well-conceived checklists designed for emergency procedures. Another is to provide the framework for sequencing or evaluating the completion of a series of ordered tasks or behaviors. Finally, checklists can provide a structure for observations of learning products and activities.

Checklist Design

The development of a checklist starts with the identification of the behavior or activity being evaluated. That behavior or activity should then be subjected to a task analysis designed to list all the steps and parts that should be completed. In addition to making a list of needed components, the developer of the checklist must also decide on the correct sequence that must be followed for optimal results. It is always best if several knowledgeable people review the final list before it is field tested prior to the actual use.

There are a few things educators should keep in mind when developing a checklist:

- Items should stress easily observable behaviors.
- Item sequence should match the natural order that will likely be followed.
- Wording should be unambiguous and clear.

- Items should provide a place to mark "X" when they have been accomplished.
- Each item should be written with consistent language and voice.
- Each item should provide only one issue to be evaluated.
- Each item should appear in only one location on the checklist.

Checklists as Frequency Records

Checklists can be designed by an early childhood educator to provide a record of the frequency of a behavior. There is an immense range of behaviors that can be assessed using this approach. Topics for assessment can include prosocial behaviors, eating habits, organizational ability, cleanliness habits, and activity level. The use of a frequency record several times during the year can provide a record of behavioral change (see example in Case in Point 5.2).

Case in Point 5.2

Classroom Behavioral Checklist

By kindergarten, children who are aggressive and demonstrate the ability to become bullies can be recognized by early childhood educators. In preparation for a parental conference on a behavior problem, a teacher may develop and use a checklist to tabulate the occurrence of inappropriate behaviors. This document can also be employed again later to assess the success of an intervention effort by the teacher and parent. That checklist could take the following form:

Child's Name ______________________Week of ___/___/___ to ___/___/___

	Frequency of Occurrence of Behavior				
	Monday	*Tuesday*	*Wednesday*	*Thursday*	*Friday*
Refuses to share with others	XXX	X		XX	XX
Pushes or hits another child	XXXXX	XX	X	XX	XXXXX
Takes other's property	XX		X	X	XXX
Calls child a nasty name	XXX		XX	XXX	XXXX
Refuses to follow directions	XXX	X			XXXX

Other concerns: ______________________________

Checklists as Mnemonic Devices

There are a range of dangerous events that can impact a preschool or public school. Such events include fires, strangers in the building, a missing child, a firearm in the building, or a weather emergency. These should each be considered in turn, and a series of steps taken by well-organized and prepared teachers. These steps should also receive approval by the appropriate authorities in the wider community including the first responders. Once rules and procedures are established, each teacher should be given a checklist of what he/she should do in the event of each emergency.

For example:

Metropolitan Primary School Weather Emergency (Tornado Warning)[5]

The following steps should be undertaken as soon as the tornado warning signal has been sounded or an administrator tells you of the emergency.
Remember STAY CALM, THINK CLEARLY, ACT QUICKLY

___ 1) Have all children immediately stop what they are doing and line up.

___ 2) As children are lining up get your roll book and keep it with you.

___ 3) Turn off any gas (laboratory classes).

___ 4) Quickly move children to the designated interior space assigned to shelter your class.

___ 5) Close but do not lock your classroom door and any other open doors you pass on the way to your class's designated shelter area.

___ 6) Have children sit on the floor with their backs to the wall.

___ 7) Use your roll book to verify the attendance for all children; note any absences and missing children.

___ 8) Always try to stay calm and composed in front of the children.

___ 9) Stay with your class at all times.

___ 10) Do not leave the assigned shelter area or release any of the children until you are told to do so by an administrator or emergency worker.

___ 11) Report all injured or missing children to an administrator at first opportunity.

___ 12) Make a note of all children who are released to the custody of parents or guardians and record who took them.

N.B. If your class is at recess, go immediately to the schoolyard, and move your children inside the school to your designated shelter area.

Sequence of Ordered Tasks

Checklists are designed to provide a way to verify the completion of an ordered sequence of behaviors (Scriven, 2007). Sequential checklists are required to operate many schools and day care centers. Every school has a large number of complex tasks that must be performed in the proper sequence to achieve the correct outcome.

The use of checklists can be as prosaic as a list of what and in what order the teacher wishes to discuss topics in a parent conference. These lists can also be quite serious and critical to the safety of children.

A good use of this type of checklist is in setting end-of-school-year closing procedures for each teacher. These checklists can have a final step that involves returning completed checklists and collecting the summer paychecks. The following is a checklist for primary grade teachers to follow at the close of the school year.

Granite Rock School System

Required End-of-Year Responsibilities for Teachers

All teachers are to complete and sign the following checklist. Please present it to the principal's office by 3:00 p.m. on the final teacher's day. A written explanation for all tasks that are in process must accompany this form.

Check the actual status of each task below.

(I) TAKE TO CONFERENCE ROOM:

Sorted materials (BUNDLED AND LABELED) for next school year by teacher/class

	COMPLETION STATUS	
	Done	In process
Locator cards	( )	( )
Cumulative folders	( )	( )
	Done	In process
Emergency health records (kids allergic to bee stings, etc.)	( )	( )
Unfinished workbooks	( )	( )
Edited e-portfolios	( )	( )

(II) TAKE TO PRINCIPAL'S OFFICE:

Remember to label and put items into the correct box.

Keys to file cabinets, desk, and classroom	( )	( )
Summer address card	( )	( )
Room repair requests	( )	( )
Teacher handbooks	( )	( )
Supply orders	( )	( )
Unclaimed student report cards	( )	( )

(III) CLASSROOM PREPARATION:

Return all AV equipment and library books to library.	( )	( )
Take computers/carts to gym for cleaning.	( )	( )
Stack empty student desks and chairs along wall in hall outside your classroom.	( )	( )
Put American flag in closet.	( )	( )
Cover all exposed cubbies and book shelves.	( )	( )
Remove all papers from bulletin boards and walls.	( )	( )
Take any unclaimed student belongings to Lost & Found box.	( )	( )
Remove all teacher's personal property.	( )	( )
Lock all windows, closets, file cabinets, and teacher desks.	( )	( )

Teacher's Name ______________________ Classroom No.________

Teacher's Signature ______________________ Date ___/___/______

Checklists can provide a tabulation of learning. This can be modified to provide a yearlong tracking system for a child's **academic growth.** For example, a preschool teacher may wish to track a 4-year-old child's letter recognition skills. In that case, the following format for a checklist can be useful:

Letter recognition, upper case letters. List all ***unknown*** *letters.*

A B C D E F G H I J K L M N O P Q R S T U V W X Y Z

January ____

April ____

June ____

Letter recognition, lower case letters. List all unknown letters.

a b c d e f g h i j k 1 m n o p q r s t u v w x y z

January ____

April ____

June ____

Published Checklists in Early Childhood Education

There are a number of published checklists designed to identify learning problems and special abilities among young children. These checklists are marketed to parents and educators as well as other professionals. The quality of data from these instruments is only as good as the background and observational ability of the person completing the form. While any person can use one of these, the information that is collected may well be meaningless unless the user has a knowledge base about what is being assessed.

The following URLs represent some of the hundreds of Internet checklists:

- Checklist of infant development for parent use: http://www.childdevrev.com/IDI_PQ_Sample.pdf
- Checklist for pediatricians in doing mental health screening for young children: http://www.brightfutures.org/mentalhealth/pdf/professionals/ec/checklist.pdf
- Checklist for English-language Learners in the primary grades: http://esol.leeschools.net/Document%20Bank/PDF/ecchecklist.pdf
- Checklist for giftedness in children. First a commercial example, then one from the Rhode Island Department of Education.
    1. Published commercially: http://austega.com/gifted/characteristics.htm
    2. Rhode Island Department of Education: http://www.ri.net/gifted_talented/rhode.html

The fact that numerous checklists about children are available in parent magazines and on the Internet has created a problem for many school administrators. In some middle class communities parents have been known to misinterpret data they collect from their children using checklists of questionable validity. Once a parent convinces him/herself that something needs to be done for his/her child, schools are subjected to intense pressure or even threatened with legal action (see Case in Point 5.3 for an example of this problem).

Case in Point 5.3

Pushy Parents and Programs for Gifted Children

The wide availability of information on the identification of academically gifted preschoolers and primary grade children has created a problem for school administrators. Some parents live through their children and see every success experienced by their child as their own. Having a child admitted into a gifted education program is a prize that a number of parents find irresistible. By using the Internet's tools they can convince themselves of the superiority of their child. This can lead to a push by the parents to have an early evaluation for giftedness by the school.

Some parents have also subverted evaluations conducted by the schools. By spending about $1,000, it is possible to have a private practicing psychologist test the young child. Once a parent has seen the evaluation materials he or she can then initiate a teaching program to teach the test protocol to his or her child.

Observational Checklists of Learning

The organization of a checklist to be used as an assessment tool in early childhood starts with learning standards. Every school should have a list of learning standards and expectations for every subject and grade. A number of schools have gone a step further and created curriculum maps. A **curriculum map** adds a timeline to specifications of learning standards and levels of expected performance.

When a checklist is used to measure early learning, a 3-point scale is often needed. The three points correspond to (1) Evident, (2) Developing, (3) Not Evident. While violating the basic principle of checklists, having simple dichotomous (binary) responses, this three-level system makes it possible to track the progress a child makes over time. This is an important concept in the area of value-added assessment (see Chapter 13 for more on the value-added model).

Curriculum Mapping

A curriculum map can be thought of as the preschool's master plan for early learning. It should be a publicly available document that captures the scope and sequence of learning objectives and activities in each content area. It is more than a curriculum guide in that it also specifies skills students will develop along with presenting a timeline. By being publically available, parents have a method of knowing what is going on and what is coming next at the early education center.

The state of Kentucky has taken a leadership role in encouraging each school system to develop and publish on the state's Web page a series of curriculum maps. Kentucky's curriculum maps cover from preschool through Grade 12 for all subjects. These maps make it possible to develop a series of evaluations that track children as they progress toward the goal of being "proficient" on the statewide mandated assessment (Glod, 2006). Student performance can be assessed in many areas by using checklists and/or rating scales. Data produced by checklists and other scales can inform the teacher of the instructional needs of each child.

Table 5.1 provides a section from the curriculum map of the Calloway County School System. It suggests the use of checklists for the assessment of preschool numerosity and basic mathematics (see Photo 5.1).

Photo 5.1 Kindergartener Being Assessed for Early Arithmetic Skills

The following URLs provide other samples of curriculum maps:

- http://www.spotsylvania.k12.va.us/cmaps/pdf/math/Math%20K.pdf
- http://www.olentangy.k12.0h.us/district/curric/map/langart/001angArts.pdf

Reliability of Checklists

The same principles true for the enhanced reliability of rating scales are also true for checklists. Checklist reliability can be found by employing an interrater method for establishing reliability. When two or more well trained people use the same checklist to evaluate an educational activity or developmental characteristic, it is possible to determine the degree of concordance for two raters. This is best done by using correlation statistics.

If there are more than two raters using the checklist, it is advisable to visualize the pattern of agreement by setting up a matrix. This can be easily done using Excel software (see Table 5.2). The various checklist question numbers should be listed along the ordinate (vertical axis) of this type of display. Names of the raters should appear along the abscissa. The resulting matrix can be used to exhibit which rater scored how many children as passing each item. The marginal total on the right side will provide how many total children passed each checklist item. The marginal total at the bottom will show which rater was more lenient and which more rigid in making judgments with a checklist.

Table 5.1 Preschool Curriculum Map in Mathematics for the Calloway County School District in Kentucky

Month	Content	Standards-Based Exit Expectations	Assessment
September	• Counting in sequence • One-on-one correspondence	Math 1.1 Demonstrates an understanding of numbers and counting	Teacher observations Rubrics Checklists
October	• More and less	Math 1.1 Demonstrates an understanding of numbers and counting	Teacher observations
November	• Shapes • Parts of a whole	Math 1.2 Recognizes and describes shapes and spatial relationships	Teacher observations Calendar Rubric Checklist
December	• Positional words	Math 1.2 Recognizes and describes shapes and spatial relationships	Teacher observations
January	• Matching • Sorting	Math 1.3 Uses the attributes of objects for comparison and patterning	Teacher observations
February	• Patterns	Math 1.3 Uses the attributes of objects for comparison and patterning	Teacher observations
March	• Measures and compares using nonstandard units	Math 1.4 Measures and describes using nonstandard and standard units	Teacher observations Science center Checklists
April	• Measures and compares using nonstandard units • Recognizes some numerals	Math 1.1 Demonstrates an understanding of numbers and counting Math 1.4 Measures and describes using nonstandard and standard units	Teacher observations Checklists
May	• Review any concepts needed	Math 1.1 Demonstrates an understanding of numbers and counting Math 1.2 Recognizes and describes shapes and spatial relationships Math 1.3 Uses the attributes of objects for comparison and patterning Math 1.4 Measures and describes using nonstandard and standard units	Teacher observations Calendar Graphs Science center Checklists
For more information contact: Sandra Dodson 500 Mero Street, 19th Floor CPT Frankfort, KY 40601 Phone: (502)564-2106 Sandra.Dodson@education.ky.gov			

SOURCE: Retrieved from http://www.education.ky.gov/KDE/Instructional+Resources/Curriculum+Documents+and+Resources/Teaching+Tools/Curriculum+Maps/cmcallowaypreschmath.htm.

Table 5.2 Example of an Excel Application for Depicting how 3 Teachers Assessed 11 Children Using a 5-Item Checklist

	Teacher 1						Teacher 2						Teacher 3						Subtotal by Child
	Q_1	Q_2	Q_3	Q_4	Q_5		Q_1	Q_2	Q_3	Q_4	Q_5		Q_1	Q_2	Q_3	Q_4	Q_5		
Abe	x	x			x			x			x		x	x		x	x		9
Betty	x	x	x	x	x		x	x	x	x	x		x	x	x	x	x		15
Craig				x	x				x	x	x						x		6
Diane		x		x	x		x	x		x	x			x		x			9
Ed			x	x	x					x	x				x		x		7
Fran	x	x	x		x		x	x	x	x	x		x	x			x		12
George									x	x					x				3
Harriet		x						x	x	x									4
Ike	x	x		x			x		x		x		x	x		x			9
Jean	x	x	x	x	x		x	x	x	x	x		x	x	x	x	x		15
Kyle			x					x	x	x					x				5

NOTE: Use the letter "X" to indicate if the child passed the questionnaire item.

Optimal levels of reliability occur when wording of the items on the checklist is clear and the decisions to be made when answering them are unequivocal. Also, best results occur when the rater(s) are familiar with what is being observed, and there is no confusion as to meanings or expectations.

Developmental Assessments

Two final areas where checklists are widely employed are on **developmental assessments** used to chart patterns of growth, and with the diagnosis of possible learning problems. The issue of developmental assessments is addressed in Chapter 7 and the issues related to special needs in Chapter 11.

Summary

Checklists and rating scales are regular components in the assessment tool bag carried by early childhood educators. These measurement devices can be used to assess complex socialization issues as well as basic learning. Rating scales can be semantic and assess the degree of agreement with a statement or the strength of feelings and attitudes about the child's progress. Rating scales can also be hierarchical and document the frequency, intensity, or strength of an activity, behavior, or the products of learning.

The reliability of these scales can be demonstrated through the use of multiple raters and using correlation to document interrater reliability. It can also be visualized as the concordance of raters as depicted on a spreadsheet. Matching the scales with the actual curriculum and learning standards can establish validity of both checklists and rating scales. One place where learning standards can be accessible to both educators and parents is on a curriculum map.

Checklists are similar to rating scales, but they are normally evaluated as a dichotomy. The binary nature of checklist answers can take the form of a simple check mark next to a description or an answer to a Yes–No question. They can be developed whenever there is list of things that a person must remember to do to ensure the safety and welfare of children. They can also be part of the evaluation of a child's learning and integrated into regular assessments specified on a curriculum map.

Discussion Questions

1. Visit an early childhood education program and ask one of the teachers to describe how he/she uses rating scales and checklists when charting and monitoring the growth of children. Bring your findings to the next class. As an alternative to this question, visit the Internet and find several checklists or rating scales developed for early childhood educators. Evaluate one for discussion with the class. What is your evaluation of the rating scale? Explain your position.

2. How could an early childhood educator use checklists in his/her classroom in nonevaluative ways?

3. What steps should an educator take to optimize the reliability of a rating scale used to assess a child's acquisition of early mathematics skills?

4. How can the validity of a rating scale used to assess children's acquisition of basic social studies knowledge be demonstrated?

5. Design a 10-item Likert-type scale or a 5-item semantic differential scale to quantify the opinion of class members on a topic of common interest (e.g., the university's bookstore, children's literature section in the library, student parking, or the university's dining options, etc.). Share your questionnaire with your classmates. What are its strengths and weaknesses?

Related Readings

Colton, D., & Covert, R. W. (2007). *Designing and constructing instruments for social research and evaluation.* San Francisco: Jossey-Bass.

Cox, J. B., & Cox, K. B. (2007). *Your opinion, please! How to build the best questionnaires in the field of education.* Thousand Oaks, CA: Corwin Press.

Douglas, D. R., & Anderson, J. F. (1974). *Questionnaires: Design and use.* Lanham, MD: Scarecrow Press.

Kallick, B., & Colosimo, J. (2008). *Using curriculum mapping and assessment data to improve learning.* Thousand Oaks, CA: Corwin Press.

Stergar, C. (2005). *Performance tasks, checklists, and rubrics.* Thousand Oaks, CA: Sage.

Notes

1. As few as 4 semantic differential items can yield useful scores; however, 10 or more items are always recommended.
2. Psychometricians use several complex systems for the development of published hierarchical scales. These include Thurstone's scale (1927), Guttman's scale (1944), and the Mokken scale (1971).
3. This is done to keep respondents honest and reading each item. It is easy for students and others to develop a mind-set and give all questions the same mark or answer. A negative valance item should appear among the first five items to make the respondent a careful reader of each question.
4. There are also more advanced statistical models that permit the permutation of correlations across all evaluators. Next, the correlations can be converted into standard scores and then averaged.
5. A tornado warning from the U.S. Weather Service indicates that a dangerous storm has been sighted on the ground and all people should seek immediate shelter. A tornado watch means that the atmospheric conditions are right for a tornado within a designated time frame.

Summative Measurements of Educational Outcomes

6

Most of what I really need to know about how to live, what to do, and how to be, I learned in kindergarten. Wisdom did not lie at the top of the graduate school mountain, but there in a kindergarten classroom.

—Robert Fulghum

Introduction and Themes

Summative assessments are a part of every early childhood education program. One key to creating a valid and useful classroom test is to base it on the approved standards for learning. Well-constructed classroom measures are planned to assess a list of learning objectives and goals and also to provide measures at different levels of cognition.

The largest national program of summative assessments was mandated in January of 2002 when President George W. Bush signed into law a requirement for annual achievement testing starting in third grade. Tests are developed by every state to measure children's progress in meeting the goal of proficiency in core subjects. The definition of proficiency is left up to each state. This opens the door to a lot of **gamesmanship** by state departments of education. When schools do not reach the required average achievement level they are quickly labeled in the local press as failing. This label can do serious harm to entire communities.

School administrators have tried a number of ways to improve scores of children from their schools. One approach has been to reward successful performance on mandated tests with cash and other prizes. Another has been to cut large chunks from the school's curriculum to make room for more time to drill children in basic skills. The best approach to improving test scores is proven to be the provision of all children with an academic summer camp or school program.

One central goal of testing mandates is the closing of the achievement gap between various identified groups of children (Asian American, African American, Hispanic, children from impoverished homes, Native American, Anglo-white, special education, and English language learners). This goal has not been met.

Winners in the new test-based approach to accountability include traditional test publishing houses. These companies have become partners with state education departments in developing, printing, distributing, and scoring new mandated tests.

With all testing programs, children with disabilities should be provided accommodations making it possible for them to perform at their optimal level.

Learning Objectives

By reading and studying this chapter, you should acquire the competency to:

- Explain the difference between summative and formative evaluations in terms of measurement goals.
- Explain the six levels of cognition as outlined by Benjamin Bloom in 1956.
- Describe how the Iowa Tests of Basic Skills differs from the other published test batteries.
- Describe the requirements of adequate yearly progress that public schools must reach.
- Discuss various penalties schools face when children do not do well on state-mandated assessments.
- Explain various accommodations that may be provided to children with a disability.
- Describe the impact of mandated high-stakes tests in third grade on primary grade curriculums.

Teacher-Designed Summative Measures

On most days, primary and preschool children are tested or in some way evaluated (Black & William, 1998). By high school graduation, it is likely a child has taken 2,000 tests, quizzes, and other written evaluations. Yet, research has shown that teachers do not have confidence in their ability to develop quality measures of achievement (Stiggins & Bridgeford, 1985).

There are three major reasons why teachers create and use quizzes and tests. At one level, these measurements are tools for documenting learning and writing **progress reports** for parents. A second reason is to provide evidence that instructional goals and objectives are being met. The third reason for a teacher to design his/her own classroom measure is to provide an introduction for children to the protocol and behaviors of high-stakes testing. Procedures required for high-stakes and other standardized tests are very different from the normal classroom practice. For example, we teach young children to share, then we tell them not to share answers during the high-stakes tests. Normally, teachers are always ready to help children when they have a problem understanding a task; but not during a high-stakes test. During standardized tests, we require children to concentrate on a single issue and work alone in silence. These protocols are all new to primary children.

Construction of quality classroom measures requires planning. The cognitive dimension is one of two central concerns that should be addressed when designing a test or assessment. When the goal of the teacher is to have children learn a fact or series of factual things, the obvious cognitive level required is knowledge. From preschool through the first two years of college, almost all questions written by teachers for examinations, tests, and quizzes are written at the knowledge level (Castelli, 1994; Finley, 1995).

Objectives for Learning

Every state has established learning standards for all students from preschool through high school (PK–12). These standards provide a framework used to develop each school's curriculum. These curriculums are then published in a guide or curriculum map. It is the task of each teacher to translate the school's curriculum documents into a series of instructional objectives and practices and design classroom assessments aligned with the standards.

When designing a summative evaluation, the teacher should work to ensure that learning standards required by the state are included on the assessment. Teachers should link each of their instructional objectives with one of the state's standards for learning. The objectives can then be turned into questions and problems for children to solve.

The best instruction is that which uses the least words sufficient for the task.

—Maria Montessori

Levels of Cognition

A question teachers address every day is the cognitive requirement expected of their students. Not all tasks and assessment activities require the same quality of thinking. In 1956, Benjamin S. Bloom and other members of a committee of the American Psychological Association provided a taxonomy or scale to describe possible levels of cognition. **Bloom's scale** or **taxonomy** defines six levels of thought that are further divided into 19 subcategories (see Table 6.1). These levels of cognition can be used to answer a test question or solve a problem.

Bloom's committee gave the name **Knowledge** to the lowest level of thinking and Evaluation to the most complex level. The level of Knowledge dominates almost all teacher-made assessments and tests in the primary grades. **Higher-order thinking** skills are rarely asked of students.

Bloom also attempted, but never finished, a fully elaborated taxonomy for educators to use with the affective domain. That taxonomy was written by David Krathwohl and includes the following broad major categories: Receiving, Responding, Valuing, Organizing, and at the most advanced level, development of a Value Concept (Krathwohl, Bloom, & Masia, 1964) (see Table 6.2).

Another unfinished project started by Benjamin Bloom was to define the psychomotor domain. The Information Technology Services Division of Pennsylvania State University (2007) recently developed a model for that domain. Table 6.3 is loosely adapted from their work.

Table 6.1 Taxonomy of the Cognitive Domain

Cognitive Level	Tasks and Operations	Assessment Verbs
Evaluation	Comparison of theories and models making discriminations using multiple evaluation dimensions. Selection of a construct that best matches criteria.	Evaluate, Compare & Contrast, Judge & Assess
Synthesis	Using analytical processes to create concepts and present new ideas and models.	Hypothetical & Deductive Thinking, Plan & Design, Organize & Provide Structure
Analysis	Envisioning a hidden pattern of information and concepts. Finding the true meaning and potential impact of concepts and ideas. Reflect and draw out the essence of a concept.	Select, Review, Breakdown, Examine, Investigate
Application	Theory and concepts put to the task of solving a problem. Using what is known to resolve a difficulty.	Calculate, Solve, Resolve, Explain, Prove, Utilize, Play
Comprehension	Translation and interpretation of meanings. Use what was learned to solve problems in various contexts.	Summarize, Interpret, Translate, Understand, Explain, Describe, Discuss
Knowledge	Recalling factual bits of information from long-term memory. Memorizing vocabulary, facts, equations, dates, faces, historical data, numbers.	Memorize, Repeat From Memory, Recall, Quote

SOURCE: Adapted from Bloom, 1956.

Table 6.2 Taxonomy of the Affective Domain

Level	Definition	Example
Value Concept	New value guides and informs behaviors.	Individual has a firm commitment to living the new value. The value becomes a defining characteristic of the individual.
Organizing	Integrating the new value into the belief system of the individual.	Priority is given to the new value and it is placed into the hierarchy of personal beliefs.
Valuing	The development of positive attitudes toward a new way of believing, acting, and approaching others.	Demonstrates a new belief and can plan social interactions and other contacts using the tenets of the new value. Joins with others in following the value.
Responding	Active attention is given to learning about the belief or value being demonstrated or explained by others.	Directed reading, active discussion, and practice by the person can lead to the acceptance of a new value.
Receiving	Person is aware of another set of beliefs or value held by others, and is willing to learn more about that value.	Being open to the opinions of others and respectful of their positions and beliefs. Being able to reflect on the belief system and values of others.

SOURCE: From Krathwohl, Bloom, & Masia, 1964.

Table 6.3 Taxonomy of the Psychomotor Domain

Level	Definition	Example
Adapting	Perfecting physical activity by tweaking fine movements.	Mentoring and careful coaching are part of bringing a physical performance to its optimal level. Practice and repetition are critical.
Practicing	Repetition and overlearning the component parts of a complex skill. Practicing the whole skill.	Each part of a skill is rehearsed until it is perfectly mastered. The entire skill sequence is then combined and rehearsed.
Imitating	Internalizing observed physical activity and attempting to reproduce the movements needed for them.	Careful instruction by a skilled coach helps the novice learn the sequence of activities and movements needed for a new skill. Learner imitates his/her coach or model.
Observing	Careful attention is paid to observing how a performance is done and the movements needed for its execution	Watching and internalizing the elements that make up a successful performance. The repeated observation of both the whole performance and its parts. These observations can occur with video support.

SOURCE: Adapted from Information Technology Services Division of Penn State University, 2007.

Each taxonomy has the potential to be useful in planning curriculum, designing instruction, and developing assessments for early education.

Blueprint (Table of Specifications) for Classroom Assessments

The combination of learning objectives and the teacher's goal for the cognitive level the child should use constitutes the two dimensions for framing a new measure. Teachers can see at a glance what items or questions are needed if they list the learning objectives on one axis of a chart, and place the desired cognitive level for the question or problem on the other (see Table 6.4).

Table 6.4 Table of Specifications for a 30-Question Summative Quiz for a Third Grade Science Unit on the Three States of Water

Level of Competence Required to Answer the Question				
Objectives	Content Emphasis	Knowledge (50%)	Comprehension and Applications (40%)	Analysis, Synthesis, and Evaluation (10%)
1. Identify major water bodies and their sizes.	9	4	4	1
2. Explain the role of the sun in evaporation.	6	4	2	
3. Compare the process of evaporation and condensation.	7	4	2	1
4. Explain the three states of water.	3	2	1	
5. Describe how the "water cycle" operates on earth.	5	1	3	1
		15 Questions	12 Questions	3 Questions
Total Test Length = 30 Questions				

Formats for Classroom Tests

When making a classroom test or quiz, primary teachers must plan with the developmental capabilities of their children in mind. The reading skills of primary children limit the types of questions teachers can use. A second concern is the length of time children can concentrate on a measurement task. Generally, primary grade children should not be expected to stay focused on a classroom test for more than a few minutes (15 to 20 minutes) (Sprenger, 2008).

Longer measures, including standardized assessments, are best broken up and given in several short blocks of time. Unfortunately, this is rarely the practice with mandated high-stakes tests (see Case in Point 6.1).

Case in Point 6.1

High-Stakes Test Time Requirements

Statewide assessments can require hours to administer. The following table of test time requirements from the Tennessee Comprehensive Achievement Test is typical.

Kindergarten	95 minutes
First grade	210 minutes
Second grade	265 minutes
Third grade	320 minutes
Fourth grade	320 minutes
Fifth grade	320 minutes
Sixth grade	320 minutes

SOURCE. http://tn.gov/education/assessment/doc/Grades_k2.pdf.

After second grade, all of the subtests take an hour to administer. An additional hour must be planned to provide time to distribute tests, complete answer sheets, and do practice questions. The total test covers four curriculum areas with 308 questions.

One strategy for classroom measurement in the primary grades involves integrating measurement into other activities. Young children need to be engaged with physical materials or provided with visual clues when they are assessed. Classroom tests can also be based on familiar workbook-like activities. Another model for a quiz can be found in materials included with unit evaluations provided by book publishers.

Directions for early childhood tests may need to be read to the children. The Grade 2 English and Language Arts Standards Test from California provides an example of this strategy (see Figure 6.1).

Figure 6.1 Second Grade Level Reading Development Test Items From California's Standardized Testing and Reporting Program (STAR)

Teacher reads: *Find and circle the word that has been divided into syllables correctly.*

(A) beg-in-ing (B) begin-ning (C) beg-inn-ing (D) be-gin-ning

Teacher reads: *Find and circle the word that has the same sound as the underlined letters in the first word.*

board (A) scared (B) card (C) boat (D) tore

NOTE: These questions were adapted from released items on the California standards test.

SOURCE: Copyright © 2008 California Department of Education (http://www.cde.ca.gov/ta/tg/sr/).

Primary grade teachers can use graphic examples to build a classroom assessment. Figure 6.2 is an example of this format for a third grade unit on time.

Figure 6.2 Primary Grade Multiple Choice Assessment of Ability to Read Time From an Analog Clock

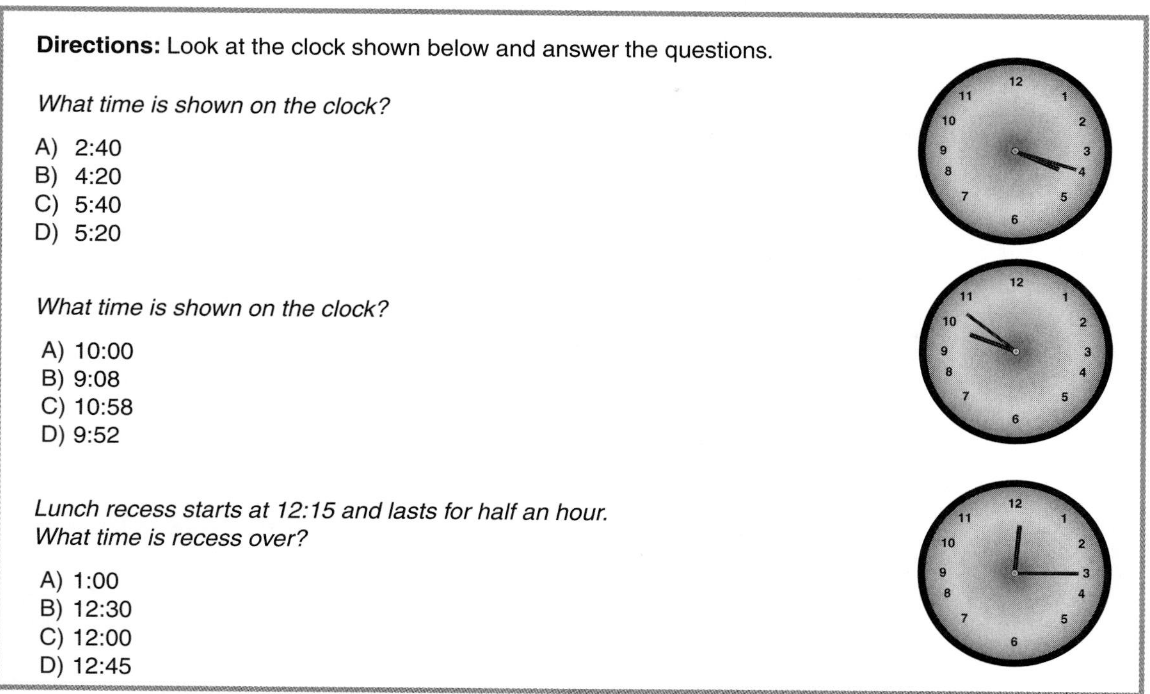

Directions: Look at the clock shown below and answer the questions.

What time is shown on the clock?

A) 2:40
B) 4:20
C) 5:40
D) 5:20

What time is shown on the clock?

A) 10:00
B) 9:08
C) 10:58
D) 9:52

Lunch recess starts at 12:15 and lasts for half an hour.
What time is recess over?

A) 1:00
B) 12:30
C) 12:00
D) 12:45

Another strategy is the use of a matching format (see Figure 6.3). With second or third graders who are developing their reading skills, matching questions can be designed requiring a minimum of reading. Teachers will need to dictate a set of directions before children answer the questions.

Figure 6.3 Matching-Format Measure of Primary Grade Reading Comprehension

Directions: On this page, you will see a list of books in a column, and another column of animals. Match the animals with the books in which they appear. Show your choice by drawing a line connecting the correct animal with each book.

Bambi	Monkey
Charlotte's Web	Wolf
Curious George	Pig
Olivia	Deer
Runt	Mouse
Frederick	Spider

One cautionary note: If more than five or six pairs are included it can be very difficult to follow the line links children draw.

Matching formats that do not require children to read are also possible. In the example below (Figure 6.4), children are asked to match animals to their habitats, and to draw a line between the animal's image and its habitat.

Figure 6.4 Matching Test Using Only Animals and Their Habitats, No Words Needed

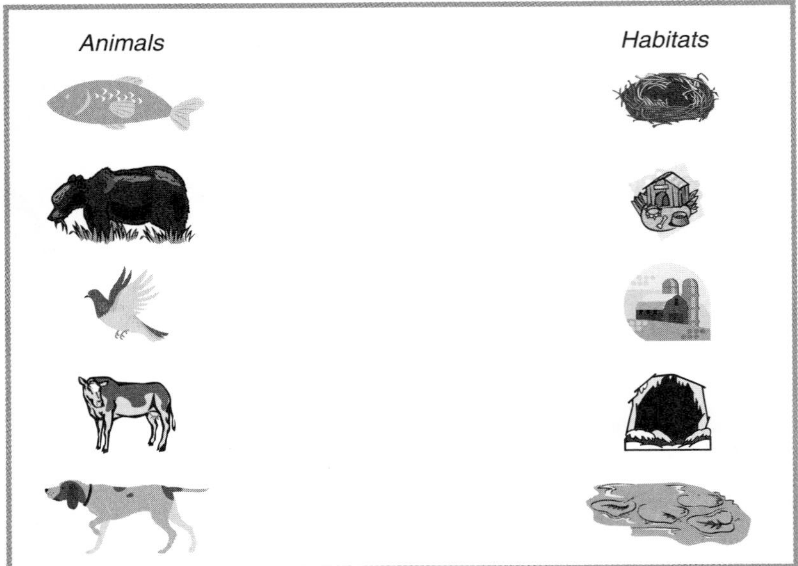

Other formats include questions asking children to mark with an "X" the picture of the correct answer. For example, a question about money can be answered by having children check coins from an array of pictured coins needed to make up a required sum of money (see Figure 6.5).[1]

Grading

A summative measure provides much more information than just an outcome score. Answers given by each child should be examined for possible patterns indicating areas where he/she is having difficulty understanding concepts or achieving skills. If several children make similar errors, there is a need to reteach. Also, examine each child's responses for strategies he/she employed (see Chapter 10).

Standardized Assessments

In the politicized education environment of the new century, educators can no longer abstain from and hope that large-scale testing will go away. Popham (1999) observed that rules for educators changed when newspapers began to report test data, and even rank schools based upon the achievement outcome of students. Today, the value of suburban homes is dependent in part on the ranking of a community's schools (Lloyd,

Figure 6.5 Test Format to Assess Primary Grade Understanding of Money

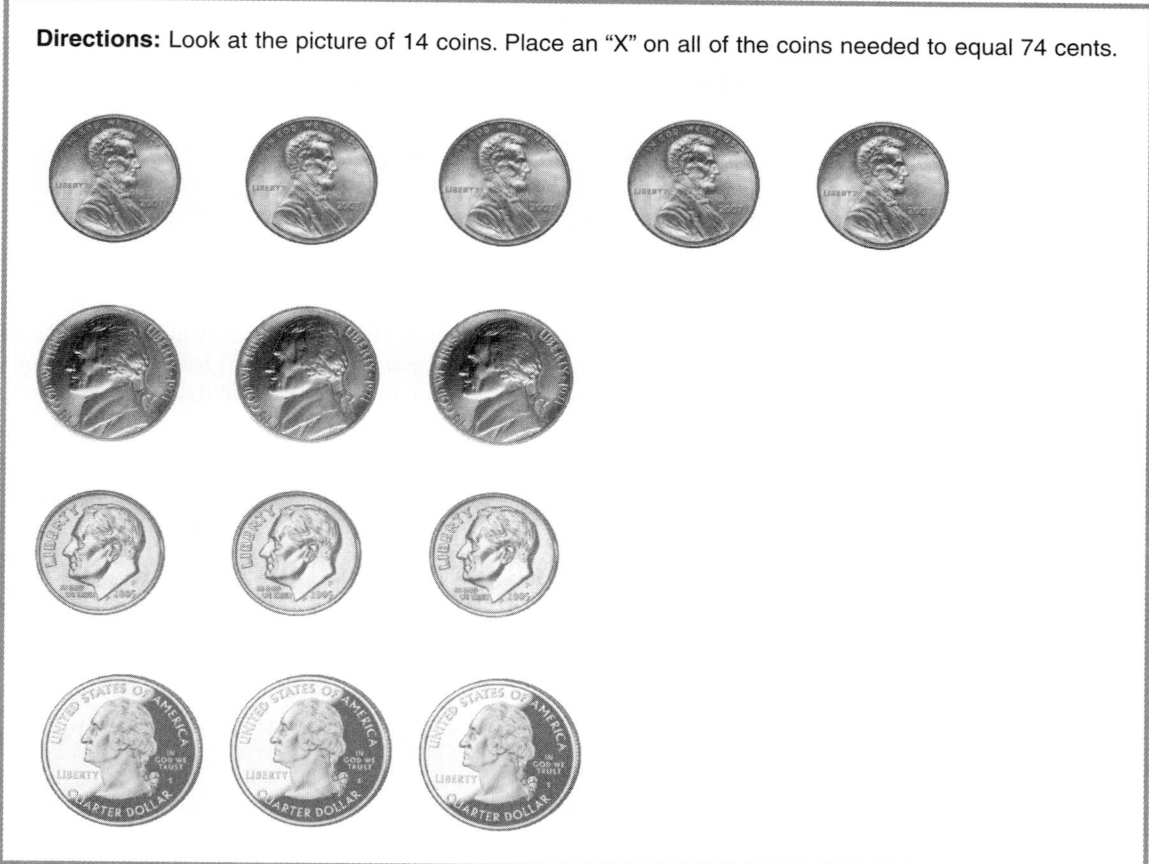
Directions: Look at the picture of 14 coins. Place an "X" on all of the coins needed to equal 74 cents.

2005; Van Moorlehem, 1998). Even divorce lawyers use the quality of neighborhood schools when arguing issues related to child custody.

Primary and preschool school children are exposed to summative measurements of achievement on a regular basis. Some are commercial standardized measures designed for individual administration (see Chapter 9). Another class of summative achievement tests includes paper and pencil measures. Included among these measures are the federally mandated standardized assessments.

Assumptions of Tests

Published assessments are built on several assumptions that few educators consider. One of these assumptions is that it is possible to systematically measure what a child knows or what skills were acquired. This is described as the **empirical** assumption of testing. The empirical assumption is the belief that by carefully observing small aspects of a child's behavior it is possible to conclude what he/she has learned or is able to do.

The second assumption is one of coverage. Assessment tasks and questions cannot measure everything a child knows or can do. All assessments measure only a small sample of the child's capabilities. Items used to make an assessment can be poorly selected and invalid. Professional test developers (psychometricians) discuss this issue in terms of item **sampling adequacy.** Quality measures assess the full range of possible skills and knowledge included in a domain of the curriculum. Teachers who design classroom assessments should be mindful of the need for appropriate coverage of the area.

Test Publishers

The testing enterprise has grown dramatically with new testing mandates. Various states spend over a billion dollars annually to meet testing requirements while being funded by the federal government for only a fraction of that. Test publishers who are in partnership with state education departments in meeting testing mandates are prospering. In 2004, Ohio spent $25 million just to develop the state test for one year (Mathis, Fleming, & Lecker, 2005). That cost does not include the price for printing, transporting test materials to all schools, and having tests returned for scoring. Nor did it account for the cost of conducting an analysis of scores, the return of data to schools, and the publishing of analytical reports.

Published Standardized Achievement Tests

The concept of a **battery** of achievement tests is an American invention of the 20th century.[2] World Book Company published the first test battery, the Stanford Achievement Test, in 1923. Book companies wanted to publish these measures to provide a closed marketing system. School leaders knew that the books their schools used were aligned with achievement tests, thereby limiting the likelihood of low scores. It also gave teachers the opportunity to see test items as they administered the tests, a knowledge that translated into new items being added to the curriculum. The result was better test scores, happy parents, and proud school boards. Figure 6.6 provides a brief description of the major standardized achievement tests used in the primary grades.

Figure 6.6 Achievement Tests and Publishers in America

- Metropolitan Achievement Test, 8th ed. (MAT-8)

  The MAT-8 is a descendant of the original Metropolitan Test first published by the World Book in 1932. Harcourt Assessment, the successor of World Book, publishes the eighth edition of the MAT. It was normed using 80,000 children from kindergarten through the 12th grade. MAT-8 has 13 different test levels (kindergarten to Grade 12), covering a wide range of curriculum areas including Reading Vocabulary, Reading Comprehension, Open-Ended Reading, Mathematics Concepts, Arithmetic Problem Solving, Science, and Social Studies. Kindergarten and primary grade subtests have a median reliability of 0.80 (Lukin & McGregor, 2005).

- Stanford Achievement Test, 10th ed. (SAT 10)

  This battery was published in 2003 and is appropriate for use with children between kindergarten and the 12th grade. Over the various grades, there are a total of 17 different subtests that make up the test battery. Some of these are only used with the primary level tests (e.g., Sounds and Letters) while others are combined scores (Total Mathematics). The SAT 10 used 170,000 children in the development and the establishment of its test battery items, and another 250,000 to establish the norm group. In kindergarten and primary grades, the SAT 10 is a moderately reliable measure with a median reliability of about 0.75 (Case, 2004).

- Terra Nova, 2nd ed. (TN-2)

  The Terra Nova, 2nd ed. (TN-2) is a new edition of what was once known as the California Achievement Test (CAT-6). CTB/McGraw-Hill published the second edition of the Terra Nova in 2002. It was developed and normed on a sample of 280,000 students. The TN-2 provides a series of different test batteries covering the grades from kindergarten through 12th grade. The teacher's manual provides a detailed content analysis of each subtest. This information makes it simple for teachers to determine if the test matches the classroom curriculums and provides "talking points" to use with parents of the tested children (Cizek, Johnson, & Mazzie, 2005). The long form of the test battery has moderate to good levels of reliability for its subtests of about 0.87.

- Iowa Tests of Basic Skills (ITBS)

  Professor E. F. Lindquist developed the ITBS at the University of Iowa. During the 1920s, he ran a summer contest for Iowa's children that rewarded academic skills. In 1935, he published the Iowa Every-Pupil Testing Program. Lindquist worked with the old-line publishing house of Houghton Mifflin (Riverside Division) to develop the Iowa Tests of Basic Skills.[4] The ITBS is an in-depth measure of academic learning. The test is available for kindergarteners through children in the ninth grade. Basic skills that the test measures are central to learning and include inference and analysis, comparison, classification, and interpretation. Higher-order thinking skills are measured by building questions using curriculum areas such as reading, mathematics concepts and estimation, mathematics problem solving and data management, social studies, and science. It also measures five areas of language arts. At the kindergarten and primary grade levels, the subtests of the ITBS have moderate levels of reliability (about 0.70 to 0.85). One advantage of the ITBS is that it provides several normative comparison groups from which a school can select. It offers norms for a national sample of public schools, a norm group for schools located in impoverished communities, and a set of norms for Catholic schools.

Accommodations

There has never been a time when so many children have been identified as needing special educational assistance. It is not just the actual number that is up, but also the proportion of children needing assistance. In 2004, the U.S. Department of Health and Human Services (USDHHS) reported 13.7% of all public school children had one or more disabling condition (USDHHS, 2005). Yet, only 9.4% of all preschool children have been identified as having one or more disability (National Center for Educational Statistics, 2007a). The difference between these numbers is a reason why early childhood educators should be vigilant with children and sensitive to signs of possible learning problems (see Chapter 11).

Early childhood teachers can provide help for children with special needs by making **accommodations** during assessments and classroom tests. It can be very challenging to find methods for collecting meaningful assessment data from children exhibiting diverse disabilities (Elliott, 2007). With classroom assessments, teachers are free to do whatever is necessary to provide a child having a disability the opportunity to work to his/her potential. Accommodations provide all children a level playing field.

Rules governing accommodations permitted for state assessments are published by each state, and must be observed. There are significant penalties for providing a child assistance that is not permitted. These penalties can cost a teacher his/her teaching license or even result in being prosecuted in state court for committing a felony.[3] A state-by-state listing of these accommodations can be found at a Web page maintained by the University of Minnesota: http://education.umn.edu/NCEO/TopicAreas/Accommodations/AccomFAQ.htm.

In a similar way, all school systems should develop and publish policies for accommodating needs of special education students on classroom tests. The accommodations a school may provide cover four main types (Salvia, Ysseldyke, & Bolt, 2007).

1. *Timing:* Children with learning problems may be provided extra time to complete the test, or frequent breaks during the testing session. It is also possible to divide extended testing sessions into smaller blocks of time. This can require several extra days for test administration.
2. *Environment:* Children with attention problems may be tested in a quiet, less distracting place such as a library study carrel or the office of the guidance counselor.
3. *Mechanics:* Children with neurological motor disorders including chronic spasticity from various forms of palsy, amputations, and musculoskeletal diseases can have their verbal responses transcribed by an adult aide.
4. *Communication:* Blind and visually impaired children can be tested with Braille versions of the assessment or with the assistance of a computerized book reader. Children having a hearing disability can have headphones for the amplification of verbal directions read by the teacher. A person can be provided who can sign directions when the child has a profound hearing disability.[5]

The cost of providing these forms of assistance must be borne by the school system. Required accommodations are also described in the child's Individual Family Service Plan (IFSP), Student Assistance Plan (Section 504 Plan), or in an Individual Educational Plan (IEP).

Achievement Gap

Over the last hundred years of standardized testing, there has been a persistent trend for Anglo-white children to, on average, have better test scores than children of both African American and Hispanic ancestry (Marchant, Morales, & Paulson, 2008).

The gap for Latino/a children is confounded by the problem of English language learners (ELL) taking tests written in a language they cannot speak or read.

Likewise, there is a persistent trend for children from middle class homes to score better than children who live in impoverished homes. These differences are well documented on state-mandated tests, and by the National Assessment of Educational Progress (Gamoran, 2007).

"This device will play arithmetic drills 24/7 to our unborn baby"

SOURCE: Cartoon by Merv Magus.

Gap Closing

In 2009, the NCLB Act was past the halfway mark toward its target date for having all children proficient in reading and math. While miniscule gains have been made toward reaching this goal between 2002 and 2008, the parallel goal of closing the **achievement gap** has not been met (Maxwell, 2008;

Viadero, 2007). There are many reasons for this, including the quality of public schools attended by minority children. Those schools tend to enroll the greatest number of children from impoverished backgrounds, have the least experienced teachers, have the highest student absenteeism, have the greatest faculty turnover and absenteeism, and have the lowest level of parent involvement (Camilli & Monfils, 2004; National Assessment of Educational Progress, 2004).

Teacher Quality

Inner-city schools enrolling many minority children tend to employ inexperienced teachers who are the least well qualified for their assignments. These novice teachers are routinely given assignments with children who are at the greatest risk for failure (Laczko-Kerr & Berliner, 2002). Also, children of the poor living in inner cities are taught by teachers previously passed over by suburban middle class schools (Sunderman & Kim, 2005). One reason for this involves complex work rules negotiated by urban teacher unions. These rules give senior teachers first choice among vacant positions within the school system.[6] Thus, urban school systems do not know until late in the summer exactly which vacancies are open for the new school year. By the time they start hiring, the pool of new teacher candidates has been picked clean by suburban school systems.

Mobility

Another reason for poorer scores among children from impoverished homes is **mobility** (Kaase & Dulaney, 2005; Lesisko & Wright, 2009; NAEP, 2004). Children of families that have moved three or more times over a two-year period had much lower achievement test scores when compared to children who never moved over the same time period.

Socioeconomic status may play a role in the achievement impact on children who live with families that move frequently. Wealthy parents move because they can. For middle and upper class families, moving is strategic and usually well planned. This is not always so for poor families who often move because they must. Therefore, moves made by children and families of poverty may be far more traumatic than is true of children with parents who move to improve their lives (Eckholm, 2008). In an effort to prevent the impact on poor families of being forced to move, New York City began a program of emergency rent assistance for families in danger of being evicted (Eckholm, 2008). The impact of the mortgage crisis of 2008–2009 is likely to have had a role in lower test scores for children (Armour, 2008).

Another type of moving occurs when parents who live in impoverished communities with notoriously poor schools smuggle their children into better suburban schools beyond their communities. This occurs frequently in suburban school systems bordering large cities and is a clear sign of both the devotion of parents to their children, and the desperation they feel toward their home school systems (Dillon, 2007).

Impact of High-Stakes Testing

The business of summative testing was dramatically changed when in 2002 the federal government began mandating achievement testing in all public schools. By linking these tests to job performance and children's grade-to-grade promotion, the U.S. Department of Education exponentially increased the pressure to improve achievement test scores. All the effort and stress on assessment in the primary grades have taken a toll on elementary schools and their teachers. These include problems in areas of curriculum, somatic illness, and the ethical practice of teaching.

Gamesmanship

One flaw in federally mandated assessment systems is that each state gets to determine what is required for a child to be proficient. Some states have very low standards for third grade children to reach to be proficient (e.g., Georgia, Idaho, Kansas, Montana, New Hampshire, North Carolina, Oklahoma, Tennessee, Texas, and Virginia), while others have high standards (e.g., Maine, Missouri, Vermont, and Wyoming). This issue of changeable standards has been referred to as measuring with a **rubber ruler** (Schumacker, 2005).

Other opportunities to stretch the envelope of testing ethics include gaming rules governing who must take the test, and which scores must be reported. The issue of privacy protection provides school leaders with an opportunity to game the results. Each state has a policy for releasing test data. States tend to set a high standard for the protection of the identity of individuals. For example, if a school enrolls only one or two racial minorities, and those disaggregated scores are released to the media it is easy to link specific children with scores. By setting a requirement that a minimum of 25 or 50 children must be in a group before their average scores are released, the state has protected the privacy of children, and also given school administrators a way to hide low-performing scores from adequate yearly progress (AYP) scrutiny. Many children fit into several of the nine categories defined by NCLB for AYP analysis (impoverished children, Anglo-whites, Asian Americans, Hispanics, African Americans, Native Americans, English language learners, and children with special needs). A child scoring low could be classified by his/her principal as a member of the AYP group that is too small to be reporting data from its members. Case in Point 6.2 illustrates a case of state gamesmanship with student scores.

Case in Point 6.2

Gaming of the AYP Report

In 2008, the schools of Virginia were required to have 73% of all children reach a level of proficient in reading and math. Privacy rules within the state do not allow disclosing data from groups of less than 50 children. This made it possible for schools enrolling a number of special education children, but less than a total of 50, to avoid reporting their data. One winner in this was the schools of Alexandria, Virginia. Seven elementary schools would have failed to meet the AYP requirement in Alexandria because less than half of the special education children reached the level of proficient on the Virginia Standards of Learning (SOL) assessments. Fortunately for those seven schools, they each enrolled fewer than 50 children with special needs. Thus, what would have been a failure to meet the AYP standard was avoided (Pope, 2008).

A related trick that state education departments have employed is with the definition used to interpret regulations governing who must be tested. Starting in third grade, every eligible child must be tested if they were in the school for a year. Some states define this to include all children who were enrolled by the fall term. Other states define it to mean that the child had to be on roll for a full 12 months. If the year is defined as a calendar year of 12 months, then a child who moved into the district during the summer or fall would not be required to take the test. This is because he/she was only enrolled 7 or 8 months (September to April), not 12 months. This calendar game was perfected in Illinois (Illinois Association of Directors of Title I, 2006). As many of the poorest families move frequently, this calendar game effectively reduced the number of children most likely to get low scores from entering the school's AYP calculation.

Curriculum Modifications

Another type of loss can be readily seen in the primary grades. What is lost is the teacher's ability to be spontaneous and to follow up in new directions when working with the children. This lack of flexibility is the result of the need to schedule more time for children to be drilled in prereading and reading skills and in basic arithmetic. The median change in each week's schedule involves about an hour and a half each week. To provide the extra 90 minutes a week for added drill sessions, other curriculum areas have been cut including the humanities, arts, and social studies (Dillon, 2006; Manzo, 2005b). Some traditional elementary school subjects such as penmanship have virtually disappeared from the curriculum (Putman, 2007).

Press for Success

In public elementary schools, the preparation for the high-stakes tests for third graders begins in kindergarten. In the past, children learned to read in first grade. Learning to read is now a kindergarten activity (de Vise, 2007b). All of this stress has taken a toll. Elementary school principals now order 20 or so extra tests from the state agency to serve as replacements for children who vomit on the state test during the examination (Toppo, 2007). Also, a significant downturn in the amount of reading for enjoyment done by children in the intermediate grades may be a reflection of the bad taste left with children who have scripted reading lessons drilled into them on a daily basis (Gifford, 2007).

Motivators

In addition to spending longer periods of time in reading drills and practice, other methods have also been employed to improve achievement test scores. Primary grade teachers have taken positive steps to motivate children to do their best work on assessments. These steps have included the full range of possibilities, from the silly to the pragmatic.

Reward programs for good or improved scores on high-stakes tests are common. Primary grade children have been given gift certificates, free restaurant meals, classroom pizza parties, tickets for the child and his or her parents to attend sporting events, and even savings bonds and cash prizes (Elliott, 2007) (see Chapter 2). Case in Point 6.3 describes an example of a "less secular" approach to improving test scores.

Case in Point 6.3

Questionable Approach to Improving High-Stakes Test Scores

In Florida, the principal of a Hernando County elementary school and five devoutly religious members of her faculty returned to school on Friday night before the high-stakes FCAT test started on Monday of the next week. They prayed over, and blessed with "Prayer Oils," student desks where children would sit to take the mandated state test on Monday morning. The oil did not evaporate and on Monday children complained to their teachers about the oily substance on their desks. Teachers reported a possible case of vandalism that appeared to have occurred over the weekend. This was resolved when it became known what the principal had done (T. Marshall, 2007).

Reading First

Prescriptive federal efforts have also been made to improve reading scores of children on standardized tests (Dillon, 2008b). The centerpiece of this effort to improve reading in primary grades has been a billion-dollar program known as Reading First. This phonics-based tutoring program for low-performing primary grade students was included as one of the federal mandates during George W. Bush's administration. Research published in 2008 indicated that this program did not work, nor did it improve skills of the primary target population of children. As a result, Congress cut the program funding in fiscal year 2008 (Manzo & Klein, 2008).

Merit Pay

One idea that has wide appeal among school boards involves **merit pay** for teachers. This idea assumes that teachers are somehow holding back from giving their full effort every day, and if teachers are given a cash prize for having their students get good test scores they will make a better instructional effort. Texas has given annual merit pay bonuses of as much as $10,000 to public school teachers. Yet, for all the publicity, there is no evidence that merit pay plans produce a significant and consistent improvement in student learning outcomes (see Chapter 2).

Summer School

Perhaps the best approach for improving the general achievement level of all elementary school children is to provide young learners with an educational program during the summer. The usual loss of achievement gains over a 10-week summer vacation is equal to about two months of academic work in reading, spelling, and arithmetic (Bennett & Kalish, 2006). This loss is greatest for children who live in impoverished conditions (Alexander, Entwisle, & Olson, 2007). Summer academic loss is especially problematic for English language learners (ELLs). It is possible for young ELL students to spend the entire 10-week summer break in Spanish-speaking communities and never hear English spoken until they return to school in the fall (see Chapter 1).

Children from middle class communities often attend private academic programs during the summer break. These include reading programs at local libraries, thematic summer camp programs (theater, science, etc.), and church-based academic enrichment and religious programs. Suburban schools that have established month-long, half-day summer programs have seen significantly better scores on their students' state assessment tests (de Vise, 2007a). Also, middle class parents are usually better educated and able to continue an informal education for their children for the 10 summer weeks.

The academic loss over the summer begins the summer following kindergarten, and becomes additive with each year thereafter (Alexander et al., 2007). Thus, by third grade the gap between children from poverty and those from middle class homes is dramatic.

There is research evidence that a summer education program can stop the summer academic slide. Ethnicity and socioeconomic conditions intersect, and many racial minorities live in poverty. This intersection implies that the test **score gap** separating ethnic groups can be reduced or closed by providing summer educational programs for all children (Cech, 2007). Research conducted with children from the inner city of Baltimore who attended a multiyear summer program revealed that they achieved test scores that were one half of a standard deviation higher than a matched group of children who did not attend (Alexander et al., 2007; Borman & Dowling, 2006). This is a very large gain and may be one way to make a real difference for low-achieving children. Where they are offered, parents see summer school programs for primary grade children as being a regular extension of the academic year (de Vise, 2007a).

Summer Schedule

The traditional summer has been from mid-June to the start of the fall term after Labor Day. A number of school systems have moved the date for the opening of the school year to the beginning of August. By making this move, schools have even more time to cram for high-stakes assessments in the spring. This early start to the school year is usually paired with several shorter vacation breaks during the year (Garner, 2007).

Neither parents nor state legislatures have missed this trend. A number of parent groups have sprung up voicing opposition to short summer vacations.

The early start also has an adverse effect on kindergarten enrollment, as fewer children reach the age of 5 by the first of August. State legislatures in four states (Florida, North Carolina, Minnesota, and Wisconsin) have passed laws requiring local public school systems start classes near or following Labor Day.

Parent Attitudes

Not all parents approve of this new emphasis on basic skills and test preparation to the exclusion of other learning activities. This is especially true for parents of children who are mentally gifted. Parents of the gifted assume their children will pass any state test and want to see an enriched and engaging curriculum for their children (Tierney, 2004). Unfortunately for them, schools have neither the resources nor time to make provisions for academically advanced elementary school children (Neal & Schanzenbach, 2007). Advanced Placement (AP) courses offered in high school usually placate parents, but primary and intermediate grade educators cannot escape criticism from these disappointed parents.

Summary

Teachers create classroom assessments for primary grade children that provide summative data. These should be based on an analysis of objectives used to organize instruction. They should also take into account the cognitive requirement of the task or questions. These two issues, objectives and cognitive levels, can be used to organize a test blueprint.

Summative tests have an increasingly important role in early childhood education. Major publishing houses all publish group-administered standardized achievement tests for children in kindergarten and the first three grades. Many schools prepare children for the mandated high-stakes assessments by using these tests.

In seven states and a number of big cities, the federally mandated assessment score is the deciding factor in determining who is promoted to fourth grade. All schools are evaluated by an examination of scores on the state-mandated assessment test for nine identified groups of students. If a school's average result does not reach the target score, it can be closed or reorganized and children transferred.

One goal for mandated assessments has been closing the gap in average achievement test scores between various groups of children. As of 2009, that has not happened. In an effort to improve scores, school administrators have tried a wide range of approaches including providing motivators for children and incentive pay for teachers. A major change made by many schools in the struggle to improve scores is with the curriculum. Large areas of the curriculum have been reduced or eliminated to provide more time to drill children in their fundamental skills. The best approach for improving scores is to provide an academic summer camp or school experience.

A problematic area for those administering summative assessments includes children with special educational disabilities. State-mandated tests provide a list of appropriate and legal accommodations that can be made in an attempt to provide a level playing field for these children.

Discussion Questions

1. Look up your state on the Internet and learn what accommodations third grade children may be provided on the mandated assessment test. After reviewing them, is anything not included that needs to be considered?

2. Design a test blueprint for a social studies or science unit test appropriate for second grade elementary school students. Bring your test blueprint to class and ask your peers for their evaluation of your blueprint.
3. After reviewing the levels of cognition as developed by Bloom's committee, discuss why so few teachers use assessment items that are above the level of "knowledge."
4. What effective steps can an elementary school administrator take to improve NCLB assessment test scores of children in his/her school?
5. How can a primary grade teacher prepare a third grade child who is an English language learner to take a reading test in English?
6. Should ELL students be allowed to be tested in their first language? When should the change to English be required?
7. Check your state's Web page and find what language alternatives are available for measuring children who are English language learners.

Related Readings

Meier, D., & Wood, G. (Eds.). (2004). *Many children left behind: How the No Child Left Behind Act is damaging our children and our schools*. Boston: Beacon.

Popham, W. J. (2001). *The truth about testing: An educator's call to action.* Alexandria, VA: Association for Supervision and Curriculum Development.

Sunderman, G. L., Kim, J. S., & Orfield, G. (2005). *NCLB meets school realities: Lessons from the field.* Thousand Oaks, CA: Corwin Press.

Tileston, D. W. (2006). *What every parent should know about schools, standards, and high stakes tests.* Thousand Oaks, CA: Corwin Press.

Notes

1. One caution: Do not use a picture of a half dollar. While still minted, this coin is not in general circulation and young children are not likely to know what it is.
2. A battery of tests is often the core component of the assessment. Batteries are a collection of tests designed to measure different parts of the curriculum, for example, mathematics, reading, or science.
3. Teachers who refuse to administer high-stakes tests mandated by schools can be fired for insubordination (Gonzalez, 2008; Shaw, 2008; Wilson, 2008).
4. The other notable product of Professor Lindquist's oeuvre was the American College Testing (ACT) program.
5. American sign language is a labor-intensive task. It is likely two sign language interpreters will be needed for a long test. It is not appropriate to expect a sign language interpreter to work more than an hour at a time. A long test may require two interpreters to work in shifts.
6. The state of California passed laws in 2006 that broke seniority rules in that state (SB 1209 and SB 1655).

Part III

Individual Screening Measures and Full Assessments

Three types of individually administered screening measures and assessments are presented in this section. The screening for developmental delay and possible medical problems is addressed. This includes six different measures used to screen for possible developmental problems from birth to preschool years. It also provides information about five different developmental inventories and curriculum-based assessments. Use of these measurements in early intervention programs is described.

Cognitive assessments are discussed in this section of the text. Measures are presented in the context of theories of human intelligence. These theories range from those of Lewis Terman to models of human ability developed by Howard Gardner and Robert Sternberg. Measures included in this section include three screening measures and six cognitive assessment batteries. The ethical use and training required to administer and interpret data from these measures is explained.

The section ends with a description of individually administered measures of early learning and academic skills. Five batteries of achievement measures are described. Six measures of language and early reading skills are also presented and discussed. Three mathematics skills measures are also described.

Technology-based assessment systems are also introduced. This includes computer adaptive assessments for young children and a description of the new mCLASS software for administering and analyzing a range of early childhood measures.

Developmental Assessments of Infants, Toddlers, and Preschoolers

7

Every generation rediscovers and re-evaluates the meaning of infancy and childhood.

—Arnold Gesell

Introduction and Themes

During a baby's first 12 months, the major concern is his/her health status and physical development. Newborns have their physical status determined in their first minute using a measurement designed by Virginia Apgar of Columbia University. Later, the focus moves to issues related to the cognitive growth and socialization of the young child.

Child development and **maturation** implies change over time. Charting the sequential changes provides a method to spot anomalies, described as developmental delays. Identification of a developmental delay triggers early intervention and special programming for the child. Interventions are designed to move children back on track and help each reach their full potential. Children's ability to move back on track is built on the concept of developmental plasticity.

Identification of a child at risk for developmental delay involves several types of assessments. Screenings are the first level in the evaluation process. Screenings are designed to be easy to administer, reasonable in cost, and require less than an hour to give. Assessment is a generic term referring to the process of gathering information needed to make a decision (McLean, 1996). Assessments normally involve a single measuring tool. An evaluation is a large-scale effort to learn about a child. It may include a collection of assessments or an assessment battery.[1] Evaluations are required when an entitlement decision is being made regarding a child.

There are a number of approaches useful in conducting assessments. A new approach to the assessment of young children involves examining how the child responds and performs in different settings including the home and child care center. This approach provides curriculum and assessments based on educational materials. Data from these environmental assessments can be used to develop service delivery plans for children with special needs. An example is the approach developed by Diane Bricker, the Assessment, Evaluation, and Programming System (AEPS) (Bricker, Capt, & Pretti-Frontcza, 1993).

Another approach is developmental and based on normative populations of children. A complementary approach for assessing child development has a behavioral focus measuring the response of an infant to the environment.

Learning Objectives

By reading and studying this chapter, you should acquire the competency to:

- Describe the first assessment infants receive.
- Make a comparison between the Assessment, Evaluation, and Programming System for Infants and Children, Revised, and other developmental assessment batteries.
- Describe three major categories for examiner education in the ethical administration of developmental screenings and inventories.
- Contrast and discuss the properties of four developmental screening tests widely used in preschools and child care centers.
- Contrast and discuss several assessment batteries measuring child development that can be used to make entitlement decisions.
- Describe how parents are used to assist in the assessment processes for infants and toddlers.

First Assessments

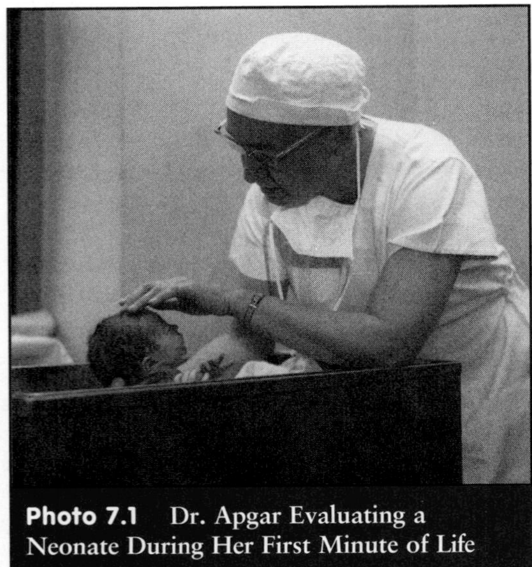

Photo 7.1 Dr. Apgar Evaluating a Neonate During Her First Minute of Life

SOURCE: Photo by Elizabeth Wilcox, courtesy of Archives & Special Collections, Columbia University Health Sciences Library.

The first and most critical concern for the newborn child is his/her medical status and physical well-being. This concern leads to the first assessment that a newborn infant faces. The attending obstetrician welcomes the newborn into the world with a formal assessment of the newborn's health and status. That medical status examination, the **A.P.G.A.R.**, is an observational rating scale administered one minute after birth and again four minutes later (see Photo 7.1). The original scale was built around an acronym of Dr. Virginia Apgar's name.[2] Her scale was designed to help young physicians in resident training remember the elements to assess with newborns. More recently, that assessment has become more sophisticated and complex. Today, the name Apgar is applied to an observational scale regarding the following factors: heart rate, respiratory effort, muscle tone, reflex response, and color.

Medical Status

The field of pediatrics has identified several warning signs teachers and child care workers should look for in their interactions with children and families. Table 7.1 is a checklist of those items.

There are many reasons a child may not achieve one or more of these developmental benchmarks, including deleterious factors related to the child's environment. These factors are described as developmental as they are open to modification. Poverty plays a major role in developmental delay children. Approximately 1 in 6 American children lives in poverty, and more than half of those live in rural communities (Save the Children, 2004). Poverty in this country is also directly related to the likelihood a young child will experience a traumatic

Table 7.1 Brief Developmental Checklist

Child Development Benchmarks for Normal Development

Failure to achieve is a warning for a child at risk for developmental or medical problems.

Birth through 3 months	*Behavior Shown*	*Not Shown*
• Recognizes caregiver	___	___
• Reflexes present (e.g., sucking, grasping, TNR, Babinski)[3]	___	___
• Visually tracking a light	___	___
• Alert to sounds in environment	___	___
• Soothes in parent's arms	___	___
• Fist sucking ends by 3 months	___	___
4 to 6 months		
• Positive control of head	___	___
• Reaching for interesting objects	___	___
• Smiles spontaneously	___	___
• Cooing sounds	___	___
• Grasping objects and mouthing them	___	___
• Falls asleep in parent's arms	___	___
6 months to 12 months		
• Primitive reflexes disappear (e.g., hand grasp, TNR, Babinski)	___	___
• Babbling behavior	___	___
• Parent bonding & stranger anxiety	___	___
• Sitting upright without support	___	___
• Determines sound source & direction	___	___
• Transfers objects from one hand to the other hand	___	___
• Looks for hidden objects	___	___
• First steps with support	___	___
12 months to 24 months		
• First spoken words by 16 months	___	___
• Sentences of 2–4 words by 24 months	___	___
• Problem solving by trial and error	___	___
• Language play and imitation	___	___
• Peek-a-boo with smiles	___	___
• Identification of hand domination	___	___
• Eye contact with caregiver	___	___
• Independent walking	___	___
• Two-word sentences	___	___
• The word *NO* enters the vocabulary	___	___
• Points to objects of interest	___	___
• Early sense of humor develops	___	___
• Climbs steps (step-upon-step) by 24 months	___	___

Persistent failures by the young child imply that the child needs further formal evaluation.

SOURCE: Adapted with permission from the Infant Parent Program, 1717 West 10th St., Austin, TX 78703.

injury (Bassuk & Friedman, 2005). Both poor nutrition and the potential for experiencing a traumatic injury are quintupled among the children of homeless families (Bassuk, Konnath, & Volk, 2006).

Optimizing each child's course of development requires that new social policy lead to improved home environments, upgraded nutrition, and the removal of dangerous components in the child's environment. Homes with educational toys, children's books, and parents interested in promoting their child's skills complete the needs for a optimally developing young child.

Other reasons a child may not reach a benchmark in a timely manner are congenital and physical in origin (Wong et al., 2001). These chronic problems may be related to a genetic anomaly (e.g., spina bifida) or exposure to an infectious disease (e.g., viruses producing a high fever, temperature ≥ 104° F).[4]

Most public schools have a school nurse who can serve as the person most responsible for the health screening of children while preschools rely on the early childhood teachers to take that responsibility. Case in Point 7.1 presents an example of how early childhood teachers can learn about medical status examinations for young children.

Case in Point 7.1

Annual Medical Status Screenings for Young Children

One university has a 75-student Child Development Center in the School of Education. In this program, the undergraduate students in the early childhood education program have a number of preservice field experiences in the center. One of these experiences involves being paired with an undergraduate student nurse taking a field-based course in pediatric nursing. These students work together under the supervision of a nursing preceptor and the children's parents. In this process, the student nurse learns to provide annual medical status screenings to young children. The teacher education student comes to better understand the medical status assessment process.

Each day, 125,000 children below the age of 5 are too sick to go to their child care program or preschool (National Association for Sick Child Daycare, 2000). A small number of child care centers provide a "sick child" care program as part of the center. These centers tend to be larger than average and are sponsored by organizations that can afford to staff a "sick bay" for children. Hospitals often provide this service for the parents who use the medical center's child care services. See Table 7.2 for a child health checklist for parents who are planning to start their child in a child care program or preschool.

Table 7.2 Back-to-School Health Checklist

For distribution to parents applying to enroll a child in a child care or preschool program.

- Have your toddler's vision and hearing screened. It is important for young children to have a vision screening by age 2. Parents can observe when toddlers have hearing problems. A child who listens to the television or music at a very high volume, or tends to favor one ear over the other when listening may be showing a sign of a hearing problem.
- Make sure your child's immunizations are up-to-date. Schools and many centers will not let a child enroll without a record of complete immunizations. Check to see if your child meets the new program's regulations.

- If you see your toddler scratching his or her scalp, it may be a sign that a case of lice was contracted during the summer. It is important that you check your child's head or show the problem to your pediatrician. Head lice will not go away without treatment, but can be cured with over-the-counter remedies.
- Child care workers and teachers must be made aware of your child's needs, especially if they are the ones who administer medicine. If your child receives medication on a regular basis for diabetes, asthma, or another chronic problem, teachers or school nurses must be informed. Work out an emergency course of action in case of a problem.
- Share any information about possible learning problems your child may have with the school or program when the child is enrolled.
- Select a developmentally appropriate backpack with wide padded shoulder straps and a padded back. Do not let him/her overfill the backpack.
- Most children are naturally anxious about being with strangers for large blocks of time. It normally takes about a month for children to adjust to new situations. Work with your child's teachers to ease your child's transition. Also, review "stranger safety" so that your child knows not to accept treats, rides, or help looking for lost pets from an adult stranger.
- Studies show that young children who eat a nutritious breakfast are more alert and learn more efficiently. Also, be sure that your child has a balanced, nutritious lunch, whether it is one you send or one provided by the school or program.

SOURCE: Adapted from Gallin, P., (2007). *Pediatrician's back-to-school health check list.* New York: Morgan Stanley Children's Hospital of New York-Presbyterian Medical Center, http://www.newswise.com/articles/view/532185.

Developmental Assessments

All parents have theories about the development of their children that include a myriad of issues. These may include the influence of family genetics, whether the child was bottle- or breast-fed, the role of birth order, the relationship among siblings, the interactions the child has with others beyond the family, child care arrangements, having a mother or father stay at home to be a full-time parent, and the toys provided to the child. These issues, and many more, are variables studied by developmental psychologists. One outcome of this science of child growth and development is the developmental inventories provided to educators, psychologists, and physicians. These instruments are carefully standardized assessments used for charting child growth and development. They make it possible to compare a child's growth status against a normative population of children who represent all children at the same age. The first of these developmental assessments was the product of Arnold Gesell at Yale University in 1940 (see Chapter 1). Once a domain of a child's development is identified as measuring below the normal expected range for the child's age, the next step in the process is to formulate an intervention plan.

Intervention plans must involve the child's parents as partners in the process. The plasticity of the developmental processes makes it possible for young children to make rapid strides toward catching up with their same-age peers. Periodic developmental screenings or even full developmental assessments should continue to be conducted to chart the child's growth toward achieving his or her full potential.

Beginning at age 3, most states require children receiving **Early Childhood Special Education** services be reevaluated every six months. Below age 3, the reevaluations are conducted in support of **Early Intervention (EI)** programs. These programs require children receiving services to have a reevaluation every six months and a full multidisciplinary team evaluation annually (see Chapter 11). Other evaluations may also be required as specified by the Individual Family Service Plan committee (see Chapter 11). See Case in Point 7.2 for an example of a clinical referral.

Case in Point 7.2

Referral Outcome

Dan, a 36-month-old child, was brought by his parents to the University Medical Center for an evaluation by a pediatric neurologist. At the age of 22 months, Danny had developed a very high fever and flu-like symptoms. His parents waited out the fever that took four days to break. By the age of 30 months, Danny's child care center director requested that he be given a developmental screening test. The results from an administration of the Bayley-III Screening test showed that Dan was significantly behind his age norm on the cognitive and language subscales.

Subsequently, a neurological assessment was conducted in the office of a licensed physician with board certification in neurology. This examination found that Danny was in the normal range, and exhibited no pathformic indications. The neurologist referred Dan to a pediatric audiologist who found that Danny had lost 70% of his hearing in the left ear and 90% in the right. The audiologist fitted Danny with two hearing aids, and his parents returned him to the child care program.[5] A follow-up developmental screening at age 3.5 years found that he was functioning in the normal range in all domains of the assessment.

Developmental Assessment Administrator Training

Testing young children presents special problems unique to their developmental level. The issues of attention span, language ability, and emotional strength must all be considered when preparing to assess a young child. Published assessment tools including developmental screening measures must be used following the protocol delineated in the examiners manual. The interpretation of scores requires the examiner to have a good understanding of statistical scoring systems and/or **criterion measures** and cut scores. No assessment tool should be used until the examiner has been educated in its use and scoring system. The best way to learn to be a test administrator with young children is by having supervised practice in the test's use.

American Psychological Association (APA) Assessment Training Levels

APA provided a three-level classification (A, B, C) of qualifications for test administrators. The APA qualification statement was a part of the association's first ethical statement published in 1950. Even though other statements on qualifications and ethics have superseded it, the original three-level model continues to be widely used today by publishing houses to limit sale of their product lines to educators and clinicians capable of correctly using testing materials.[6]

Level A: Qualification requires that the individual has an ethical need to use these measures. No specialized education in testing and assessment is required. This level of qualification includes most classroom teachers. The types of measures appropriate at this level include curriculum probes and standardized group-administered tests.

Level B: Educators qualified to use B-level tests and assessments must have earned a master's in education or psychology (or related field), and have specific training in measurement including measurement statistics.

Teachers with collegiate education in child development and early childhood assessment may also qualify at Level B without a master's degree. Membership in a professional organization requiring its members be well qualified in test administration and interpretation also qualify at Level B. These organizations include, among others, the American Counseling Association, the International Reading Association, and the American Speech-Language-Hearing Association. Level B includes most group-administered tests of intelligence, **attention deficit disorder (ADD)** scales, and developmental measures.

Level C: These measures require the individual be highly educated and have had advanced training in educational and psychological measurements. Typically, these people hold a doctorate in educational or school psychology, or a have a Ph.D. in a clinical field in psychology. They hold advanced licensure from a state agency and are members of professional associations such as the American Psychological Association or the National Association of School Psychologists. These professional associations require adherence to an ethical cannon related to education and training of those using C-level tests. These measures include most individually administered tests of intelligence and personality.

Developmental Screening Assessments

There are a number of widely used developmental screening assessments appropriate for evaluating young children (see Photo 7.2). This chapter provides a description of six measures designed as **developmental screening assessments**. These screening assessments are designed to require a short time to administer and score, and be less expensive to purchase and use than the larger developmental inventories and assessment batteries.[7]

Photo 7.2 Child Completing a Developmental Screening Test

Early Screening Inventory–Revised (ESI-R)

ESI-R is designed to measure children at risk for school failure. It has two forms, one for children between the ages of 36 and 54 months, and one for children up to 6 years. ESI-R[8] has both English and Spanish language versions (Meisels, Marsden, Wiske, & Henderson, 1997). The test assesses three areas of child development: Visual Motor-Adaptive, Language and Cognition, and Gross Motor. ESI-R provides a method for combining scores from three areas into a single score. Additionally, the measurement provides a supplemental parent questionnaire. ESI-R is published by Pearson Education and requires a Level B education to administer. The 2009 cost for the test is $134.95 for each of the two parts in English or Spanish (3 years to 4½ years, and 4½ to 6 years).

ESI-R requires 20 minutes to administer and can identify children who may need special education and/or early intervention. It provides first-time users with inservice information via video. A national sample of 6,000 children was used to establish its statistical basis. Test–retest reliability is also at an appro-

"My Thaddeus was assessed by a child psychologist and found to be developmentally superior in every area but the 'social emotional' dimension"

SOURCE: Cartoon by Merv Magus.

priate level, resulting in low standard error of measurement values. The interrater reliability correlations are very high. ESI-R demonstrates concurrent validity with other instruments. ESI-R was described by one reviewer as the "gold standard" of screening measures (Kimmel & Paget, 2001). As a screening instrument, it is only a first step in the process of collecting the data needed to make entitlement and placement decisions.[9]

Neonatal Behavioral Assessment Scale, 3rd ed. (NBAS-III)

NBAS-III is an assessment of the developmental status of newborn infants. It is designed to measure infants below 2 months of age. It requires a significant amount of advanced or graduate-level training in its use by professionals in child development or medicine (Brazelton & Nugent, 1995). This screening measure focuses on the infant's behaviors clustered in seven areas: Reflexes, Autonomic System, Organizational Status, Regulation Status, Motor System, Habituation, and Social-Interaction. There are seven supplementary items that are able to assess the impact of fetal alcohol and or drug exposure.

The authors do not provide information about the scale's normative sample. It is also lacking information about reliability and validity. This makes the NBAS-III an assessment that must be interpreted with caution (McGregor, 2001). The screening assessment requires about 25 minutes to administer by a well-trained medical professional. It is published by Oxford University Press and sold for $64.95 (2009).

Bayley Scales of Infant and Toddler Development, 3rd ed., Screening Test (Bayley-III Screening)

This individually administered screening test is a quick assessment of children between the ages of one month and 42 months. It was originally designed to provide an indication of whether a child is progressing normally, or at risk for a **developmental delay** and needing further evaluation. It provides three subscales: Cognitive, Language, and Motor Abilities. The Cognitive subtest has 33 items in four domains: exploration, response to novelty, problem solving, and play-related tasks. The Bayley-III Screening Language Development subtest includes 24 items measuring receptive language. Another 24 items that measure expressive language skills are part of the Language Development subtest.

Its Motor Abilities subtest is composed of 27 fine and 28 gross motor items. The administration requires 20 minutes for children under the age of 12 months and 30–40 minutes for children over one year of age. Any teacher can administer the Bayley-III Screening, but only a person with a B level of training should interpret the scores from its administration (Bayley, 2006). Pearson Education sells the Bayley-III Screening for $205.00 (2009).

Bayley-III Screening was standardized on a sample of 1,700 infants and toddlers (Doggett & Johnson-Gros, 2007). This standardization group was selected to match the U.S. Census data for family location, socioeconomic status (SES), and ethnicity. The reliability (internal consistency) of the scales is good, ranging around $r = 0.82$. It was also used with a population of children ($N = 622$) born with a range of neuromotor and developmental disabilities and found to be a highly reliable measure. Test–retest (7-day interval) found the Bayley-III Screening to be a stable measure ($r = 0.83$). Also, interrater reliability with independent assessors is very high ($r = 0.96$).

Denver Developmental Screening Test, 2nd ed. (Denver-II)

This individually administered screening measure is used with children between birth and 6 years. Denver-II is widely used in pediatric practice, where it assesses infants at risk for developmental delay (Frankenburg, 1974). The Denver-II is also employed as a screening method for the development of language skills and physical abilities of infants, toddlers, and young children in child care centers. The test materials are quotidian, and highly appealing (Frankenburg et al., 1990). Administrators of this test should be well trained (Level B) and have specific training in using the Denver-II. Its administration requires 25 minutes plus time for scoring and interpretation. Denver-II is also published in Spanish by Denver Developmental Materials, and either version costs $111.00 (2009).

Denver-II provides 125 items covering four developmental dimensions: Personal-Social, Fine Motor Adaptive, Language, and Gross Motor (Hughes & Mirenda, 1995). It was normed on a sample of 2,096 children representative of the population of Colorado, giving the norming sample good Hispanic representation. The scoring system provided age points where 25%, 50%, 75%, and 90% of the sample (at that age) passed the item. There are also five behaviors assessed through guided observations: Attention Span, Fearfulness, Interest in Surroundings, Compliance, and Typical Behavior.

What is missing from the assessment is a measure of receptive language. Another problem with the administration and scoring of the Denver-II is that it tends to underestimate the possibility that a child is at risk. Some of the tasks that the child is asked to do during the test's administration require previous learning. For example, one task requires the child build a tower by stacking three one-inch blocks upon each other. If children have never played with blocks, this may be an issue causing failure, when with a little practice the youngster could do the task.

Ages and Stages Questionnaire, 3rd ed. (ASQ-III)

This developmental screening measure is a series of 19 questionnaires each with 30 questions completed by parents. Each of the 19 questionnaires assesses child development for one particular age group from 4 to 60 months. Every two to six months, the ASQ-III questionnaire changes, reflecting the child's age (Boyce & Poteat, 2005). ASQ-III is a system for monitoring a child's development and screening for potential problems.

ASQ-III was developed to complete the picture of a child provided by developmental screenings (see a page from the ASQ III in Figure 7.1). Its authors aver that medically oriented developmental screening measures, such as Denver-II, do not predict which children will experience problems in school (Bricker et al., 1999).

The ASQ-III's questionnaire items cover five major dimensions:

1. *Communication.* Recognition of the names for body parts, sentence formation, explaining a picture, and so on.

2. *Gross Motor.* Running, stair climbing, jumping, and so on.

3. *Fine Motor.* Use of a crayon to draw lines and circles, cutting with scissors, and so on.

4. *Problem Solving.* Can recreate an array of blocks, use of tools (step stool), and so on.

5. *Personal-Social.* Dressing, eating behavior, recognition of mirror images, and so on.

Figure 7.1 A Page From the ASQ-III Questionnaire at 48 Months

Communication

Be sure to try each activity with your child.

	Yes	Sometimes	Not Yet
1. Does your child name at least three items from a common category? For example, if you say to your child, "Tell me some things that you can eat," does your child answer with something like, "Cookies, eggs, and cereal"? Or if you say, "Tell me the names of some animals," does your child answer with something like, "Cow, dog, and elephant"?	❐	❐	❐
2. Does your child answer the following questions: "What do you do when you are hungry?" (Acceptable answers include "Get food," "Eat," "Ask for something to eat," and "Have a snack.") Please write your child's response: ____________ "What do you do when you are tired?" (Acceptable answers include "Take a nap," "Rest," "Go to sleep," "Go to bed," "Lie down," and "Sit down.") Please write your child's response: ____________ Mark "sometimes" if your child answers only one question.	❐	❐	❐
3. Does your child tell you at least two things about common objects? For example, if you say to your child, "Tell me about your ball," does he/she say something like, "It's round. I throw it. It's big"?	❐	❐	❐
4. Does your child use endings of words, such as "s," "ed," and "ing"? For example, does your child say things like, "I see two cat*s,*" "I am play*ing,*" or "I kick*ed* the ball"?	❐	❐	❐
5. Without giving help by pointing or repeating, does your child follow three directions that are unrelated to one another? For example, you may ask your child to "Clap your hands, walk to the door, and sit down."	❐	❐	❐
6. Do your child use all of the words in a sentence (for example, "a," "the," "am," "is," and "are") to make complete sentences, such as "I *am* going to *the* park," or "*Is* there *a* toy to play with?" or "*Are* you coming, too?"	❐	❐	❐

More of the ASQ can be accessed at http://www.agesandstages.com/.

SOURCE: Adapted from http://www.pbrookes.com/store/books/bricker-asq/faq.htm.

ASQ-III provides an early warning of a possible developmental disorder (Bricker et al., 1999). Its primary goal is making early intervention on behalf of the child possible. ASQ-III is available in English, French, Korean, and Spanish; the English language version is available online from the University of Oregon (see http://www.uoregon.edu/~eip/asq.html). This online process takes about 15 minutes for parents to complete. Later, parents are sent an analysis of the child's developmental status. Within a few days, other information including suggestions of activities that parents can complete with the child are sent online. Questionnaires can also be mailed back to the scoring center.

The unusual approach of having the child's parents serve as the sole source of data from the questionnaires was one that was well tested and found to have **concurrent validity** (Knobloch, Stevens, Malone, Ellison, & Risemburg, 1979). It is appropriate for all SES levels employing language below the sixth grade reading level. ASQ-III had marginal reliability (Cronbach alpha ≅ 0.67). Questionnaire stability (reliability) improves with the age of the child.

ASQ-III normative samples are based on 18,000 questionnaires that have been returned for scoring. No clear data are available on the 2009 ASQ III as to the normative breakdown of that sample of tested children. The publisher only states that the questionnaire has "high reliability with an alpha over > 90." Hispanic children were underrepresented with the English language version of the measure, and Native Americans were oversampled with the older edition (Boyce & Poteat, 2005). Teachers with an A level of education can use it.

Validity of the earlier version, the ASQ-II, was found as the concordance of placement recommendations based on ASQ-II scores and the placement recommendations from other recognized assessments—the Bayley Scales of Infant and Toddler Development and the Stanford-Binet Scales of Intelligence. ASQ-III is published by Brookes and costs about $249.95.[10]

Child Development Inventory (CDI)

The CDI is a developmental screening assessment designed for children between 15 and 75 months. CDI requires between 30 and 60 minutes to administer. Its first edition, Minnesota Child Development Inventory, was published in 1968. It was redesigned and republished in 1992 as the Child Development Inventory (CDI) (Ireton, 1992). The CDI's manual was revised and updated in 2005 (Harold Ireton, personal communication, February 2008). Criticism is focused on the narrow normative group sample (569 white children from Minneapolis–St. Paul) (Kirnan & Crespo, 1998). The author defended this sample by reinstating the arguments of Arnold Gesell—that the best norm is one that demonstrates what is typical for development.

The normative sampling problem was addressed in part by Joseph Byrne, Joseph Backman, and Jane Bawden (1995), who used the CDI to assess 1,322 Canadians (Nova Scotia) between 12 and 49 months old. These data never became part of the CDI scoring system but provide another source for comparison. While adding to the available comparative data, the problem of ethnic and geographic diversity is still unaddressed.

CDI requires as long as an hour to administer and score by a teacher with an A level of education. It measures eight domains of development and provides a general development score. Subtests include Social, Self-help, Gross Motor, Fine Motor, Expressive Language, Language Comprehension, Letters, and Numbers. Its kit includes a 300-item parent questionnaire. Cost is a major advantage of the CDI; a complete kit costs $82.40 (2009). Pearson Education publishes the CDI.

For a summary of these screening measures covered in this section, see Table 7.3.

Table 7.3 Developmental Screening Assessments

Measurement	Measurement Subtests	Age Range	Time to Administer	Publisher	Cost (2009)
Early Screening Inventory–Revised (ESI-R)	Visual Motor-Adaptive, Language and Cognition, and Gross Motor	3 to 4½ years, and 4½ to 6 years	20 minutes	Pearson	$134.95
Neonatal Behavioral Assessment Scale, 3rd ed. (NBAS-III)	Reflexes, Autonomic System, Organizational Status, Regulation Status, Motor System, Habituation, and Social-Interaction	Birth to 2 months	25 minutes	Oxford University Press	$64.95
Bayley Scales of Infant and Toddler Development, 3rd ed., Screening Test (Bayley-III Screening)	Cognitive, Language, and Motor Abilities	Birth to 42 months	20 to 40 minutes	Pearson	$205.00
Denver Developmental Screening Test, 2nd ed. (Denver-II)	Personal-Social, Fine Motor Adaptive, Language, and Gross Motor	Birth to 6 years	25 minutes	Denver Developmental Materials	$111.00
Ages and Stages Questionnaire, 3rd ed. (ASQ-III)	Communication, Gross Motor, Fine Motor, Problem Solving, and Personal-Social	4 months to 6 years	15 minutes	Brookes	$249.95
Child Development Inventory (CDI)	Social, Self-help, Gross Motor, Fine Motor, Expressive Language, Language Comprehension, Letters, Numbers, and General Development	15 months to 6 years	30 to 60 minutes	Pearson	$82.40

SOURCE: Adapted from the following manuals: *Neonatal Behavioral Assessment Scale 3rd ed.*, (Oxford University Press), *Bayley Scales of Infant and Toddler Development, 3rd ed.* and *Screening, Child Development Inventory* (Pearson Education), *Denver Developmental Screening Test, 2nd ed.* (Denver Developmental Materials), and *Ages and Stages Questionnaire, 2nd ed.* (Brookes Publishing).

Developmental Inventories and Curriculum-Based Assessment

Once a screening test indicates a child may be at risk for a developmental delay, the next step involves a larger evaluation of the child. This chapter describes five measures that are large-scale **developmental inventories** or batteries. Developmental inventories are age normed based on a large population to provide a reliable method for differentiating between children and provide valid data for making entitlement decisions (see Case in Point 7.3 for an example of the use of screening instruments).

Case in Point 7.3

Use of Screening Measures and Developmental Assessments

Toni (age 36 months) was having difficulty listening and following directions at her preschool. Her teacher felt there was a possible problem with her receptive and expressive language skills. With parental approval and assistance, her teacher used a screening measure to make an initial assessment of Toni's status at 40 months using the Bayley-III Screening. This administration was while Toni attended her prekindergarten located in a public elementary school. A fully certified teacher carried out testing with Toni's mother in the room.

Toni scored below average on the three subtests of the Bayley Scales of Infant and Toddler Development, 3rd ed., Screening Test. Toni was then referred to the University Medical Center, Division of Pediatric Medicine, for further evaluation.

The assessment materials used by the psychologist at the University Medical Center included the Mullen Scales of Early Learning (Mullen), the Assessment, Evaluation, and Programming System for Infants and Toddlers, Revised (AEPS-R), the Adaptive Behavior Assessment System, 2nd ed. (ABAS-II), and the Childhood Autism Rating Scale (CARS) (see Chapter 11). The evaluation also included an examination by a board certified child psychiatrist. Clinical observations were made of Toni's muscle tone, balance, coordination, motor planning, postural control, attention to task, and quality of movement. The child psychiatrist also interviewed her mother. A state board certified audiologist conducted an audiological examination. Data from all of these assessments were summarized in a final evaluation report from the Division of Pediatric Medicine. That report noted that all of Toni's scores were in the low-normal range. It concluded that Toni presented no clear evidence suggesting a significant cognitive or neurological problem.

The final decision was not to recommend placement in early special education. A reevaluation was recommended in six months.

NOTE: Abstracted from an actual case report.

Unlike the developmental inventories, curriculum-based assessments are designed using items that have a high educational value and therapeutic relevancy. These items can diagnose a problem and provide a key to remediation. Their use can support and provide a model for understanding the developmental problems identified by the developmental inventories.

Assessment, Evaluation, and Programming System for Infants and Children, Revised (APES-R)

The APES-R is a curriculum-based assessment of the developmental progress of a child and a method of intervention. Brookes Publishing sells it for $239.00 (2009). AEPS-R has two tests; one is for birth to age 36 months, and the other for 3 through 6 years. It provides content needed to write objectives and goals for Individual Family Service Plans, and a way to track a child's progress. It can be a standalone measure but during evaluations is typically paired with developmental assessment.

AEPS-R provides scores covering six domains of development: Fine Motor, Gross Motor, Adaptive Behavior, Cognitive, Social-Communication, and Social Development (Bricker et al., 1993). The AEPS-R and the ASQ-III share an author, Diane Bricker. While the ASQ-III requires little background to administer, she recommends teachers receive specific training before using the AEPS-R. AEPS-R involves a series of activities and toys for the child to manipulate. Each of the six areas is scored as 0 indicating the child is not ready for the task or skill, 1 indicating the child is partially able to do the task, and 2 indicating mastery. The scores are combined in each of the six areas to create subtotals (Bricker & Cripe, 1992). Cut scores are published with the material to provide a standard needed to make entitlement decisions (Bricker et al., 2007).

Cut scores were established by testing a sample of 1,381 normal children and 662 children enrolled in early intervention and early special education. Comparing scores on the six domains between the two groups analyzed, the AEPS demonstrated the validity of its scores. AEPS-R must be interpreted with caution as the reliability of scores and the details of the two samples are not described.

Brigance Inventory of Early Development, 2nd ed. (IED-II)

IED-II is a developmental inventory designed to assess children between birth and the **developmental age** of 7 years. It is a complex instrument requiring examiners to have a B level of education, and complete training with the Brigance IED-II. It is sold by Curriculum Associates for $259.00 and the scoring software is another $99.00 (2009).

IED-II measures five broad domains and 14 subdomains of development (Brigance & Glascoe, 2004). It uses a criterion-based scoring system providing information useful in monitoring and evaluating children with special needs.

IED-II also provides **composite scores** based on a marginal normative sample of 1,171 children (A. Davis & Holmes, 2007). While nationally representative, the sample was skewed by an excess of at-risk children identified by **Child Find**[11] and too few children between 5 and 7 years. Test–retest reliability (1 week) found the IES-II to be stable, and it has good internal consistency ($r = 0.85$) (A. Davis & Holmes, 2007).

In addition to direct measurement of the child, administration of the full IED-II battery requires an examiner interview both parents and teachers and observe the child's behaviors. The requirement for observational data implies specialized education is required for examiners. The IED-II does not provide information as to the degree of agreement (**concordance**) between two or more observers (interrater reliability).

The Brigance IED-II has had several of its components adopted by state education departments and large city school systems as the assessment tool of choice for the evaluation of state-funded preschool programs and for monitoring young children receiving special education intervention.[12] The Brigance IED-II can be used in the development of an Individual Family Service Plan (IFSP) (see Chapter 11 for more about special education). The IED-II can be used to follow the growth and development of **special needs children** once a child and his/her family are receiving services through Early Intervention.

The Brigance is a well-known, widely used assessment tool appropriate for infants, toddlers, and preschool-age children. It has a superior manual that can be purchased separately for $99.00 and a software-based report writing system for $59.95.

Bayley Scales of Infant and Toddler Development, 3rd ed. (Bayley-III)

Goals for the Bayley-III are to identify and evaluate deficits in a child's development, and to assist in intervention planning. The Bayley-III is a comprehensive assessment battery providing five scales measuring Adaptive Behavior (Conceptual, Social, and Practical), Cognitive Development, Language Development (Expressive and Receptive), Motor Skills (Fine and Gross), and Social-Emotional. It can be used in assessing children between one month and 42 months. The Bayley-III also provides a system for charting a child's growth over time, and calculating a reliable growth score. This feature makes the Bayley-III a good instrument in Early Intervention programs for documenting the impact of the efforts.

The Bayley-III is priced by Pearson Education at $1,039.00 (2009), and requires a high degree of education (Level C) to purchase and use. Bayley-III requires from one and a half to two hours to assess children over one year in age (Bayley, 2006).

The scales for measuring Social-Emotional development and Adaptive Behavior functioning use a parent questionnaire. Other subtests, Cognitive, Language, and Motor, collect data in playlike situations involving the child and his/her parents. This format optimizes infant or toddler performance on the tasks. The parent presents tasks on some subtests, while the test administrator collects data concurrently.

The Bayley-III is well conceived and technically sound. Its norm base of 1,700 was well selected and is representative of the American population (Tobin, Hoff, & Venn, 2007). Its subtests have high internal consistency, and high reliability is reported for different age groups (average $r \cong 0.86$). The Bayley-III manual presents studies describing score patterns with various special populations of infants and toddlers. The Bayley-III has found a special niche in helping children of parents who are on military deployments (see Case in Point 7.4).

Case in Point 7.4

Measuring the Impact of Parental Separation

The ongoing wars in the Middle East have brought with them an emotional toll being paid by families back home. By 2010, approximately 1 million of the troops deployed into war zones in Iraq and Afghanistan were parents (Ramirez, 2009). About a quarter of them have been deployed into combat two or more times. About 11 out of 12 of the deployed parents are the fathers of young children.

All deployments to a war zone can be disruptive and anxiety provoking to young children; but multiple deployments can be emotionally damaging on children, especially preschool children. Army pediatricians have reported an increase in stress-related illnesses among young children on posts where many parents are being shipped out (Glod, 2008). The greatest negative impact occurs among children between 3 and 5 years of age (Chartrand, Frank, White, & Shope, 2008). These children exhibited increased levels of acting out behaviors including hitting, biting, and hyperactivity.

A new *Sesame Street* video for military families depicts the Muppet character of Elmo turning to his mom and friends for support during his dad's deployment. A second video portrays a bilingual Muppet character, Rosita, being reunited with her father who returned from his deployment in a wheelchair (Jowers, 2008).

Preschool counselors on a number of bases have begun to employ standardized measures of social–emotional development to track changes ongoing in children when a parent is going in harm's way.[13] Among these measures is the Bayley-III subtest for Social–Emotional Development. Family counseling combined with individual play therapy are frequently used if the child scores low on the assessment.

Battelle Developmental Inventory, 2nd ed. (BDI-2)

The BDI-2 is an individually administered, criterion-referenced, developmental assessment that has been standardized for children from birth to age 7 years, 11 months (Newborg, 2005). BDI-2 is a large assessment requiring over two hours to administer and score. It provides scores in five different dimensions: Cognitive (COG), Adaptive (ADP), Personal Social (P-S), Communication (COM), and Motor (MOT). Each has several scored subdomains (see Table 7.4). The total assessment contains 450 items, but each age level is measured with different subdomain tests. It provides a 100-item, quick-screening assessment (20 items from each domain) requiring a half hour to administer.

Table 7.4 Battelle Developmental Inventory, 2nd ed.: Domains and Subdomains

Domains	Subdomains
Cognitive (COG)	Attention and Memory (30 items) Reasoning and Academic Skills (35 items) Perception and Concepts (40 items)
Adaptive (ADP)	Self-care (35 items) Peer Interaction (25 items)
Personal Social (P-S)	Adult Interactions (30 items) Peer Interaction (25 items) Self-concept and Social Role (45 items)
Communication (COM)	Receptive Communication (40 items) Expressive Communication (45 items)
Motor (MOT)	Gross Motor (45 items) Fine Motor (30 items) Perceptual Motor (25 items)

SOURCE: Adapted from the following manual: *Battelle Developmental Inventory, 2nd ed.*

Criteria used for item selection included whether it measures a skill or ability important for the child's normal functioning and whether it was an area that could be improved through intervention. BDI-2's criterion-referenced format is a good format for following up with children receiving special education services.

BDI-2 is a complex test requiring a B level of education, plus specific training in its administration. Because of its length and complexity, young children will need rest periods during testing. Examiners can encourage and praise the child as a motivational method during the assessment. It is normal for a parent to be present during the administration of the BDI-2 to preschool children.

This assessment is widely used by child development specialists working for state agencies on tasks related to identifying and providing service to young children at risk for developmental disabilities. It is used in writing Individual Family Service Plans (IFSPs) and monitoring children's progress prior to public school kindergarten.

Research has demonstrated BDI-2 to be a valid and reliable assessment for the identification of toddlers experiencing developmental delays or at risk for cognitive disability (McLean, McCormick, Bruder, & Burdg, 1987). It is a proven and appropriate method for screening infants for disabilities (Boyd, Welge, Sexton, & Miller, 1989), and to identify speech and language disabilities in early childhood (Mott, 1987). The test was standardized on a sample of 2,500 children modeled around the U.S. population but missing children with disabilities (Athanasiou, 2007).

Overall, BDI-2 is an excellent developmental assessment that is an effective method for identifying and monitoring infants and young children at risk for a serious disability. It provides output keyed to the Head Start Outcome Framework (learning standards). It also provides a user-friendly score report for parents and teacher. This is an expensive measuring system, costing $985.00 for a full BDI-2 kit (2009).

Mullen Scales of Early Learning, AGS ed.

This developmental assessment covers the child's first 68 months. Mullen Scales requires test administrators to have a high level of preparation at Level C (Pearson Assessment Technical Support, personal communication, July 22, 2008). Testing requires about a half hour with children under 3 years and about an hour for older children (Mullen, 1995).

Children between birth and 33 months are measured along five domains of development: Gross Motor, Fine Motor, Visual Reception, Receptive Language, and Expressive Language. Between 34 months and 68 months, the scale does not measure Gross Motor functioning. The overall score is standardized and easily interpreted with a mean of 100 and standard deviation of 15. Its manual recommends that a score 1.5 standard deviations below the mean on the total scale (7th percentile) is indicative of developmental delay. Also, subtest scores two standard deviations below the mean (second percentile) indicate developmental delay (Mullen, 1995).

Mullen Scales's reliability is good ($r \cong 0.80$) with interrater reliability very high ($r \cong 0.95$). The norm group is dated but was very representative of the population of 1,849 children in 1990 (Chittooran & Kessler, 2001).

Overall, the Mullen Scales of Early Learning is a good assessment of early cognitive and motor skills. It is available from Pearson Education for $770.00 (2009).

For an overview of the assessments in this section, see Table 7.5.

Table 7.5 Developmental Inventories and Curriculum Assessments

Measurement	Measurement Subtests	Age Range	Time to Administer	Publisher	Cost (2009)
Assessment, Evaluation, and Programming System for Infants and Children, Revised (APES-R)	Fine Motor, Gross Motor, Adaptive Behavior, Cognitive, Social-Communication, and Social Development	Birth to 36 months, and 3 to 6 years	30 minutes	Brookes	$239.00
Brigance Inventory of Early Development, 2nd ed. (IED-II)	Motor Skills (Fine and Gross), Language Skills, Academic/Cognitive, and Daily Living, Language Skills, and Academic/ Cognitive	Birth to 7 years	No time frame published	Curriculum Associates	$358.00
Bayley Scales of Infant and Toddler Development, 3rd ed. (Bayley-III)	Adaptive Behavior, Cognitive Development, Language Development, Motor Skills, and Social–Emotional	One to 42 months	From 1.5 to 2 hours	Pearson	$1,039.00
Battelle Developmental Inventory, 2nd ed. (BDI-2)	Cognitive, Adaptive, Personal Social, Communication, and Motor	Birth to 8 years	2 hours	Riverside	$985.00
Mullen Scales of Early Learning, AGS ed.	Gross Motor, Fine Motor, Visual Reception, Receptive Language, and Expressive Language	Birth to 68 months	30 to 60 minutes	Pearson	$770.00

SOURCE: Adapted from the following manuals: *Assessment Evaluation and Programming System for Infants and Children* (Brookes Publishing), *Brigance Diagnostic Inventory of Early Development, 2nd ed.* (Curriculum Associates), *Battelle Developmental Inventory, 2nd ed.* (Riverside Publishing), *Mullen Scales of Early Learning, and Bayley Scales of Infant and Toddler Development, 3rd ed.* (Pearson Education).

Summary

Medical workers are the first to assess and make professional judgments about the growth and development of infants. The child psychologist and pediatrician, Arnold Gesell, first published standardized measures of child development in the 1920s. An alternative approach to developmental assessments is provided by curriculum-based approaches to evaluation. The Assessment, Evaluation, and Programming System for Infants and Children, Revised, provides an example of this alternative.

Screening tests are employed to make a quick assessment that can identify children who warrant a more detailed assessment with a developmental inventory. Among these are Early Screening Inventory–Revised (ESI-R); Neonatal Behavioral Assessment Scale, 3rd ed.; Bayley Scales of Infant and Toddler Development, 3rd ed., Screening Test; Denver Developmental Screening Test, 2nd ed.; the Ages and Stages Questionnaire, 3rd ed.; and the Child Development Inventory.

Age-normed developmental assessments reviewed for the chapter are the Assessment, Evaluation, and Programming System for Infants and Children, Revised; Brigance Inventory of Early Development, 2nd ed.; Bayley Scales of Infant and Toddler Development, 3rd ed.; the Battelle Developmental Inventory, 2nd ed.; and the Mullen Scales of Early Learning, AGS ed.

Discussion Questions

1. Should child care centers be required to employ a certified school nurse? If you agree to this approach, how much should parents be charged for the extra service?
2. Should the parent of a sick child stay home from work to provide care or place the young child in the "sick bay" at their child care center? Explain your reasoning. How can a center pay for a "sick-bay?"
3. What are the advantages and disadvantages to using a developmental assessment such as the Bayley-III Screening with all incoming 2- and 3-year-old children in a child care center?
4. Families can be stressed by a number of circumstances including the deployment of a parent into a war zone. What signs should a teacher of toddlers use to identify a child's possible high level of personal stress?
5. How do measures like the Bayley-III differ from curriculum-based assessments?

Related Readings

Mertler, C. A. (2007). *Interpreting standardized test scores.* Thousand Oaks, CA: Sage.
Salkind, N. J. (2004). *An introduction to the theories of human development.* Thousand Oaks, CA: Sage.
Sprenger, M. B. (2008). *The developing brain: Birth to age eight.* Thousand Oaks, CA: Corwin Press.

Notes

1. A battery describes a measurement tool composed of two or more related, but independent, components.
2. Virginia Apgar was the first woman to be promoted to full professor of medicine at Columbia University's College of Physicians and Surgeons. In 1952, Dr. Apgar used her name as an acronym for the five subtests of her new measure of the status of newborn babies: A = appearance, P = pulse, G = grimace, A = activity, R = respiration. Her work was honored 20 years after her death in 1994 by the U.S. Postal Service when a stamp was issued in her honor (see http://www.u-s-history.com/pages/h1704.html).

3. At birth, infants exhibit reflexes that disappear over time. One is the tonic neck reflex or TNR. When placed on his/her back, the infant extends one arm out and turns the head in that direction. Another is the grasping reflex. When an adult finger or just a dowel is placed flat into the infants palm, his/her fingers automatically close on the adult's finger and squeeze with a reflexive strength that, once lost at three months, won't return in voluntary form for five years (Lowrey, 1974). The Babinski reflex (or Plantar reflex) occurs when an infant's heel is touched or a touch runs down the side of the child's foot. The infant's toes first spread, then close in a grasping movement (to see an example of the Babinski reflex go to http://video.google.com/videoplay?docid=7289405551860373128&ei=NzIsSpL3LYrcrgKM_4SmCg&q=Babinski+Reflex). Other primate species have similar reflexive mechanisms in their newborns. Among humans, these reflexes are thought to be vestiges of skills needed for survival among our quadrumanous ancestors (Thies & Travers, 2000).
4. In July of 2008, two researchers at the Howard Hughes Medical Center of the Harvard University School of Medicine identified a possible genetic cause for autism (Morrow et al., 2008). The characteristic appears to be a recessive anomaly.
5. Adults with similar levels of hearing loss often use only one hearing aid. Young children learning to locate sounds in a stereophonic environment are always fitted with two hearing aids.
6. Pearson Education, the country's largest test publisher, uses a similar system for qualifying people to use its products. The Pearson system has four levels. In addition to the old APA standards, the Pearson Company added a level Q for medical practitioners.
7. Several academic pediatricians have developed a developmental screening assessment. It is being marketed over the Internet directly to parents at a cost of $9.95 (2008). This online developmental screening for young children is designed to be answered by the parents. This screening is for children between the ages of 18 months and 48 months. It reports itself as being normed on a sample of 1,000 children and to have a reliability of 0.85. All of this would be more interesting if the authors had not elected to remain anonymous. The Web pages for this assessment can be found at http://www.forepath.org/index.php.
8. The acronym for this test, ESI-R, is often pronounced as "easy-r."
9. Assessments are measures on at least one dimension. A test is an assessment. An evaluation involves more than one assessment of a child. Evaluations are needed prior to making an entitlement decision regarding a child. For more on this, see Chapter 2.
10. The price includes all forms, license to reprint, training materials, and user's guide.
11. Child Find is a state-by-state mandated program under the 1997 reauthorization of the Individuals With Disabilities Education Act. The requirements are that each state initiate and follow through with programs designed for the early location, identification, and referral of children with disabilities and their families to Early Intervention services and/or early childhood special education services.
12. Those states and cities include Connecticut, New Hampshire, New York City, Oklahoma City, and Philadelphia.
13. Counselors working with children of active duty members of the armed services can never be dismissive of the real danger being faced by the parents who enter war zones. A mute testimony to these dangers can be seen in Zone 60 of Arlington National Cemetery, a section reserved for those killed in the Iraq and Afghanistan wars.

Cognitive Assessment of Young Children

8

There is no such [thing] as intelligence; one has intelligence of this or that. One must have intelligence only for what one is doing.

—Edgar Degas

Introduction and Themes

There are several reasons young children may need to have their cognitive ability assessed, including identification of problematic areas in cognition, and educational programming for children with special needs. Among the reasons why young children may have low levels of cognitive functioning are environmental influences, physical injury, diseases, and congenital abnormalities.

The first measure of cognitive ability was designed to help school officials in France identify children needing special education services. A century ago in America that French assessment took on a new form and role and quickly earned the sobriquet, IQ Test. This measure was used to support the notion of a meritocracy, whereby the best and brightest (as measured on an IQ test) were placed in advanced programs and tracked into college preparatory curricula.

In the United States, the assessment of cognitive ability began with the assumption of a general factor or core to all intelligence. Numerous psychologists, including contemporary writers such as Howard Gardner and Robert Sternberg, challenged this single-factor concept.

Recent editions of large-scale cognitive assessments report scores using multiple factors of ability. There are several screening tests that can be used by classroom teachers and counselors.

Learning Objectives

By reading and studying this chapter, you should acquire the competency to:

- Explain why the cognition of young children is measured.
- Describe several causes of low cognitive development among young children.
- Trace the development of the first measures of general cognitive ability.
- Discuss the concept of multiple factors of intelligence, and the writings of contemporary theorists including Howard Gardner and Robert Sternberg.

- Explain how screening tests and cognitive assessments are similar and different from one another.
- Explain why a false negative finding is more dangerous for a child than a false positive.
- Describe the measurement scales of the two versions of the current edition of the Stanford-Binet Intelligence Scales, and two of the Wechsler Intelligence Scales for Children.

Rationales for and Against Cognitive Assessments

Standardized measures of **cognitive ability** have been gatekeepers for getting a child needed special educational support. They also serve as the ultimate Ridwaan, selecting children for admission into academically gifted and talented programs.[1] Requirements for their use are part of special education regulations in the Individuals With Disabilities Education Act (IDEA, 1997). The reauthorization of the law (2004), known as the Individuals With Disabilities Education Improvement Act (IDEIA), opens the door to using alternative approaches to assessment when making entitlement decisions.

Cognitive assessments can also be used in program planning for a child needing special education. Smaller screening tests cannot fulfill this role, but larger assessments like the Woodcock-Johnson-III can be used to track a child's progress.

The use of screening measures and larger assessments of **mental ability** or cognitive functioning with children below the age of 4 can provide very misleading information (Neisworth & Bagnato, 2004). Traditional standardized ability measures are notoriously unreliable with children between ages 2 and 4. This reflects the rapid growth the child is experiencing in all cognitive dimensions.

Use of cognitive ability tests to label a child implies a belief in biological determinism. One result of the identification process can be lower expectations and the assumption that nothing more can be done. While there are congenital and intractable problems that can result in low test scores, for example, Down's syndrome, most cognitive problems can be remediated. Even more severe cognitive difficulties like those caused by Down's syndrome can be improved through early intervention (Wybranski, 1996).

Early screening of children can provide a quick and low-cost method of spotting children in need of a more thorough assessment. A downside of screening tools is possible errors and wrong calls. False positives from a screening (likely problem) are a minor concern, as the child will be identified correctly on a large cognitive assessment. False negatives (no problem) are a major issue. If a child is delayed in receiving needed interventions, small problems can become larger.

Environmental Factors in Cognitive Development

A child's cognitive screening indicating delayed or low cognitive development would normally be followed by a parent–teacher conference where the findings are explained. Next, with parental approval, he/she would be evaluated using full cognitive and developmental assessments.[2]

Causes of low cognitive functioning can be environmental. Children exposed to small amounts of **heavy metals** including lead (Pb^{++}) may experience cognitive loss. Lead may enter the child's blood when a toy or household object is mouthed. As little as 10 micrograms of lead in a deciliter of blood (10 µg/dl) causes neurological damage in children (Department of Health and Human Services, 2007b). Lead is found in the trim paint in older homes.[3] In addition, there were millions of toys manufactured in China that had to be destroyed because they were colored with lead paint (Lipton & Barboza, 2007). Lead has also been found in imported toothpaste, children's books, and furniture. Between 3 and 4 million American people have neurological damage caused by Pb^{++} poisoning, including 310,000 young children (Alliance for Healthy Homes, 2006). Other environmental hazards that adversely affect young children include arsenic (As^{+++}) used to treat lumber and in manufacturing insecticides and fertilizers (see Table 8.1 for data on inner-city heavy metal poisoning).

Table 8.1 Ten Top Cities for Lead Poisoning in 2003

City	Number Tested at ≥ 10 mcg/dl	Percentage Tested at ≥ 10 mcg/dl	Number of pre-1950 Housing Units	Percentage of pre-1950 Housing Units	Number of Children Tested	Percentage of Children Tested
Cleveland	2,329	14%	142,817	66%	16,461	36%
Philadelphia	4,384	11%	386,382	57%	38,767	33%
Buffalo	675	10%	106,351	73%	6,702	27%
Providence	992	9%	39,800	59%	11,008	75%
Milwaukee	1,999	9%	116,338	47%	22,904	40%
St. Louis	936	8%	95,091	65%	12,011	42%
Detroit	2,104	7%	210,588	56%	31,516	34%
Chicago	6,691	6%	602,934	52%	103,701	40%
Baltimore	1,030	5%	113,955	65%	20,294	41%
New York City	3,526	1%	1,642,098	51%	304,130	47%

SOURCE: Data from the Alliance for Healthy Homes, 2006, available at http://www.ehw.org/Lead/LEAD_home3.htm.

Hospitalization

Cognitive assessments are routinely included in a hospitalized child's medical status report. At the beginning of the 20th century, it was not uncommon for young children to die of illnesses, or traumatic injuries. Now, there are fewer mortalities, but many children still need hospitalization. Periodic reassessments typically follow hospitalization to monitor the child's recovery and progress.

Traumatic head injuries, including concussions, cause both short-term and long-term cognitive loss. Rules for how children are allowed to play have evolved to reduce such injuries. Today, children wear helmets when on bicycles, when playing baseball and football, and when on inline roller skates. These precautions reflect recent information about appropriate safety practices.

Impaired cognitive functioning may result from high fevers during childhood illnesses, neurological infections, and congenital brain abnormalities. Diseases most likely to cause cognitive loss and neurological damage are those related to *Haemophilus influenzae*, including bacterial meningitis. High fever (oral temperature ≥ 104° F) can accompany many childhood illnesses including diphtheria, tetanus, pertussis, polio, bacterial ear infections, measles, mumps, and rubella. The good news is that the risk of childhood diseases can be eliminated through vaccinations begun during early childhood. Unfortunately, many parents are eschewing vaccinations and exposing their children to illnesses out of a misguided fear that several vaccination series (DTaP, PCV IPV, and MMR) somehow cause autism.[4]

See Case in Point 8.1 for another potential influence on the development of cognitive ability.

Case in Point 8.1

Impact of Poverty on Infant Development

Cognitive neuroscientists have identified a link between the development of an infant's neurology and the environment of the child's home (Farah, Noble, & Hurt, 2005). The impact of an impoverished environment on an infant's developing neurology is equivalent to being born addicted to crack cocaine. When children were tested for IQ at school age, the Philadelphia-based researchers found that children of working class families born addicted to cocaine and those born into poverty without exposure to drugs both had average **IQ scores** of 79 (Monastersky, 2008). This is a borderline score indicating the child is functioning in the 9th percentile in cognitive ability.

Another environmental cause of low or abnormal cognitive functioning is prenatal maternal malnutrition. A child who has a low birth weight (less than 5.5 lbs.) is at increased risk for lower cognitive ability and at a higher risk for autism (Schendel & Bhasin, 2008).

First Measures of Cognition

In 1900, there were no dependable methods to assess cognitive functioning. This all changed when a lawyer, turned research psychologist, published the first workable assessment system for identifying children having a low potential for success in schools (Siegler, 1992). That psychologist, Alfred Binet, and his doctoral student, Theodore Simon, designed the first workable measure of cognitive functioning. The French government and La Société Pour l'Etude Psychologique de l'Enfant commissioned research that led to this publication in 1905.[5, 6] It also led to Alfred Binet being appointed to the prestigious Ministère Français de l'Instruction Publique.[7]

The Binet assessment was designed to estimate the mental age of children. This involved a collection of 30 tasks (*arrêts mentaux*, or mental stunts) beginning with the easiest that all neurologically sound children could do with success (e.g., the visual tracking of a light). Each item a child could pass led to the next slightly more difficult task, for example, "Show me your thumb." The point in the progression where the child could not pass any more items was used to set the child's upper cognitive limit. If a child was tested and passed all items up to what a typical 6-year-old should complete, but could not go beyond that point, he/she would earn a score of "Mental Age 6.0 years." In other words, he/she was measured as having the capacity to solve mental tasks at a level equivalent to that of a 6-year-old.

Binet never felt his measure could assess the great variety of ways cognitive ability is expressed in the many dimensions of a person's life (Du Bois, 1970). He died in 1911 before he could take a position on how the American version of his test had morphed into what was being described as a measure of genetically given intelligence.

It did not take long for the measurement designed to identify French children in need of special education to be changed into something very different. First, Henry H. Goddard, director of research of the Vineland Training School for Feeble Minded Boys and Girls (New Jersey), made a simple English translation of the Binet scale (Goddard, 1920). He then distributed 22,000 copies of that anglicized and lengthened Parisian measure to schools and hospitals throughout the country. The Goddard version increased the number of mental tasks from 30 to 58 to expand its scope into other age groups. Goddard never conducted measurement research needed to ensure test validity. His measure was not well standardized and its item difficulty levels of questions translated from French to English were inconsistent. This notwithstanding, he was positive that he could identify mentally defective people of any age with his instrument.

Figure 8.1 provides a slide rule used by psychologists in the 1920s to calculate IQ using mental age and chronological age.

Figure 8.1 The IQ Slide Rule First Developed by Samuel Camin Kohs of Reed College (1918)

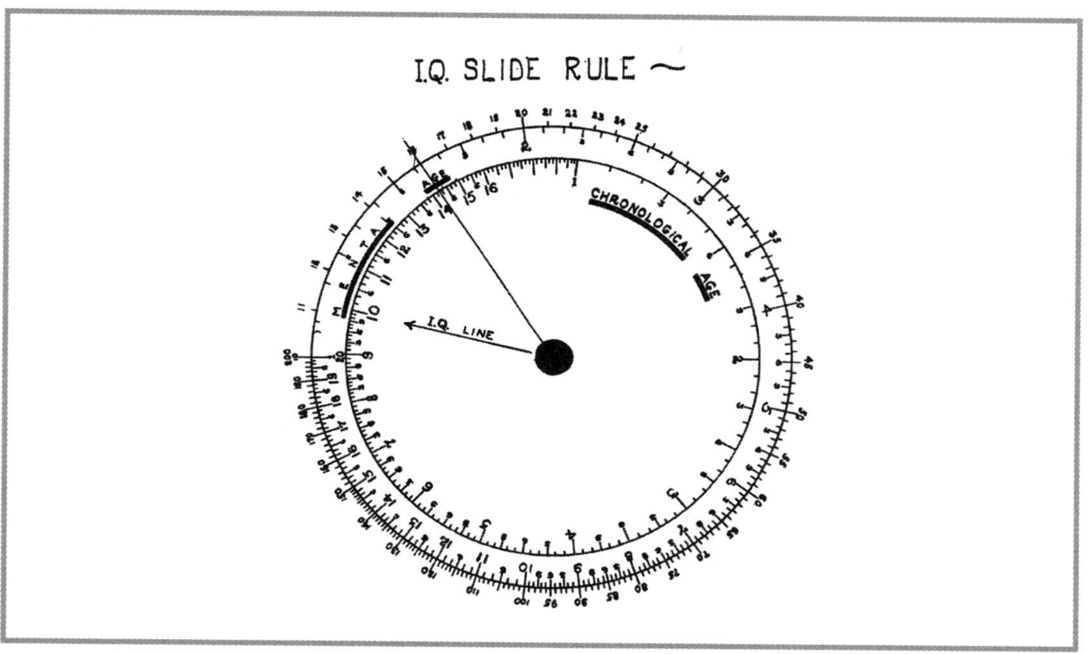

SOURCE: From Kohs, S. C. (1918), "Educational Research and Statistics", *School and Society. Vol. VIII*, Ed. J. McKeen Cattell. New York, NY: The Science Press.

Goddard introduced the "technical" terms for individuals with impaired levels of mental ability. These labels ranged from the lowest, the idiot (IQ = 0 to 25), to mid-level retardation of the imbecile (IQ = 26 to 50), to the mildly retarded moron (IQ = 51 to 70). The addition of these words to the scientific literature did not stop their use in the general vernacular. These terms, while commonly used by psychologists from 1920 to 1960 to describe levels of retardation, never appear in contemporary psychological reports. Instead, we have the following classification system:

- IQ at or above 130 (mentally gifted)
- IQ between 71 and 129 (normal ability)
- IQ between 50 and 70 (mild retardation)
- IQ between 35 and 49 (moderate retardation)
- IQ between 20 and 34 (severe mental retardation)
- IQ below 20 (profound mental retardation)

SOURCE: American Psychiatric Association, 1994.

Lewis M. Terman of Stanford University, another student of G. Stanley Hall, created the first American version of the Binet scale that was statistically normed on an American population of

2,300 California children. The Stanford Revision and Extension of the Binet-Simon Intelligence Scale (Terman, 1916) provided a scoring system age graded and appropriate for children between 2 years and 14 years (see Figure 8.2). It was similar to the original Binet scale but with a recognizable American flavor (Du Bois, 1970). Terman's goal was to efficiently track children in school and place them into curricula where they could learn. The dark side of this is that each year the child's track became more rigid and difficult to escape.

American psychologists of that era assumed that mental ability was an inherited characteristic. IQ tests became a method to identify young members of an American **meritocracy**. This meritocracy, much like Plato's philosopher kings of 2,500 years ago, was destined to provide our leaders, scientists, and artists. The rest of the population was destined to work to support those in the leadership (Marks, 1974).

Figure 8.2 Items Similar to Those From the 1916 Version of the Stanford Revision and Extension of the Binet-Simon Intelligence Scale (at age 5)

Vocabulary Test	The child must define words for common items as they are read to him/her, for example, a scarf, an oven, and a ball.
Pre-Mathematics Skills	Demonstrates the ability to count from 1 to 5 while pointing at 5 coins placed in a line.
Auditory Memory	Determine if the child can repeat verbatim (without errors) the following sentences: (1) Bill has lots of fun playing cards with his sister. (2) Susan wants to build a big castle in her playhouse.
Fine Motor	Determine if the child can use a pencil and copy the drawing of a square (about 2 inches per side) on another piece of paper.

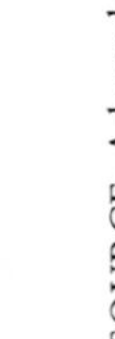

SOURCE: Adapted from Terman, 1916.

Reliability and Validity of Early Childhood Tests of Mental Ability

Reliability and stability of mental ability scores increase as children grow and become older. That growth can occur in a number of dimensions including receptive and **expressive language**. Language is central to mental ability, but its relentless growth makes it difficult to design a reliable (stable) measure of mental ability for children below the age of 5 years old. While cognitive measures are unstable during the preschool years, they firm up after the child enters school (Kranzler, 1997).

Cognitive measures used with 2- and 3-year-old children are designed to minimize the need for verbal answers. Verbal skills become the backbone of most IQ tests with children aged 4 and older. What is measured with 2-year-olds is not what is measured with 5- and 6-year-old children. Validity for measures of mental ability is usually expressed as how well ability test scores relate to school performance. This type of validity assessment is not possible for children below the age of 3 or 4 years old.

The idea of using a simple physical measurement to assess human cognitive ability has always been of interest to scientists. See Case in Point 8.2 for examples of this idea.

Case in Point 8.2

Brain Size and Mental Ability

The physical size and development of the human brain and cognitive ability has been the subject of research since the 19th century. Bogus research methods of the 19th and early 20th centuries described the large brains found in White men as an indication of their superiority over smaller-brained women and people of other ethnic groups (Gould, 1996). The French neuroanatomist Paul Broca once speculated that women have smaller brains because for eons they have not had to use them as intensively as have men. This was thought to be an explanation why women were considered to be less intelligent.

Research into the link between IQ and brain weight is done one of two ways. One involves the use of MRI imaging of living people (R. Lynn, 1994; Peters, 1995); the other approach is to study the brain postmortem (Witelson, Beresh, & Kigar, 2006). Data from both genders show that there is a significant correlation between human brain size among boys and men and measures of intelligence (r = 0.50). This correlation between the two (size and IQ) is diminished in adulthood. Also interesting is the fact that the correlation between brain size in girls and women is not significantly correlated with their mental ability.

One Versus Many Factors of Mental Ability

Lewis M. Terman

Early theorists writing about mental ability, including Terman, held a strong belief in the existence of a single core or general factor, central to all intelligence. This "g" **factor** was thought of as a reserve of mental energy, directed by the conscious mind, to solve problems and perform tasks. The concept of a single "g" factor made it easy to view intelligence as inherited. Thus, when the child is born he/she enters the world with a quantum of this mental energy determined by his/her DNA. It follows that if groups of children have different average levels of this g factor, those differences indicate genetic differences between the groups. Recent examples of theorists supporting this position include Richard Herrnstein and Charles Murray (1994), and Arthur Jensen (1999).

Louis L. Thurstone

An early critic of the single-factor theory, L. L. Thurstone (1927, 1938, 1947) developed a model for mental ability including seven primary factors: Verbal Comprehension (V); Word Fluency (W); Number (N); Spatial Visualization (S); Associative Memory (M); Perceptual Speed (P); and Reasoning (R) (Thurstone, 1947). Thurstone published a test of Primary Mental Abilities (PMA) in 1938 that made it possible to see variations in the patterns of mental abilities of children. This system went far beyond the single IQ score available through the measures developed by Terman. Using the PMA, educators could see where the child excelled and identify what dimensions were not areas of strength.[8] The PMA is now out of print, but it ushered in a number of other conceptualizations of multiple intelligences.

Raymond B. Cattell

Cattell, a professor of psychology at Columbia University, opened the door to the role that environment plays in the elaboration of human intelligence. Cattell proposed that the general factor of intelligence is made up of two parts: one a fluid, or **genetically given factor of intelligence** (Gf), and the other a **crystallized intelligence factor** (Gc) of ability given structure by the environment and elaborated through learning (Cattell, 1963). The relationship between the two changes as the person moves through life. In early childhood, they are similar, but the differential life experiences of individuals result in ever-greater disparity between the two over time.

Recently, the original two-factor model was transformed into a multifactor theory of mental abilities known as the **Cattell-Horn-Carroll** (C-H-C) taxonomy of human cognitive abilities (McGrew, 2003). This model is now the theoretical foundation upon which the Stanford-Binet, 5th ed., and the new Early Stanford-Binet are based. It is also the theoretical basis for the Woodcock-Johnson III NU, Test of Cognitive Abilities.

C-H-C provides for three stratum of human intellect. The highest stratum (III) is composed of the general factor "g" of ability. Stratum II includes 10 broad cognitive skills, including fluid and crystallized intelligences, quantitative reasoning, processing speed, and vocabulary. There are 70 other specific cognitive skills that make up Stratum I. Most published IQ tests measure 2 or 3 of the 10 Stratum II abilities.

Ask not is this child smart, but how is this child smart?

—Howard Gardner

Howard Gardner

Recent multiple-factor theories include those of Robert Sternberg and Howard Gardner. Most educators are familiar with the **multiple intelligences model** (MI) of Howard Gardner (1999). This reflects the fact that the model has an intuitive appeal for educators who must cope with the broad array of deficiencies and abilities young children bring with them. Gardner's model focuses on eight unique human intelligences. Gardner describes these intelligences as evolutionary products, created over the 200 millennia that it took for the evolution of the human species. These evolutionary products became part of our mental schema, and they make possible our efficacious interaction with the environment.

The MI model is optimistic and allows for continual refinement and improvement by the growing child making it very different from a fixed intelligence, or "g" factor model. Gardner's position is that no two children have the same pattern of intelligences (H. Gardner, 1998). He argues even monozygotic twins possess different patterns of abilities. Effort and instruction can improve any of the domains of intelligence; but great levels of a particular intelligence require both a generous genetic contribution and appropriate environmental interactions.

MI theory assumes individuals have unique abilities and suggests teachers use multiple channels when teaching new concepts and when assessing what children can actually do. For example, poetry or music may be appropriate vehicles for helping a struggling child learn mathematics. The goal for instruction should be to give each child the opportunity to learn in ways that are harmonious with their unique set of abilities (H. Gardner, 1995). The whole concept of multiple intelligences is one that fits well with the approach to teaching known as differentiated instruction (Northwest Regional Educational Laboratory, 2005).

Lesson Planning for Early Childhood Classes Employing the Various MI Levels

Logical/Mathematical: Most of the mathematical concepts described by Piaget are related to this area of intelligence, including serration and one-to-one correspondence, additivity, **reversibility,** and continuous quantity problems. Teaching methods include practice with manipulative instructional toys, including counting toys, measuring toys, and mechanical toys.

Linguistic: To develop expressive and receptive language skills children need to be encouraged to use and expand their language. Have children make up and relate personal stories, answer all questions asked by children, and while teaching, provide a running narrative describing each step being taken. Also provide better and expanded descriptive terms for children to use in their speech. Introduce children to art prints and encourage them to develop a narrative about what the painter wanted to say.

Spatial: Develop the child's ability to understand their place in space and their location in relation to other people and places through experience. Teach basic mapping skills: classroom, school, street, trip from school to home, and giving location directions to others. The child's spatial ability also has a linguistic component and practicing the terms in, on, out, above, below, and so on can help in this development.

Interpersonal: This involves helping children become cooperative partners with others. There is a clear developmental component to this area, yet it can be encouraged several ways. Teachers can teach children conflict resolution practices and provide games that require children share and cooperate with others. Encourage individual children to explore how others feel about their behavior.

Intrapersonal: Helping children better understand their own feelings and attitudes is something early childhood teachers can accomplish. One goal is to have children become able to quiet their emotions and soothe themselves. Help children verbalize their feelings of hurt, anger, or other emotions. Ask children to tell their preferences, and explain their wishes and wants. When the child is afraid, help him/her express that fear.

Musical: A sense of rhythm and a love of music can be part of all classrooms. Several things that can enhance this development include introducing rhythmic children's songs, and making recordings for the children to hear over again of their own voices. Experiments have demonstrated that quietly played classical music in the background can improve the amount children learn (D. Dawson, 2003). Early childhood classrooms should be equipped with rhythm sticks, recorders, glockenspiels, and other instruments to use each day.

Body/Kinesthetic: This describes the child's ability to move smoothly and with grace through the environment. This is related to the child's skill at games and the appearance of general coordination and physical prowess. In many ways, it portends later aestheticism. Teachers can encourage this development by providing daily physical (preferably outdoor) activity. Large muscle games and activities should be a regular part of each day.

Naturalist: This intelligence is centered on understanding and being sensitive to the natural world. It implies the child recognizes his/her place and role on the planet. Teachers can introduce natural events and processes to the children. Good teachers have a working knowledge of environmental biology and how to introduce children to it. Small gardens, hamsters or gerbils, flower bulbs, ant farms, and other items should be part of classrooms.

A criticism of the MI model is that there is no way to measure it and that it stands as an unproven theory. Gardener has argued that the fact that there is no measure of his model is its strength. He argues that the various intelligences of MI are not fixed and measurable, but are evolving and are continually being developed. This flexible nature of the model works against accurate measurement (H. Gardner, 1998).

Robert Sternberg

Sternberg has proposed that the question of the amount of intelligence an individual possesses is trivial unless that intelligence is successfully employed. His point is that only the individual can define success in his/her life. Sternberg has developed a three-factor model to explain human cognition (Sternberg, Wagner, Williams, & Horvath, 1995). One of the three pillars of Sternberg's **triarchic model** (three factor) of human intelligence is "**practical intelligence.**" This area of ability involves the contexts in which the individual acts. It expresses how well the individual relates to the external world. The growth and elaboration of intelligence, as described by Sternberg, is a developing expertise linking mental ability to mental activity (Sternberg, 1999). Mental ability expresses the individual's capability for adapting to current circumstances and thriving. His model has no place for a race factor in ability; indeed, Sternberg has discounted the whole issue of race by describing it as a social construct (Sternberg, Grigorenko, & Kidd, 2005).

Another mental ability identified by Sternberg is "**analytical intelligence,**" made up of analytical and verbal skills. These two factors are in line with other major theories of ability. The final factor of the triarchic model is "**creative intelligence,**" which, as its name implies, is an experiential aspect of human mental ability. Creative intelligence provides direction whenever the individual responds to novel situations and stimuli. Additionally, it contains a number of aspects related to leadership and interpersonal skills. A person with high creative intelligence can see opportunity where others do not.

Recently, Robert Sternberg (2008) and his colleagues at Tufts University have been developing a variation on his triarchic model, the WICS, or Wisdom, Intelligence, and Creativity Synthesized. The focus of the research has been on college admissions tests. To date, there are no published measures of either the triarchic model or the WICS initiative.

Screening Tests of Mental Ability

There are two published cognitive screening tests appropriate for use by teachers and counselors and a measure of **relational concepts** reviewed below (see Table 8.2 for a summary). These instruments are appropriate methods for approximating a child's mental ability at one moment in time, but cannot be the basis for entitlement decisions. The ethical use of these screening instruments assumes examiners have a B level of education (see Chapter 7).

Table 8.2 Screening Tests of Cognition

Measurement	Type of Measurement	Measurement Subtests	Age Range	Time to Administer	Publisher	Cost (2009)
Slosson Intelligence Test–Primary (SIT-P)	Screening Test for Cognitive Ability	Crystallized Verbal Ability and Performance Fluid Ability	2 to 7 years	15 to 30 minutes	Western Psychological	$168.00
Kaufman Brief Intelligence Test, 2nd ed. (KBIT-2)	Screening Test for Cognitive Ability	Crystallized Verbal Ability and Matrices Problem Solving, Fluid Ability	4 to 90 years	20 to 40 minutes	Pearson	$232.00
Boehm Test of Basic Concepts, 3rd ed., Preschool (Boehm-3)	Screening Test for Relational Concepts	76 Basic Relational Concepts	3 to 6 years	20 minutes	Pearson	$166.00

SOURCE: Adapted from the following manuals: *Slosson Intelligence Test—Primary* (Western Psychological Services, Inc.), *Kaufman Brief Intelligence Test, 2nd ed.*, and *Boehm Test of Basic Concepts—Preschool* (Pearson Assessment).

Slosson Intelligence Test–Primary (SIT-P)

The SIT-P is an individually administered brief test of children's intelligence between the ages of 2 and 7 years old sold by Western Psychological Services for $168.00 (Erford, Vitali, & Slosson, 1999). SIT-P provides two test forms: one for children below the age of 4, and one for children between 4 and 7 years. It requires about a half hour to individually test a kindergarten age child. Testing a 3-year-old requires 15 minutes.

SIT-P provides Verbal Ability and Performance Ability scores and a total mental ability score. The publisher also describes the verbal items on the SIT-P as measuring Crystallized Verbal abilities. It is composed of test items covering Vocabulary, Similarities and Differences, Digit Sequences, Sentence Memory, and Quantitative Skill. **Performance test** items are described as measuring Fluid Ability. Items for the latter dimension are Fine and Gross Motor Skills, Block Design, Perceptual Motor Speed, and Visual-Motor Integration.

There is one reliability study reported in the literature that was written by the test's author involving 1,337 children (Erford & Pauletta, 2005). Families included in the sample were better educated than the American population; the sample was appropriately designed to match the American ethnicity, but not the country's geography.

SIT-P has good internal consistency reliability ($r \cong 0.98$). It is stable over a 30-day time frame ($r \cong 0.90$) with children over 48 months old. The SIT-P correlates moderately well with the Wechsler tests ($r = 0.74$) and less well with the Stanford-Binet ($r = 0.65$).

Overall, it is a good basic screening test for the level of cognitive functioning of young children (see Photo 8.1).

Photo 8.1 Kindergartener Being Assessed for Her Cognitive Ability

Kaufman Brief Intelligence Test, 2nd ed. (KBIT-2)

This cognitive ability screening measure can be used with children as young as 4 years old and with school-age populations. It requires about a half hour to administer and an additional 10 or 15 minutes to score. It is user-friendly, employing a desktop flip chart format and printed in full color. KBIT-2 provides a measure of verbal ability (crystallized intelligence), matrices problem solving (nonverbal, **fluid intelligence**), and a full-scale IQ score (Kaufman & Kaufman, 2004b). Pearson Education publishes the test for $232.00 (2009).

KBIT-2 was standardized with a norm group of 2,120 English-speaking individuals from the southern states. There is a Spanish language set of directions and responses, but no norm sample of Spanish-speaking children. While the test is very reliable ($r = 0.93$) for school-age children, it is only marginally reliable ($r = 0.78$) with preschool children.

Overall, KBIT-2 is convenient and easily administered and can be used to screen children in kindergarten and the primary grades. It is less expensive and far easier to interpret than large-scale cognitive assessment tests normally used by school psychologists.

Boehm Test of Basic Concepts, 3rd ed., Preschool (Boehm-3)

Boehm-3 is not designed to assess mental ability or IQ; instead, it provides a measure of children's understanding of basic relational concepts essential for school success including size (shortest and tallest), direction (in front and behind), classifications (all), temporal quantity (before and after), spatial reasoning (nearest and farthest), quantity (many and few), and general use relational terms (another and between). Boehm-3 is designed for use with children between 3 and 6 years of age (Boehm, 2001). The Boehm-3 requires about 20 minutes to administer. It involves 76 concepts assessed by showing the child arrays displayed on a flip chart–style manual. A Spanish language version is available.

The Boehm-3 was standardized using 660 children between 3 and 6 years old, from all races, both genders, all socioeconomic levels, and from across the nation (Boehm, 2001). Scores for the concepts being assessed are presented in percentiles based on how well children of that age group perform. It is reliable ($r = 0.90$), and has a small standard error of measurement, between the 2.0 and 2.9 percentiles (T. Graham & Kutsick, 2005). One advantage of the Boehm-3 is that it is available from Pearson Assessment (2009) for only $166.00.

Case in Point 8.3 describes a consulting role for early childhood teachers regarding cognitive ability.

Case in Point 8.3

Nature of Gifted Children

Many parents view preschool teachers as a resource of information about child development. In this role, it is common for parents to ask about their child's academic potential. The National Association for Gifted Education has a Web page with information for parents who think their child may be gifted at the following URL: http://school.familyeducation.com/child-psychology/gifted-education/38808.html.

In general, academically gifted children follow the same physical development pattern as their same age peers. The difference between academically gifted preschool children and others include areas of cognitive and emotional growth.

Cognitive differences include greater curiosity and a desire to know how and why things work. The academically gifted have sharp memories of past incidences, and can focus on problems for longer time blocks than their peers. They have larger, more elaborated vocabularies, exhibit good reasoning skills, can solve more complex puzzles, and have an easier time learning new material. Gifted children often make friends and play with older children. This is done to have interactions with children of an equal mental age. They have a better grasp of the meaning of jokes and riddles than others and have a more advanced sense of humor.

Very bright preschool children have the ability to sense emotions of others and can even become distressed when bad things are reported or pictured on news shows. They experience intense emotional levels, including being very happy, and, occasionally, they are intensely sad or fearful.

Assessment Batteries for Measuring Cognitive Abilities

There are six major, individually administered assessment systems for measuring the cognitive ability of preschool children. They are expensive and complex measuring tools each requiring the highest level of academic preparation and assessment training to ethically administer and interpret (see Table 8.3 for a summary).

Table 8.3 Cognitive Assessments

Measurement	Measurement Subtests	Age Range	Time to Administer	Publisher	Cost (2009)
Kaufman Assessment Battery for Children, 2nd ed. (KABC II)	18 subtests available Luria: 4 Domain Scores C-H-C: 5 Domain Scores	3 to 18 years	1 to 1.5 hours	Pearson	$850.00
Wechsler Preschool and Primary Scale of Intelligence, 3rd ed. (WPPSI-III)	Three Factor Scores: 1. Verbal 2. Performance 3. Processing Speed These are based on 12 subtests plus the two combined scores. Combination scores provide total Verbal Ability and Performance Ability	2.5 to 7 years	1 to 2 hours	Pearson	$1,005.00
Wechsler Intelligence Scale for Children, 4th ed. (WISC-IV)	Four Factor Scores: 1. Verbal Comprehension 2. Perceptual Reasoning 3. Working Memory 4. Processing Speed A total of 15 subtests Two Combined Scores: Verbal Intelligence Performance Intelligence	6 to 17 years	2 hours	Pearson	$1,010.00
Stanford-Binet Intelligence Scales, 5th ed. (SB-5)	1. Nonverbal Fluid Reasoning 2. Verbal Fluid Reasoning 3. Nonverbal Knowledge 4. Nonverbal Quantitative Reasoning 5. Verbal Visual-Spatial Processing 6. Nonverbal Working Memory 7. Verbal Working Memory 8. Verbal Knowledge 9. Verbal Quantitative Reasoning 10. Nonverbal Visual-Spatial Processing	2 to 90 years	2 hours	Riverside	$1,048.00

(Continued)

SOURCE: Adapted from the following manuals: *Kaufman Assessment Battery for Children, 2nd ed., Wechsler Preschool & Primary Scale of Intelligence, 3rd ed., Wechsler Intelligence Scale for Children, 4th ed.* (Pearson Assessment), *Stanford-Binet Intelligence Scales, 5th ed., Stanford-Binet Intelligence Scales for Early Childhood 5th ed.*, and *Woodcock-Johnson, Test of Cognitive Abilities, 3rd ed.* (Riverside Publishing).

Table 8.3 (Continued)

Measurement	Measurement Subtests	Age Range	Time to Administer	Publisher	Cost (2009)
Stanford-Binet Intelligence Scales for Early Childhood, 5th ed. (Early-SB-5)	1. Knowledge 2. Quantitative Reasoning 3. Visual-Spatial Processing 4. Working Memory 5. Short-Term Memory 6. Procedural Knowledge 7. Picture Absurdities 8. Form Patterns 9. Block Span 10. Fluid Reasoning	2 to 7 years	5 hour to 1 hour	Riverside	$369.00
Woodcock-Johnson NU Test of Cognitive Abilities, 3rd ed. (W-J NU-III)	1. Verbal Comprehension 2. Visual-Auditory Learning 3. Spatial Relations 4. Sound Blending 5. Concept Formation 6. Visual Matching 7. Numbers Reversed 8. Incomplete Words 9. Auditory Working Memory 10. Visual-Auditory Learning-Delayed	2 to 90 years	2 hours	Riverside	$1,296.00

Kaufman Assessment Battery for Children, 2nd ed. (KABC II)

The KABC II measures the cognitive abilities of children between 3 and 18 years (Kaufman & Kaufman, 2004a). The full battery consists of a combination 18 core and supplementary subtests. The core subtests are used to compute both the Mental Processes Index (MPI) and the Fluid Crystallized Index (FCI). Supplemental subtests provide measures of the specific cognitive abilities assessed as the core subtests. These supplemental subtests facilitate the computation of the Nonverbal Index (NVI). Different combinations of these subtests are required at different age levels. Pearson Assessment distributes the KABC II to qualified users for $850.00 (2009).

The theoretical perspective of the examiner also influences which subtests are not included. One approach examiners may take is based on the work of Alexander R. Luria, a Russian neuropsychologist. The Luria scoring model for the KABC II is designed to identify deficits and diagnose neurological syndromes (Tupper, 1999). The second scoring option is based on modern cognitive theory and employs the Cattell-Horn-Carroll (C-H-C) approach. The authors call this confusing presentation of two completely different conceptual frameworks the "duel theoretical model" of the human intellect.

Unlike the Wechsler and Stanford-Binet scales the KABC II manual does not provide research-based evidence that the KABC II is an appropriate source of data for guiding educational support and interventions. The KABC II is an appropriate instrument for measuring cognitive abilities and making diagnostic statements. However, the meaning of the scores derived from the use of the KABC II is not well-defined (Braden & Thorndike, 2005). The pattern of scores on various subtests has not been linked to an explanation under either the Luria or C-H-C theoretical models.

The KABC II was standardized using a sample of 3,025 children selected to match U.S. Census data in 2001. The sample also includes children who have been classified and receive services, for example, children who are learning disabled or who are academically gifted (Kaufman & Kaufman, 2004a). It is a reliable instrument with good internal consistency ($r \cong 0.80$). The lowest reliability coefficients occur with the youngest children in the normative sample (Braden & Thorndike, 2005).

Wechsler Scales of Intelligence

The most widely employed measures of cognitive ability used today are two tests of the Wechsler system. David Wechsler developed the Wechsler Intelligence Scale for Children (WISC) in 1947, and the Wechsler Preschool and Primary Scale of Intelligence (WPPSI) in 1967. The fourth edition of the former was published in 2003, as the WISC-IV, and the third edition of the latter as the WPPSI-III in 2002. Both assessments require about two hours to administer and score. They are expensive, each costing $1,005.00 from Pearson Education.

WPPSI-III is actually two measures—one of cognitive functioning for children between 2½ and 4 years and the second for cognitive functioning for children between 4 and 7¼ years. Elements of the measure for the younger group are also part of the assessment of older children (Wechsler, 2002). The WPPSI-III is made up of seven core subtests: Block Design, Information, Matrix Reasoning, Vocabulary, Picture Concepts, Word Reasoning, and Coding, and supplemental subtests of Symbol Search, Comprehension, Picture Completion, Similarities, Receptive Vocabulary, Object Assembly, and Picture Naming.

These subtests are combined into three major factor scores: Verbal, Performance, and a factor called Processing Speed (see Figure 8.3).

WPPSI-III also provides a full-scale IQ score with a mean of 100 and standard deviation of 15. It is very reliable and was standardized using a representative sample of 1,700 children (Madle & Meikamp, 2005; Sattler & Dumont, 2004). The supplemental subtests of the WPPSI-III and WISC-IV give the measures great flexibility

Figure 8.3 Factors and Subtests of the WPPSI-III

Verbal Factor	Performance Factor	Processing Speed Factor
Information	Block Design	Coding
Vocabulary	Matrix Reasoning	Symbol Search*
Word Reasoning	Picture Concepts	
Similarities*	Object Assembly*	
Comprehension*	Picture Completion*	

*Supplemental subtests.

NOTE: A General Language Score is also possible and found by combining the Receptive Vocabulary and Picture Naming subtests.

SOURCE: Adapted from: Wechsler, D. (2002). *Wechsler preschool and primary scale of intelligence, 3rd ed., administration and scoring manual.* San Antonio, TX: The Psychological Corporation.

in the evaluation process. The full-scale IQ score has a very low standard error of measurement (*SEM* = 2.92). It has also been shown to be a valid assessment capable of identifying children with disabilities and children who are cognitively gifted (Wechsler, 2002). WPPSI-III examiners should be educated to the C level, and familiar with testing children using the WPPSI-III.

WISC-IV is composed of 10 core tests: Block Design, Similarities, Digit Span, Picture Concepts, Coding, Vocabulary, Letter-Numbering Sequencing, Matrix Reasoning, Comprehension, and Symbol Search (Wechsler et al., 2003). Core tests are supplemented with another five supplemental subtests: Picture Completion, Cancellation, Information, Arithmetic, and Word Reasoning. These subtests are then combined to create four factor scores including Verbal Comprehension, composed of Similarities, Comprehension, and Vocabulary (or Information), and Perceptual Reasoning, composed of Picture Concepts, Matrix Reasoning, and Block Design (or Picture Completion). The third factor is Working Memory, composed of Letter-Number Sequencing, and Digit Span (or Arithmetic). The final factor is Processing Speed, composed of Coding and Symbol Search (or Cancellation) (see Figure 8.4).

Figure 8.4 The Structure of the Subtests of the WISC-IV

Full-Scale IQ Score			
VCI[a]	PRI	WMI	PSI
(5 subtests)	(4 subtests)	(3 subtests)	(3 subtests)
Similarities	Block Design	Digit Span	Coding
Vocabulary	Picture Concepts	Letter-Number Sequencing	Symbol Search
Comprehension	Matrix Reasoning	Arithmetic[b]	Cancellation[b]
Information[b]	Picture Completion[b]		
Word Reasoning[b]			

a. Verbal Comprehension Index (VCI); Perceptual Reasoning Index (PRI); Working Memory Index (WMI); and Processing Speed Index (PSI).

b. Supplemental subtests.

SOURCE: Adapted from: Wechsler et al. (2003). *Wechsler intelligence scale for children, 4th ed., technical and interpretative manual*. San Antonio, TX: The Psychological Corporation.

A full-scale IQ score can be determined from the various core and supplemental subtests. The mean and median full-scale IQ is 100 (*SD* = 15). Thereby, half of all children have an IQ less than 100, and 68% of all scores fall between an IQ of 85 and 115. Only 2% of the IQ scores from a normal population will be two standard deviations above the mean (gifted IQ of 130 or more) or below the mean (mentally retarded IQ of less than 70).

The WISC-IV was normed with a nationally representative sample of 2,200 children (Wechsler et al., 2003). It is designed for assessing children between the ages of 6 and 17 years. In 2008, Pearson Education distributed the basic kit for $1,010.00. There is also a WISC-IV designed and normed for Spanish-speaking children. The WISC-IV is a complex measure, the ethical use of which requires a C level of education.

In addition to the Spanish language version of the Wechsler, Pearson Assessment also provides a Wechsler Nonverbal Scale of Ability, 4th ed. (WNS-IV). This variation uses up to six of the nonverbal subtests: Matrices, Coding, Object Assembly, Recognition, Spatial Span, and Picture Arrangement provide a cognitive assessment for children from any language background. It is designed for children between the ages of 4 and 7 years. Pearson lists this 2009 publication for $699.00.

Technically, the WISC-IV is a highly reliable measure that is very stable over time. The four factor scores each have standard error scores around 4.0 points. The full-scale IQ has a standard error of 3.0 (Madle & Meikamp, 2005).

Stanford-Binet Intelligence Scales, 5th ed. (SB-5)

SB-5 was published in 2003 as a measure of mental ability for individuals between 2 years and adulthood. This wide range of age groups means the instrument can be used to diagnose exceptionalities across all ages of school children (Roid, 2003). It is a complex and technical measurement the ethical use of which requires a Level C education and specialized training. Riverside Publishing sells it for $1,048.00 (2009).

SB-5 provides subtest scores in 10 domains: Nonverbal Fluid Reasoning, Verbal Fluid Reasoning, Nonverbal Knowledge, Nonverbal Quantitative Reasoning, Verbal Visual-Spatial Processing, Nonverbal Working Memory, Verbal Working Memory, Verbal Knowledge, Verbal Quantitative Reasoning, and Nonverbal Visual-Spatial Processing. Subtests can be combined providing total scores in Nonverbal IQ, Verbal IQ, and Total IQ (Roid, 2003). Subtest score patterns can reveal possible learning problems and disabilities. Unlike its single-factor predecessors, SB-5 is based on a five-factor model of human intelligence composed of Fluid Reasoning, Knowledge, Quantitative Reasoning, Visual-Spatial Processing, and Working Memory. The evaluation of a child using SB-5 requires two hours to administer and score.

SB-5 was normed with 4,800 children and adults representative of the population of the United States. It is a highly reliable measure with a small standard error of measurement (3 IQ points) (D'Amato, Johnson, & Kush, 2007). Overall, the SB-5 is an appropriate test of mental ability for use with preschool and early education students.

Stanford-Binet Intelligence Scales for Early Childhood, 5th ed. (Early-SB-5)

This 2005 early childhood version is appropriate for assessing children between 2 and 7 years of age. It employs the SB-5's scoring system and provides an observational checklist for recording the child's behaviors and problem-solving strategies. Early-SB-5 differs from the longer version by including more items, not requiring children to respond verbally, more child-friendly test materials, and a shorter protocol (Sink, Eppler, & Vacca, 2007). Full-scale administration of the Early-SB-5 requires about an hour.

The Early-SB-5 was normed using a representative sample of 3,160 children, and provides comparison groups for gifted children, and children with learning disabilities and/or mental retardation (Roid, 2005). Its reliability ranges from a low of $r = 0.70$ for one of the subtests with 2-year-old children to $r = 0.96$ with 6-year-old children. Riverside sells Early-SB-5 for $369.00 (2009).

Woodcock-Johnson NU Test of Cognitive Abilities, 3rd ed. (W-J NU-III)

There are two assessments included in the Woodcock-Johnson. One is a test of cognitive ability and the other a measure of achievement. The latter component is reviewed in Chapter 6.

W-J NU-III provides two cognitive measures. One is a quick (10 minute) screening measure, the Brief Intellectual Ability (BIA) test, that is based on three cognitive measures, including Visual Matching, Concept Formation, and Verbal Comprehension. The W-J NU-III was designed to match the Cattell-Horn-Carroll

"It is simply S. O. P. for us to test each child and let you know if we see signs of Ivy League potential."

SOURCE: Cartoon by Merv Magus.

theory of cognitive abilities (Woodcock, McGrew, Mather, & Schrank, 2001). The Woodcock-Johnson is the only published cognitive ability test to measure all 10 of the Stratum II abilities of the C-H-C model (Kranzler, 1997).

In addition to the 10 subtests, Woodcock-Johnson NU-III scores fall along three battery clusters: Verbal Ability, Thinking Ability, and Cognitive Efficiency. Through analysis of the subtests, a total of 16 possible Factor-Cluster-Scores assessing dimensions of cognitive processing are available. W-J NU-III also provides a comprehensive fluid intelligence or total mental ability score, a "g" score.

W-J NU-III is highly reliable and valid with a low standard error of measurement (Woodcock et al., 2001). It was normed on a population of 8,818 people including 1,843 preschool-age children. The norm data provide month-by-month standards for early childhood. The normative sample provides a good representation of the population of the United States and Canada.

W-J NU-III requires over two hours to administer and score. It is the most complex measure of cognitive ability, providing highly nuanced information about how children think (Cizek & Sandoval, 2003). Its ethical use requires an education background at a C level and specific training in its administration. W-J NU-III is user-friendly with all questions mounted on desktop flip charts. In 2009, Riverside Publishing sold it at a cost of $1,296.00.

Summary

Young children have their level of cognitive ability assessed for a number of reasons, for example, to screen them for a possible cognitive loss due to trauma, illness, or the ingestion of environmental toxins.

The reliability of mental ability measures improves as the age of children being tested increases. Language is central in ability measures used with young children. Increasing language skills are related to the improvement in reliability of mental ability measures.

The first theories of mental ability were based on an assumed single core of intelligence. In America, the measurement ideas of Binet and Simon were taken to another level in the development of the Stanford-Binet Scales of Intelligence. More recently, theorists including Howard Gardner and Robert Sternberg proposed models for intelligence including several factors of ability. The day-to-day experiences and observations of classroom teachers may explain the popularity of Gardner's MI model with educators.

Discussion Questions

1. Why do preschools screen new enrolling children for cognitive functioning during their first program year?
2. Design an inservice program to teach parents about Gardner's MI model. Provide a list of things parents can do at home with their youngsters to encourage multiple forms of intelligence.

3. What in an infant's home environment can impair neurological growth?
4. How do single-factor and multiple-factor theories of mental ability differ in terms of scores, administration, and information about children?
5. Why are reliability levels for mental ability tests generally lower with younger children?
6. Analyze and explain which of the three assessments, KBIT-2, Boehm-3, or SIT-P, provide teachers with the most valuable information?

Related Readings

Gardner, H. (1999). *Intelligence reframed: Multiple intelligences for the 21st century.* New York: Basic Books.
Gould, S. J. (1996). *The mismeasure of man.* New York: Norton.
Sprenger, M. (2008). *The developing brain: Birth to age eight.* Thousand Oaks, CA: Corwin Press.
Sternberg, R. J. (Ed.). (1999). *Handbook of creativity.* New York: Cambridge University Press.

Notes

1. Ridwaan is one of the 10 angels of the Mohammedan faith. Ridwaan is the guardian of the gates to paradise, a job held by Saint Peter for Christian believers.
2. Testing a young child's cognitive functioning may be the result of an infant or toddler being referred through Child Find. These assessments and possible referrals for services are a mandate of the Individuals With Disabilities Education Improvement Act of 2004, Part C. The IDEIA Part C requires each state to identify young children at risk for developmental disabilities and provide multiple levels of educational, medical, psychological, and social services (see Chapter 11).
3. Lead-based paint was outlawed on January 13, 1971. Homes in many of the nation's largest cities were built between 1850 and 1950. Old lead paint (e.g., white trim) may have several coats of newer latex-based paint over it, but the old lead is still in place.
4. A genetic model for the cause of the autism spectrum disorders was published in 2008 (Morrow et al., 2008).
5. Society for the Psychological Study of the Child.
6. The Ministry of Instruction (France) needed a method of identifying less able children needing an alternative educational program. In some ways, the use of a test of cognition for the identification of children requiring special education has not changed much over the past century.
7. French Ministry for Public Instruction.
8. Parts of the PMA are still used by medical professionals. Neurologists use the subtests for Spatial Visualization (V) and Perceptual Speed (P) in making differential diagnoses. The Associative Memory (M) subtest is frequently used to chart people with Alzheimer's.

Standardized Assessments of the Early Academic Skills of Young Children

9

To succeed, you will soon learn, as I did, the importance of a solid foundation in the basics of education—literacy, both verbal and numerical, and communication skills.

—Alan Greenspan

Introduction and Themes

Prior to World War I, the word achievement was only used in agricultural contexts, for example, "yield in bushels achieved in a growing season." In the 1920s, the word was applied to the quantification of learning. In 1923, Lewis Terman met with Casper W. Hodgson, president of the World Book Company, and presented him with the printing plates for the first achievement test, the Stanford Achievement Test.[1] World Book was the country's largest publisher of school textbooks, making it a logical choice as the publisher of the first achievement tests.

The first achievement tests were group administered, paper and pencil measures. Individual achievement tests were not developed and published until 1946 with the publication of the Wide Range Achievement Test (see below). Individual achievement tests and screening instruments are better suited for measuring the development of learned skills and knowledge in a preschool setting than are group administered tests.

Federal law now requires all 2.85 million third grade children attending a public or charter school be assessed for achievement in reading and mathematics every year. In every one of the 89,252 public elementary schools in the United States, these high-stakes tests now drive the curriculum (McMurrer, 2008). Core curriculums for all primary and early childhood education now increasingly emphasize prereading, reading, and early arithmetic skills (Louvouezo, 2008).

This pressure for early skill development and achievement was given a structure in 2002 when each state was required to set learning standards for early childhood education. This was part of what was named the Good Start, Grow Smart initiative. This law was written as a supplement to the No Child Left Behind (NCLB) Act.

Following the passage of that initiative there has been a lot of activity by state departments of education in developing and publishing standards for learning in early childhood centers. By 2008, all states, federal territories, protectorates, Washington, D.C., and the Commonwealth of Puerto Rico had published written standards for learning for young children. Altogether, 27 states identify and publish learning standards for children between the ages of 3 and 5 or 6 years; other states provide standards for infants, toddlers, and preschoolers (U.S. Department of Health and Human Services, 2006). Each of these statements includes the development of prereading and early mathematics. The individual state standards can be read at the Department of Health and Human Services Web page at http://www.nccic.org/pubs/goodstart/elgwebsites.html. This standards-based academic structure has made the use of various literacy and early mathematics achievement measures more common than prior to the 2002 laws.

A second reason for the use of one-to-one achievement tests is to meet the ongoing assessment needs of children receiving special help. Programs that use a response to intervention approach need continuous monitoring of the child's progress.

An important new application for emerging technology is with the screening and monitoring of academic progress among young children. One technological system uses personal data assistants (PDA) to record and track student learning. Another is the online testing of children by computer adaptive testing software.

Learning Objectives

By reading and studying this chapter, you should acquire the competency to:

- Describe and discuss the standards for early learning and why they were mandated by the Department of Health and Human Services.
- Describe the changing nature of early childhood curriculums since the passage of the NCLB Act in 2002.
- Describe the role of the child's family in his or her language development.
- Explain the relationship between the primary language of a child's family and the child's early mathematics skills.
- Describe measures that an early childhood educator can create to assess a child's acquisition of the conservation of number concepts as described by Piaget.
- Explain how a personal data assistant can assist in the assessment of young children's early learning.
- Describe the use of CAT in assessment in early childhood.

Assessment Batteries for Early Achievement

Each of the following five achievement assessments requires the examiner have knowledge about the specific test, and Level B education (see Chapter 7). There is a problem associated with interpreting reliability statistics from individually (one-on-one) administered tests. These measurements use a scoring system that involves finding a **ceiling-level** and a **basal-level.** Questions on these tests are sequenced from easy to hard and the basal-level is assumed to be the score below which the child would not make an error. Once identified as a basal-level, no questions at a lower difficulty level are asked. Likewise, a ceiling-level score is assumed to be the point at which the child will not be able to answer more complex questions or solve more difficult problems. When reached, no other questions of greater complexity are attempted. This truncates the range of possible scores for test takers, and inflates test reliability. Internal consistency is also improved because unanswered items are wrong (ceiling and above) or right (basal and below). The only range of questions where statistical variance (needed for reliability) can occur is between the basal and ceiling scores (Browning, Salvia, & Ysseldyke, 1979).

Developmental Indicators for the Assessment of Learning, 3rd ed. (DIAL-III)

DIAL-III has been around in its present form for a number of years (last revision, 1998), but it continues to be used with children between 3 and 7 years. It provides five subtests assessing Language, Concepts,

Motor, Self-Help Development, Social Development, and a total score. Normative data are too old to be appropriate for children in 2009–2010. Pearson Education markets DIAL-III for $530.95 (2009).

DIAL-III requires a half hour to administer by a team of teachers with a B level of education (see Chapter 7) and knowledge of the scoring system. Testing requires a team approach designed to measure three children at one time. Team members observe the children and record their behaviors and answers to questions posed. The test room should look like any preschool or kindergarten room, and testing should be done in a game-like atmosphere. Children being evaluated move from one station (teacher) to the next. One station is for Motor Assessment, one for Concepts Assessment, and one for Language Assessment. DIAL-III assessment also includes a parent questionnaire asking about the child's socialization, health, and self-help needs. An abbreviated version of DIAL-III requiring about half the time of the full test was given the whimsical name Speed DIAL.

DIAL-III was normed with a national sample population of 1,560 children. A Spanish language version was normed with a sample of 650 children. The **norms** for the Spanish-speaking children are not representative of the Spanish-speaking population of the United States (Cizek & Fairbank, 2001). This assessment uses assessment activities that are engaging and hold the attention of children. DIAL-III has good reliability ($r \cong 0.90$) (Czadnowski & Goldenberg, 2001). DIAL-III is less appropriate for screening after kindergarten (Cizek & Fairbank, 2001).

Peabody Individual Achievement Test, Revised (PIAT-R)

The PIAT-R battery was standardized in 1998 for children ages 5 through 19 years. The test itself has not been revised since 1989 (Cross & Fager, 2001). Pearson Assessments sells the PIAT-R for $440.00 (2009). The 1998 standardization included 3,184 children. It was representative of the U.S. population between kindergarten and 12th grade. PIAT-R provides subtests for Reading Recognition, Reading Comprehension, Mathematics, Spelling, Word Expression, and General Information.[2]

Reliability evidence must be taken from the 1989 first edition (Benes & Rogers, 1992).[3] Only the Word Expression subtest is unreliable, lacking stability over time. Today, primary grade children are taught a very different curriculum than they were 20 years ago. The normative scores need to be recalculated (Cross & Fager, 2001).

The PIAT-R is an easy **assessment battery** to administer with user-friendly features. It requires about an hour to administer and score and may be used when making placement decisions; but caution must be used in interpreting the scores.

Qualls Early Learning Inventory (QELI)[4]

This screening battery consists of measures of General Knowledge, Oral Communication, Written Language, Math Concepts, Work Habits, and Attentive Behavior. It is appropriate for kindergarten and first graders.

This brief, 10-minute observational instrument is completed by teachers (Qualls, Hoover, Dunbar, & Frisbie, 2003). It presents 44 questions scored using a 4-point ordinal scale (see Chapter 4). QELI's normative sample included 2,108 children from a national sample matching U.S. Census data. It is consistent and stable with good reliability (median $r \cong 0.85$). QELI is distributed by Riverside and sells for $35.50 (2009).

Wechsler Individual Achievement Test, 3rd ed. (WIAT-III)

WIAT-III is an achievement measure that provides scores for the achievement domains of Reading, Mathematics, Mathematics Fluency, Written Language, and Oral Language. It does this with nine subtests and seven supplementary subtests. This well respected measure was published in 2009. The assessment was standardized using 2,950 children and youth (4 to 19 years) and is representative of the American population. The four domain scores are stable over time and consistent (reliable). These reliability coefficients are based on retesting after 10 days ($r \cong 0.85$).

The WIAT-III requires 45 minutes to administer to preschool children and 1.5 hours with children between first and sixth grades. Examiners should have specific instruction in administering the WIAT-III and a B level of education (see Chapter 7). Pearson Assessment markets it for $500.00 (2009).

Table 9.1 provides a summary of the tests covered in this section.

Table 9.1 Individual Achievement Test Batteries for Early Childhood

Measurement	Dimensions of Measurement	Age Range	Time to Administer	Publisher	Cost (2009)
Developmental Indicators for the Assessment of Learning, 3rd ed. (DIAL-III)	Language, Concepts, Motor, Self-Help Development, Social Development	3 to 7 years	30 minutes	Pearson	$530.95
Peabody Individual Achievement Test, Revised (PIAT-R)	Reading Recognition, Reading Comprehension, Mathematics, Spelling, Word Expression, and General Information	5 to 19 years	1 hour	Pearson	$440.00
Qualls Early Learning Inventory (QELI)	General Knowledge, Oral Communication, Written Language, Math Concepts, Work Habits, and Attentive Behavior	5 to 7 years	10 minutes	Riverside	$35.50
Wechsler Individual Achievement Test, 3rd ed. (WIAT-III)	Reading, Mathematics, Mathematics Fluency, Written Language, and Oral Language	4 to 19 years	45 minutes to 1.5 hours	Pearson	$500.00
Woodcock-Johnson III NU Tests of Achievement (WJ III NU Ach.)	48 brief tests of achievement covering Oral Expression, Listening Comprehension, Written Expression, Basic Reading Skills, Reading Comprehension, Reading Fluency, Math Calculation Skills, and Math Reasoning	2 years to old age	2 hours	Riverside	$573.00

SOURCE: Adapted from the following manuals: *DIALIII, PIAT-R, WIAT-III* (Pearson Assessment), and *QELI, WJIII, Ach.* (Riverside).

Woodcock-Johnson III NU Tests of Achievement (WJ III NU Ach.)

Paired with the Woodcock-Johnson, Test of Cognitive Abilities, 3rd ed., is the WJ III NU Ach. The Tests of Achievement require a B level of education (see Chapter 7).

Woodcock-Johnson III NU Tests of Achievement determine an individual's level of learning, and describe the status of his/her academic strengths and weaknesses (Mather & Woodcock, 2001). Combined with the Woodcock-Johnson-III cognitive test (see Chapter 8), the two batteries provide data necessary to assess over- or underachievement and examine patterns of intra-individual discrepancies. This is possible because the two assessment batteries were normed using the same subjects. A combined kit with both measures can be purchased from Riverside Publishing for $1.296.00.

WJ III NU Ach. provides a series of brief (5 minute) measures covering 48 dimensions divided into 12 subtests, making it an ideal measure for **response to intervention** approaches for supporting at-risk learners. WJ III NU Ach. requires 2 hours to administer and another hour to score. Of the 8,818 people used as the normative group, 1,843 were toddlers and preschoolers as young as 24 months. It is highly reliable and valid for assessing early achievement and making placement decisions.

The cognitive tests are based on the model for human intellect known as the Cattell-Horn-Carroll (C-H-C) model while the model used to develop the achievement subtests is not clear (Cizek & Sandoval, 2003). The test was developed using a psychometric rather than a theoretical model. The full achievement battery is marketed by Riverside for $573.00 (2009).

The First "R"

While oral language acquisition is a natural process (Chomsky, 1972), the acquisition of reading skills is neither intuitive nor easy, reflecting the lack of a biological imperative for reading. Five percent of children learn to read without formal instruction, and 35% have little difficulty learning to read in school. Forty percent of children learn to read only with considerable effort, and 20% find learning to read the most difficult task they have ever faced (Lyon, 1998; Michigan Department of Education, 2008). Severe cases of reading disability occur in about 4% of children and can involve mirror-image (dyslexic) reading (American Psychiatric Association, 1994).

"Where she get off telling us our Bonnie got bad grammer? We should-a just got up and went home."

SOURCE: Cartoon by Merv Magus.

Tasks a child masters to become a reader follow those needed for speech. The first spoken words, however, are not the first words children learn to read. To read, children must learn the symbols used to represent the **phonemes** of our language. These letters and blends are a critical learning step. Next, the child must learn how combinations of phonemes construct **morphemes.** Those blended sound combinations can be expressed as the written letter combinations that represent words. The idea that written symbols on a paper can be used to represent the sounds of oral language is an astounding concept to learn.

Step one in the process is **phonemic awareness**, describing how children must learn that written letters represent the phonemes used to speak. This major educational task occupies much of the informal and formal instruction in preschools. Parents who patiently read with their young children at home set the stage for this learning. The wide variation of home backgrounds is a reason why children have vastly different levels of prereading skills in kindergarten.

Step two (kindergarten to second grade) is when children learn to sound out the letter combinations making up simple morphemes. With practice, this process becomes faster and the child's efficiency as a reader improves (**fluency**). It is also a time when children memorize a number of simple words they can recognize on sight, thereby creating a sight vocabulary of words immediately available to the young reader. See Case in Point 9.1 for a method for tracking the development of early reading skills.

Case in Point 9.1

Running Records for Reading

One technique for tracking the emergent reading skills of young learners is a technique known as the **"running record."** This requires the classroom teacher spend about 10 minutes with each child assessing his/her reading skills. This assessment should occur more frequently with poor readers (every 3 weeks) and less frequently with youngsters reading fluently at grade level (4 times a year). The running record requires the child read a short passage from an unfamiliar text at his/her reading level. The teacher follows along marking a copy of the text material copied on a running record form to indicate how the child attacked each word in the passage. Errors are recorded by the teacher and corrected for the child. Teachers also record their observations as to how the child determines the meaning of unfamiliar words. The question for the teacher is whether the child acquires an understanding of the word(s) through meaning in context, structure, or visual cues (M, S, V). For a tutorial on this method, see http://www.readinga-z.com/guided/runrecord.html.

Early Literacy

Early literacy skills, abilities children acquire through instruction, are needed prior to reading. Toddlers of parents who read to them have a great advantage over their peers who do not have reading parents. Children read to on a regular basis will be more likely to develop a love for the process of reading and will have their own favorite books. Two and 3-year-old children will sit with a parent for hours while being read to, even if the same book is read over and over (see Photo 9.1).

Photo 9.1 A Mother Reading to Her Young Children

Language develops when an infant's parent plays **verbal contagion** games with a baby.[5] By cooing and babbling back and forth with the baby, the infant learns that communication is a two-way street and develops an enjoyment of speech. When parents elaborate on the questions their children ask and provide careful answers to all childish enquiries, they improve their young child's early literacy level. The development of these early literacy skills are directly linked to later reading ability, verbal reasoning, and academic success (Parents as Teachers National Center, 2005) (see Photo 9.2).

It is hypothesized that infants and young children have an inborn drive to understand and organize language sounds that surround them from the moment of birth (Chomsky, 1975). The assumption behind this idea is that there is a genetic key impelling the young child to create rules of language from what is heard. The production of oral language begins with the first morpheme (word) at about 12 months and progresses to two-word utterances around the second birthday (R. Brown, 1974). Verbs enter the child's lexicon before the age of 3 ("walk more" . . . meaning let's walk together a bit more) or ("read book" . . . meaning please read this book to me). The grammar of toddlers is economical, avoiding prepositions, articles, and conjunctions.

Children are inventing language and its rules as they go along. There are both pragmatic reasons (being satisfied) and biological reasons (a genetically impelled capability) for the child to construct language. Parents do not teach this form of baby grammar. The syntax parents use around their babies and toddlers does not become an early part of the child's language.

Toddlers can understand the meaning of their parents' speech even though they cannot speak using adult syntax. Likewise, parents can understand the meaning that their child is conveying when using "baby talk." Between 36 and 48 months, the child's grammar expands and sentences become more complex by co-joining two sentences addressing the same topic (without using a preposition). For example, the child may explain, "I tired Liam . . . no more play" or "Like Daddy car . . . more ride" or "Nikki loves Mommy . . . Mommy makes sticky waffles." Toddlers know when adults are mocking them, and recognize when grown-ups are using "baby talk." See Case in Point 9.2 for an example from your author's experience.

Photo 9.2 Young Child Enjoying a Book

Case in Point 9.2

Language Understanding and Production

A colleague and his wife have a 3-year-old son. The first time the wife and their little boy visited our office area, I asked the child what his name was. The child responded, "Maffu." I replied, "You are Maffu?" He became cross with me and said, "No, Maffu!" I then replied "Oh! You are Matthew." He then said, "Yes, Maffu." With that, he had had enough of me and headed across the hall to his father's office.

While he could not pronounce his name and produce the dental fricative phoneme "th," he knew what his name should sound like and did not like me mispronouncing it.

The sequence of language development is consistent, but the rates of acquisition vary enormously making the interpretation of standardized tests of oral language very difficult (Peisner-Feinberg & Maris, 2005).

Screening Tests for Literacy Skills

Teachers with a basic knowledge of testing can use literacy screening tests to estimate how well children's reading skills are developing (see Chapter 7). A note of caution is needed when using one-on-one tests of early reading. Children can understand printed words internally before they can read them verbally (German & Newman, 2007). Most individually administered early reading and literacy screening and assessments require the child to orally read passages or name objects (see Table 9.2 for a summary of the tests discussed in this section).

Table 9.2 Individual Achievement Screening Tests

Measurement	Dimensions of Measurement	Time to Administer	Age Range	Publisher	Cost (2009)
Dynamic Indicators of Basic Educational Literacy, 6th ed. (DIBELS)	Sound Fluency, Letter Naming Fluency, Phoneme Segmentation Fluency, Nonsense Word Fluency, Oral Reading, Oral Retelling Fluency, and Word Use Fluency	15 to 20 minutes	PK to 3rd grade	University of Oregon	$1.00 per child
Early Reading Diagnostic Assessment, 2nd ed. (ERDA-2)	Phonological Awareness, Phonics, Vocabulary, Comprehension, and Fluency	65 to 110 minutes	5 to 8 years	Pearson	$318.00 per kit, or 4 kits for $1,272
Early Literacy Skills Assessment Kit (ELSA)	Comprehension, Phonological Awareness, Alphabetic Principle, Alphabetic Letter Recognition, and Concepts About Print	15 to 20 minutes	3 to 5 years	HighScope	$149.95 per kit, 2 kits
Expressive Vocabulary Test, 2nd ed. (EVT-2)	Expressive Vocabulary and Word Retrieval	10 to 15 minutes	5 to 11 years	Pearson	$399.00
Peabody Picture Vocabulary Test, 4th ed. (PPVT-4)	Receptive Vocabulary Level	10 to 15 minutes	2.5 years to adulthood	Pearson	$399.00
Process Assessment of the Learner, 2nd ed. (PAL-2)	23 short measures of Language Development, Early Reading Skills, and Reading	30 to 60 minutes	5 to 11 years	Pearson	$468.00
Test of Early Reading Ability, 3rd ed., (TERA-3)	Alphabet, Meaning, and Conventions of Printed Language	45 minutes	3.5 to 8.5 years	Pearson	$274.00
Wide Range Achievement Test, Expanded Early Reading Assessment (WRAT-ERA)	Pre-Reading Skills and Reading Skills	20 to 40 minutes	PK to 1st grade	Psychological Assessment Resources	$248.00

SOURCE: Adapted from the following manuals: *ERDA, EVT-2, PAL, TERA-3, EMDA, KeyMath, 3rd ed.* (Pearson Assessment), *ELSA* (High/Scope), *WRAT-ERA* (Psychological Assessment Resources), and *TEMA III* (Pro-Ed).

Measurement	Dimensions of Measurement	Time to Administer	Age Range	Publisher	Cost (2009)
Early Math Diagnostic Assessment (EMDA)	Math Reasoning, Numerical Operations	20 to 30 minutes	PK to 3rd grade	Pearson	$209.00
KeyMath3 Diagnostic Assessment (KM III)	Basic Concepts, Operations, and Applications	30 to 90 minutes	4.5 to 21 years	Pearson	$540.00
Test of Early Mathematics Ability, 3rd ed. (TEMA-III)	Numbering Skills, Number-Comparison, Number Literacy, Mastery of Number Facts, Calculation Skills, Understanding Concepts	Untimed	3 to 9 years	Pro-Ed	$320.00

Dynamic Indicators of Basic Educational Literacy, 6th ed. (DIBELS)[6]

DIBELS is widely employed as a measure of early literacy for children in prekindergarten through third grade (Manzo, 2005a). It measures Sound Fluency, Letter Naming Fluency, Phoneme Segmentation Fluency, Nonsense Word Fluency, Oral Reading, Oral Retelling Fluency, and Word Use Fluency. DIBELS is a good predictor of how well a child does on the standards-based reading tests. DIBELS also provides a method of monitoring the developing skills of children receiving learning support. Administration and scoring of the DIBELS, 6th ed., is complex (Brunsman, 2005). Many subtests require examiners time the child's responses, while counting the fluency and accuracy of responses. The recent development of scoring system software by Wireless Generation makes scoring and recording the DIBELS, 6th ed., easier (see below).

The measure is distributed by the Center on Teaching and Learning at the University of Oregon. Using a federal grant, the DIBELS materials are distributed for the nominal cost of $1.00 per year per child being assessed.

Early Reading Diagnostic Assessment, 2nd ed. (ERDA-2)

ERDA-2 provides a diagnostic assessment of five components of early reading: Phonological Awareness, Phonics, Vocabulary, Comprehension, and Fluency (Psychological Corporation, 2003).

In that several subtests require clinical judgment to score, examiners should be well educated at level B (see Chapter 7) and familiar with the ERDA-2 (Whitehead & Shaw, 2005). The full assessment with primary grade children requires between one and two hours to administer. There is an abbreviated version used as a screening test requiring 20 minutes for administration.

ERDA-2 was normed on a representative sample of 800 children between kindergarten and third grade. It reports modest internal consistency reliability but good stability reliability over time (median $r \cong 0.85$). Pearson Assessment distributes the ERDA-2 at a price of $318.00 for each of the four kits, kindergarten through Grade 3. The total for all four kits is $1.272.00 (2009).

Early Literacy Skills Assessment Kit (ELSA)

HighScope Educational Research Foundation designed ELSA as a standardized screening measure for children between 3 and 5 years. Its five scales are Comprehension (Connecting, Retelling, Predicting),

Phonological Awareness (Rhyming, Phonemic Awareness, Segmentation), Alphabetic Principle (Sense of Word), Alphabetic Letter Recognition (Letter Sound Correspondence), and Concepts About Print (Orientation, Story Beginning, Direction of Text). HighScope distributes ELSA at a cost of $149.95 (2009) for each of two kits. Two kits make it possible to use the screening with the same child over two years.

Testing involves reading a story with the child and asking questions about embedded material. It is a **criterion-referenced measure** based on the assumptions of the HighScope Early Childhood Curriculum, providing three levels of criterion-referenced scores. These include (low) Emergent-Exploration, Emergent-Awareness, and (high) Competent Emergent-Application (DeBruin Parecki, 2005).

ELSA was standardized (normed) with a **sample of convenience** from 31 classrooms across three states enrolling 630 preschoolers. With the exception of the Phonological Awareness, the other four scales have good reliability ($r \cong 0.87$).

Expressive Vocabulary Test, 2nd ed. (EVT-2)

EVT-2 is an assessment of expressive vocabulary and word retrieval normed with children from 2½ years through adulthood. The EVT-2 is normally used with the Peabody Picture Vocabulary Test, and the two measures were co-normed on the same sample of 2,725 people. EVT-2 uses a flip chart format presenting 38 labeling questions requiring children to provide an object's name from its picture. Another 152 items ask children to provide synonyms for depicted items. Overall, EVT-2 is a reliable measure of expressive vocabulary, easy to administer, and with only one total score, easy to interpret.

Peabody Picture Vocabulary Test, 4th ed. (PPVT-4)

PPVT-4 is a screening measure used to determine the receptive vocabulary level of children beginning at age 2½. When combined with the EVT-2, it can assess verbal ability (Williams, 2007). PPVT-4 has 204 test items based on arrays of full-color pictures presented using a desktop flip chart (Dunn & Dunn, 2007). The PPVT-4 requires 15 minutes to administer.

The PPVT-4 can track the language learning progress of children who are English language learners (ELL), and provide the follow-up measurements of receptive vocabulary in a response to intervention program. It was standardized using 3,540 individuals selected to approximate the U.S. population. PPVT-4 is a reliable ($r \cong 0.95$), widely used early childhood measurement (Early Childhood Measurement and Evaluation Resource Center, 2008). Pearson Assessment markets it for $399.00 (2009).

Process Assessment of the Learner, 2nd ed. (PAL-2)

This screening measure provides 23 measurements related to Language Development, Early Reading Skills, and Reading with children in kindergarten through Grade 6 (Berninger, 2007). Virginia Berninger designed the battery based on a neurodevelopmental model for language and reading skills. Each measurement is brief, designed for programs using a response to intervention approach. PAL-2 provides detailed data about the English language strengths and weakness for elementary school children.

PAL-2's subtest scores are reported in deciles[7] (Jennings, 2005). The battery requires about 40 minutes to administer with primary grade children. Pearson Assessment markets PAL-2 at $468.00 (2009).

The screening battery was normed using performance data from a sample of 868 children between the ages of 5 and 13 years. The sample was not representative of the population of children in the United States by including too few girls (♀ = 46%, ♂ = 54%). The short nature of the 23 measures reduces scale reliability. The median internal consistency reliability is ($r \cong 0.71$). Scores from the PAL-2 and the PPVT-4 are not correlated, and it is only marginally correlated with the WIAT-III, raising questions about the concurrent validity of the PAL-2.

Test of Early Reading Ability, 3rd ed. (TERA-3)

This screening measure published by Pearson Assessment requires a B level of education (see Chapter 7) and costs $274.00 (2009) to purchase. It was last published in 2001 and is used to assess young children between 3½ and 8½ years. TERA-3 provides three subtest scores (Alphabet, Meaning, and Conventions of Printed Language) requiring 45 minutes to administer and hand score. The normative group is small but well engineered to represent the population (N = 875) (deFur, 2003). TERA-3 is easy to administer, reasonably priced, and was designed to meet the standards set by the National Reading Panel.

Wide Range Achievement Test, Expanded Early Reading Assessment (WRAT-ERA)

ERA is a measure of prereading and beginning reading skills for children between 5 and 7 years (Robinson, 2005). WRAT-ERA is norm referenced providing two subtest scores, Pre-Reading Skills and Reading Skills. Pre-Reading Skills includes items designed to measure letter-word discrimination and letter-sound discrimination (phonemic awareness). Reading Skills includes items to measure word reading and sentence reading (early comprehension). There are 40 items on each subtest.

WRAT-ERA has good internal consistency reliability (median $r \cong 0.85$). Its normative sample of 600 young children aligns with U.S. Census data in terms of socioeconomic status and ethnicity. Families that made up the sample for the younger children were more educated than the population in general, and the total sample was skewed toward the southern United States (Lukin & McCabe, 2005).

ERA requires a Level B educational background (see Chapter 7) and is distributed by Psychological Assessment Resources at $248.00 (2009).

See Case in Point 9.3 for a new oral language environmental assessment being used by the parents of infants today.

Case in Point 9.3

Baby's Language Environment

A new worry for middle class parents is the quality of the language around their developing infant. This is a reflection of recent research demonstrating that the language development of infants and young children is correlated with the quality and quantity of oral language directed to the child by parents and others in the environment (Bhattacharjee, 2008; Hart & Risley, 1995, 1999). Later school success is directly correlated with the language skills acquired during infancy and early childhood. Building on this concern, Infoture of Boulder, Colorado, created and markets a small device that analyzes the language environment around children. The device, LENA (language environment analysis), costs about $400.00 and is clipped to the infant's clothing (see Photo 9.3). It listens to all the language in the environment; then, it separates out oral language directed to the infant and the sounds that the infant makes in response. At the end of the infant's day, the LENA device is plugged into the home computer and it provides a chart of how much productive language was directed to the child, and how many responses the child made.

The Third "R," Growth of Mathematical Concepts

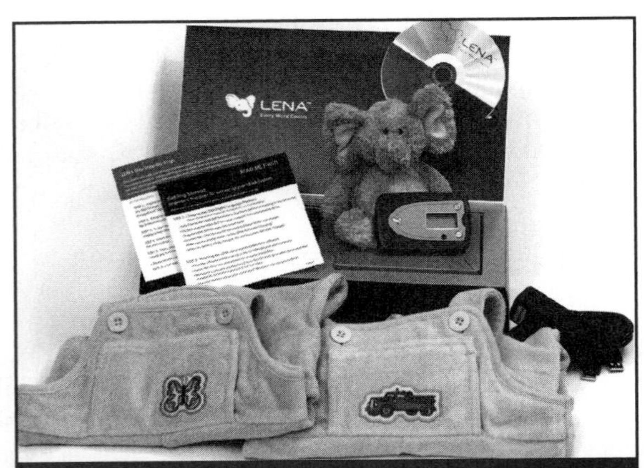

SOURCE: Infoture, Inc. Used with permission.

Photo 9.3 The Infoture LENA (Language Environment Analysis) Device and System

Young children explore and use mathematics concepts to understand their world during their early years. Children learn to balance their body weight, build and balance Froebel blocks, compare amounts, find patterns, and learn the floor plan of their environments. Mathematics helps children make sense of their world outside of school and helps them construct a solid foundation for success in school (National Association for the Education of Young Children, 2002). Children first learn mathematics from their own bodies, then generalize principles to other occasions (see Case in Point 9.4 and Photos 9.4a and 9.4b for examples of this principle).

Case in Point 9.4

Development of Early Numerosity

Anyone who has carefully watched a young infant knows that a day occurs at about the age of 10 weeks when the infant recognizes his/her hand and can coordinate its movement in reaching and grasping. From this point in the child's development the infant's hand becomes an integral tool for exploring and understanding mathematics.

The fact that humans are endowed with 10 fingers and toes contributes to why we have invented a system of mathematics based on the number 10. If we had only 6 fingers and toes, like the rhinoceros, it is likely that we would have adopted a number system based on the number 6.

Digits of the base 10 1, 2, 3, 4, 5, 6, 7, 8, 9, 10, 11, 12, 13, 14, 15 . . .

Digits of the base 6 1, 2, 3, 4, 5, 6, 11, 12, 13, 14, 15, 16, 21, 22, 23 . . .

Systems for rapid mathematical calculation known as finger counting have been used throughout Europe since medieval times (Menninger, 1992). These systems were all built on the base 10 numbering system.

There is evidence that children raised in homes where English is the primary language are at a disadvantage when developing an understanding of mathematics. A central concept for children to learn is the concept of number. Asian languages, including Japanese, Korean, and Mandarin, provide the number 12 with a logical name: ten two. English and other European languages use irregular linguistic rules to name numbers over 10. Words like eleven and twelve are much more difficult to understand and conceptualize (Park & Leung, 2003; Wang & Lin, 2005).

Photo 9.4a Infant Playing With His Fingers

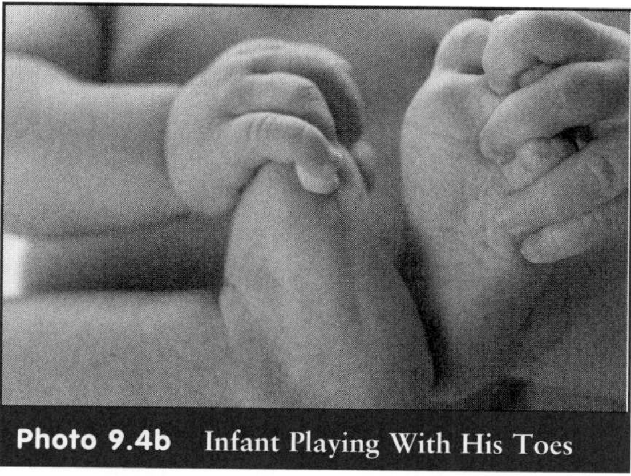

Photo 9.4b Infant Playing With His Toes

Most preschool children learn to repeat "their numbers" as a verbal exercise before they attend kindergarten. The ability to count from 1 to 100 does not imply a conceptual understanding of number. Much as the young child's ability to repeat the alphabet does not imply reading comprehension, being able to count does not imply the child has acquired the concepts needed to understand number (Piaget, 1965). See Case in Point 9.5 for an example of Piaget's math testing method.

Case in Point 9.5

Piaget's Conservation of Quantity Applied to Mathematics

A 5-year-old child can easily count seven quarters arranged in a row. A parallel row of seven more quarters can be set out on the same surface and arranged across from the first row. Have the child count each row. Ask if one row has the same number of quarters as the other; or if one has more?

Once the child agrees both have the same, rearrange one row. Make it twice as long as the first by spreading the quarters farther apart along the line. Repeat the question, does one row have the same number of quarters as the other? Or does one have more?

Typically, children below the age of 6 years will argue the longer appearing row has more. This logical fallacy demonstrates young children lack the concept needed to reverse an operation and see objects as they were before being transformed. Also, they cannot **decenter** from their dependence on visual cues and therefore hold the perspective that longer is more.

Mathematics (Conservation Reasoning) Tasks Developed by Jean Piaget

Continuous quantity: http://www.youtube.com/watch?v=MpREJlrpgv8

Conservation of mass: http://www.youtube.com/watch?v=WKL4trUNAlk

Groups and classes: http://www.youtube.com/watch?v=tYtNk0BotRE&feature=related

Conservation of length: http://www.youtube.com/watch?v=glDIMWRYu_k&feature=related

Teachers develop ways to help children construct their own conceptual frameworks for number concepts (Van de Walle & Lovin, 2005). Learning mathematics requires they be learned in a variety of ways, and frequently repeated in different contexts (Kilpatrick, Swafford, & Findell, 2001). Teachers need an understanding of what each child knows (formative assessment) and adjust the learning activities to optimize learning (R. Wright, Martland, & Stafford, 2006). Children's acquisition of mathematics concepts flourishes when new learning experiences are meaningfully supported by prior learnings (NAEYC, 2002). In other words, assessment is part of teaching early mathematics.

Measures of Numerosity and Early Mathematics Skills

Three of the reviewed batteries of assessments used to assess early learning include a mathematics subtest (Peabody Individual Achievement Test, Revised; Qualls Early Learning Inventory; and the Wechsler Individual Achievement Test, 3rd ed.). The Early Math Diagnostic Assessment is a prekindergarten to third grade assessment. At school age (6 years old), there are several stand-alone measures of mathematics achievement, including the KeyMath, 3rd ed. (KM-III), and the Test of Early Mathematical Ability, 3rd ed. (TEMA-III) (see Table 9.2 for a summary of these measures). There is also a mathematics assessment for early learners in the technology-based mCLASS system for assessments (see below).

Early Math Diagnostic Assessment (EMDA)

EMDA is a norm-referenced screening test created from one of the subtests of the Wechsler Individual Achievement Test, 3rd ed. It provides two subtest scores, Math Reasoning and Numerical Operations. EMDA was normed to be used with children between 5 and 8 years. It requires 20 to 30 minutes to administer and can be scored as a criterion-referenced measure (Below Basic, Basic, Proficient), or in standard score form (Mean = 100, Standard Deviation = 15) (Psychological Corporation, 2002). EMDA is distributed by Pearson Assessments for $209.00 (2009).

EMDA is a stable and reliable instrument ($r = 0.93$) that was normed using a stratified sample of 1,374 children representative of the U.S. population. It is user-friendly, and easy to administer and score. EMDA provides an important and useful diagnostic measure of early math skills (Gierl, Tan, & Olivarez, 2005).

KeyMath3 Diagnostic Assessment (KM-III)

KeyMath3 provides a total score combining three subscales: Basic Concepts, Operations, and Applications and 10 subtest scores (Connolly, 2007). KeyMath3 uses 372 individual mathematics assessment questions, arranged in a sequence of increasing difficulty, and presented using a flip chart format.[8]

The scores from the third edition are based on a national sample of 4,000 children and young adults between the ages of 4½ and 21 years. It is an appropriate diagnostic measure that can be used with early childhood aged children. The content of the test has been revised to match the standards for learning endorsed by the National Council for Teachers of Mathematics (Connolly, 2007). The measure is easy to administer (Level B) (see Chapter 7), and the scoring system is not difficult to follow. The basic KeyMath3 is sold by Pearson Assessment at a cost of $540.00 (2009).

KeyMath3 reports reliability for the total score as 0.90. The subtests (strands) are less reliable ($r \cong 0.70$). The KeyMath3 does provide valid and reliable diagnostic data that can be used in the development of IEPs and IFSPs.

A new online edition of the KeyMath3 test was also published in 2007. This version also provides a very wide measurement range from 4.5 years through age 21.

Test of Early Mathematics Ability, 3rd ed. (TEMA-III)

TEMA-III (2003) was designed as a measure of early mathematical ability for children between 3 and 9 years. It was standardized with a sample of 1,228 (Form A) and 591 children (Form B) drawn from selected regions of the nation in the year 2000. The sample is not an accurate representation of the population of young children in the United States. The basic test kit from Western Psychological costs $320.00 (2009) and requires administrators to have a B level of training (see Chapter 7) (Ginsburg & Baroody, 2003).

TEMA-III is untimed and requires about an hour to administer and score. Its reliability is very high (median $r \cong 0.95$), and it is a valid assessment of mathematics ability levels of young children. Its theoretical basis is consistent with research in children's development of mathematics understanding (Crehan & Monsaas, 2005). The TEMA-III reports scores for the following subtests: Numbering Skills, Number-Comparison Facility, Number Literacy, Mastery of Number Facts, Calculation Skills, and Understanding of Concepts.

Technology for Assessing Early Academic Skills

There are two directions technology is taking in providing teachers with assessment help. One direction for new and emerging technology is the interface of individually administered screenings and assessments with personal digital assistants (PDA) and classroom computers. This provides an integrated method of recording, storing, and reporting assessment data. Handheld systems are now replacing flip charts and clipboards of more traditional approaches (see Photo 9.5). A major player in this field is the company, Wireless Generation and its mCLASS systems (Mobility Classroom) for assessment.

Photo 9.5 PDA Being Used by Teacher in a Math Assessment

SOURCE: Wireless Generation, Inc. Used with permission.

mCLASS

The **mCLASS** software is written to permit early childhood teachers to give formative assessments and individually administered assessments to children between preschool and third grade. In 2008, over 150,000 teachers used it across the country to assess 2 million children. New mCLASS software is used by 16 states in their early childhood assessment programs. Table 9.3 provides an overview of these technology-focused assessment systems.

mCLASS Reading 3D

The reading assessment system, mCLASS Reading 3D, combines the DIBELS measures (discussed earlier) with an observational assessment based on Text Reading and Comprehension. This system provides ongoing progress monitoring (Andrea Reibel, vice president of Wireless Generation, personal communication, August 11, 2008). mCLASS software also provides a system for monitoring Individual Educational Plan progress with a PDA-based response to intervention (RTI) system. This RTI approach employs the DIBELS, 6th ed., software.

Table 9.3 Technology-Assisted Assessments

Measurement	Brief Description	Assessment Areas	Grade Level	Format for Scoring	Software Vendor
mCLASS Reading 3D	Developed by Wireless Generation	Text Reading and Comprehension	K to 5th grade	PDA	Wireless Generation
Texas Primary Reading Inventory (TPRI)	Developed at the University of Texas as a statewide measure of Reading and Language Arts Development	Phonemic Awareness, Phonics, Fluency, Vocabulary, and Comprehension	PK to 3rd grade	PDA	Wireless Generation
TejasLEE	Developed at the University of Texas Health Science Center, Houston, as a Spanish language Reading Skills Assessment	Prereading and primary reading skills in Spanish	K to 3rd grade	PDA	Wireless Generation
Indicadores Dinámicos del Éxito en la Lectura (mCLASS)	A Spanish language version of the DIBELS from the University of Oregon	Measures all the areas covered in the English language version of DIBELS	K to 3rd grade	PDA	Wireless Generation
mCLASS: Math	Developed by H. Ginsberg as a measure of early mathematics; similar to TEMA-III	Computation, Concepts, Missing Number, Number Facts, and Quantity Discrimination	K to 1st grade, 2nd and 3rd grades	PDA Written Test	Wireless Generation
STAR Early Literacy	Developed by Renaissance Learning Co. of Wisconsin (Rapids, WI)	44 subtests of Reading and Language Skills presented as 7 domain scores	PK to 3rd grade	CAT	Renaissance Learning

SOURCE: Adapted from the following manuals: *PALS, TPRI, TejasLEE, Indicadores Dinamicos del Exito en la Lectura, mCLASS: Math* (Wireless Generation), and *STAR Early Literacy* (Renaissance Learning).

In addition to providing software for the DIBELS assessment and monitoring system, Wireless Generation also developed software for Scott Foresman's Reading Street Series.

Texas Primary Reading Inventory (TPRI)

mCLASS individualized assessment software has also been designed for the Texas Primary Reading Inventory (TPRI). The TPRI describes itself as being a valid and reliable assessment tool that provides a picture of a student's reading/language arts development. TPRI was normed for use with students in prekindergarten through Grade 3. It is a quick screening keyed to work with a longer inventory. This combination makes it possible for primary grade teachers in Texas to identify strengths and problem areas as well as monitor progress in each child's reading skill development. Another advantage of the TPRI system is an instructional solutions guide in the form of the *Intervention Activities Guide* included in each classroom kit. The subtests of the TPRI match the Texas state mandates by including Phonemic Awareness, Phonics, Fluency, Vocabulary, and Comprehension (Texas Education Agency, 2006).

TejasLEE

Another measuring tool developed in Texas to measure reading skills and comprehension in Spanish is the TejasLEE. This mCLASS software provides an individually administered measure of reading skills covering four grade levels, kindergarten through Grade 3 (University of Texas Health Science Center at Houston, 2005). Figure 9.1 contains some of the topics in this assessment.

Figure 9.1 **Examples of Subtests in the TejasLEE**

Kindergarten

- Conocimiento de la Letra Impresa (Book and Print Awareness)
- Identificación de las Letras (Letter Naming)
- Conocimiento de los Sonidos (Letter Sound Identification/Sound-Symbol Correspondence)
- Conocimiento Fonológica (Phonological Awareness includes Syllables/Phonemes)
- Reconocimiento de las Palabras (Decoding/Single-Word Reading)
- Comprensión Auditiva (Listening Comprehension)

First Grade

- Conocimiento de los sonidos (Letter Sound Identification)
- Conocimiento Fonológica (Phonological Awareness includes Syllables/Phonemes)
- Comprensión Auditiva (Listening Comprehension)
- Exactitud de Lectura (Reading Accuracy)
- Proporción de la Fluidez de la Lectura (Reading Fluency)
- Comprensión de la Lectura (Reading Comprehension)

Second Grade

- Dictado (Spelling)
- Exactitud de Lectura (Reading Accuracy)
- Proporción de la Fluidez de la Lectura (Reading Fluency)
- Comprensión de la Lectura (Reading Comprehension)

Third Grade

- Dictado (Spelling)
- Accentuación y Diéresis (Application of Accents and Diaeresis)
- Fluidez en el Reconocimiento de las Palabras (Single Word Reading Fluency)
- Exactitud de Lectura (Reading Accuracy)
- Proporción de la Fluidez de la Lectura (Reading Fluency)
- Comprensión de la Lectura (Reading Comprehension)

Indicadores Dinámicos del Éxito en la Lectura (mCLASS IDEL)

The mCLASS software was designed for use in the administration of the Spanish language version of DIBELS, the Indicadores Dinámicos del Éxito en la Lectura (mCLASS IDEL). This individually administered measure can be used in conjunction with DIBELS to provide a method of monitoring the skill development of young children learning to read in both English and Spanish (Good, Cummings, & Baker, 2004).

mCLASS: Math

mCLASS also provides a brief **math screening** measurement system for early childhood designed by Herbert Ginsberg, coauthor of the Test of Early Mathematics Ability (TEMA) (see above). Ginsberg's math screening assessment is designed for one-on-one use with children in kindergarten and first grade (H. Ginsberg, 2007). A second version provides a written math screening measure that is given to groups of children. That screening for second and third grade provides scores in Computation, Concepts, Missing Number, Number Facts, and Quantity Discrimination. Once the class has completed the test, the teacher enters the scores online to mCLASS and receives back a class report for the five subtests.

The second direction is seen in **computer adaptive testing (CAT)**. This approach actually does all of the testing of young children and reports scores to the teacher. The teacher's role is to introduce the child to the testing protocol and then the computer takes over the assessment process with the child. Computer adaptive testing requires that the test publisher's item file stored in the computer be graded for item difficulty. When a child logs on to the system, the difficulty level of the items a child experiences are selected by the computer software based on what the system remembers about the child's previous learning. If the child gets all the items correct, the computer software presents the child with more and more difficult questions and tasks. It stops only when the child has reached a high level of proficiency, or is making errors and getting items wrong. If the software finds the child cannot handle the level of questions, it begins lowering the item difficulty until it finds the appropriate level for the child's understanding.

Computer adaptive testing is replacing paper and pencil, high-stakes, state-mandated tests (Way, 2005; R. Wright, 2008). Other versions of this CAT system include an early literacy assessment, the STAR Early Literacy.

STAR Early Literacy

STAR Early Literacy is an online CAT approach to the measurement of developing reading skills among children between prekindergarten and Grade 3. The full assessment includes 44 areas for testing and provides seven scores. Graphophonemic Knowledge, General Readiness, Phonemic Awareness, Phonics, Comprehension, Structural Analysis, and Vocabulary. The average time required for the assessment is 13 minutes (T. Graham & Ward, 2005). If the young child being tested is not familiar with the use of a computer mouse and clicking on answers, the STAR software provides a developmentally appropriate tutorial.

The STAR Early Literacy is designed to select increasingly difficult items in each of the seven domains being tested. It stops the testing when the child is getting less than 75% of the computer stimulus queries right. The system has good reliability with a test–retest reliability of 0.87. STAR Early Literacy is a criterion-referenced measure and does not report scores on a norm-referenced or standardized score system. The standardization of the test was based on a sample of 11,000 children in 84 different schools. That sample was skewed toward the southeast states and is underrepresentative of the northeast states (T. Graham & Ward, 2005). It also included too few children from families at the upper end of the socioeconomic scale.

Overall, it is a user-friendly system that provides a good alternative to the one-on-one screening tests. Renaissance Learning sells schools a license and software package for an initial cost of $149.00. Each year, after purchasing the license, there is a per child cost of $0.39 (2009).

A sample of the items on the STAR Early Literacy is available online at http://www.renlearn.com/sel/test.aspx.

Summary

Administering and scoring one-on-one achievement assessments are a regular part of the job for early childhood educators. Two central areas for concern with early achievement are prereading and reading skills and early mathematics. These dimensions are the central focus of many assessment tools. Neither learning to read nor acquiring the skills to understand arithmetic operations come naturally to most children. Careful teaching by parents and teachers is essential for the child to progress and be a successful learner. Part of the process of teaching is having a good understanding of just what each child's level of skill acquisition is and what he or she is ready to learn. This implies a need for specific information about skill development.

In addition to the many one-on-one assessments available for measuring early achievement, there are also new innovative ways to measure the achievement status of children that are technology based. A growing number of assessments are designed to be recorded and analyzed using software loaded into PDAs. Computer adaptive testing is also making inroads into both the early childhood classroom and as the platform for statewide assessments under testing mandates.

Discussion Questions

1. What are the strengths and weaknesses of using a CAT model for early assessments in achievement areas like reading and mathematics?
2. If you were to provide a short talk to a parent group at your preschool, what would you tell them about their role in improving prereading skills?
3. What advantages does using a clipboard and test record form have when individually assessing a child?
4. Explain why it is, or is not, a good idea to use a measure of reading skill development in Spanish with children who come from homes where Spanish is the language of choice?

Related Readings

Cerra, C., & Jacoby, R. (2007). *Test talk! Understanding the stakes and helping your children do their best.* Hoboken, NJ: John Wiley.

Sunderman, G. L., Kim, J. S., & Orfield, G. (2005). *NCLB meets school realities: Lessons from the field.* Thousand Oaks, CA: Corwin Press.

Tileston, D. W. (2006). *What every parent should know about schools, standards, and high stakes tests.* Thousand Oaks, CA: Sage.

Wright, R. J., Martland, J., & Stafford, A. K. (2006). *Early numeracy: Assessment for teaching and intervention.* Thousand Oaks, CA: Sage.

Notes

1. When told by Terman that he was carrying the lead plates to print an achievement test, Cap Hodgson, president of World Book, is said to have replied, "What's an achievement test?" (Tom Fitzgibbon, former president of Harcourt Brace Jovanovich, the successor of World Book, personal communication, November 2006).
2. For example: What should you do if you scrape your knee in a fall?

3. There are no current statistics on reliability for the 1998 standardization.
4. Before 2006, QELI was known as the Iowa Early Learning Inventory.
5. Verbal activities with a baby can include explaining what is being done with him/her when being bathed or cared for. It can also involve singing songs when around the child, or even describing what the adult is doing or sees in the environment.
6. In Chapter 2, the DIBELS was described in some detail.
7. Decile is a percentile band including 10% of the population. A decile score of 6 on a subtest indicates that the child did as well as, or better than, 60% of the referent sample of children.
8. See the note of caution on interpreting reliability values from tests where children do not take all test items early in this chapter.

Part IV
Parent Communication and Special Needs Children

One central point of communication between parents and teachers is progress reports that take the form of periodic report cards. Report cards are now given at every primary grade level including kindergarten. Most schools have begun to employ a standards-based reporting system complete with rubrics and benchmarks covering 40 or more areas of skill and achievement.

The war on social promotion has increased the role of high-stakes tests in determining a child's eligibility for grade-level promotion. Report cards present special problems when children with disabilities and English language learners are graded. Also, problems arise with transfer children.

Technology now plays an increasingly important role in grading and reporting to parents. As schools become more computer capable, parents have the ability to be in daily contact with early childhood educators.

Open and ongoing communication is needed with parents of children experiencing learning difficulties. The process of meeting requirements of Section 504 of the Rehabilitation Act and requirements of the Individuals With Disabilities Education Improvement Act requires ongoing parental involvement. Services provided under early intervention are channeled through the at-risk child's family. Even the Individual Family Service Plan must be developed in the context of the child's family.

This section provides descriptions of major problems children may experience that interfere with normal development and learning. The identification of attention deficit/hyperactivity disorder (AD/HD) and the spectrum of autism disorders are explained.

Chapter 12 describes how preschools and primary grade schools can improve the level of parental engagement in the school's programs. Evidence of the positive impact on early learning as a function of engaged parents is described. Two forms of engagement, school based and home based, are discussed in terms of optimizing every child's academic skills. The section also addresses the special problem of improving the level of engagement with ethnic and language minority families.

Evaluating, Grading, and Reporting to Parents

10

We all get report cards in many different ways, but the real excitement of what you're doing is in the doing of it. It's not what you're gonna get in the end—it's not the final curtain—it's really in the doing it, and loving what I'm doing.

—Ralph Lauren, *Designer*

Introduction and Themes

The first use of report cards occurred in American colleges during the 18th century. This practice spread to all public schools and eventually to early childhood education. Reporting systems have taken a number of forms, but one of the most persistent has been the use of letter grades. Today, letter grades are being supplanted by standards-based systems of grading. New report cards present parents with a checklist of the child's achievement of the learning standards for the grade level.

Report cards serve as legal documents and must be completed by primary grade teachers. These reports can be tempered by the careful use of comments about the child. There is no one right format for report cards, and they can be designed to best meet the needs of local communities.

Another direction for making progress reports to parents is the use of carefully structured written narrations by the teacher. These narratives describe the progress and successes of children to their parents.

Perhaps the most effective way to inform parents of their child's progress is through the use of parent conferences. Teachers who are well prepared and organized have the most productive parent conferences. Parent conferences can be especially important for keeping parents of children receiving special services informed of their child's progress and growth.

The decision to promote a child to the next grade has traditionally been made by teachers and parents. Each child's progress as described on his/her report card was weighed in that promotion versus retention decision. High-stakes tests have changed all this for tens of millions of children. These tests have taken promotion decisions away from parents and teachers.

There is little evidence to support the policy of retaining children in their grade as a way to improve academic achievement. This policy is also related to the likelihood that a child will eventually drop out of school.

Learning Objectives

By reading and studying this chapter, you should acquire the competency to:

- Debate the use of standards-based grades on early childhood reports versus the use of narrative reports.
- Describe various report card formats in use today in early childhood education.
- Explain how the movement to stop "social promotion" has impacted schools and children in the third grade.
- Write high-quality narrative format progress reports.
- Provide guidance to novice teachers about writing effective report card comments.
- Organize and conduct a successful series of parent conferences.
- Describe the problems associated with providing progress reports to the parents of children receiving special education services.

First Grading Systems

Use of report cards is as old as our nation. The practice of providing ordinal grades on a report card started in higher education and was designed to provide a method of selecting students for honor society membership.[1]

Growth of public education throughout the 19th century was accompanied by the adoption of grading models copied from higher education. Educators adopted the familiar 100-point scale, developed at Harvard College, to provide "progress reports" for the parents. Progress reports gave parents a number selected to represent how much a child learned from the banquet of knowledge presented by the teacher (Kingston, 2005, p. 5). One hundred-point systems imply a percentile for learning. Even though the 100-point system is rarely, if ever, used in early childhood education, its vestige is still there in some public schools in the form of requirements for letter-grades to equal the "percentage of the curriculum learned" (e.g., A = 90–100, B = 80–89, C = 70–79, D = 60–69, Below 60 = F).

Report Card Checklists

Most school systems require primary teachers summarize everything in each child's portfolio into some form of ordinal sequence of grades on a checklist. The format for report cards has changed dramatically in this era of standards-based education. Today's report card marks are not the global letter grades for an entire discipline, for example, Arithmetic "B," Reading "A," which were ubiquitous until 1998. Now, primary grade report cards describe the child's achievement of specific learning standards and objectives. This grading process is summative and is required several times each year. All report cards are legal documents and part of the school's required database during state audits.

Altering Grades

The ultimate authority over a child's report card is in the hands of the school system's superintendant. While classroom teachers in every grade between kindergarten and high school assign grades and write report cards, any grade can be changed by the school system's administration.

The following statement appears in the regulations of the Education Department of the State of New Mexico:

New Mexico Register / Volume XIX, Number 13 / July 16, 2008

6.30.10.5 **Effective Date:** July 16, 2008, unless a later date is cited at the end of a section.

6.30.10.6 **Objective:** The purpose of this rule is to establish minimal requirements for those school districts and charter schools that seek to permit changes to a student's final course grades, and to require that school districts and charter schools adopt written policies for any change to a student's grade. While a change in a final course grade should be the exception and not the rule *once a classroom teacher has issued a final course grade, the enactment of written policies coupled with consistent application of those policies should result in the changing of grades only when warranted* and should lead to increased public confidence in the process.

Standards-Based Report Cards

The original No Child Left Behind Act of 2002 (P.L. 107-110) mandated the development of standards-based education for every public and charter school in the country. Paralleling the development of state standards for learning has been the conversion of report cards for most school systems to standards-based reporting systems. This change reflects how schools are working to provide parents with information about their child's progress expressed in the form used by the state to judge schools. At first, these **standards-based report cards** confused as many parents as they helped (Guskey, 2002; Pemberton-Butler, 1999). See Figure 10.1 for an example of this new format for a primary grade report card.

Along with new report cards have come revised methods for grading. These "new grades" are similar to the following adopted by schools in Albuquerque, New Mexico:

- Advanced
- Proficient
- Nearing proficient
- Emerging

See http://ww2.aps.edu/ for more on the Albuquerque schools.

The Palm Beach School System (Florida) began using a 3-point scale for grades in 2006.

- At or above grade level.
- Less than one year below grade level
- Far below grade level

See http://www.palmbeach.k12.fl.us/cotaylores/PntSdtInfo.html for more about Palm Beach public schools. Other good examples of this model of report card can be seen at the following URLs:

Sample Kindergarten Report Card Employing a Standards-based System from the Federal City Schools, Washington: http://www.fwsd.wednet.edu/cur/tlc/

Sample Kindergarten Report Card Employing Rubrics from Harrison County, South Dakota: http://www.harrisoncsd.org/pdf/rubrics-k.pdf.

Figure 10.1 Kindergarten Report Card, Walnut Creek School District

Walnut Creek School District
Kindergarten Report Card

School Name:

Academic Year: 2005–2006

Academic Legend: Grade level Expectations for the End of the Trimester	
Exceeds Standards – *Consistently grasps, applies, and extends key concepts, processes, and skills. Works beyond stated goals.*	**ES**
Meets Standards – *Grasps and applies key concepts, processes, and skills. Meets stated goals.*	**MS**
Approaching Standards – *Beginning to grasps and apply key concepts, processes, and skills. Making less than expected progress.*	**AS**
Needs support – *Not grasping key concepts, processes, and essential skills. Area of concern that requires support.*	**NS**
Not assessed at this time	**X**

Language Arts Standards	**T1**	**T2**	**T2**
Reading			
a. Identifies upper case letters: /26 | /26 | /26			
b. Identifies lower case letters: /26 | /26 | /26			
c. Identifies letter sounds: /26 | /26 | /26			
d. Produces rhyming words			
e. Discriminates beginning sounds			
f. Hears and blends sounds			
g. Identifies concepts of print (left to right, spacing, words, top to bottom)			
h. Reads basic sight words			
i. Comprehends and retells a story			

Student Name:

Teacher Name:

Attendance	**T1**	**T2**	**T2**
Total Days			
Days Tardy			
Days Absent			

Mathematics Standards	**T1**	**T2**	**T2**
< indicates area of need			
Number Sense			
a. Understands 1 to 1 correspondence			
b. Compares sets with up to 10 objects each by using the teams more than, less than, and equal to			
c. Identifies numbers to: ☐ 10 ☐ 20 ☐ 30			
d. Counts to: ☐ 10 ☐ 20 ☐ 30			
e. Orders numbers to: ☐ 10 ☐ 20 ☐ 30			
f. Demonstrates the concepts of add / substract using manipulatives			
g. Recognizes when estimates are reasonable			

Language Arts Standards	T1	T2	T2
Writing			
a. Writes first name			
b. Forms upper / lower case letters correctly			
c. Uses phonetic sounds for temporary spelling in words and sentences			
d. Writes left to right, top to bottom			
e. Writes short vowel words from dictation			
Listening & Speaking			
a. Follows one and two step oral directions			
b. Speaks in complete and coherent sentences			
c. Expresses ideas in front of a group			

History/Social Science Standards	T1	T2	T2
a. Geographic concepts (maps, symbols, relative location – near/far)			
b. Historical concepts (past and present, people and events)	**Taught but not formally assessed**		
c. Community concepts (self, family, jobs, and citizenship)			

Mathematics Standards	T1	T2	T2
Algebra & Functions			
a. Sorts/classifies objects by 1 attribute			
Geometry & Measurement			
a. Tells time to the hour			
b. Compares length, weight, and capacity of objects			
c. Identifies geometric shapes ■ ● ▲ ▬			
d. Identifies 3-dimensional shapes (sphere, cone, cube)			
Statistics, Data Analysis & Probability			
a. Understands and uses pictographs			
b. Describes/identifies patterns			
c. Extends patterns			
Mathematical Reasoning			
a. Demonstrates and explains simple story problems using manipulatives			

SOURCE: Walnut Creek School District, Walnut Creek, CA, 94597. Used with permission.

Whose Report?

The central reason for requiring report cards is to meet the needs of the parents by providing accurate information about each child.[2] Until children reach their 18th birthday, all report cards are written to and for parents. Parents want report cards with which they can be comfortable and that are easy to understand. As a general principle, parents are more comfortable with the report card format they grew up seeing. This explains why it took a number of years for schools to move away from global letter grades (A, B, C, etc.) and adopt **standards-based grades** (Clarridge & Whitaker, 1997).

Parent comfort notwithstanding, the problem with standards-based grades is they are easily misinterpreted by both parents and children (Marzano, 2000). They also take more time for teachers to complete. A significant gap exists between what a teacher means in assigning an ordinal achievement value on a report card and what parents think they are being told (Waltman & Frisbie, 1994). Report card grades are beyond the conceptual understanding of children below the second grade and cannot have a reward effect because young children cannot understand them. What can be of great significance in the life of a primary grade child is a letter sent home. An example of this is given in Case in Point 10.1.

Case in Point 10.1

Power of Positive Reinforcement

What has a significant impact on a young child is a short note sent by mail or e-mail expressing the teacher's pleasure regarding some aspect of the child's learning. That type of communication will quickly find itself mounted by refrigerator magnets in a prominent spot. This little reinforcement can even be more powerful if the preschool's director or school principal signs the note.

One principal I know makes it a point to check with all his teachers on a regular basis to learn which children have done something especially well, or who have accomplished a difficult learning. Once known, he visits classrooms during quiet seatwork time, crouches down next to the child, and whispers a message of kudos about the child's success. He then gives the shocked youngster a sealed letter for the parents expressing his pleasure with the child's work. Small gestures like this can be the most powerful motivator for future effort that could be given.

Teachers of the school appreciate this type of support and have created a verb, *Blackburned,* after the name of the principal. In the lexicon of that school, it describes the glow a child has after being reinforced this way by the principal. After the classroom visit, the child has been Blackburned.

Attitude Grades

Perhaps the most confusing grades on report cards of the recent past are those for attitude and nonacademic behaviors. **Attitudinal grades** reported to parents on report cards have included dimensions such as Deportment, Citizenship, Cooperation, and Work Habits. These were, and in many cases still are, purely the subjective opinion of the classroom teacher. It is easy to visualize a parent trying to determine what a grade of "75" in deportment was all about, or what a "C" in work habits meant.

Attitudinal measurements have been replaced on primary report cards with variables providing qualitative descriptions of how children go about learning. These look a lot like comments from 50 years ago, including Punctuality, Cooperation With Peers, Organization, Focus and Attention on Tasks, Exhibiting Concern for Others, Class Participation, and Compliance With Rules. See Figure 10.2 for an example of this type of reporting system for attitudes and behaviors.

Figure 10.2 Primary Report Card Items for Attitudes and Behaviors

Personal Planning

- Identifies a number of activities that contribute to a healthy lifestyle
- Explains how physical activity contributes to health
- Understands how eating the right foods can keep a person healthy
- Progress in personal planning in relation to learning outcomes

Work Habits

- Shows a positive attitude toward learning
- Demonstrates consistent effort
- Focuses on tasks
- Begins learning activities with little support from the teacher
- Progress in work habits relative to expectations

Social Responsibility

- Cleans up area when finished using materials
- Treats classmates fairly and respectfully
- Able to identify simple ways to improve the classroom
- Recognizes and responds to the needs of others

Grade Level Promotion/Retention

Report card grades provide information needed to decide about a child's promotion to the next grade. Heretofore the decision to retain children was made by educators in close consultation with the child's parents. That approach is now being replaced by reliance on high-stakes test scores to make the decision.

In the recent past, being the one who did not move on with his/her peers opened the child up to personal embarrassment and ridicule.[3] Being "left back" was a traumatic occurrence in the life of a child. Schoolyard taunts were common and the psychological pain of public failure was insufferable. The stigma of "flunking the grade" changed as a function of the testing mandates of 2002. When so many children were retained-in-grade, the sting of failure was removed. The U.S. Department of Education (USDOE) estimates that about 15% of all children in public school have been retained-in-grade one or more times (National Center for Educational Statistics, 2006). The number retained is even greater in states and cities where grade promotion is contingent on passing a high-stakes test. These estimates by the USDOE have been disputed by the National Association of School Psychologists, which estimates that between 30% and 50% of all children are retained-in-grade at least one time before they graduate or leave school (National Association of School Psychologists, 2003).

The War on Social Promotion

In his state of the union address in 1999, President Bill Clinton called for the end of **social promotion**[4] (Clinton, 1999a, 1999b). One outcome has been the use of high-stakes tests by seven states and a number of large city school systems to retain children who do not test at a proficient level.[5] The goal of requiring **grade retention** for children with low scores on high-stakes tests was stopping social promotion. The focal year for this process is Grade 3. Grade 3 was targeted as being the last year when elementary teachers teach reading skills.

Retention and Equity

An issue with grade retention is that it occurs more frequently among minority students (Massachusetts Department of Education, 2005). Overall, approximately three out of four children retained-in-grade are members of minority groups. African American children are the group most likely to be retained-in-grade. Two times as many African American children are retained-in-grade compared to their Anglo-white peers (National Center for Educational Statistics, 2006). Another group that has a disproportionately high number of children retained-in-grade are English language learners (ELL), especially children of Hispanic heritage (Hauser, 2001). An analysis of Florida data by Jay Greene of the conservative Manhattan Institute concluded that black and Hispanic third graders are retained-in-grade because of something related to their race, not just lower average achievement test scores (Matus, 2009).

Value of Grade Retention

More children are retained in their grade for an extra year in the United States than in any other industrial nation in the world (Holmes, 2006). Yet, for all the expectations of state legislatures, there is no evidence that grade retention has any lasting positive effect.

Thirty years of research have never provided proof of an academic achievement advantage through the grade retention of young children (Kelly, 1999; Nichols, Glass, & Berliner, 2006; Thompson & Cunningham, 2000; J. Wright, 1979). It appears that children retained-in-grade lose ground, not make it up (Roderick & Nagaoka, 2005). In states requiring a minimum score on a high-stakes test for promotion, the number of retained children is increasing (Georgia Association of School Psychologists, 2003; Kindergarten Readiness Issues Group, 2003). The National Association of School Psychologists (2003) condemned the whole concept of grade retention as inappropriate and ineffective.

A study of data from Florida has shown that one outcome of the war on social promotion has been a slight improvement in the average Florida Comprehensive Achievement Test (FCAT) scores after third grade. Third grade is the first grade requiring a passing score on the FCAT for promotion. This improvement was praised by then Governor Jeb Bush (1998–2006) as showing how the "tough-love" of Florida's no social promotion policy improved the schools (Matus, 2007).

What on first examination appeared to be an improvement in the average score of fourth graders was a statistical artifact. The fourth grade increase happened in schools with high failure rates among third grade children taking the test. The result of removing all low-scoring children from the population in fourth grade was to create an artificial improvement in the achievement scores of fourth graders. The average state test scores for subsequent grades beyond fourth also benefited from the policy of retaining third graders for one or two extra years (Haney, 2006). However, the price paid for the improvement occurred in the third grade where average scores fell and a population of retained students dramatically increased the grade-level enrollment. The Florida data are described in Case in Point 10.2.

Case in Point 10.2

Causalities in the "War on Social Promotion"

In 2005–2006, 8,000 children in Florida (one of the first states to mandate promotion tests) spent a third year as third graders. In an attempt to prevent a buildup in the number of children stuck in third grade, Florida began to put repeating third grade children into fourth grade halfway through the school year. Each school district was given permission to decide how to determine if a retained child was able to move on to fourth grade. The sad truth was that many of these children still could not be promoted at midyear because they were unable to pass the local assessment test. In 2005, one county school system in Florida gave 750 repeating third graders early promotion into fourth grade only to find that 84% failed the mandated fourth grade examination and ended up repeating that grade (Harrison, 2005). Richard Stiggins observed that our obsession with high-stakes testing is causing major segments of our student population to be *left behind* because the mandated measures are causing many kids to give up in hopelessness (Stiggins, 2002).[6]

Test-based grade promotion in primary education is not well received by many educators. In Georgia, there was a clear effort to circumvent the required retention of thousands of 9-year-old children who failed the third grade high-stakes test. Conservative critics castigated educators as being lawbreakers (Green, 2008).

A Price to Pay

The decision to end social promotion by requiring a score of proficient on a statewide high-stakes test is not an inexpensive one. The cost of adding an extra year to the education of a child costs an average of $8,500, and is much higher for some states (National Center for Educational Statistics, 2008). Table 10.1 depicts this cost for North Carolina.

Table 10.1 Data From North Carolina on the Cost of Grade Retention in 2002

Kindergarten Retained = 6,758	Extra year of education = $51,468,928
Grade 1 Retained = 6,860	Extra year of education = $52,245,760
Grade 2 Retained = 3,756	Extra year of education = $28,605,696
Grade 3 Retained = 4,969	Extra year of education = $37,843,904
Total cost (2002) of primary grade retention in North Carolina = $170,164,288	

SOURCE: FPG Child Development Institute, The University of North Carolina, Chapel Hill, available at http://www.fpg.unc.edu/~pir/retention_brief.pdf

States opting to prevent social promotion are not alone in paying a high price for their choice. New York City's schools new policy of requiring third grade children pass a test to be promoted to fourth grade cost $115 million the first year (Fair Test, 2007).

Interpreting Report Card Grades

Report card grades or checklist scores are not as straightforward as they may seem. Each grade represents a composite picture of the child. Even though report cards give teachers space to write comments to the parents, this does not prevent nonacademic factors from affecting the grades on progress reports.

Standards-based grades can be influenced by individual educator's perceptions of a child's effort, alertness, attention to detail, penmanship, and actual achievement. Most primary teachers consider process as well as outcome when assigning grades (Marzano, 2000). Teacher opinion and attitudes can have an impact on report cards for children on the cusp between two rating scale levels (Brookhart, 1991). This makes the meaning of report cards idiosyncratic and murky at best (Clarridge & Whitaker, 1997). Grades represent many pieces of student work, weighted and combined into a single statement. From kindergarten through the second grade, most teachers try not to emphasize report cards, preferring other ways to communicate with parents. By third grade, report cards play a larger role in the child's overall assessment and reporting to parents.

It is not uncommon for a third grader who receives a grade of "Below proficient" to ask his/her teacher what would be necessary to get a grade of "Proficient," only to be told to "work harder." This may reflect the fact that the teacher is unclear of what his/her expectations really are for the child. It can also mean that the teacher has a vague feeling of what the child is able to do, and wants to leave room for improvement. This type of nonanswer for the child's question provides him/her with virtually no guidance, and reflects how report card grades have an almost ephemeral nature (Clarridge & Whitaker, 1997).

At best, report cards can be viewed as presenting estimated summations of what children have learned and can do. Report cards tell nothing of efforts and difficulties students experience in learning new material or acquiring new skills. Most report cards do not demonstrate a child's strengths nor do they elaborate on the child's areas of weakness (Brookhart, 1991). See Case in Point 10.3 for a traditional report card system still employed in the public schools.

Case in Point 10.3

Local School Report Card

Local school systems create grading systems and design report cards that best serve their community's needs. One result for American education is there are thousands of variations in place for meeting the basic need to record and report achievement. One of them was developed to serve Tangipahoa Parish, Louisiana. Starting with first graders, that district requires letter grades be recorded for all subjects based on the following standards:

A = 94 to 100%

B = 87 to 93%

C = 78 to 86%

D = 70 to 77%

F = 0 to 69%

The district does not provide teachers with guidance as to what the percentage values are linked to, but it does provide detailed information for calculating a grade point average starting with first graders. These grade points are then linked to the school's "Honor Roll." Thus, children from the first grade onward can be on the honor roll for the school. Kindergarten children in Tangipahoa Parish are graded with the following system:

M = Skill has been mastered. This is defined as 80 to 100%

I = Improving. This is defined as 70 to 79%

N = Needs improvement. This is defined as 0 to 69 %

To see the full report card model go to: http://www.tangischools.org/handbk/grading.pdf.

Stickers and Stars

Grading the quality of learning achieved by young children and reporting that information to parents is a complex instructional task. First, when grading young children the process should be developmentally appropriate (Brumbaugh, 2008). One developmental need for young children is the acquisition of a sense of competence and ability to cope (White, 1959).

Children respond well to positive reinforcement including praise by the teacher. A simple statement by a kindergarten teacher to a class such as, "*I like the way Darlene has cleaned up her table and is ready for . . .*" will result in others following suit and cleaning their areas and preparing for the next activity. Primary grade classroom teachers are the central players in children's lives for the hours spent in school. Praise from a teacher is a powerful motivator. Similarly, young children take pride in workbook pages or worksheets on which the teacher placed a sticker to indicate good work. Primary grade children will practice drawing pentagrams (stars) for hours until they have mastered the crayon strokes needed to produce this mark that the teacher uses on only the best student work.

Wise teachers know how to use this power of positive reinforcement to facilitate learning and control behavior. Likewise, good early childhood educators know how to resist the temptation of overcorrecting children or using many red marks on the student's work. Consistent criticism will wear a child down and produce the opposite effect from what is desired. In all endeavors, young children need to be guided toward the desired end in a way that minimizes criticism by focusing on what is being done correctly.

Self-Esteem and Report Cards

One of the links between teacher behavior and developing personalities of young children involves self-esteem. The picture children carry within themselves as to who they are, and how others see them, forms their **self-concept.** This concept can be right on target, or it can be way off base. The evaluation by the child of the concept of the self which he or she holds is known as **self-esteem,** and is an expression of the child's sense of self-worth (Coopersmith, 1967; Reeve, Deci, & Ryan, 2004). There is clear evidence that for elementary age children one element of self-concept and esteem is how well they do in school (Phye, 1996). Also, research has shown that the young child's self-concept and esteem level are very malleable during the early years (Poole, Miller, & Church, 2004). Middle class children today typically have many after school activities. See Case in Point 10.4 for examples.

Case in Point 10.4

A Child's Daily Schedule

School represents only a fractional part of the child's day. After school activities also make a major contribution to the growing child's self-concept. Middle class parents schedule their child's free time as tightly as the schedule of a corporate lawyer. Young children learn to play musical instruments, play soccer, tap dance, play pee wee football, ice skate, play ice hockey, do the ballet, and play T-ball. All of these activities and the myriad of others in which young children are enrolled involve learning new skills and rules. Each of these contributes to the self-confidence, poise, and self-concept of the developing child.

Report Card Comments

Nonacademic factors about how children work in the classroom are of concern for both teachers and parents and should be included in the comment section of the report card. Writing comments on report cards is a labor-intensive job that most educators dislike. Comment writing takes a long time because each word must be carefully considered. It is all too easy for the parents to misread teacher's intentions and miss the point the teacher was making. Yet, these comments are important links in the chain of communication between the home and school. Report cards are legal documents and a permanent record for the child; these comments must be carefully crafted and well written.

Valley Elementary School

"I got an "A" in Gym Class, and a "C" in both Arithmetic and Reading, and a "D" in Language Arts. I guess that makes me a "B" student. Pretty good, don't ya think?"

SOURCE: Cartoon by Merv Magus.

Space is limited on the report card comment area; therefore, the comments need to be pithy, accurate, and succinct. Appropriate comments are specific and address an identifiable issue. Comments can provide kudos and reinforce children's positive self-images. Positive comments may contain words such as efficient, thorough, committed, caring, cheerful, follows directions, helpful, listens carefully, and insightful. Likewise, the comment section can provide parents with insight into problems the child is experiencing. Comments such as the following can direct parents to these areas needing attention: has difficulty with . . . , must be reminded to . . . , needs to be urged . . . , cries frequently . . . , has failed to master . . . , and continues to struggle with . . .

There are no absolutes in education. For that reason, the use of words and phrases implying an absolute should be avoided. Such words include never, cannot, refuse, will not, is unable to, inevitably, and always. A number of school systems have developed an approved list of comments teachers can select from for report cards. These are typically part of a computerized report card system. Internet locations offering hundreds of comments are also available for teachers to use when writing report cards. The following are four of these:

http://www.teachersnetwork.org/ntol/howto/align/reportsam/

http://www.teachnet.com/how-to/endofyear/personalcomments061400.html

http://www.teachervision.fen.com/page/6964.html

http://www.education-world.com/a_curr/profdev/profdev148.shtml

Narrative Reports

Most preschools and many primary level elementary schools employ narrative reports in lieu of, or along with, report cards. Written reports fill gaps left behind by simple letter grades and provide parents with a multifaceted assessment of their child. Writing a thoughtful narrative about each child in a primary grade classroom is very labor intensive (Francis, 2006). Spending 15 minutes writing a well conceived description of a child is a daunting task when done for 25 children four times a year. There is also the question of copy-editing narratives before they go to the parents (see Case in Point 10.5).

Case in Point 10.5

Grammar Counts

A suburban elementary school began sending brief narrative reports home with the school's standards-based report cards. This policy was enacted by the school district as a requirement for all primary grade level children. The policy change occurred when the district reduced the class size in all primary grades to a maximum of 18 children.

An elementary school administrator was surprised to find a parent of a first grader in her office the day after report cards went home. She assumed that the parent was there to complain about the child's grades. The mother handed the principal a narrative report that accompanied the standards-based report cards. As the principal read it, she quickly realized the problem. The teacher had made both spelling and serious errors in syntax in writing the document that went home. The parent, a secondary school teacher, had used a red pen to correct the narrative, and added comments about the quality of writing. The parent went on to ask the principal to move her daughter to a classroom with a more literate teacher.

Some schools provide an outline or structured list of topics for the teacher to address when composing narrative reports (see Figure 10.3).

Other schools and child care centers provide teachers with wide latitude in deciding what dimensions to address in a narrative report. Written reports should give parents an accurate, balanced, and impartial picture of their child in school (McAfee & Leong, 1994). It should be evidence based and able to be documented using portfolio and test data. Additional data can be found by making systematic observations and through discussions with other teachers, administrators, and specialists having contact with the child.

Figure 10.3 Garnet Rock Elementary School Narrative Report

Grade 1

Name of Child ______________________________

Teacher & Classroom No. ______________________________

Date of Report ______________________________

Scheduled Date & Time for Parent Conference ______________________________

Cognitive Learnings and Skill Development

Reading Skills

Writing Skills

Mathematical Knowledge and Skills

Scientific Understanding and Reasoning

Creative Arts

Social Skills and Emotional Development

Interactions With Other Children

Cooperation With Teachers and Staff

Attention and Focus on Tasks

Organization and Planning

Efficiency and Time Use

Organization and Work Habits

Physical Education and Development

Large Motor Skills

Fine Motor Skills

General Comments and Issues

The narrative report should begin with a positive statement about the child. This can include a description of the unique characteristics of the child and a list of his/her special talents and skills. Next, the narrative should describe the progress being made toward reaching the curriculum goals for the grade level. These factual statements can be enhanced with examples, such as,

> She has made much progress so far this year in arithmetic. At this point she has learned the concept of addition and understands addition with single digits. She also recognizes that a number does not change when counted objects are rearranged and appear to be different. We are now working on the concept of two-digit numbers by adding digits to 10 or more.

A copy of the narrative report should be saved in the child's portfolio. Points described on the document can be revised into goals for the child to achieve and discussed during the next parent conference.

Parent Conferences

Parent conferences are a regular part of the school year for all preschools and elementary schools. A current trend is for more communication to occur between parents and educators through e-mail. However, the 30-minute parent conference will be part of the preschool or elementary school program for years to come. In primary grades, it is important to hold the first parent conference prior to the first report card. This schedule provides teachers an opportunity to explain the system he/she uses for progress reporting.

Online Report Cards

Written report cards will soon be viewed as a quaint educational technique from a bygone era. The trend today is to use online parental communications, including the use of **online report cards.** Web-based systems can facilitate continuous communication between parents and each child's teacher during online office hours. Early childhood teachers can be in daily contact with parents of children needing extra help. Primary teachers can post daily homework assignments making it possible for parents to check student assignments. Preschool teachers can describe lessons completed that day, and introduce new ideas to be introduced in the near future.

Another new electronic report card software feature makes it possible for parents to track their child's daily progress. Thus, there are no surprises when parents have a conference with their child's teacher. Some new systems can even make it possible for parents to see into the teacher's grade book.

The time teachers spend recording achievement scores and determining how each child is doing compared to state standards can be greatly reduced by technology. Electronic report cards can be generated automatically, saving teachers time (Francis, 2006). However, there is no available technology that can make the subjective decisions required to write good narrative descriptions of children.

Educational technology has some problems. One involves computer security, and having the entire school community wired and online. Secondly, when an online reporting and communication system is implemented, it is critical that no family be left behind. Parents must be computer literate and check the system daily. Inservice education for parents and help in parents' acquisition of home computers must be addressed by school systems moving in this direction. One thing that is helping in this effort is the development of a new generation of very inexpensive computers,[7] and Wi-Fi access being provided to entire cities.

Below are several commercial software models for online grade reporting.

http://www.engrade.com/

http://www.thinkwave.com/

http://www.mygradebook.com/

http://www.ahisd.net/gradespeedparent.htm

Some school systems have developed their own "in-house" online grade reporting systems. For example, the Montgomery County School System (MD) has developed and implemented a two-tier system known as the "Online Achievement and Reporting System" (OARS) that provides a computerized grade book for all teachers and also an e-mail link for all parents. OARS can be reviewed at: http://www.montgomeryschoolsmd.org/departments/oars/faq.shtm#Staff_WhatIsOars.

Online reporting systems are well suited for the new standards-based report cards. The software is very costly but the model is growing in use.

Transfer Students

Teachers recognize that once the school year is under way a new child is a potentially disrupting influence on a well-organized classroom. Transfer students need a lot of attention and help to learn routines of school and classroom. This takes a significant amount of the teacher's time. Time must also be spent administering and evaluating various assessments needed to determine appropriate learning groups for the new arrival.

Moving from school to school is no small matter in the United States. Overall, about one family in six moves to a new home each year (El Nasser & Overberg, 2007). About half of the moving is done within the same county or parish, and almost all moves occur among families with parents in their 20s and 30s.

Deleterious impacts from frequent moving can be seen in graduation rates. Children from families who do not move, and who live in the same school district for all 13 years (K to 12), have a 95% graduation rate. With children who have changed residences one time in the 13 years, the graduation rate falls to 68%, and those who moved three or more times have a graduation rate of 30% (Bracey, 1989).

There are a number of reasons why a family moves and transfers children to new schools. Some families move frequently because they are in the military. Military personnel are frequently rotated to different duty stations and take their families with them. The military community of families is well organized and ready for the inevitability of moving. Research has shown that children with parents in the armed forces do not suffer from the experience (Smrekar & Owens, 2003). This may reflect many support systems in place for members of our armed services.

Middle class families tend to move for strategic reasons related to jobs and opportunities (Horvath, 2004). These families normally plan ahead and try to make a smooth transition for their children to new schools.

Children of impoverished families are most likely to experience school problems related to moving. Often, poor families move because of life's circumstances, not because they want to move. Middle class families can hire tutors and pay for academic summer camps to make the transition to a new neighborhood and school easier for their children. This is not an option for most impoverished families. As a result, children of the poor frequently have lower levels of achievement than their more fortunate peers (Jencks & Phillips, 1998).

Early childhood teachers should work closely with parents of transfer children. All efforts should be made to make the transition as smooth as possible. This can mean not posting standardized test scores for these children on permanent records. If that is not possible, teachers can place a comment on the child's cumulative record explaining why scores that year are highly suspect and likely to be unreliable. Report cards should also have a special notation explaining that the child had less than a full school year to learn the school's curriculum. Likewise, no child should be forced to repeat a year as a result of transferring during the year.

Report Cards for English Language Learners

The goal of report cards is to provide an understandable progress report for parents. For teachers to provide parents with comments and reports they can understand, school districts have developed report cards and rubrics in the primary language of the community's families. The New York City school system now provides report card translations for Arabic, Bengali, Mandarin Chinese, Haitian Creole, Korean, Spanish, and Urdu (see Figure 10.4).

Figure 10.4 An Example of a Report Card Written in Spanish

ROUND ROCK ISD

PRIMER GRADO
BOLETA DE CALIFICACIONES

4	Excediendo el Nivel de las Expectativas del Grado			
3	**Cumpliendo con las Expectativas para la Salida del Grado**		Estudiante:	
2	Progresando para Dominar las Expectativas al Nivel del Grado en un Tiempo Apropiado		Maestro/a:	
1	Experimentando Dificulatad		Escuela:	
N/A	No Evaluado		Directo/a:	

Artes de Lenguaje	**Periodo de Reporte**			
Lectura	**10**	**20**	**30**	**40**
El alumno se desempena al ñivel o sobre el nivel del grado				
Comprende el texto al nivel de la expectativa				
Responde a varias lecturas verbalmente y por escrito				
Lee texto familiar con fluidez				
Descifra palabras desconocidas efectivamente				
Alumenta vocabulario que ve con frecuencia				
Escritura				
El alumno se desempena al nivel o sobra nivel del grado				
Genera ideas antes de escribir				
Apunta ideas y reflexiones				
Usa estrategies bàsicas de capitalizatión y puntuación en su tarea				
Usa estrategies de deletreos en su trabajo escrito				
Sigue el proceso de escritura desde borrador a Publicacion				
Usa caligrafió legible				

Matematicas	**Periodo de Reporte**			
Matematicas	**10**	**20**	**30**	**40**
El alumno se desempena al nivel o sobre el nivel del grado				
Numeraciones				
Lee, escribe y compera numberos hasta 100				
Usa valor del puesto				
Describe partes fraccionales				
Aplica hechos de sumar y restar hasta 18				
Usa palabras y numeros para describir el valor de las Monedas				
Resolviendo Problemas				
Usa un modelo para resolver problemas conectados a experiencias diarias				
Selecciona una estrategia para resolver problemas				
Comunica la explicación de la estrategia y la solución				
Probabilidad y Estadisticas				
Colecta, separa, organiza, y usa información para contester preguntas				

(Continued)

SOURCE: This is from the Round Rock School District, Texas. For more about Round Rock reporting system see http://www.roundrockisd.org/home/index.asp?page=1581.

Figure 10.4 (Continued)

Artes de Lenguaje	**Periodo de Reporte**			
Lectura	**10**	**20**	**30**	**40**
Escuchando y Hablando				
Escucha al orador				
Escucha y hable para ganar conocimientos				
Hable apropiadamente enfrente de una audiencia				
Comunica ideas, experiences y necesidades				
Ciencia				
Comprende conceptos, destrezas y aplica procesos				
Usa destrezas de pensamiento critico para investigar usando una variedad de recursos				

Matematicas	**Periodo de Reporte**			
Matematicas	**10**	**20**	**30**	**40**
Modelos				
Identifica, crea, y extiende modelos				
Usa patrones para contra				
Geometria				
Usa, compara, y contrasta caracteristicas de formas y sólidos				
Medidas				
Usa unidades de tiempo estandar y estandar de largo, area, peso, y capacidad				
Estudios sociales				
Entiende conceptos presentados y aplica aptitudes de proceso				
Usa destrezas criticas de pensamiento para organizer y usar informacon de una variedad de recursos				

Report Cards for Special Education Students

Both **case law** and federal legislation require that children receiving special educational services be provided all educational opportunities provided to their peers. The task of special education in early childhood (PK–3) is to provide learning support and assistance so that children can reach the goal of an equivalent, appropriate education.

Since 2002, federal testing mandates require all children be tested using the same standards-based achievement test. Every child in an age cohort (even those with IEPs) is tested together. Before 2002, an interdisciplinary child study team prescribed the educational program for children with special needs. Necessary interventions were documented in the child's Individual Educational Plan (IEP). New testing mandates in 2002 and the passage of the Individuals With Disabilities Education Improvement Act (IDEIA) in 2004 changed the rules. Federal testing mandates now take precedence over requirements of IDEIA regarding testing programs. The lone exception to the high-stakes testing mandate was made for 3% of the population of children with severe disabilities. That exception makes it possible to employ developmentally appropriate evaluations for the assessment of children with significant disabilities. Federal mandates for schools require even the most profoundly impaired children show progress from year to year (see Chapter 11). All other children with disabilities must take the same high-stakes assessment test used with nondisabled children in their age cohort.

There is no federal mandate for the use of report cards. Schools are free to design progress reports appropriate for children with special needs. Children having significant learning problems can be expected to have low grades when their success is measured in terms of other children. For that reason, standards-based reports can be problematic for children struggling to reach a basic level of proficiency.

Parents of children with special learning needs can be expected to be upset and angry if they are sent a report card showing an array of areas of the curriculum graded "Far below grade level."

One approach that can be used with progress reports for children receiving special educational services is to report academic growth. Each of the educational goals enunciated on the child's IEP can be addressed using this format. Children with special needs are evaluated frequently as part of the normal monitoring system, thereby providing ample material for making meaningful growth-based report cards. Report cards for children receiving special educational services are more complex than most for teachers to complete. This reflects the fact that special education is a cooperative effort among a team of teachers and specialists. See Table 10.2

Table 10.2 Growth- and Improvement-Based Report Card

Reading Section of a Growth-Focused Report Card for Kindergarten Children

Reading (Mark "X" on the line to indicate the level of the child's learning)

Level 1	Level 2	Level 3	Level 4	Level 5
Pretend reading/ inconsistent with picture	*Pretend reading/ consistent with pictures*	*Independent reading/reading single words*	*Independent reading/reading simple sentences*	*Independent reading/reading multiple sentences*
____________1	____________2	____________3	____________4	____________5 (January)
____________1	____________2	____________3	____________4	____________5 (April)
____________1	____________2	____________3	____________4	____________5 (June)

Sight vocabulary (Mark words that child can recognize and pronounce)

a all am and are at big can for go have I in is it like me my on see the this to up with you

January Total ____________

a all am and are at big can for go have I in is it like me my on see the this to up with you

April Total ____________

a all am and are at big can for go have I in is it like me my on see the this to up with you

June Total ____________

SOURCE: Adapted from original work by Barbara J. Szagola. Used with permission.

for a growth-focused report card that can be used in kindergarten or with special education students in the primary grades.

One teacher should be designated as the primary contact educator for collecting information needed for the special education report card for each child. This includes responsibility of collecting comments and grades from various specialists working with each child, and writing composite reports.

Summary

Report card grades have been used in American education since the founding of the Republic. One role that grades played in the past was to provide information useful in making retention or promotion decisions. In many large cities and seven states that decision is now made on the basis of high-stakes test scores. This policy has been ineffective in improving achievement. Minority children and children of poverty have significantly lower scores on these high-stakes tests, and are retained-in-grade far in excess of their middle class, White peers.

Report cards are written for and to parents. Standards-based grades are now widely used to report student progress. Many standards-based reports are checklists with added comments. These standards-based report cards are keyed to the state's standards for student learning.

There are problems in using high-stakes tests with children who have transferred into the school setting during the school year. It takes a year to prepare a child for the high-stakes tests. Another problem area for both testing policy and report cards is with children who are receiving special educational services. Children with special needs should have their growth or improvement reported to their parents in lieu of using standard report cards.

Discussion Questions

1. What are advantages and disadvantages of having honor rolls in the primary grades?
2. What reasons are there for and against retaining a child in grade for an extra year?
3. What provisions should be made for report cards of primary grade children who are receiving special education services?
4. What are reasons for and against using letter grades on report cards?
5. What can be done to assist children who transfer into a primary classroom in the middle of the year to keep them from being misgraded?
6. Visit a local school, or search the Internet, and review the report card used in a kindergarten and/or primary grade school. What is good and bad about this report card?

Related Readings

Azwell, T., & Schmar, E. (1995). *Report card on report cards: Alternatives to consider.* Portsmouth, NH: Heinemann.

Brookhart, S. M. (2004). *Grading.* Upper Saddle River, NJ: Prentice Hall.

Clarridge, P. B., & Whitaker, E. M. (1997). *Rolling the elephant over: How to effect large scale change in the reporting process.* Portsmouth, NH: Heinemann.

Guskey, T. R. (2002). *How's my kid doing? A parent's guide to grades, marks, and report cards.* San Francisco: Jossey-Bass.

Sunderman, G. L., Kim, J. S., & Orfield, G. (2005). *NCLB meets school realities: Lessons from the field.* Thousand Oaks, CA: Corwin Press.

Thomas, M. R. (2005). *High-stakes testing: Coping with collateral damage.* Mahwah, NJ: Erlbaum.
Wagner, E. N. (2002). *A parent's guide to high stakes testing.* New York: Learning Express.

Notes

1. Phi Beta Kappa was established on the campus of the College of William and Mary in 1776 and was soon followed by chapters at Yale (1780) and Harvard (1781). The first grading system was introduced at Yale University when it issued report cards to its students. Achievement was reported using a four-point ordinal scale that ranged from the best grade of *Optimi* (very good) to the lowest grade of *Pejores* (very bad). In between these two anchor points were grades of *Second Optimi* (less than good) and *Inferiores* (further down) (Smallwood, 1935). Harvard soon followed with a grading system based on a 100-point ordinal scale.
2. When students reach their 18th birthday, their parents can only see their grade reports with the consent of the student. The only outside agency that can examine any student's record at any time (without a court order) are recruiters for the U.S. military.
3. Children who were enrolled in special education and learning support programs were free from the specter of "flunking the grade."
4. "Social promotion" describes the policy of promoting a child to the next grade level to keep him/her together with same age peers. The promotion is made even in the case of low achievement.
5. These states and cities include Delaware, Florida, Georgia, Mississippi, Missouri, Texas, and Wisconsin, and the cities of Chicago, New York, and Philadelphia.
6. There are three loopholes for parents to use if they want to avoid having their child retained-in-grade based on a test score. All three require that parents move the child to another educational environment. One is to remove the child and home school him or her. In some states this can be done with the assistance of virtual schools taught over the Internet. Another involves enrolling the child in a parochial school. The final answer is the most costly, and involves enrolling the child in a private preparatory school or independent school. None of these options require the child to pass a test.
7. In 2005, the Massachusetts Institute of Technology and Nicholas Negroponte announced the development of a $100 computer. This computer and variations on its design are now entering many American schools and will soon be available everywhere. There is more about this in Chapter 12.

Identification of Young Children With Special Needs

11

Instruction does much, but encouragement does everything.

—Goethe

Introduction and Themes

The total number and the percentage of the population of children with a significant disability have never been greater. Early childhood educators are the first to refer most of these children for evaluation.

Prior to the 1970s, there was no uniform requirement for public schools to provide special education for children with disabilities. Passage of Section 504 of the Vocational Rehabilitation Act (1973) and the Education for All Handicapped Children Act (1975) changed this. In 1986, amendments to the latter (P.L. 99-457) extended requirements for educational services to children as young as 2 years old. A recent version of Public Law 94-142, the Individuals With Disabilities Education Improvement Act (IDEIA, 2004), made many of the testing provisions of 94-142 subservient to federal testing mandates passed in 2002 (P.L. 107-100, No Child Left Behind Act). IDEIA also introduced use of response to intervention (RTI) as a normal step for the identification of children with attention deficit/hyperactivity disorder (AD/HD). It also expanded early special education to toddlers and their families.

Identification of a disabling condition is not sufficient proof for a child to receive special education services. There must also be proof that the normal development and education of the child is being impaired by the condition.

Learning Objectives

By reading and studying this chapter, you should acquire the competency to:

- List major classifications of disabilities experienced by school children in the United States.
- Explain the legal basis for the case law that has led to the passage of special education legislation.
- Explain requirements of Section 504 of the Rehabilitation Act as to the services schools must provide children experiencing a learning problem.

- Describe various forms that Public Law 94-142 has taken between the 1975 Education for All Handicapped Children Act and the latest version as the Individuals With Disabilities Education Improvement Act.
- Explain the difference between assessment using response to intervention and curriculum-based assessment.
- Describe methods that can be used to identify young children with AD/HD.
- Describe methods that can be used to identify young children with Asperger's disorder and other pervasive developmental disorders.

Special Education Population

The number of children receiving services for special education in this country has never been greater, nor has it ever represented a larger proportion of the population of students. In 2005, there were 6,109,000 children enrolled in special education programs (see Table 11.1 for a breakdown). The total public school population that year was 50 million. Thus, 12% of the school-age population receives special education services.[1]

Table 11.1 Children Being Provided Special Education Services in 2005

- Specific Learning Disabilities (LD and AD/HD) 2,780,200
- Speech or Language Impairments 1,157,200
- Mental Retardation (all levels) 545,500
- Emotional Disturbance and Conduct Disorders 472,400
- Multiple Disabilities 133,900
- Autism Spectrum Disorder (including Asperger's disorder) 193,000
- Hearing Impairments 72,400
- Orthopedic Impairments 63,100
- Major Health Impairments 561,000
- Traumatic Brain Injury 23,500
- Vision Impairment (including blind and low vision) 26,000
- Deaf and Blind 1,600
- Developmental Delay (incomplete data from states) 79,100
- Approximate total of all children with a disability 6,109,600

SOURCE: U.S. Department of Education, 2007, available at http://www.ideadata.org/index.html.

Between 80% and 90% of children with disabilities were not identified until they began school (Barkley, 1998; Mash & Dozois, 1996). Disabilities most typically identified prior to starting public school include developmental delay, orthopedic disabilities, genetic abnormalities, major illnesses, and traumatic injuries (Raber & Frechtling, 1985). Some disabilities not normally identified until the child is of school age include **attention deficit/hyperactivity disorder** and learning disorders (American Psychiatric Association, 1994). The critical point is that early childhood educators have a central role to play in early identification of children who will need special assistance. The necessity for teachers to be vigilant for, and have sensitivity to, signs a child may need special support cannot be overstated.

Identification

The primary goal for early identification of possible learning problems is to direct services to the child and his/her family (Scarborough et al., 2004).

Preschool teachers are better equipped than parents to identify children exhibiting potential learning problems. Parents lack broad experience with many children at different levels of ability and from different backgrounds. This parochial viewpoint limits what parents know about what early childhood behaviors are within the normal range.

The problem faced by preschool teachers is the possible harm done by a failure to follow up and determine that a child needs special support services. Likewise, if the decision by the early childhood educator is to pursue a full-scale evaluation, and that effort shows there is no difficulty present, it is possible the child's parents will have been frightened for no reason. Likewise, valuable resources (in terms of staff time) will have been used without good cause.

This difficult decision for teachers about the identification of children possibly needing special education has been resolved by two pieces of federal legislation that clearly describe steps to be followed whenever a possible learning problem exists. These specific steps were provided to ensure the validity and fairness of the process.

The first step in the process of providing young children with extra help for their learning involves **identification.** Once the early childhood teacher senses a child may need special educational services, a screening for the possible problem must be conducted. Table 11.2 presents steps in the identification and assessment processes.

Table 11.2 Steps in the Process of Identifying Children Requiring Special Services

Step	Decision to Be Made
1. Screening	Whether or not a **referral** for further assessment is needed
2. Assessment	What is the area of learning or developmental difficulty? Referral to Instructional Support Team[2]
3. Multidisciplinary	Eligibility for special services and instructional program planning team evaluation
4. Monitoring of child	Decide if the intervention is working or requires modification

Intervention

Early intervention can make a major difference in the life of a young child. Follow-up research has shown the expense of early intervention for preschool-aged children with special needs is cost effective. Early identification can reduce long-term supplemental educational expenses for assisting children with disabilities later in their educational careers. While working with a sample of children identified with Down's syndrome, Nancy Wybranski (1996) found the amount of preschool support they received was inversely related to the amount of assistance they needed as second graders. The point is, early intervention provides support and improves the likelihood a child will have a successful school career.

Legal Basis

The 14th Amendment to the U.S. Constitution provides the basis federal courts have referenced when requiring school systems provide children with disabilities an education equivalent to what is received by others. Court decisions make up what is known as case law. Federal courts are free to use cases that come before them to create policies having the force of law. The U.S. Supreme Court has decided that every child has a Constitutional right to an appropriate education. In other words, no school can refuse to provide a child with an appropriate educational program. Federal legislation has followed the leadership of the courts in this matter.

> **U.S. Constitution, Amendment 14, Section 1:**
>
> *No State shall make or enforce any law which shall abridge the privileges or immunities of citizens of the United States; nor shall any State deprive any person of life, liberty, or property, without due process of law; nor deny any person within its jurisdiction to the equal protection of the laws.* Ratified July 9, 1868.

Case Law[3]

Several critical court decisions led to policies taken for granted today. For the most part, these cases have been based on the requirements for **equal protection** and **due process**. Before the 1970s, public schools could, and often did, refuse to provide a free public school education for children with significant disabilities. Children with less obvious disabilities were allowed to attend school and languish in regular education classrooms. Eventually, these children dropped out of school. If parents of children with disabilities wanted to ensure their children were appropriately educated, it was their responsibility to find private schools and pay the tuition. Public schools believed they had no role to play in the placement or education of children with disabilities.

That all changed with a federal court decision from the case *Parents Association for Retarded Children (PARC) v. the Commonwealth of Pennsylvania.* In October 1971, Pennsylvania accepted a consent decision mandating that "All children, handicapped or otherwise, are entitled to a free and appropriate public education." Subsequent case law by the Supreme Court of the United States made it illegal to change the status of any child without providing the child and his/her family with procedural due process (*Gross et al. v. Lopez et al.*, 1975).

Thus, children cannot be expelled from school unless there has been an open hearing when the child's parents could provide evidence and be represented by counsel. Additionally, all placement decisions, including whether or not special education is to be provided to a child, must make provisions for the child's parents to have input into the process. See Case in Point 11.1 for a description of an unfortunate incident with a special needs child in kindergarten.

Case in Point 11.1

Inappropriate Disciplinary Method

Most early childhood educators are prepared to teach in an inclusive classroom. The mix of children with special needs and children without disabilities in the same early classroom requires a skillful and patient teacher.

On May 28, 2008, local television news carried the story of a kindergarten teacher in Port Saint Lucie, Florida. She was frustrated by the behavior of a disabled student (Asperger's disorder). She had the troublesome child stand in front of the kindergarten class and asked each class member to tell the child why they did not like him. The teacher then belittled the problematic kindergartener herself. Next she asked her class to vote on whether the offending child should be sent out of the classroom or be allowed to remain. The kindergarten class voted 14 to 2 to have the child removed.

The child's parents were not amused by this behavioral management approach. During a stormy conference with the school's principal, the child's mother was told her boy needed to be disciplined and learn to follow rules. The mother contacted local media when she thought the school's principal was not hearing her. The school district became involved, and the teacher was asked to explain her management approach to the superintendent of schools.

The kindergarten teacher defended her behavior as an appropriate disciplinary approach. The administration of the Port Saint Lucie School District did not agree, and the teacher was disciplined. Meanwhile, a nationwide online petition by parents of children with Asperger's disorder collected thousands of names of people demanding action by the Saint Lucie County School District (Fox News, 2008).

Federal Statutes

The federal government passes laws with mandates for schools to follow; but each state develops local laws needed to enable the federal plans.[4] For example, each state is required to develop regulations for school systems to conduct screenings for possible learning and/or health problems including sensory screenings for possible problems of hearing and vision. Additionally, measures of achievement and cognition are also required as part of ongoing screenings. Early screenings for possible problems are a first step in the process of making an **entitlement decision** (Wolery, 1994).

Education of the Handicapped Act (P.L. 91-230, 1970) and Related Legislation

Programs set up by the Bureau for Education of the Handicapped[5] were consolidated into the first federal legislation for special education in 1970 with the passage of Public Law 91-230. Later that decade another significant law, the Education of the Handicapped Act Amendments of 1974 (P. L. 93-380) provided subventions (grant totals of $15 million) directly to local school districts designed to improve educational programs for children with disabilities.

Section 504 of the Vocational Rehabilitation Act (1973)

This law signed by President Richard M. Nixon in 1973 ensured equal access to a free and appropriate education for all children needing special education services between 3 and 22 years old.

It was written to protect all individuals (including children) from any form of discrimination based on having a disability. Section 504 mandates include the use of an **Instructional Support Team (IST)**. The team includes the child's parent(s), classroom teachers, a guidance counselor or child development specialist, educational specialists (e.g., reading, art, music, and physical education teachers), a school nurse (if on staff), and the principal or director. See a sample referral form for a student assistance team in Figure 11.1.

Figure 11.1 Sample Referral form for a Student Assistance Program Team Review

Name of Student ______________________________ Gender ___(M) ___(F)

Date of Birth (mm/dd/yyyy) ____/____/______ Grade(s) repeated ______________

Attended preschool program? ___(Y) ___(N) If yes which? ______________

If yes, how many months of fulltime preschool enrollment?_____ How many months part-time ________

Attended day care (nonacademic) ___(Y) ___(N) If yes, which? ______________

Most recent test scores: Date of Test ______________ Test form ____ Level ____

Standardized Achievement: ______ Reading Total ______ Reading Vocabulary _______ Reading Comp.

______ Arithmetic _______ Arithmetic Problem Solving _______ Writing Mechanics _______ Spelling

Other test scores ______________________ When given?____________

Name (Print) of Referring Teacher ______________________________

School Building ______________ Grade level(s) __________ Phone __________

*****

Describe the learning problem.

Associated areas of problematic behavior.

*****

Part II

Student Assistance Committee Recommendations Date ____/____/______
Instructional Activity and Materials

Benchmark for Success

Duration of Intervention ______________________________

Signature Referring Teacher ______________________________

Signature School Administrator ______________________________

Signature Lead Teacher ______________________________

The IST should meet shortly after a referral is received, and not wait to see "how things work-out." ISTs address educational problems children are experiencing even when the problems are not severe. Their goal is to identify alternative solutions for students having difficulty.

Schedule

ISTs should meet regularly to review the child's progress and discuss educational strategies with the teacher. Periodic IST meetings (four times a year) provide a forum where the classroom teacher can express his/her concerns when/if the efforts do not appear to be working. It is usual that toward the end of the school year the final IST committee meeting includes the teacher(s) who will work with the child in the next grade. Additionally, the child's progress for the year should be summarized and ideas for parents and child to work on over the summer be presented and discussed.

Individuals With Disabilities Education Act (The Education for All Handicapped Children Act) (P. L. 94-142, 1975)

This law provides three mandates regarding children with disabilities including a **free and appropriate educational program.** Second, special educational services should be provided in the **least restrictive educational environment.** The third requirement mandates development of a written individual education plan with clear objectives and indicators of success.

SOURCE: Cartoon by Merv Magus.

The requirement for a free and appropriate education for all children with disabilities forced many school systems to change their policies and approaches. Parents can take school systems to court and force compliance for failing to provide services children need (Katsiyannis & Herbst, 2004).[6]

The second mandate defining the best placement for children with disabilities as the least restrictive environment changed the nature of special education in schools. **Inclusion classes** that pair special education and regular education teachers replaced dedicated special education classrooms. Today, all teachers instruct children with special needs every day (Alvarado, 2006; Gaetano, 2006). In early childhood settings, children needing special services learn in inclusive early childhood education settings.

Individual Educational Plans (IEPs) are written to describe goals for special education services, approaches to employ with instruction, and benchmarks for success. Each IEP is the product of a **multidisciplinary team** and includes the full involvement of the child's parents. Under the requirements of **procedural due process,** parents who are not in agreement with the outcome of the multidisciplinary team can appeal the decision (see Chapter 12).

Communications with the child's parent(s) must be in the language they understand. This can be a challenge because over 50 different primary languages are common among those attending public schools in America (Salvia et al., 2007).

Instructional and Assistive Technology

The Communications Technology Amendments of the Rehabilitation Act of 1998 (P.L. 105-220) required computers provide adaptations for users with disabilities. Technology makes it possible for children with disabilities to communicate with others, read books, and listen to their teacher's presentation. Adaptations include modified keyboards and a user-friendly computer "mouse." Software modifications now provide accommodations for children with orthopedic disabilities and help those with sensory impairments by providing larger font sizes, higher sound levels, and speech recognition.

The IEP Process

When the IST's interventions are not effective, a second more formal referral is initiated. The referral organizes and presents the initial IST committee's materials and instructional support plan, interim reports, and recent assessment scores. The guidance counselor, or the lead teacher, may coordinate this effort. The Individual Educational Plan (IEP) is the next step for children with disabilities between 3 and 21 years. Figure 11.2 provides a sample referral form for an IEP Committee.

Figure 11.2 Sample IEP Committee Referral Form for Primary Grade Children

Name of student ______________________________ Gender ___(M) ___(F)

Date of birth (mm/dd/yyyy) _____/_____/_______ Grade(s) repeated ______________

Attended preschool program? ___(Y) ___(N) If yes, which? ______________________

If yes, how many months of full-time preschool enrollment?_____ How many months part-time _____

Attended day care (nonacademic) ___(Y)___(N) If yes, which? ______________________

Academic and cocurricular development and activities.

Disciplinary referrals past two years.

Grades for major subjects for past two years:

From Year ________ to Year ________

Reading ________ ________

Mathematics ________ ________

Science ________ ________

Social Studies ________ ________

Most recent test scores: Date of test ___/___/_______ Test form ____________ Level ____________

Standardized Achievement: ______ Reading Total _______ Reading Vocabulary ______ Reading Comp.

______ Arithmetic _______Arithmetic Problem Solving ______Writing Mechanics ______ Spelling

Most recent NCLB scores: Date of test ___/___/_______

(Abv) = Above, (Pro) = Proficient, (Bgn) = Beginning, (Blw) = Below Proficient

Percentile Reading ____% (Abv) ___ (Pro) ___ (Bgn) ___ (Blw) ___

Percentile Math ____% (Abv) ___ (Pro) ___ (Bgn) ___ (Blw) ___

Percentile Science ____% (Abv) ___ (Pro) ___ (Bgn) ___ (Blw) ___

Other test scores ______________________ When given? ____________

Name (Print) of Referring Teacher ______________________________

School Building ____________________ Grade level(s) ________ Phone ________

*****

Describe the interventions initiated by the Student Support Team (SAT) or the Instructional Support Team (IST).

Dates of SAT/IST intervention: Start ___/___/______ End ___/___/______

Describe outcomes from the (SAT/IST) committee.

Does the child qualify for extended school year services? ___(Y) ___(N)

Describe the current learning problem.

Associated areas of problematic behavior.

Unmet annual goals for growth in each dimension of achievement specified in the curriculum:

Goal(s)	Benchmark(s)
1.	1.
2.	2.
3.	3.
4.	4.

IEP Format

IDEIA (2004) requires an Individual Educational Plan but does not prescribe a format to follow (see Figure 11.3 for the required elements). A critical requirement for IEPs is documentation proving the child's learning is negatively impacted by the identified condition or disability.

Figure 11.3 Required Elements of an IEP

1. Child's current educational **performance level** across all areas of the curriculum and a description of how the disability affects the child's involvement and progress in school.
2. List of reasonable annual goals that can be accomplished during the school year.
3. Special education and related services that will be provided to the child including any modifications, and program supports the child will receive.
4. Description of the extent to which the disabled child will participate in regular classroom activities with nondisabled peers.
5. Modifications or accommodations needed for the child to take mandated standardized tests.
6. Start date when special education and related services will be provided to the child and the frequency and duration of these activities and support services.
7. Provision for the transition of the child into life after school. (This component must be in place before the child reaches the age of 14.)
8. Provision for counseling about the rights that the child will accrue upon reaching the age of 18.
9. Description of how progress toward annual goals will be measured, and how the child's parents will be kept appraised of that progress.

SOURCE: Adapted from http://www.ed.gov/parents/needs/speced/iepguide/index.html.

NOTE: For more information about IEPs, see http://www.ed.gov/parents/needs/speced/iepguide/index.html.

Most local school systems have developed their own IEP formats. Educational software vendors now sell computerized IEP writing software. One advantage of computerized IEPs is they ensure all documents are similar in quality and follow a common structure (Margolis & Free, 2001). Example software can be reviewed at the following URLs:

Tera Systems
http://www.einet.net/review/3494-234948/IEP_Software_Special_Education_Software_by_Tera_Systems_Inc.htm

Chalkware Educational Solutions
http://www.iepware.com/

Maximus/Tienet System
http://www.maximus.com/corporate/pages/tienet.asp

The decision to provide testing accommodations during statewide tests and whether the child qualifies for **extended school year services (ESY)** is normally addressed during the meeting of the multidisciplinary team that writes the IEP. This recommendation is then included in the IEP.[7]

Response to Intervention (RTI)

RTI provides a systematic method to monitor progress once an IEP has been developed. It requires the careful charting of how a child with special needs responds to interventions. The approach is very similar to the use of **curriculum-based assessment (CBA)** (see below).

RTI begins early in the school year when every child is screened for possible educational deficits (Samuels, 2008). Once children at risk have been identified through screening, standardized assessments are employed to evaluate them. Children with serious educational needs are then presented with selected instructional interventions keyed to their specific difficulties. This takes place through the "504" committee. Children are periodically retested and if there is no improvement, they are normally referred to the **IEP Committee** for evaluation.

Curriculum-Based Assessment (CBA)

Curriculum-based assessment is a specialized form of measurement that identifies the child's actual capability to perform tasks required for learning. Once the child's capabilities are identified, remediation requirements can be established by analyzing the discrepancy between the child's performance levels and the performance of others. CBA measures, known as curriculum probes, are locally produced reflecting local curriculum goals (Fuchs & Fuchs, 2004). For example, probes may involve testing the number of words the child can read in a minute; or, briefly testing the child's ability to solve multiplication problems. CBA identifies skills needing improvement and suggests remediation, while providing data that may be needed later to develop an IEP. Combining probes with more traditional measurement dimensions such as normative achievement and cognitive/intellectual ability provides the full curriculum-based assessment (Lichtenstein, 2002).

Individual Family Service Plan (IFSP)

In 2004, the Individuals With Disabilities Education Improvement Act (IDEIA) extended special education services to infants and toddlers. The vehicle for planning the delivery of specialized services is the Individual Family Service Plan (IFSP). Referral for evaluation and possible services can originate from medical professionals, social workers, or caregivers (IDEIA, 2004).

The child is evaluated within his/her family context, and a plan developed for the family designed to optimize the child's development. This starts with a series of early childhood evaluations and family interviews carried out by a child development specialist or early childhood teacher.

Social service agencies lead the process of writing the Individual Family Service Plan. IFSPs address the abilities and limitations of the child, while providing a plan of action to remediate areas of developmental delay (Bruder, 2003/2004). IFSPs include family members and take into account the natural environment in which the child lives. The key required elements of an IFSP are provided on Figure 11.4.

Figure 11.4 Required Elements in an IFSP

1. Child's present level of physical, cognitive communication, social/emotional, and adaptive development.
2. Family's resources, priorities, and concerns relating to the development of the disabled child.
3. Major outcomes to be achieved for the child and the family; the criteria, procedures, and timelines for determining progress, and a timeline for deciding about modifications in the plan that may be needed.
4. Specified list of early intervention services for the child and family including a statement of the beginning, frequency, and intensity of such services.
5. A description of the natural environment in which the child lives. If a change is indicated, a detailed justification for not providing services in the natural environment of the child and family.
6. Name and contact information for the person with the responsibility to coordinate service delivery to the family.
7. Transition plan from early childhood preschool or day care to public school, including a provision for parents to provide input in the development of the IEP.

SOURCE: Advocating for the Educational Needs of Children in Out-of-Home Care: Training Curriculum for Child Welfare Caseworkers and Supervisors. Colorado Department of Human Services, Denver, CO. More information available at http://muskie.usm.maine.edu/helpkids/pubstext/COEducation.doc.

Rapidity of normal growth and development during early childhood years is one reason why assessment findings reported in the IFSP must be reviewed every six months. This **biannual review** requirement reflects the marginal test-retest reliability for early childhood assessments (Bricker, Yovanoff, Capt, & Allen, 2003).

Accommodations for Children With Disabilities

The goal of providing accommodations to special needs children during tests is to ensure the evaluation is of what the child has accomplished and can do, not what disabilities prevent him/her from doing. Each state has its own set of guidelines for testing accommodations. The goal for providing accommodations is not to give some children an advantage, but to make it possible for children with special needs to fully participate. A list of approved accommodations can be found at a Web page from the University of Minnesota: http://education.umn.edu/NCEO/TopicAreas/Accommodations/AccomFAQ.htm.

All school systems should also have an approved set of policies for accommodating needs of special education students on classroom tests and examinations.

Identification of Learning Disabilities

Assessment of Reading Problems

Reading is a core skill for every child. The third grade, with its high-stakes reading test, can be a nightmare for children who have fallen behind in the development of this skill. More referrals are made for reading problems than for any other curriculum area (Lyon, 1998) (see Chapter 9).

Environmental Factors

Reading problems do not imply neurological or psychological abnormalities. Most children having difficulty learning to read had little exposure to reading materials and no preliteracy experiences prior to kindergarten. Children surrounded with numerous books and caregivers that play rhyming games, read aloud, and work to expand the child's vocabulary tend to learn to read without difficulty. The National Reading Panel published a list of parental linguistic interactions that facilitate a child's learning to read including talking and listening, reading children's books aloud, talking about books, learning to recognize letters of the alphabet, and demonstrating the letter–sound link (Armbruster, Lehr, & Osborn, 2003).

Assessment of Numeracy Problems

The second most common disability involves **numeracy problems** and learning mathematics. This area for learning is closely linked to the child's cognitive development. The connection between cognition and the development and measurement of mathematics concepts is described in Chapter 9.

Identification of AD/HD

Attention deficit/hyperactivity disorder (AD/HD) is a disability associated with learning problems that impacts the largest number of children. This disorder interferes with neurological executive functions of the brain including the ability to focus and attend to tasks (McLean, Wolery, & Bailey, 2003). Children who cannot attend to learning tasks lack the ability to focus on classroom instruction. This form of AD/HD is named attention deficit/hyperactivity disorder, predominantly inattentive type by the American Psychiatric Association (1994). When combined with hyperactive behaviors it becomes attention deficit/hyperactivity disorder, combined type. AD/HD frequently occurs along with learning problems including poor reading skills (American Psychiatric Association, 1994). Symptoms associated with AD/HD diminish but never disappear as the individual matures. It may still have an adverse effect on the life of adults in college and at work (T. Brown, 2005).

Tourette syndrome is a neurological disorder that manifests as uncontrolled **motor** and/or **verbal tics**. It is usually first evident when the child is between 5 and 7 years; however, it can be obvious among younger children (Evans, King, & Leckman, 1996). A mild form of Tourette syndrome appears in 1% of all children, and one in a thousand have severe involvement. The likelihood a child will have AD/HD if he or she is diagnosed with Tourette syndrome is very high (Walkup, 2006).

Incidence

Over 40% of all special education entitlement decisions involve AD/HD or a related learning problem (e.g., learning disability [LD]). Only 20% of the children identified with AD/HD are girls (Committee on Quality Improvement, 2000). Of the children identified with AD/HD, about two out of three are also hyperactive.[8] There is evidence for a genetic component to the problem of AD/HD (Chang, 2005).

The diagnosis of AD/HD is typically compounded with anxiety, conduct disorder, and/or severe oppositional behavior (Hardman, Drew, & Egan, 2008). Attention deficit/hyperactivity disorder is also found among children with problems in language and speech development and those with reading problems.

Before 2007, the best method for screening a child for possible AD/HD involved using observational checklists.[9] Checklists used in the identification of AD/HD include items to be answered by both parents and teacher. Having a child exhibiting the behaviors associated with AD/HD changes parenting behavior and must be considered in developing the IEP (Lin, 2001). A clinical interview of the parent(s) by the school's psychologist can provide these data. Entitlement decisions for special education for children with AD/HD must include a clinical diagnosis by a highly trained professional.

A pediatric allergist published a book in 1975 that described a link between the diet children eat and the likelihood that they will exhibit AD/HD symptoms. That book by Benjamin F. Feingold was extraordinarily popular among parents of young children. His recommendation was to eliminate artificial coloring agents and preservatives from the food that young children eat. Recent research in Great Britain has supported Feingold's original hypothesis. See Case in Point 11.2.

Case in Point 11.2

The Feingold Diet and AD/HD

Following publication of the Feingold Diet in 1975, many parents of children with AD/HD tried to control their child's symptoms through diet. The items removed include all foods and patent medicines containing:

- Artificial (synthetic) coloring
- Artificial (synthetic) flavoring
- Aspartame (Nutrasweet, an artificial sweetener)
- Artificial (synthetic) preservatives BHA, BHT, TBHQ

Anecdotal reports support this approach to treating AD/HD (Brody, 2009). Recently, a team of medical researchers in the United Kingdom was able to document that this dietary approach inhibits the symptoms of AD/HD in young children (McCann et al., 2007). That research used a double blind research approach and was able to both increase and decrease the level and severity of AD/HD symptoms through dietary control.

Instruments for Identification of AD/HD

Diagnostic guidelines provided in the *Diagnostic and Statistical Manual of Mental Disorders* (American Psychological Association, 1994) provide the basis for published AD/HD checklists. An entitlement decision requires a licensed clinical specialist make the diagnosis.

The American Psychiatric Association suggests that a child may be AD/HD if he/she persistently exhibits an array of these behaviors in both school and home settings:

1. Inattention
   a. fails to follow through and complete tasks
   b. is easily distracted by the environment and others in it
   c. finds it hard to concentrate on schoolwork or sustain attention
   d. does not listen when spoken to
   e. is forgetful and tends to lose items (homework, lunch, books, etc.)
2. Hyperactivity
   a. will climb and roam
   b. constantly shifting from one task to another
   c. talks excessively
   d. is constantly on the go as if driven by a motor
   e. is restless and cannot remain seated for a long period
   f. does not play well with others (few friends)
3. Impulsivity
   a. acts without thinking or planning
   b. frequently calls out in class
   c. frequently interrupts others and butts into conversations
   d. cannot wait before taking a turn
4. Early Onset

There is an early onset of the disorder, with the symptoms occurring before the age of 7. Symptoms must have persisted for more than six months.

A medical treatment for the symptoms of ADHD involves the use of psychotropic medications. See Case in Point 11.3 for information on this pharmacological approach to controlling symptoms.

Case in Point 11.3

Psychotropic Drugs and AD/HD

A common medical approach to treating children identified as having AD/HD includes the prescription of methylphenidate. This drug goes by the brand name Ritalin. Today, about one million children are treated with Ritalin or similar drugs (atomoxetine and dexamfetamine).

The concern is that the use of psychotropic stimulant medication may lead to drug and alcohol addiction later in adulthood. Longitudinal research evidence has not found this to be true (Wilens, Faraone, Biederman, &

Gunawardene, 2003). There are serious side effects associated with long-term use of these powerful stimulants. One is that methylphenidate can increase blood pressure, reduce appetite, cause stomach pain, increase nervousness and anxiety, and make it more difficult for the child to sleep. *Many parents are reluctant to give their children this powerful medicine.*

The advantage is that the drug can give the child the ability to focus attention on learning. It also improves the child's receptive language ability (R. T. Brown, Perwien, Faries, Kratochvil, & Vaughan, 2006). The key to the successful use of methylphenidate is careful titration of the child's serum and close monitoring by a board certified child psychiatrist.

There are over two dozen published observational scales for identification of AD/HD. Five observational scales commonly used to gather data about children experiencing learning problems related to attention deficit are listed below.

Behavior Assessment System for Children, 2nd ed. (BASC-2)

BASC-2 is described as a multidimensional approach to assessing a range of childhood disorders including AD/HD. It is published by Pearson Education ($124.00, 2008) and is used with children between 2 and 21 years old (Reynolds & Kamphaus, 2004).

It includes teacher and parent self-report questionnaires, a formal student observation system, and forms for collecting the child's developmental history. BASC-2 assesses the possibility of impairment in the child's "executive function."[10] The BASC-2 was well normed and corrected for gender differences. It requires the professional interpreting it be educated at a B level (see Chapter 7). A version of the BASC-2 was published in Spanish and validated on a sample of children from Puerto Rico (Perez & Ines, 2004). To review a sample parent report, see the following URL: http://www.agsnet.com/Group.asp?nGroupInfoID=a30000.

Brown Attention Deficit Disorder Scales for Children and Adolescents (Brown-ADD)

The Brown-ADD Scales for Children includes a teacher questionnaire, parent questionnaire, and a semi-structured clinical interview. Administration of the questionnaire requires examiners to be trained at a B level (see Chapter 7). Pearson Assessment sells the Brown Scales for $235.00 (2009).

It was normed for use with a population between 3 and 12 years old and provides comparative and diagnostic tables up to age 18. Unfortunately, the sampling process used by T. Brown (2001) opened the measure to criticism as having a potentially biased normative base (Jennings, 2003).

Conners' Rating Scales–Revised (CRS-R)

Multi-Health Systems of Canada designed the Conners' Rating Scales–Revised for use with children between 3 and 17 years (Conners, 1997/2000). Pearson Assessment distributes the CRS-R in the United States for $276.00 (2009).

CRS-R provides a global index score as well as scores that align with the fourth edition of the *Diagnostic and Statistical Manual of Mental Disorders* (*DSM-IV*, 1994) AD/HD classification. Scoring and interpretation of the CRS-R is limited to educators who have a B level of measurement education (see Chapter 7).

There are seven subscale scores that are a part of the CRS-R: Oppositional, Cognitive Inattention and Problems, Hyperactivity, Anxious-Shy, Perfectionism, Social Problems, and Psychosomatic (Hess, 2001).

Early Childhood Attention Deficit Disorders Evaluation Scale (ECADDES)

The Early Childhood Attention Deficit Disorders Evaluation Scale is appropriate for children between the ages of 2 and 6 years. ECADDES was designed by Stephen McCarney and Nancy Johnson (1995) to align with diagnostic characteristics listed in the *DSM-IV* (1994). Hawthorne Educational Services lists ECADDES for $178.00 (2009).

Two observational checklists make up this instrument, one for use in the school and the other for use in the child's home. Data from the observations in two settings (home and school) are used to derive scores on two subscales, Inattentive and Hyperactive-Impulsive. Observational checklists take less than half an hour to be completed by the preschool teacher and the parent. The ECADDES was standardized on a sample of almost 2,900 children. The sample was not nationally representative with an underrepresentation of children from ethnic minority groups and an overrepresentation of children from rural settings in the upper Midwest (L. Cohen, 2001; H. Keller, 2001).

Scales for Diagnosing Attention Deficit/Hyperactivity Disorder (SCALES)

Gail Ryser and Kathleen McConnell (2002) developed this instrument that can identify children and adolescents (5 through 18 years) who exhibit AD/HD behaviors. Pro-Ed lists this measure for $98.00 (2008).

Questionnaires are completed by teachers and parents and are to be scored by a B level administrator (see Chapter 7). The 39 Likert-type scale questions on two forms yield three subscale scores aligned with *DSM-IV* (1994) criteria, vis-à-vis inattentiveness, hyperactivity, and impulsivity. The validity of the three subscale scores was well established by factor analysis (Law, 2001). This measure is a good screen for AD/HD and is also an appropriate device to use to monitor students who have an IEP for attention deficit/hyperactivity disorder.

The Quotient AD/HD System

This system is a 15- to 20-minute individualized assessment for AD/HD. It is given on a computer screen and involves three infrared projectors, motion tracking devices, and a high-speed computer presentation of test stimuli. The system is enclosed in a study carrel and has a large screen for the child to watch. The computer-presented stimuli are flashed for 0.02 seconds every 2 seconds. The stimuli flashed on the screen are geometric shapes. Children are instructed to tap a key when one designated shape is presented, and ignore the others. The infrared systems trace the child's head and leg movements during the assessment process. The computer also tracks the child's latency of responses and errors. Altogether the system observes and collects data about the child 50 times per second on 19 different variables. These measures are analyzed by the corporation center over a secure Internet link. Data are analyzed at the offices in Cambridge, Massachusetts, which sends a report back about the child within a minute. That report is based on a normative sample of 2,000 children.

These 2,000 children were from schools in New England that volunteered to participate in a standardization study. The sample did not include children who were receiving psychotropic drugs, and included children of all ability levels between kindergarten and Grade 8 (Eric Gordon, CEO, personal communication, August 21, 2008). Test–retest reliability after a five-day latency was very good ($r \cong 0.90$).

If the child's response and movement patterns significantly depart from the norm along a series of parameters, the clinician can make diagnostic statements about the dimensions included in the diagnostic criteria of the American Psychiatric Association, hyperactivity, impulsivity, and inattention (Behavioral Diagnostics, 2008).

The instrument is very new, and the publishers have set a three-year total lease price of $14,220.00 (2009). There is also a $50.00 fee for each assessment administered.

Pervasive Developmental Disorder (PDD)

Children with a **pervasive developmental disorder** experience severe and pervasive impairment in reciprocal social interactions and communications. These disorders are chronic and will last for the child's whole life. As children with PDD grow up and become adults, many learn to cope with their disorder and live normal lives. Naturally, many adults with severe disabilities spend their adult lives in assisted living environments or in other institutional settings. This was well depicted in the movie *Rain Man* (Guber & Levinson, 1988).

Frequently, children with PDD exhibit stereotyped behaviors, activities, and interests (American Psychiatric Association, 1994). Of the five disorders classified by the American Psychiatric Association as being pervasive developmental disorders, two have recently been identified by early childhood educators with increasing frequency. These are **autistic disorder** and **Asperger's disorder.**

In 1990, only two children in a thousand were diagnosed with Asperger's disorder or with autism. Today, that number is closer to one in 80 children and about half of the cases are identified as being of the Asperger's type (Gillberg, 2006). One of the differences between the two disorders is mental ability. Asperger's has been described as a high-functioning form of autism (Klin, McPartland, & Volkmar, 2005).

Asperger's Disorder

There is both anecdotal proof and clinical evidence that there is a genetic vulnerability or link to Asperger's disorder and/or autism (Hardman, Drew, & Egan, 2008; Morrow et al., 2008). Parent advocacy groups have claimed that these disorders are caused by childhood vaccinations. Yet, to date there is no scientific evidence of a causal link between vaccines and this form of disability. Case in Point 11.4 provides a true description of a child with this disorder.

Case in Point 11.4

Case of a Child With Asperger's Disorder

A few years ago, a child named Alex was referred by a third grade teacher for assessment by the IEP Committee. Alex was a tall, thin, 10-year-old boy. He did not socialize well with others, and in October asked his teacher to be seated in a back corner of the classroom. That corner was where a series of social studies posters were hung on the walls.

During class a month later, the teacher asked if any child knew their state's flower. Alex did, and then went on to list the state flowers of the other 49 states. To the teacher's amazement he also knew every state capital and official animal.

An extensive evaluation provided the documentation needed to identify the child as having Asperger's disorder. Interestingly, when his mother heard the description of her son she said that Alex had a younger sibling who exhibited all the same behaviors.

Identification of Asperger's Disorder

Highly educated clinicians normally diagnose Asperger's disorder through interviews with the child and his/her teachers and parents. In 2008, a new identification system developed by Marilyn Monteiro was announced.

Monteiro Interview Guidelines for Diagnosing Asperger's Disorder (MIGDAS)

MIGDAS is a highly scripted series of interviews and structured observations of the child. Western Psychological lists it for $149.00 (2009). In addition to the base price, it requires the examiner purchase a number of toys and other stimuli material for the assessment process.

Guidelines provide structured conversations that a team of clinicians should use with the child, his or her parents, and teachers in collecting data. It also includes a series of stimuli that are age appropriate for children of different developmental levels. Scripted interviews are also provided for the child's teacher and parents. The MIGDAS is a labor-intensive diagnostic system. It requires a team approach to interviewing the child, parents, and teachers.

The MIGDAS provides a series of scores based on data collected during interviews. These include qualitative descriptions of the child covering Language and Communication, Social Relationships and Emotional Responses, and Sensory Use and Interests. The MIGDAS does not provide data about its normative subjects or its reliability and validity. For that reason, it must be only viewed as a way to organize qualitative clinical impressions.

Autistic Disorder

The spectrum of related **autistic spectrum disorders (ASD)** include Kanners disorder, Rett syndrome, childhood autism, infantile autism, and Asperger's disorder (National Institute of Mental Health [NIMH], 2007). Children with autism can be identified as young as 18 months. As infants and toddlers, they squirm away from being hugged or cuddled by a parent. They do not seem interested in what their parents have to say, and rarely speak themselves. Some of these children are identified when their parents have them tested by an audiologist as possibly being deaf. As preschool children, bright lights, new sights, and loud sounds can agitate them. Head banging and severe tantrums are common behaviors among children with autistic disorder.

Manifestation

Autism is usually paired with low cognitive ability (American Psychiatric Association, 1994). In addition, children with autism typically have problems interacting with other people. Children with autism are usually reluctant to make eye contact or smile, and have no interest in playing with others or making friends. At school, children with autism tend to engage in solitary activities. Cognitively low-functioning children with autism may also be classified as having **Kanners disorder** (NIMH, 2007).[11]

Correlational research has demonstrated that children born with low birth weight (less than 2.5 kg) are at a greater risk for developing autism than children in the normal weight range at birth. This effect is most pronounced for boys. Girls born early (less than 33 weeks gestation) are at higher risk for autism, but not boys (Larsson et al., 2005). In general, girls with autism tend to have lower levels of mental ability than is true of boys with the syndrome (Osborne, 2002).

There is also evidence that extreme sensory deprivation during infancy and early childhood can induce an "environmental autism."[12] See Case in Point 11.5 for a true case of a child being deprived to the point of inducing autism.

Case in Point 11.5

Environmentally Induced Autism

On July 13, 2005, a Plant City, Florida, police officer found a filthy, undernourished 6-year-old girl who had lived in a house surrounded by her own feces and covered in bugs. She could not speak, walk, or focus her eyes. The girl could only take nourishment and water through a baby bottle. She was the daughter of a woman who had a low level of mental ability and various mental issues. The girl had lived in a closet, without clothing or even a bed to sleep upon. The first time she ever left the house was when the police officer carried her to the patrol car and drove her to the emergency room of a medical center.

A pediatric team at Tampa General Hospital cleaned her up and fed her intravenously. She had no discernable physical or neurological problems, but was developmentally far below normal in most dimensions. She was diagnosed as having environmental autism, Kanner's type.

After three years of patient parenting by a concerned family, she was able to use the bathroom with assistance, and she could feed herself, but was still without speech and she had other symptoms of severe autism (DeGregory, 2008).

Autism can also be paired with a great talent and give an otherwise mentally deficient child an unexplainable ability to play musical instruments, memorize complex lists such as airline time tables, or do higher calculus while a primary grade student. This combination of autism, low IQ, and a great talent is known as **autistic savant disorder.**

Asperger's disorder is a variation on autism. Children with Asperger's disorder frequently have better social skills than autistic (Kanner's syndrome) children and have above average levels of mental ability. Young children with Asperger's disorder exhibit all the same behaviors of other children, but do so to an extreme level or in an inappropriate format or location. Children with Asperger's disorder also tend to concentrate on a single issue or area of learning and develop a true expertise on the topic. Asperger described these children as, *"kleine Professoren mit einem unglaublichen Wissen von diesem oder von diesem Thema"*[13] (Osborne, 2002). This dimension of Asperger's can lead the child to a productive and full life.

Summary

As recently as the 1970s, children needing special educational services were frequently denied access to public schools. Most children with disabilities ended up being educated in private specialized schools at the expense of parents.

Federal legislation in the 1970s and the record of case law since that time have brought about major policy changes for our schools. Today, the approach known as response to intervention (RTI) is widely employed with young children. It involves having all children screened for possible problems. Children identified with potential learning problems are referred to assistance teams or committees. These are committees of teachers and other specialists. The job of the committees is to recommend alternative instructional approaches for children who require educational assistance and support. If the instructional intervention does not work, he/she can then be referred to a multidisciplinary, individual educational program committee.

Special education is designed to work within an inclusive educational environment structured to provide children with an appropriate educational experience that sets goals for learning and benchmarks for success. Special education is carried out in a minimally restrictive learning environment.

There has been an unexplained spike in the number of children identified with a pervasive developmental disorder. New evidence points to a genetic link as a cause of many forms of PDD. The most common PDD being identified by early childhood educators includes the autism spectrum disorders.

Discussion Questions

1. Contact a local school system (or use the district's Internet database) to determine the number of children receiving special education services. Compare this to the district's total population of students. Is the district's data similar to the national data? Identify any differences you have found.
2. How are Section 504 Committees and IEP Committees similar and different? What are the goals of each?
3. What are the advantages and disadvantages of the response to intervention (RTI) approach to assessment?
4. In what ways are children with AD/HD, and children with a reading disability but without AD/HD similar and different?
5. What are the differences between characteristics of children with a PDD such as autism and children with AD/HD?
6. What are reasons a parent of a child with AD/HD would not have the child prescribed a psychotropic drug?

Related Readings

Gargiulo, R. M. (2008). *Special education in contemporary society: An introduction to exceptionality* (3rd ed.). Thousand Oaks, CA: Sage.

Osborne, L. (2002). *American normal: The hidden world of Asperger's disorder*. New York: Copernicus Books.

Ostrosky, M. M., & Horn, E. (Eds.). (2002). *Assessment: Gathering meaningful information* (Young Exceptional Children Monograph No. 4). Missoula, MT: Council for Exceptional Children.

Pierangelo, R., & Giuliani, G. A. (2005). *Assessment in special education* (2nd ed.). Upper Saddle River, NJ: Allyn & Bacon.

Pierangelo, R., & Giuliani, G. A. (2007). *The educator's diagnostic manual of disabilities and disorders*. Hoboken, NJ: John Wiley.

Wright, P. W. D., & Wright, P. D. (2007). *Special education law: Wright's law* (2nd ed.). Hartfield, VA: Harbor House Law Press.

Notes

1. Not all 6 million children with special needs are enrolled in public schools. Private schools for children with severe disabilities enroll about 1.5 million.
2. Various names are used for this team of educators and specialists including Student Assistance Team (SAT).
3. Courts can define how and when a law is applied through the interpretation of original statutes. Case law can also be created in answer to a suit of law based on existing statutes and the Constitution. Case law made by the U.S. Courts of Appeals and the U.S. Supreme Court has the force of law for the nation as a whole. Twelve Circuit Federal Courts and the 94 District Federal Courts can make case law for their region of the country. State courts can make case law for their state. Each state has its own supreme court that can make case law for that state, provided it is not in conflict with federal laws or case law.
4. Parent support and advocacy groups for children with disabilities date back to the 1930s; but it was not until the 1960s that needs of disabled children began to be addressed in legislation (Pardini, 2002). In 1965, Title VI of the Elementary and Secondary Education Act included a provision for the establishment of the Bureau for Education of the Handicapped. That small office provided a resource for future legislation that had a huge impact on the education of American children with disabilities.

5. Education was not established as a cabinet-level department of the federal government until the Jimmy Carter administration in 1979 with the passage of Public Law 96-88.
6. State courts, where most cases are heard, have been reluctant to make school systems pay punitive damages when they lose special education cases. For that reason, school systems have been aggressive in challenging parents who want expensive placements for their children with disabilities.
7. Special education services can be provided during the summer break to children with special needs. To qualify for a summer program, the IEP committee must believe the child may lose his/her newly learned skills over summer months unless they are given added summer services. The IEP committee must determine the need for ESY services.
8. The American Psychiatric Association classification is AD/HD, Predominantly Inattention Type, and AD/HD, Predominantly Hyperactive-Impulsive Type. The total package is described as AD/HD, Combined Type.
9. A new system for collecting and quantifying empirical data for the differential diagnosis of AD/HD was developed in 2002 at McClain Medical Center and by physicians at Harvard University's College of Medicine. The behavioral Diagnostics Company in Cambridge, Massachusetts, has marketed that system since 2007. This is the Quotient ADHD System, a computer-assisted individualized measure.
10. The executive function is a cognitive construct describing a mental system that controls and manages other mental processes. Abilities to plan ahead and concentrate are directed by the executive function.
11. Dr. Hans Asperger, a pediatrician in World War II Austria, made the original diagnoses of autism and Asperger's disorders. This went unnoticed for years in English language journals. An American psychiatrist, Dr. Leo Kanner, independently identified the same disorder in 1943. His name was associated with this disorder for the next 50 years. The name of Asperger became the dominant label for the disorder during the 1990s.
12. The first record of experimentally induced autism occurred in the 13th century when Holy Roman Emperor Frederick II had several year-old infants locked away and cared for by a silent order of nuns who were ordered to minimize contact and never speak to, or around, the children. Frederick wanted to see what language God would impart to those not influenced by worldly speech. By adolescence, the members of the silent group were mute and exhibited autistic-like behaviors.
13. Little professors with an incredible knowledge of this or that topic.

Family Involvement and Engagement 12

. . . if public education does not take into consideration the circumstances of family life, and everything else that bears on a man's general education, it can only lead to an artificial and methodical dwarfing of humanity.

—Johann Pestalozzi

Introduction and Themes

Between 80% and 90% of a primary grade child's life is spent at home with his/her parents. Regular constructive contact between parents and a child's teachers is correlated with superior standardized test scores. Not all parents have the time flexibility to be engaged in their child's education. Family and work obligations can make it difficult for many parents to attend parent–teacher conferences.

In addition to parental engagement, other family-oriented factors in achievement test scores are the education of the parents, the organization of the home, and the values of the parents. The family's SES level is an important predictor of how well children do on standardized tests.[1] Children who receive a **free or reduced cost lunch** tend to have lower average scores than do children of middle class homes.

While a number of family-based factors influence the achievement of children, only one, parent engagement, can be directly influenced by educational policy. All preschools and public elementary schools schedule parent–teacher conferences. Teachers should be highly prepared for these conferences and work to make them comfortable for parents. Parent involvement should include the child's father as well as the maternal caregiver. Possibly the most difficult of all parent conferences for teachers are those associated with special education placements. One new direction for the traditional conference at school is the videoconference. The technology necessary to support this approach is readily available, but not always the best approach when discussing a child's special needs.

To improve the quality and quantity of parent–school contacts, schools have begun to develop new approaches. One new direction is the establishment of transition programs for children making a major educational move (e.g., preschool to kindergarten). Another is the adoption of a team approach to community and family outreach. This can be especially useful for children of minority groups including ELL children.

Learning Objectives

By reading and studying this chapter, you should acquire the competency to:

- Present evidence as to the importance of parents in the early education of children.
- Describe home and family factors that influence achievement test scores of young children.
- Explain the qualification for a child to receive a free or reduced cost lunch.
- Develop a plan to increase the engagement of Hispanic parents in a school's programs.
- Design an inservice program showing teachers how to prepare for parent conferences.
- Describe how a team approach to parent involvement in a school's programs can work to increase parental engagement.
- Discuss ideas for helping children with special needs make transitions from early intervention to a school-based program.

Train a child in the way he should go, and when he is old he will not depart from it . . .

—Book of Proverbs 22:6

Parent's Role in Early Education

Today, the number and range of advice books for parents on the education and rearing of children has reached over a hundred-thousand English language volumes.[2] These books cover the range of ideas for raising children and are often contradictory with each other. Perhaps the best-selling book ever written on child care is *Baby and Child Care* by the pediatrician and psychiatrist Benjamin Spock (1957). This book, first published in 1946, became the standard for parents of the baby boom generation and sold over 50 million copies. His principle point was that parents should use their own common sense and treat their children with respect.

Pundits providing parental advice have come and gone over the past 50 years, but the importance of the parental role in each child's academic development remains unquestioned.[3] Federal legislation in 2002 required all schools have a parent involvement policy designed to engage children's parents in school (Jacobson, 2008c). The law also mandates parents have an opportunity to serve in leadership and advisory roles with parent–school committees (Epstein & Sheldon, 2006).

Parental Impact

Children enrolled in the primary grades experience about 1,000 hours of classroom instruction each school year. This represents about 11% of a child's life. The other 89% of the time children are in the custody and care of their parents.

The important role of parents in the education and academic development of their children begins with establishing a climate that nurtures and supports the child's academic growth. Laurence Steinberg (1996) has argued that the goal of every parent should be to develop children who are truly engaged in learning. Parenting philosophies as well as parental characteristics correlate with the measurable academic success of young children.

Parents' Engagement and Early Achievement

Achievement research has shown that one thing parents can do to encourage academic development is visit the child's school on a regular basis. Starting in preschool, when children see their parents meeting with their teachers, the concept that the school and the home are connected becomes ingrained (Michigan Department of Education, 2001). One critical issue in the relationship between parenting and the academic achievement of young children is the quality of parent–school **engagement.** This variable is more than a simple count of how many school activities are attended by the child's parents or the number of parent-initiated contacts made with the child's teachers.

When parents work with the child's school to resolve learning problems, the child learns important coping strategies. By seeing his or her parents working along with teachers, the young child learns that education is important and valued by the parents. There is also evidence children are given more attention by their teachers when parents are engaged with the school (Pomerantz, Moorman, & Litwack, 2007). Case in Point 12.1 presents an example of how a school can engage parents.

Case in Point 12.1

Idea for Parental Engagement

Engagement of parents can start on their child's first day as a kindergartener. One elementary school has an active parent organization that sets up a reception for "first day" parents. After parents drop their children off for the first day of kindergarten, the parents are invited to attend a reception and breakfast set up in the school's library. Here, members of the parent organization, educational specialists, and the school principal all can meet informally with the first day parents. At the breakfast, parents learn about programs and activities geared to help them, and get to ask questions about the school and its programs. Parents are encouraged to network with each other, and the parent organization sets up parent support programs in the evenings that all of the first day parents are encouraged to attend.

The first day of kindergarten can be an emotionally draining experience for parents. The parent group sponsoring the reception provides many boxes of Kleenex, and shoulders-to-cry-on as needed. This first day reception has been given the sobriquet, the "Boo-Hoo Breakfast" by the local newspaper (Smith, 2007).

Parents of Children With Special Needs

Children with disabilities experience a number of **transitions** in their programs. These transitions can be very stressful for both children with disabilities and their parents (Mawdsley & Hauser-Cram, 2008). If a child is identified as being at risk for a developmental problem during infancy, the focus of the child's program of assistance is directed through the family. These services are defined in Part C of the Individuals With Disabilities Education Improvement Act of 2004 (IDEIA) (see Chapter 11).

The first transition occurs when the child is placed in a prekindergarten or child care program at age 3. At that point, the program is focused on the child, and the family plays a supporting role. This service is described as early childhood special education and is elaborated in Part B of the IDEIA.

Transition into school reinforces the central role special educators play in providing educational assistance and monitoring of the child's growth and development. It also can increase the tension felt by both the young child and his/her parents (Schulting, 2008).

Parents who worry excessively about the transition between Part C and Part B (preschool and beyond) tend to have children who have difficult transition experiences (Mawdsley & Hauser-Cram, 2008). For that reason, special attention should be paid to parents of young children with disabilities as they move between educational levels.

School Transitions

There are a number of educational practices in preparation for a transition that have been shown to improve achievement levels of all young children. Well-planned transition experiences have been shown to be especially beneficial for children from impoverished homes (Schulting, 2008). These activities include holding open house receptions for children and their families and having the new teacher (kindergarten) visit with the child and his/her parents in his/her home. These should all occur prior to the kindergarten roundup described in Chapter 2.

Large-scale research has shown that children and families that experience kindergarten transition programs had better achievement test scores at the end of the kindergarten year (LoCasale-Crouch, Mashburn, Downer, & Pianta, 2007). Two variables, parent engagement and student achievement, were found to show the largest amount of change for children from homes at low and middle socioeconomic levels. There was little change for children from upper SES levels. The many advantages children of the upper classes have make transition programs superfluous (Schulting, 2008).

Home Environment

While conferences between parents and the child's teachers are important, it is the engagement of the parent with the school and teachers that supports early achievement. Engagement provides opportunities for early childhood educators to share ideas and give support to parents who wish to reinforce the school's learning activities.

Parents can be engaged with the school in a joint effort to improve the educational motivation and academic interests of their children. This goal can be achieved in part by parents who provide an academically conducive home environment. An academically conducive home environment is one where parents monitor how the child's time is spent. For example, the amount of time the young child spends playing computer games is limited as is the amount and type of television shows the child can view. About 15% of the variation in children's standardized test scores is the product of these two variables: time spent watching TV and playing computer games (Holbrook & Wright, 2004). Watching excessive amounts of TV during the child's first 3 years has been demonstrated to have a negative impact on his/her attention span and ability to focus on learning tasks at age 7 (Christakis, Zimmerman, DiGiuseppe, & McCarty, 2004).

Parental Education and Expectations

The best thing parents can do for their children's academic development is provide a positive academic role model. It is not the possession of high school diplomas and college degrees that is the causal factor in the achievement of young children; it is the parental attitude toward education, and expectations held for their child. Children of parents who express lofty goals for education achieve better scores on the **National Assessment of Educational Progress (NAEP)** examinations than children who have indifferent parents (Halpern, 2006).

Consistent increments (monotonic trends) occur in the assessment test scores of children as a function of increasing levels of parental education (Abbott, Joireman, & Stroh, 2002; NAEP, 2004). Research by the Rand Corporation in California provides documentation of large average achievement test score differences among groups of first and second grade children (Cannon & Karoly, 2007). A significant factor linked to measured achievement differences between children was parental education. In the Rand study, parents with "some college" had children with significantly better levels of reading achievement in first grade and better levels of English language arts, reading, and mathematics skills at second grade than did children with less well educated parents. The education level of parents correlates with other dimensions including home reading and educational expectation level for children (Holbrook & Wright, 2004). This makes a cluster of variables, including parental education, home reading, TV and game limits, and educational expectations that predict the achievement level of children.

Home Reading

Another powerful home influence on how much a child learns is home reading. Parents who value reading and who have at least 25 books and several newspapers and magazine subscriptions have children who perform better on state assessments (Levitt & Dubner, 2005). This variable, books in the home, has been shown to account for more than 20% of the variance in NAEP reading test scores. Books are a sign that parents value reading, and read for their own needs and enjoyment. Parents who like to read tend to read to (and with) their young children. Parental role models are a powerful influence on growing children and their habits. This influence is evident as early as kindergarten where early reading skills have been shown to correlate with the degree of engagement parents have with their children's reading (Chae, 2008).

Impact of Socioeconomic Status

The family's socioeconomic status (SES) is also directly related to reading ability of young children. It is possible this is an artifact of other correlated variables including those noted above; however, measures of SES have shown that at first grade there is a consistent reading skill advantage experienced by children of the middle and upper social classes (Stephens, 2006).

A likely factor causing SES differences in reading ability among primary grade children is parental behavior. Two out of three middle class kindergarteners are read to at home every day while this is true for only 36% of children qualified to receive a free or reduced cost lunch.[4] Testing in first grade shows that middle class children have an ability to read twice as many words in context compared to children receiving a free or reduced cost lunch (National Center for Educational Statistics, 2005). This difference in reading vocabulary can have a profound impact on a child's experience in primary grades. Table 12.1 presents the 2009 income qualification levels for free and reduced price lunches.

One of the most telling factors in the test score gap between children from middle class families and children from impoverished families is the child's vocabulary (Hart & Risley, 1995). Longitudinal research has demonstrated that by the age of 3, children born into middle class families have vocabularies twice as large as vocabularies of children born into impoverished homes. The tipping point is reached around the age of 18 months when the size of a toddler's vocabulary begins to grow exponentially (McMurray, 2007).

The quality of interactions children experience and the richness of the vocabulary they experience has much to do with this growth. Differences in vocabulary size among young children are correlated with SES levels. Vocabulary is a core component on almost all measures of mental ability. For this reason, vocabulary differences are reflected in early cognitive ability test scores, and are linked to the score gap between children of different SES levels. Vocabulary differences are caused by the amount and complexity of the language used by the young child's parents on a day-to-day basis (Hart & Risley, 1999).

Table 12.1 Qualification Needed to Receive a Reduced Price School Lunch (2008–2009)

Size of Family Unit	Maximum Family Income to Qualify for a Reduced Cost Lunch (2008)
1	$19,240
2	$25,900
3	$32,560
4	$39,220
5	$45,880
6	$52,540
7	$59,200
8	$65,860

SOURCE: U.S. Department of Agriculture. More information available at http://www.fns.usda.gov/cnd/lunch.

NOTE: Reduced cost lunches are priced at $.50 per day. Free lunches require a maximum family income 30% lower than that required for a reduced cost lunch.

Children living in a nuclear family including both a father and mother have better early academic skills and achievement than children who live in single parent families (D. A. Dawson, 1991; National Center for Educational Statistics, 2007b). Yet, 44% of children born in the United States to women below the age of 30 were born out of wedlock in 2007 (Barton & Coley, 2007). Thirty percent of all school-age children live in a single parent family, and as many as 40% of children from single family homes live in poverty (U.S. Census Bureau, 2007). A longitudinal study of elementary school children in Canada found significantly better achievement for young children of two parent families compared with children living with one parent (Adams & Ryan, 2000). This finding was more intense for families that were less wealthy.

One outcome of divorce is often the impoverishment of the single parent living with children (J. Allen, 1985). By the time young people grow to become high school seniors, the effect of living in a single parent family is even more pronounced. High school students from intact families have far better school attendance and thereby better grades and achievement than do children of divorce (Ham, 2003). Also, there is evidence that the impact on children and youth of living in a single parent family is greater on girls than it is on boys (Keen, 1998; McLanahan & Bumpass, 1988).

The role of the father in child development and education has received very little research interest over the years (D. Lynn, 1997). Yet, there is evidence that fathers who read to and with their children have children with better levels of reading skills in primary grades (Gadsden & Ray, 2003). Successful efforts have been made by community groups to get African American fathers to participate in the education of their children. One successful effort is the "Million Father March." This project started in Chicago and has spread to 200 cities around the country (Lyons, 2007). National role models like President Barack H. Obama provide a template for other fathers to follow in raising children who reach their optimum academic potential and achieve success in life.

Anna Freud was a child psychologist who studied the impact of fathers being away from home on young children. Case in Point 12.2 is about her work.

Case in Point 12.2

Research Into the Impact of Father Separation

Anna Freud (youngest child of Sigmund Freud) published the first psychological study of children separated from their fathers by war. She collected data from children enrolled in a residential school she established in wartime London, the Hampstead Wartime Nursery for Homeless Children. Her findings about the deleterious impact of separating children from their families have influenced social policy since that era. Our reticence to remove children from their homes and place them in institutions is one example of her influence. She was a powerful advocate for supporting troubled children within their families.

Communication

The communication between parents and children about schoolwork is also an important factor in student test scores. Dysfunctional families that have poor lines of communication between parent(s) and children have youngsters with more school problems, lower levels of achievement, and poor test scores (Beach, 1995). NAEP scores are significantly higher for children who report talking about school with a parent every day. Scores from children who report they "hardly ever discuss school" with their parents had NAEP achievement scores below the national average (NAEP, 2004).

Increasing Parent Involvement

Definition

Increasing parent involvement in schools is one of six areas for educational reform mandated under the original No Child Left Behind Act from 2002. It provided for two dimensions of parental involvement. The first was school-based involvement including attending meetings and conferences, volunteering, and participating in school governances. The second is home-based involvement including talking about school with the child, helping with assignments and projects, reteaching skill areas, reading with the child, and providing a quiet place for the child to read and do schoolwork (Pomerantz et al., 2007).

Rationale

When parents are involved with their child's school, the child will develop better early skills and have better achievement test scores. Involvement includes belonging to the parents association, volunteering to assist on field trips and outings, assisting during classroom celebrations and parties, and having regular conferences with the child's teacher. Only 56% of parents attend teacher conferences and only 40% review what their children are learning in school (Markow & Martin, 2005; National Center for Educational Statistics, 1998). A statistical analysis of longitudinal data by the economist Steven Levitt confirms the role of parent involvement in the success of children in school (Levitt & Dubner, 2005). The education critic Chester Finn once averred, "What's most important for all parents is to share responsibility with the schools for how well their children learn" (Finn, 1991, p. 271). This parent involvement effect is a consistent one that works no matter how wealthy or poor a family may be. Figure 12.1 provides goals for parent involvement in the schools.

Figure 12.1 National Standards for Parent/Family Involvement

1. Communicating—Communication between home and school is regular, two-way, and meaningful.
2. Parenting—Parenting skills are promoted and supported.
3. Student learning—Parents play an integral role in assisting student learning.
4. Volunteering—Parents are welcome in the school, and their support and assistance are sought.
5. School decision making and advocacy—Parents are full partners in decisions that affect children and families.
6. Collaborating with community—Community resources are used to strengthen schools, families, and student learning.

SOURCE: Adapted from Epstein, Coates, Salinas, Sanders, & Simon, 1997.

The only reason I always try to meet and know the parents better is because it helps me to forgive their children.

—M. Louis Johannot
Head Master of Ecole Le Rosey
Canton Du Vaud, Switzerland

Parent Conferences

Even though **parent conferences** take a great amount of time and can become very tedious for the teacher, they are critically important. Primary grade elementary schools tend to set parent–teacher conferences in the early fall of the school year about a month prior to American Education Week.[5] Preschools usually hold two formal parent–teacher conferences each year. These are frequently supplemented by the occasional informal meeting over a cup of coffee. Goals for both preschool and primary grade teachers are to facilitate two-way communication and mutual sharing of information. Case in Point 12.3 discusses the father's role in home-school communications.

Case in Point 12.3

The Father's Role in School Programs

One of the tasks that early childhood educators have is to get both parents engaged in the school's efforts on behalf of the child. The high rate of marital failure may preclude involving the child's father in the school's programs. However, every effort should be made to encourage his participation whenever possible.

All families are different, and respond in their own unique ways to the tasks of child rearing. Research into these issues only provides generalizations about the roles that parents assume. From that research we know that fathers spend a quarter to a third of the time parenting their children, as compared to mothers. Mothers are generally more accessible to their children. In a two-parent home, it is typically the mother who stays with the child when he/she is sick. Likewise, it is the mother who makes important decisions for the child such as whether to take piano lessons, attend ballet class, or go to a summer camp.

The role of the father in the development of a child is complex and nuanced (D. Lynn, 1997). While both parents play with their children, it is usually the father who engages in loud, creative, and expressive play, and in emotionally arousing forms of play. Mothers are typically the keepers of the language, and provide the child with vocabulary and syntax. Fathers who have an interest in teaching their child, and who encourage their child to learn, can have a powerful and positive impact on the growing child's cognitive ability (Lamb, 2003).

Preparation for Parent Conferences

Teachers need to spend time preparing for scheduled parent conferences. Also, teachers can only see two or three parents in an hour. For primary grades, the whole process can add the equivalent of two or three days of work to the teacher's schedule. The preschool teacher has a smaller number of children, but must meet parents more often, so the time commitment is about the same. Because of parent work schedules, much of the time for parent conferences must come in the evenings and on weekends. However, parents need to meet and get to know the teacher who is responsible for their preschool and elementary age child. Parents want to feel that the teacher really knows and cares for their youngster. This is all the more reason for careful preparation by teachers prior to conferences.

In addition to the preparation done by the teacher, parents should also be guided so they know what they could do to get ready for the conference. To facilitate this, early child educators can provide parents with suggestions for things that parents can ask teachers during conferences. Remember to suggest that parents ask their child what subjects they like and which are not their favorites. Also, parents should ask their child if there is something that the parents should talk over with the teacher. The following is a short list of questions that parents may want to have their child's teacher answer:

1. What social skills is he/she expected to master this year?
2. How do you evaluate children? Do you explain grades to the children?
3. How well does my child get along with others?
4. How is my child's attention span? Does he/she listen to directions, and so on?
5. Do you sense any sensory difficulties? Eyes? Hearing?
6. Is he/she on track developmentally with others of the same age?
7. What are my child's greatest strengths?
8. What dimensions of my child are the least advanced and need attention?
9. What can we do at home to reinforce what you are doing at school?
10. Does my child take part in group activities and games with others?

Preparation for the conference by the teacher should include a review of all files and information sources about the child. If the conference is scheduled early in the school year, this preparation may involve a review of last year's work. A précis should be written on a card where it can be quickly reviewed between parent conferences. The information should be drawn from:

1. The child's teacher last year
2. The school nurse
3. The child's health file
4. The guidance counselor
5. Attendance records
6. The child's portfolios
7. Standardized test scores
8. Lunchroom and recess playground aids
9. All teacher-made test results

In addition to these, the teacher should make a brief description of important "talking points" that he or she wishes to remember to discuss with the parent. One thing to remember is to have several suggestions of ways that parents can help with the education of their child at home.

Conducting a Parent Conference

During the conference, the first priority is to put the parent(s) at ease and prevent any feelings of confrontation (Mendler, 2006). This may be achieved by encouraging parents to discuss their observations and raise any questions they may have. Early childhood teachers should ask parents about the child at home. Getting a feel for the child's schedule and activities away from the classroom can provide teachers with important information. This includes an approximation of the child's time spent with computer games and watching TV, and the amount of time the child sleeps at night.

Teachers should be positive when describing the child's work habits, social interactions, and academic gains. The conference is an excellent time to remind parents to keep lines of communication between home and school open. Depending on school policy, the teacher can share his/her e-mail address with parents and let them know policies of the school regarding online contacts.

A new direction in parent conferences involves the use of video conferencing technology. Modern home computer systems are frequently equipped with video cameras making the two-way meeting an easy step. This application of technology is actually a videophone system connecting the school computer equipped with a video camera with a similar unit at the home or office of the parent. Stand-alone videophones can be bought today at many electronics stores and added to the office and faculty rooms of schools and child care centers.

Inclusion of Children in Conferences

There are some authors who advocate for having children attend the parent–teacher conference (Stiggins, 2007; Wortham, 2008). The argument for this approach is that the child can present his/her portfolio to the parent in front of the teacher and talk about what has been learned. This can provide the child with enhanced communication skills with his/her parents.

This author disagrees with this approach. The open discussion of the child's progress in front of him/her is likely to become stilted and cryptic. Young children can become bored with the "adult talk" going on and become a distraction. It is also likely that any conversation between parents and the teacher will be misinterpreted and not correctly understood by the young child. If the parent–teacher meeting is held at night it may interfere with the child's schedule.

Pre-Assessment Conference

Classroom teachers and elementary school counselors are people who all-too-frequently are responsible for meeting with a child's parents and discussing the possibility that their child may need extra help. In the minds of many misinformed people, children with special needs are seen as being damaged goods, or somehow dangerous. Many parents may already have concerns with the way their child must work extra diligently just to keep up with his/her peers. Thus, the call requesting an in-school meeting may not be well received. Parents may ask for a quick diagnostic statement about their child over the phone during that call. Teachers should avoid falling into this trap. Tell the parents that the information should only be explained and shared in person.

Conducting a Pre-Assessment Conference

The key to a successful parent meeting is to make the theme one of "finding a solution" and helping the child stay with his/her peers. Having a positive **pre-assessment conference** will make it possible for the child's parents to become more supportive and engaged with the school. Successful parent conferences also send a positive message to children that the school and home are working together (Pierangelo, 2004).

During the pre-assessment meeting, parents should meet with only the teacher and no more than one other educator.[6] It is normal for educators to rely on statistical evidence and test scores to "prove to the parents that something must be done." This approach is wrongheaded and can lead to poor school–home relations. Allow the parents to tell you what they know first, do not interrupt their descriptions, and withhold judgments about what they say. The following is a brief list of things a teacher can do to facilitate a parent–teacher pre-assessment conference:

- Schedule a long block of time for the meeting. It is essential that parents do not feel hurried or rushed into making a decision about their child.
- Never "talk down" to parents or ascribe blame to them or their home lifestyle. By being pejorative, educators can create unnecessary resentment that blocks progress with the child.
- Try to meet in a room around a table (preferably a round one) and avoid sitting behind a desk when talking with parents. Educators should never sit in a position of power (e.g., head of the table).
- Be sure to provide parents with a pad and pen so they can take notes about the meeting if they wish.
- Start by building parent confidence. Parents should be encouraged to describe their child's typical day.
- Ask parents to describe their child's greatest strengths.
- Ask parents to describe any academic or other problems the child seems to be having.
- Describe strengths that teachers see in the child. Try to make a positive statement about the child.
- Review major curriculum goals for the grade level, and the progress the typical child is making toward those goals.

- Describe the child's status as a learner, and what problems he/she is experiencing.
- Describe the next steps the school plans to take to improve the child's learning including the next level of assessment.
- Discuss the role that parents can play with the team that will be assembled to discuss the child and a support program designed for him or her.
- Never close a meeting without sharing something with parents. This can be a handout listing support groups and their contact points, or a list of books that have good ideas for parents to follow in helping their child. Also, provide parents with a description of the school's pupil services division and various offices and agencies that are part of the total team. It is important to provide parents with a statement describing their legal rights in the assessment and placement process.
- Provide a summary for parents of what was covered during the meeting and what the next steps are.

Entitlement Conference

By the time parents are asked to attend an **entitlement conference** (IEP team), they have already attended several other meetings about their child's learning needs. Parents will have attended a pre-assessment meeting, a student Instructional Support Team (IST) meeting, and an initial Individual Educational Plan (IEP) Committee meeting. The agenda for the first entitlement meeting is the development of an Individual Educational Plan for the child (see Chapter 11).

The role of parents on the IEP committee is to serve as equal partners and team members. Parents should be viewed as assets who know more about the child than the other committee members. They also are invaluable adjuncts to the educational process for the child. With their help, and with their reinforcement of the child's educational program, the child with a special need can make the most improvement.

If the committee asks parents to provide help for the child at home, the request should be as specific as possible. Likewise, when educators have suggestions for how parents can assist the child's development at home it should be highly practicable. The IEP Committee should never assume that parents are teachers and can understand specific educational jargon (educationese). Perhaps the best approach is for the parent to be given printed material describing things that can be done at home to support the educational program.

Parents of children with special needs will be asked to attend annual conferences with members of the IST to discuss progress and review the child's IEP. These may also involve reviewing the response to intervention (RTI) data collected during the year.

Technology and Parent Communications

One way a school can support healthy parental involvement is to invest in a computer server that makes it possible for ongoing communication with each child's family. That system can also be used to share school news on a computer bulletin board and provide e-mail interaction between the school's staff, teachers, and the school's parents. Special events, lunch menus, upcoming field trips, projects, and homework assignments can be posted for parents to see.

Naturally, this system requires parents have a computer and knowledge of computers and how to use the Internet. This may require another investment on the part of the school system to provide parent education and free computers for those in need. There are computer systems for indigent families that now sell for about $200. The international version is sold in Africa and South America for about $100. A cheap, reliable computer for those who cannot afford technology was the idea of Nicholas Negroponte, a professor and director of the Media Laboratory at Massachusetts Institute of Technology. Negroponte's computer is manufactured and marketed by Quanta Computer, a leading manufacturer of portable computers. In 2008, Daewoo announced the sale of a new classroom computer that costs less than $400.00 (A. Elliott, 2008). In 2010, a number of discount companies sell laptop systems for less than $350.00.

One way to improve parent engagement with the school is through educational programming designed for parents offered in the evenings and/or on weekends. One good topic for parents is how to communicate with the school over the Internet. This type of class can be taught in the school's computer center.

Parent Organizations

There is a long history of parent involvement in American education. In 1897, Alice McLellan Birney and Phoebe Apperson Hearst started an organization of mothers of school children. A call to action by the leadership of this group led to the first national meeting in Washington, D.C., in 1897 that was attended by 2,000 parents and educators. By 1919, the Parent Teacher Association had 37 state charters for affiliated chapters to work for the betterment of children's lives (Minnesota Parent Teacher Association, 2008).[7]

Team Approach

School policymakers have long recognized the need to find ways to get parents involved. Yet, teachers and building principals cannot do this alone. Central to improving parental engagement with the school is leadership. The process of building a community-based program to support parent engagement requires multilevel leadership from the school system (Epstein & Sheldon, 2006).

Schools committed to engaging parents need to examine how they reach out to parents. All contacts between the school and parents must be designed to foster a trusting and mutually respectful approach to parent participation.

All schools hold open houses and most primary schools schedule parent conferences. These tried-and-true techniques can be off-putting for many parents who see schools as intimidating and foreboding places. This parental attitude can reflect their school problems from years ago; or, it can be the product of being poorly treated during an earlier contact.

To break this cycle, Joyce Levy Epstein and her colleagues at Johns Hopkins University suggest an approach that stresses informal contacts with parents (Epstein, Sanders, Salinas, Jansom, & Voorhis, 2002). That model is part of the National Network of Partnership Schools (NNPS) (Dessoff, 2008). Epstein's approach has been developed and implemented for the past 20 years. It includes several types of involvement that schools should work to establish with parents.

One activity that can be done over the Internet or during a back-to-school night is a survey. Parents should have input as to the type of informal and structured (formal) activities they would like to see the schools provide for the community. Parents should also be surveyed for ways they can volunteer or help the school and its programs. Figure 12.2 provides a sample parent volunteering survey.

Schools should print brochures advertising plans for informal activities and use local shopping outlets and community churches to distribute information to parents of a community. Direct mail and Internet advertisements are other approaches for local schools to use to get the word out about informal activities. If appropriate, all advertisements and the school's Web page should be bilingual.

Figure 12.2 Survey of Potential Areas for Parent Participation and Volunteering

Name ______________________________ Phone(s) ______________

Name of child (children) in the school ______________________________

Name of the child's (children's) homeroom teacher(s) ______________________________

____

I am able and interested in helping at school...

____(Y) ____(N) helping supervise children on field trips.

____(Y) ____(N) running booths at school fairs and fund-raising activities.

____(Y) ____(N) providing secretarial assistance (envelope addressing, letter stuffing, etc.) to support the parent organization's activities.

____(Y) ____(N) helping run the copy equipment and collating teacher worksheets.

____(Y) ____(N) reading stories to small groups of children.

____(Y) ____(N) individually tutoring a child who needs extra help.

____(Y) ____(N) writing (block printing) the story as a child dictates it.

____(Y) ____(N) demonstrate a hobby or craft to children.

____(Y) ____(N) show and explain the native costume from another culture.

____(Y) ____(N) assist during a class party, or social event.

____(Y) ____(N) give a talk on "career day."

"Sometimes I wish our school did not try quite so hard to get parent involvement."

SOURCE: Cartoon by Merv Magus.

Informal activities for improving parent engagement include opening school resources to the community (e.g., swimming pools, libraries, computer centers, vocational guidance, and topical education programs). Other activities include setting up interactive (Internet or telephonic) homework assistance, holding monthly student recognition award assemblies that give parents a participatory role, and creating informal channels for educators and parents to meet. Informal channels may include holding a picnic or barbecue during the week prior to the school's opening. Hold a family story reading day when parents and other family members are invited into the classroom to read stories to small groups of children. This can occur several times during the school year with different parents reading to the children each time. Each of these ideas will facilitate educators meeting with parents. One school's method for getting parents involved in their child's schoolwork is described in Case in Point 12.4.

Case in Point 12.4

Parents as Reading Volunteers

One elementary school reading teacher worked with the school's parent organization to organize an early morning reading program for young children. In this program, the reading teacher trained two reading aids (Title I–funded positions), and had them open up the school's library an hour before the school day started. This provided parents who had early morning jobs a safe alternative for their children. It also provided a time for extra instruction in reading. The reading teacher recruited unemployed parents to volunteer as aides in the program.[8]

Hispanic Families

The problem of finding ways to increase the engagement of Hispanic parents is one that is critical. Hispanic parents frequently find they face daunting barriers when they try to become involved with the education of their children. Barriers are more than just language, and include cultural expectations, and familiarity with cultural norms established for American education (Arias & Morillo-Campbell, 2008).

The problem that Latino(a) parents face is a significant concern because Hispanic children represent the fastest growing minority group in our schools.

There are several ways schools can build bridges to reach parents of children who are English language learners (ELL). A first step is the inservice education of teachers and members of the support staff with the culture and history of the ELL children in the school. Another is to work to hire as many bilingual teachers and staff members as possible. Finally, establish nontraditional involvement activities that are reciprocal between the school, parents, and the wider community (Arias & Morillo-Campbell, 2008). An example of this kind of outreach is described in Case in Point 12.5.

Case in Point 12.5

High School Role Models as Reading Coaches

One elementary school principal worked through the school district's high school coaches to recruit African American and Hispanic high school varsity athletes. The elementary school served a high-poverty community, and 90% of those enrolled were from minority groups. These high school athletes read stories to children in kindergarten and first grades. It provided student athletes with a service learning experience while providing primary grade children with role models for reading. On the second or third return visit to the elementary school, a number of student athletes brought their parents and/or siblings along to see them "teach." The high school students took great pride in working with, and being a role model for, young children. That year they grew in their abilities as oral readers during the year.

A reciprocal program is one that develops parents as volunteers in the school. This makes it possible for parents to feel a sense of *orgullo* (personal pride). Research has shown that schools that reach out and invite parents to volunteer and assist in schools can be very successful. When Hispanic parents were asked why they became school volunteers they answered that schools were respectful of them and provided for their needs. Small gestures were important in making this possible. Little courtesies such as a separate room for volunteers were powerful motivators. Language is another motivator. Hispanic parents appreciate school staff and administrators who try to speak some Spanish (Quintanar & Warren, 2008).

Summary

Books offering advice to parents as to how to raise and educate their children now number in the tens of thousands. Parents play a central role in determining how well children do in preschool and in primary grades. The impact of parents can be seen in the correlation of the achievement test scores of their children and parental education levels, socioeconomic status, reading habits, and the amount of time they permit children to enjoy computer games and watch TV each day. A major factor in how children learn is the amount and quality of the contacts that parents have with their children's school. This parent–school contact issue is especially important, as it is one that schools can influence.

One traditional form of parent contact with schools is the parent-teacher conference. Successful conferences involve good preparation by both parties, that is, teachers and parents. It can be facilitated or augmented by video conferencing. This option is most useful for parents with complex work schedules.

Parent involvement in pre-assessment conferences, and as members of Individual Educational Plan Committees, requires that educators exhibit a high degree of sensitivity and respect for the input of the child's parents. These conferences require careful planning, and can never be handled as a videoconference.

Schools can improve the level of parent engagement by employing a team approach that elicits community involvement in programs and resources of the school. Nontraditional, reciprocal programs can be useful in bringing minority parents, especially Hispanic parents, to greater levels of involvement in the school and the education of their children.

Discussion Questions

1. Prepare a list of all artifacts that a teacher should review when planning a parent–teacher conference for a child. How much time would you need to discuss these items?
2. What are six nontraditional activities that a preschool could employ to encourage parental involvement with their program?
3. If you were the teacher of a child who was determined by the IEP Committee to need special education for a serious learning disability related to AD/HD, what handouts would you prepare to share with parents at the entitlement decision meeting?
4. What role should technology play in supporting parent engagement with the school?

Related Readings

Epstein, J. L., Sanders, M. G., Salinas, C., Jansom, N. R., & Voorhis, F. L. (2002). *School, family, and community partnerships: Your handbook for action* (2nd ed.). Thousand Oaks, CA: Corwin Press.

Epstein, J. L., & Sheldon, S. B. (2006). Moving forward: Ideas for research on school, family, and community partnerships. In C. F. Conrad & R. Stein (Eds.). *Sage handbook for research in education: Engaging ideas and enriching inquiry* (pp. 117–138), Thousand Oaks, CA: Sage.

Mendler, A. N. (2006). *Handling difficult parents: Successful strategies for educators.* Rochester, NY: Discipline Associates

Steinberg, L. (1996). *Beyond the classroom: Why school reform has failed and what parents need to do.* New York: Touchstone.

Notes

1. SES represents socioeconomic status. It is a composite statement about a person's income, education level, occupation, and social standing within the community.
2. An Internet search of the word "parenting" on the Amazon book list turned up 103,259 titles on January 21, 2009.
3. Parents are referred to throughout the chapter. It must be recognized that this includes the person(s) who care for and nurture the child. Such people may be parents, grandparents, legal guardians, and foster parents.
4. Children who qualify for a free or reduced cost lunch live in impoverished conditions. In 2008, about 11% of America's children lived in households designated as being "food insecure." That proportion goes up to a third of the children living in African American homes. A total of 19% of all children qualify for a free or reduced cost lunch on the basis of poverty.
5. In the fall of 1921, the National Education Association in cooperation with the American Legion promoted the first National Education Week to celebrate American teachers and the job that they do for children and society. The annual celebration normally occurs the second week of November and is a time when the public is invited into schools to see education in action. Today that week is called the American Education Week.
6. It is important to note that all meetings related to special education and entitlement decisions with parents cannot be conducted via teleconferencing.
7. The Parent Teacher Association is a large national organization with thousands of affiliates. Some schools have formed local, unaffiliated parent organizations under various names. One is the "Parent Teacher Organization." Like the PTA, these organizations are working for the betterment of lives of children.
8. These volunteer activities require a great deal of careful planning. Parents and others coming into the classroom must first have a background check. Next, appropriate books must be selected for the visiting family members to read. Finally, a short inservice should be provided for the parents to teach them how to read dramatically with young children.

Part V

Evaluation of Early Childhood Programs and Schools

This short section of the text provides various models for the evaluation of early education centers and schools. Evaluation models appropriate for responding to federal and state requirements are explained with examples. The evaluation of teachers and programs using a value-added approach are described along with descriptions of strengths and weaknesses of value-added evaluations.

Two models for the accreditation of child care centers and early education programs are explained. The section concludes with a presentation of issues and concerns parents may have when selecting a preschool or child care provider.

Program Evaluation and Planning 13

Not everything that counts can be counted, and not everything that can be counted counts.

—Albert Einstein

Introduction and Themes

Evaluation of early childhood education is a recent phenomena that is here to stay. One of Lawrence Schweinhart's keys to a quality prekindergarten is a well integrated program of continuous assessment of program quality and children's development (Schweinhart, 2008).[1]

Forty-three states provided some form of support for preschool education programs in 2009. Whenever state funds are involved, there will be a need to be "accountable" and an evaluation will be required. This has resulted in a series of statewide assessment programs being initiated to evaluate centers and preschools receiving state funding.

Early primary education is often supported (in part) with federal funds under Title I of the Elementary and Secondary Education Act (2004), the reauthorization of No Child Left Behind. To receive federal support, the school must submit an application including a detailed plan for the evaluation of the program or project to be funded.

The administration of President Lyndon B. Johnson introduced the discipline of educational evaluation and made it an integral part of all early childhood education programs receiving external funding. One source of guidance for how to conduct evaluations is provided by the U.S. Department of Education in the form of Education Department General Administrative Regulations (EDGAR).

The newest approach to the multifaceted problem of evaluating an early childhood education program is one based on test scores and examines academic growth. This approach, the value-added approach to the evaluation of education, looks at where the child begins, not just where he/she ends up at the end of the school's program year.

Many early childhood centers and preschool programs are "**tuition driven**" and must compete in the private marketplace for children to fill their enrollment needs. This provides another type of evaluation, the decision of parents as to which preschool to select for their child.

To meet evaluation requirements of state agencies and parents, preschool and child care centers pursue accreditation and recognition by professional societies. By meeting operational standards established by an organization such as the National Association for the Education of Young Children, care providers or preschools can document their quality. In 2008, a total of 10,000 early childhood centers had achieved accreditation by NAEYC.

Learning Objectives

By reading and studying this chapter, you should develop the ability to:

- Explain which forces made the evaluation of early childhood education programs necessary.
- Discuss what parents are looking for in selecting a preschool or child care program for their young child.
- Explain problems of basing an evaluation of early childhood education solely on test scores.
- Describe major "indicators of effectiveness" that are part of the NAEYC guidelines for the assessment of early childhood curriculum and program effectiveness.
- List and describe the seven steps for conducting a systematic evaluation of an educational program.
- Describe the concept of P-16 as it relates to preschool education.
- Explain how a systematic program evaluation is different from a value-added assessment.

We begin with learning. Every child must have the best education that this Nation can provide. Thomas Jefferson said that no nation can be both ignorant and free. Today no nation can be both ignorant and great.

—President Lyndon B. Johnson

Impact of Quality Preschool Programs

A large-scale study by the National Institute of Child Health and Human Development of the long-term impact of early child programs demonstrated that quality child care and preschools have a beneficial impact on the educational development of children (NICHD, Early Child Care Research Network, & Duncan, 2003). It reported the percentage of children experiencing child care prior to school was 80%, an all-time high.[2] The study found children in third grade who were enrolled in a quality preschool when they were 4 years old had an achievement advantage in math and reading compared to their peers who had no day care experience. This advantage was most pronounced with children from impoverished homes (Duncan & Gibson-Davis, 2006).

The role of evaluation and accreditation is to ensure that child care and preschools are providing a high-quality experience for young children. By regular evaluations, funding agencies and parents can be assured of program quality.

Why and Who Evaluates Early Childhood Education?

Child care centers and preschools are evaluated as part of their state licensing applications. Head Start programs are evaluated against educational performance standards established by each state (Stipek, 2006). Parents evaluate child care providers and preschools as they make a decision to place their child in a program (American Academy of Pediatrics, 2002). In addition, schools and programs that receive funding from private foundations and/or state agencies must have a thorough evaluation of efforts they made with the funding.

The Money Trail

Love of money is said to be at the root of all evil. Whether that demonic view is true or not, we know that money is the principle reason for the development of modern approaches to educational evaluation.

Our federal government's effort to imporve the education of America's children came as a part of President Lyndon B. Johnson's "War on Poverty." In 1965, he announced the goal of creating a "Great Society," free of poverty and its pernicious effects on children (Johnson, 1966). Funding was provided to schools to improve basic education and test innovative educational ideas and methods. That year Congress also passed laws creating the Head Start program.

For the fiscal year 2008, the amount of money for federally supported education programs had grown from the $1.0 billion of the Johnston administration to $66.2 billion including $7 billion for Head Start. This enormous amount of money is but a fraction of what states spend to run public education. That total is now about a half trillion dollars per year. This mammoth amount of expenditure creates a need for schools to be "held to account." Between 2003 and 2007, the number of 4-year-olds enrolled in tax-supported preschool programs increased by 40% (Barnett, Hustedt, Friedman, Boyd, & Ainsworth, 2007). In 2009, there were over one million preschool children in 38 states that attended state-funded preschools. That represents 22% of the population of 3- and 4-year-old children. The per-child per-year expenditure of the states was $3,650.00 for a total of $3.7 billion (Barnett et al., 2007). Only 12 states do not provide support for preschool education.[3] With 70% of women in American households now employed outside of the home, there is a great need for child care in this country, and the pressure on states to provide ever more preschool service will only increase (Rust, 2003).

Governmental Mandates

Today, accountability based on test scores is an established part of American education. Early childhood educators have resisted this move, basing their opposition on the likelihood that educational programs would suffer. Their concern has been that developmentally appropriate instruction would deteriorate into so much mind-numbing, repetitious drill (Government Accountability Office, 2005; Stipek, 2006).

State Assessments of Early Education

The accountability movement and associated testing programs in early education are not going to disappear anytime soon. State governments have become committed to improving early education and see accountability with testing as central to their efforts. Not unexpectedly, in states with test-based accountability many early education and child care centers teach children by a rote learning method designed to prepare them for the high-stakes test (Stipek, 2006).

The use of individually administered tests is seen by state education officials as being more cost effective than the use of evaluation teams working in situ. One examiner visiting a school and spending two days individually testing preschoolers is less expensive than sending an evaluation team to the school to observe and evaluate the range of educational activities that are ongoing. A simple test is far less complex for a state examiner to score than is a child's portfolio filled with educational **products**. The use of high-stakes tests in preschools under a state mandate is described in Case in Point 13.1.

Case in Point 13.1

High-Stakes Testing in Florida's Preschools

An example of the ascendancy of high-stakes testing in preschools happened in the state of Florida. A voter initiative was passed in 2002 that forced a reluctant Governor Jeb Bush and a conservative state legislature to provide a voluntary prekindergarten education for all 4-year-old children (Zigler, Marsland, &

(Continued)

(Continued)

Lord, 2009). Florida did not establish a new level of public schools for prekindergarten, but used existing private day care and preschool providers. The $350 million state budget for prekindergarten education requires that all Florida's private preschools and day care centers using state money participate in an evaluation based on a high-stakes assessment program. The early childhood education law passed by the legislature included a preschool testing program.[4] The focus of Florida's high-stakes assessment is **"kindergarten readiness."**

The test used in Florida is the Florida Kindergarten Readiness Screener (FLKRS) (Moreno, 2008). This assessment is given to over 100,000 4-year-old children in Florida each year.

The following are components of this assessment (FLKRS):

- From the Dynamic Indicators of Basic Early Literacy Skills (DIBELS)
  1. Letter Naming Fluency (LNF) probe
  2. Initial Sound Fluency (ISF) probe
- Early Childhood Observational System (ECHOS)
  1. Approaches to Learning (1 probe)
  2. Social and Emotional (2 probes)
  3. Language and Communication (1 probe)
  4. Emergent Literacy (4 probes)
  5. Cognitive Development and General Knowledge (9 probes)
  6. Motor Development (2 probes)

The scoring system is weighted so that two DIBELS probes (2 minutes each to administer) account for 66% of a child's total score. The state has set a score level for the FLKRS described as equaling "kindergarten readiness." The reason for selecting that particular score is murky, and the whole testing and scoring system is patently invalid (Moreno, 2008). The FLKRS evaluation model provides no allowance for children from impoverished backgrounds, chaotic homes, or for children with health problems. Yet, the "readiness rate" (percentage of children scoring as kindergarten ready) is critical for early childhood education providers. A low percentage of children (below 70%) scoring as kindergarten ready causes the state to label the early childhood school or center as being a "low-performing provider." That designation means the provider must provide a written improvement plan to the state followed with progress reports every quarter. "Kindergarten readiness" rates for various preschools and day care centers are distributed to the media and published in local newspapers. Three years on the low performing list and the provider becomes ineligible to receive state funds.

Pew Task Force

The Pew Charitable Trust's task force report focused on state efforts to assess and improve early childhood learning. That report provided a call for states to work to establish a robust, positive, and rigorous culture for early childhood accountability (Schultz & Kagan, 2007). The Pew report identified seven states with high-quality models: Arkansas, Maryland, Michigan, New Jersey, New Mexico, Ohio, and Pennsylvania.

The Pew task force reported most state evaluations of preschool programs involve employing a combination of observational tools and direct child assessment measures. Observational systems focus on several dimensions of the center's operation, including quality of the program's leadership, overall environment, and instructional activities. Each of these three dimensions can be assessed using a checklist system such as the Early Childhood Environment Rating Scale, Revised (ECERS-R) (Harms, Clifford, & Cryer, 1998). This is a widely used measure designed to provide a structure for observing and evaluating early childhood programs. This measure consists of 43 checklist items covering seven dimensions of a center's operation: space and furnishings, personal care routines, language-reasoning, activities, interactions, program structure, and parents and staff. A summary of the advantages and disadvantages of observational and direct measures in early childhood are presented in Figure 13.1.

"Now that we have settled on the preschool, what language option do you want for her high school curriculum, and have you a college major in mind"?

SOURCE: Cartoon by Merv Magus.

Figure 13.1 Approaches to Evaluation and Assessment in Early Education

Observational Tools (Strengths)

- Available tools cover all domains of child development and learning.
- Assessors have benefit of multiple opportunities to observe children over time in a variety of contexts to confirm their ratings.
- Assessment process is unobtrusive and does not require removing children from their classroom or interrupting learning activities.
- Since teachers use this assessment format for instructional purposes, much data are available and additional costs/burdens are minimal.
- Risks of coaching/"**teaching to the test**" are minimized because assessments are not composed of individual questions.

Observational Tools (Limitations)

- Assessors must be well trained in order to carefully observe and analyze children's behavior, discourse, work samples, and other evidence and generate consistent and accurate ratings.
- Bias in teacher ratings can occur if teachers do not share the same cultural and linguistic background as children they are assessing.

(Continued)

Figure 13.1 (Continued)

- The accuracy of teacher ratings can decline over time or suffer from "rater drift" (see Chapter 4).
- Teachers may inflate ratings to show more rapid progress or higher end-of-program outcomes if assessors perceive that results will influence the reputation of their local agencies or lead to changes in funding levels.

Direct Child Assessment Measures (Strengths)

- Due to the structured nature of questions and the method of eliciting direct responses from children, there is lower risk of errors based on the assessor's judgment.
- Use of common questions, similar to standardized assessments used with older children, create the perception that results are more objective than ratings generated by observers.
- The scope, depth, and costs of training are typically lower than training for observational tools.
- Allows programs to compare the performance of children to norms for nationally representative samples of similar-aged children.

Direct Child Assessment Measures (Limitations)

- Assessors must be trained to ensure consistent administration of questions, recording of responses, developing rapport with children, and addressing behavioral challenges.
- Some children may be distracted or may not perform at their best if they are not comfortable with the assessor.
- Children must be able to process language well.
- Cultural differences among children and a program's pedagogical practices may influence how children respond to questions or tasks.
- Requires removing children from their classroom and assigning and/or compensating staff to administer the assessment.
- These assessments are not appropriate for measuring some important goals, notably social and emotional development.
- Reliance on a specific set of questions creates the risk that, if items become known, teachers can coach children on questions to inflate outcomes.

SOURCE: Schultz & Kagan, 2007, Figure 5, p. C-86.

Coordination of preschool evaluations within the state's approved standards can provide a smooth transition from preschool to primary grades and beyond. This becomes the beginning of what is known as a **P–16 model** for education.

P–16

The preschool to Grade 16 model is an approach that states now employ to link all three levels of education, preschool, kindergarten to Grade 12, and higher education (Chamberlin & Plucker, 2008).[5] The idea is to create a seamless integrated educational system for the children of a state beginning with funded preschools and flowing through a four-year degree from a state university. Part of the effort is to strengthen preschool educational programs and reduce the achievement gap between children from different social and ethnic groups.

In summary, public financing is an important driving force for program evaluations. This started with the expansion of the federal government into education during the 1960s and continues today in the form of state support for prekindergarten programs. Efforts by various states are moving toward use of a combination of direct measures of children and observational assessments of learning environment and processes. Case in Point 13.2 describes a statewide program for assessing preschool education programs.

Case in Point 13.2

Standards, Training, Assistance, Resources, and Support (STARS)

Pennsylvania began a voluntary system to improve the quality of early learning in the Commonwealth's 6,325 early childhood programs in 2002. A total of 4,300 programs agreed to participate and use the standardized rating tool selected by Pennsylvania, the Early Childhood Environment Rating Scale, Revised (ECERS-R). In addition to the ECERS-R, Pennsylvania standards for early education include requirements for teacher qualifications and staff development, leadership, community and family relations, and instructional quality. The STARS system matches many standards set for accreditation by the NAEYC. The STARS acronym represents **S**tandards, **T**raining/Professional Development, **A**ssistance, **R**esources, and **S**upport.

The system awards early childhood programs with stars on the basis of the evaluations. Up to two stars can be awarded on the basis of a self-study report. To earn three or four stars, programs must complete self-evaluations and also be evaluated by an external team. Three stars also requires that the program be able to document that the curriculum being used is aligned with approved standards for early childhood (Pennsylvania Department of Education, 2007). The state also published a "crosswalk" that demonstrated how Pennsylvania standards, NAEYC standards, ECERS-R items, and Head Start standards can be aligned with one another. The Commonwealth added $46 million to the state's budget to cover costs of this assessment initiative.

To see Pennsylvania's standards and the Keystone STARS program, see http://www.dpw.state.pa.us/PartnersProviders/ChildCareEarlyEd/KeyStoneStarChildCare/.

Formal Evaluation Models

Title I (NCLB, 2002, P.L. 107-110) funding in support of their reading and other skill development efforts for children at risk began in 1965. These funds provide early childhood schools with extra faculty and specialists as well as educational materials.[6] Application for these funds requires that a school include a carefully developed systematic plan for the evaluation of the Title I program once it is funded.

It has been argued that many variations of how to conduct an evaluation of an educational program can be organized into three empirically defined domains (Ryan, 1988). These three domains are **critical–theoretical, interpretative,** and **empirical–analytical.**

Critical–theoretical evaluations are based on a large view of society as a whole. They examine how the educational program fits within the larger social system of our communities. This approach is more than just an effort to determine how an educational system works, but rather how it can be used to improve conditions for all children.

Interpretive evaluations embrace several philosophical methodologies including phenomenology and hermeneutics. Evaluation questions developed under this paradigm focus on gaining an understanding of the social context and culture through analysis of language and interactions.

Evaluation as a discipline grew from traditions of empirical–analytical research. It comes from the philosophical position of logical-positivism. Tools of this approach are mathematical and rational. Evaluation questions are posed in terms of quantifiable, objective data.

In most educational evaluations, a combination of these methods is employed. The combination of several paradigms makes it possible for the evaluator to examine multiple facets of an educational project.

Critical evaluation of aspects of American education is nothing new. Case in Point 13.3 describes an evaluation that took place in the 19th century.

Case in Point 13.3

Joseph Mayer Rice: Early Critic of American Education

The 19th century saw the publication of a series of articles by Joseph Mayer Rice, a disgruntled physician who studied teacher education in Germany at Jena and Leipzig universities. Working alone, he used his German experiences as a perspective to evaluate American education. This massive study took him to 35 American cities where he assessed 125,000 children and interviewed 1,200 teachers. His writing was highly critical of American educational practice. He saw schools as being controlled by corrupt politicians and incompetent administrators. Even teachers were not immune from his criticisms. "The office of teacher in the average American school is perhaps the only one in the world that can be retained indefinitely in spite of the grossest negligence and incompetency" (Rice, 1893, p. 15). The reforms Rice urged for schools of the United States provided a wedge for reformers of the progressive movement including John Dewey to use in urging new approaches to educational policy, organization, and procedures (P. Graham, 1966).

Evaluation Standards

Diversity in evaluation methodologies did not prevent a committee representing academic disciplines involved with evaluation from developing a set of standards for conducting evaluations (Stufflebeam, 1981). These **evaluation standards** were updated again in 1994. Standards are presented in four broad areas:

1. Utility—describes the evaluator's credibility, the **stakeholders'** identification, the clarity of the writing, and the evaluation's impact.
2. Feasibility—addresses questions of a practical nature such as cost and local politics.

3. Propriety—concerns human relations among those who are party to the evaluation including subject rights and evaluator responsibility.

4. Accuracy—involves the quality of data and analysis in the report and the justifiability of conclusions.

More is available on these standards for evaluations from http://www.ericdigests.org/1996-1/the.htm.

To provide a more uniform model for the evaluation of Title I and other federally funded programs, the U.S. Department of Education published a set of evaluation guidelines known as the Education Department General Administrative Regulations (**EDGAR**). These guidelines (Title 34, Code of Federal Regulations, Parts 74–86 and 97–99) are something with which all early childhood education administrators should be familiar. A current copy should be available in the center's or school district's office. To learn more about the EDGAR guidelines, see http://www.ed.gov/print/policy/fund/reg/edgarReg/edgar.html.

Evaluation of educational programs involves following a well-conceived and systematic plan. Evaluation plans typically account for between 10% and 35% of points awarded during the review and selection process involving federal grants for education. Each evaluation plan must address two dimensions, one involving products (outcomes), and the other, the processes followed.

Analysis of products involves answering a series of evaluation questions through an analysis of data. This is a summative assessment of what happened during the funded project. Process questions are answered as the project goes along and are formative in nature. The final project report normally includes both types of information.

External funding through a governmental agency can improve the quality of services and education being provided to children. Grants can provide funding to hire specialists and child care aides, and/or purchase new educational materials and equipment. External funding will always have a string attached: that string is an evaluation of what the agency or school did with the money.

Steps in Systematic Educational Program Evaluation

- **Goal Identification:** Primary goals for the evaluation are the first items to be set. This makes it possible to determine parameters upon which the evaluation will focus. This also makes it possible to identify stakeholders and to determine the audience for the evaluation.
- **Objective Writing:** Starting with elaborated goals for the evaluation, a series of objectives must be developed. This process should involve representatives from all stakeholder groups.
- **Management Plan:** Tasks required to meet each objective must be identified and the sequence for their completion determined. Also personnel responsible for each task must be identified.
- **Data Collection:** These processes follow a sequence of tasks listed in the management plan. Data sources are both formative and summative. Formative data collection is ongoing and can be used to provide ongoing guidance to the project.
- **Data Analysis:** Analyses use both summative (statistical) and formative (qualitative) data for the final project report.
- **Publication:** Various stakeholders and audiences should be informed of evaluation conclusions and recommendations.
- **Dissemination:** Once a final report is written, it should be distributed according to specifications of the management model (R. Wright, 2008).

Teachers and center staff are often included on the list of stakeholders when an evaluation is planned for an early childhood education program. Also, teachers are the source of much of the data needed to complete the evaluation process. Other stakeholders are parents, members of the school's governing boards, community leaders, and local political leaders. Figure 13.2 presents an example of a required evaluation as part of the application for a federal grant.

Figure 13.2 Example of a Required Evaluation From a Federal Grant Application for the Year Starting October 1, 2008

Title: Technical Assistance Center on Outcomes No. 84.326L for Infants, Toddlers, and Preschool Children With Disabilities.

From: Competition CFDA, Office of Special Education and Rehabilitative Services; Notice Inviting Applications for New Awards for Fiscal Year (FY) 2008

(c) A plan, linked to the proposed project's logic model, for a formative evaluation of the proposed project's activities. The plan must describe how the formative evaluation will use clear performance objectives to ensure continuous improvement in the operation of the proposed project, including objective measures of progress in implementing the project and ensuring the quality of products and services.

SOURCE: Competition CFDA, Office of Special Education and Rehabilitative Services; Notice Inviting Applications for New Awards for Fiscal Year (FY) 2008. Government Document.

Value-Added Assessments

A statistical method (data based) for evaluation of educational programs and schools has become available for policymakers. It involves an assessment of growth occurring within the learners over time (Linn, 2007). This approach, the **value-added** model for assessment, uses test scores to define educational quality. Its appeal is based on the appearance of being scientific, and free from the potential biasing effect of classroom observations and portfolio assessments. **Value-added evaluations** have become the favored method for measuring the effectiveness of schools in a number of states.

A common concern of teachers opposed to having student test scores provide the basis for evaluations is that some schools enroll students who are far more difficult to teach than are children in other schools. Proof for this was provided in 2006 through a statewide Ohio study of 5-year-old children. It was found that readiness scores for children entering kindergarten in 2005–2006 reflected the same well-documented ethnic and socioeconomic gap that exists on other achievement tests (Ohio State Board of Education, 2006). There is no debating the fact that educators working with children from upper socioeconomic backgrounds living in supportive home environments will see high assessment test scores. Likewise, children from the lowest strata of the socioeconomic scale will not do as well on assessment measures. Thus, from the outset the idea of evaluating schools on the basis of assessment test scores seems somehow inherently flawed and unfair (Popham, 2000).

Cross-Sectional Evaluation

High-stakes testing programs measure each child once, usually during the spring of the year. On the basis of those scores, teachers and schools are evaluated. This is a **cross-sectional evaluation** model that assumes all classrooms start with the same basic type of children, and it is the teacher and the instructional program that cause any differences seen in the spring. Educators know this is a false premise, and there are numerous differences between children that contribute to the amount they will learn and the depth of understanding they will achieve in a school year. Research by the National Center for Educational Statistics has provided an estimate that the primary grade teacher's effect on standardized test scores accounts for between 4% and 18% of the variation (statistical variance) between standardized test scores (Resnick, 2004). This impact is greater for low-achieving students and lower for high-achieving students.

Recent data suggest the role of preschool teachers may be considerably more important in a child's educational and conceptual development than the kindergarten and primary grade teachers. This conclusion was based on research led by Andrew Mashburn of the University of Virginia. He found that good teachers provide children with feedback about their ideas, comment in ways that extend and expand their skills, and frequently use discussions and activities to promote complex thinking. Such teachers use "how and why" questions to expand the conceptual bases of their students. These effective prekindergarten teachers are constantly linking what is happening in the classroom with other aspects of the child's life (Mashburn, 2008).

While the basic impact of a single primary grade teacher is not great, the cumulative effect of several teachers over years is very powerful. In other words, the teacher factor is additive. Large achievement differences happen after three or four years of consistently good or consistently ineffective teaching. Measurable effects on achievement test scores for at-risk children taught by good teachers have been documented in all grades beginning with first grade (Hamre & Pianta, 2005). A worry for educational leaders is that the best teachers may find the current emphasis on repetitive, mind-numbing drilling of children in the basic skills to be stultifying. The fear is that these highly effective teachers will be led to retire early (Winerip, 2004).

Sanders's Value-Added Evaluation

School impact can be found by using value-added analysis of achievement test data. The required statistical model to do this was derived from agricultural statistics by a biostatistician at the University of Tennessee, William Sanders. Using public school test data, he applied a mixed-model regression analysis to the task of identifying and measuring the effectiveness of classroom teachers, schools, and school districts (Sanders & Rivers, 1996). Sanders's method involved using **longitudinal data** collection to determine the amount of achievement growth each child experienced and what part of that achievement could be assigned to the educational program.

William Sanders described value-added assessment as being similar to the way parents track the physical growth of their children. He noted it is common for parents to record the height of their growing child by making annual pencil marks on a doorframe. This series of height marks can be thought of as one type of repeated measurement of the child. Marks on the door frame are similar to annual school assessment tests that are also repeated measurements. A glance at the door frame shows parents which years saw the most growth, and which years saw little growth. Sanders's statistical model uses this same principle (Sanders, 1998; Sanders, Saxton, & Horn, 1997).

One outcome from a value-added assessment can be a report indicating how much change has occurred with children that a particular teacher taught. In the case of primary grade elementary teachers who teach several areas that are tested (reading, arithmetic), value-added reports are generated for each.

Use of a value-added assessment system is expanding and is now used in North Carolina, Pennsylvania, Tennessee, and Texas. Additionally, several large cities have bought into this approach to evaluation (Hu, 2007). Statistical software for conducting a value-added assessment is available, but there has been little research into possible problems with its use (Amrein-Beardsley, 2008). To learn about this statistical package, see http://www.sas.com/govedu/edu/services/effectiveness.html.

Limitations of Value-Added Assessment

Educational applications of **value-added assessments** are "test bound." This describes the condition where the entire data source is based on test scores. The scaling of test items and the psychometric characteristic of tests can influence the local outcome score reports (Viadero, 2008a). Test item quality determines the quality of the assessment conducted of schools and teachers (Lockwood et al., 2007; Resnick, 2004).

To make longitudinal decisions about instructional quality, test scaling must be carefully balanced each year. A change of one point in a year must be equal to the change of one point in ensuing years. This implies that all test items at every grade level have the same relative difficulty level. Achievement test publishers have never met that psychometric requirement.

Value-added assessments based on student test scores are sensitive to statistical variance and are therefore impacted by class size. Large classes have less variance and are therefore more sensitive to significant instructional changes, whereas small classes have more variance making value-added assessments less sensitive to the instructional environment (Amrein-Beardsley, 2008; J. Cohen, 1988).[7]

Related to this is the very large statistical range (**confidence interval** size) associated with making causal statements about educational efficacy of educational programs (H. Braun & Wainer, 2007). For these reasons, Henry Braun and Howard Wainer suggest that value-added assessments are best employed as an initial screening system. In order to make personnel decisions such as tenure and merit pay, more data should be part of the evaluation. Additional data can include teacher portfolios and results of traditional teacher observations.

There is also evidence that value added teacher ratings can be manipulated by assigning certain students in a teacher's classroom (Viadero, 2009).

It is the supreme art of the teacher to awaken joy in creative expression and knowledge.

—Albert Einstein

Licensing and Accreditation

In 1985, the National Association for the Education of Young Children began to accredit preschools and day care providers based on new program standards. The NAEYC accreditation process requires about two years to complete and involves a lengthy self-study and follow-up site visit by professionals of the NAEYC. Case in Point 13.4 presents the first set of national standards for American preschools.

Case in Point 13.4

First Standards for Early Childhood Education

In 1929, a committee of the forerunner of NAEYC, the National Association for Nursery Education, published the first standards for American nursery schools. That year there were only 157 independent nursery schools following standards in this country (Meek, 1929). Those standards required nursery schools to elaborate their objectives for the following areas:

1. Motor and sensory control
2. Social adjustment

3. Development of interests and drives
4. Power to imitate, to choose, and to be occupied constructively
5. The ability to find a medium for expression of feeling
6. Appreciation
7. Physical development

Standards also addressed group sizes, ages for enrolled children, and staff size and training. The 1929 standards did not require teachers have any amount of formal education; but suggested that teachers have a wide background of experiences, and be of good character.[8] They wanted teachers to form "genuine" relationships with children. The standards espoused an indirect approach to teaching. This was to be done by setting the learning environment and standing aside while children went about the job of learning.

The original standards also called for an environment rich in materials and equipment, and an ample supply of storybooks and musical and rhythmic items. It called for plants and small animals to be kept in classrooms. The standards also called for vigilance in health matters and the removal from the school environment of any child exhibiting symptoms of illness.[9]

NAEYC

The programmatic evaluation for preschool education and child care is an evolving field. In 2006, the National Association for the Education of Young Children published a revised set of guidelines for program accreditation. There are now over 10,000 centers and preschools that have achieved accreditation by the NAEYC (M. Ginsberg, 2008).[10]

NAEYC uses 10 standards in the accreditation process. In an average month, about 100 new applications for accreditation are evaluated by the NAEYC and 87% pass on the first attempt. Accreditation is carried out using a simple 3-point scale, "Not Met, Partially Met, and Fully Met." To see the full set of NAEYC standards for accreditation visit the following URL: http://www.naeyc.org/academy/pursuing/overview.

NAEYC Accreditation Standards for Early Childhood Education

Standard 1: Relationships. The goal is to establish positive relationships among children and adults and develop a sense of community. This standard is assessed using evaluation questions covering six areas including relations among adults and children, friendships among children, and behavior management.

Standard 2: Curriculum. This area assesses the extent to which the program implements a curriculum aligned with the program's published goals. Curriculum is evaluated in eleven separate areas: overall completeness and appropriateness, social–emotional development of children, physical development, language development, and

(Continued)

(Continued)

cognitive development. Cognitive development should be fostered through the inclusion of instruction in early literacy, early mathematics, science, technology, creative expression and art appreciation, social studies, health and safety education.

Standard 3: Teaching. All teaching and instructional activities are appropriate and designed to accomplish the program's goals. The evaluation examines seven dimensions of teaching and instructional behaviors. Several of these evaluation questions deal with a consideration of appropriateness issues including those of culture and linguistics. The evaluation strives to determine if learning by children occurs in a caring and supportive environment. Teachers work to make learning interesting and meaningful for each child.

Standard 4: Assessment of Progress. The goal of this standard is to ensure that there is a plan in place for the formal and informal assessment of children and their progress. Evaluation questions examine if an appropriate plan is in place for the evaluation of children and whether there is reciprocal communication about the assessment with the parents. Throughout the NAEYC document, there is no mention of the measurement of academic tasks by high-stakes achievement tests.

Standard 5: Health: Accreditation evaluations focus on three areas related to the physical well-being of children including ways that the program promotes the protection of children's health and nutritional well-being. It also addresses environmental issues related to concerns about the spread of infectious and viral diseases.

Standard 6: Teachers. The accreditation evaluation focuses on the background and education of faculties and staff. At least 75% of the teachers must hold a bachelors or higher degree in an appropriate field (early education, special education, child development, etc.).[11] All assistant teachers must hold or be working toward a Child Development Associate degree (at any time no less than 50% hold a CDA). All aides have a high school diploma or the equivalent. Also, there must be an ongoing staff development and evaluation system in place.

Standard 7: Families. NAEYC evaluators examine the relationship between staff and parents. The goal is to see a collaborative relationship between the early childhood program and each child's home involving outreach efforts by the staff, and a multifaceted effort to keep parents informed and engaged.

Standard 8: Community Standards. Evaluators look for a series of reciprocal relationships with other institutions and community agencies. Early childhood programs must be able to document that they are a positive part of the neighborhood and wider community.

Standard 9: Equipment. There are four areas of concern related to the physical plant and the appropriateness of the building's design in meeting the program's goals. There are questions about both outdoor equipment and indoor furnishings. The overall "health" of the building is also evaluated in terms of airflow, temperature control, molds, old paint, and plumbing problems. Finally, all programs must be housed in a completely smoke-free building, including secondhand smoke from adjacent areas.

Standard 10: Leadership and Management. This evaluation goal is to determine if the program has effective policies that support stable high-quality faculties and staff. NAEYC looks to determine if the program is on a secure financial foundation and can provide children and their families with a quality educational experience.

SOURCE: Adapted from the NAEYC Academy for Early Childhood Program Accreditation.

Qualistar

A second evaluation for early childhood programs is the **Qualistar** Rating System. This integrated system of early childhood program assessment and child placement assistance is from the Colorado Department of Human Services. Qualistar is a method for assessment providing a 5-point rating system including measures of the learning environment, family partnerships, staff training and education, adult-to-child ratios and group size, and accreditation. Centers with NAEYC or similar accreditation are given full point value on this fifth component of Qualistar. The rating system is user-friendly for parents in search of a quality prekindergarten experience for their child. Each evaluated center is awarded a number of Qualistar stars. More on this system is available at http://www.qualistar.org/.

Evaluation by the Marketplace

In the United States, there are about 19.6 million children under 5 years old. Only 6.3% of these attend a licensed preschool and less than another 3% are enrolled in Head Start. Day care providers enroll another 13.5% of the population of preschoolers (U.S. Census Bureau, 2008). On average, the annual cost of enrolling a child in a full-time preschool was about $7,000/child in 2005.

Nationally, there are 74,000 liscensed providers of early childhood education and day care (NAEYC, 2006). While there are a number of highly visible and oversubscribed preschools near our large cities, the vast majority of providers of early education and child care are dependent on enrollment and tuition payments. Less-competitive programs must advertise and actively recruit parents with young children.

When parents of a prospective enrollee visit a child care center or preschool they are engaged in an evaluation. That evaluation has multiple facets and includes considerations such as cleanliness, staff attitude and appearance, toys and educational equipment, food services, the mix of children, distance from home or work, hours of operation, and cost. There are a number of easily seen markers of a quality child care center or preschool that parents can use in their evaluation. One of the most obivous of these markers is the staff to child ratio. The American Academy of Pediatrics (AAP) recommendations for staffing are presented on Table 13.1.

Table 13.1 Staffing Recommendations of the American Academy of Pediatrics (2007)

Child's Age	Staff to Child Ratio	Maximum Group Size
Birth to 12 months	1 to 3	6
13 to 30 months	1 to 4	8
31 to 35 months	1 to 5	10
3-year-olds	1 to 8	14
4- and 5-year-olds	1 to 10	16
6- to 8-year-olds	1 to 10	20

SOURCE: Used with permission of the American Academy of Pediatrics, *Choosing Quality Child Care: What's Best for Your Family?* Copyright © 2007 American Academy of Pediatrics, updated 11/07.

The AAP recommends that parents also ask about the provider's policy regarding parents visiting and observing. The AAP published a list of things for parents to look for during a visit to a child care provider or preschool. The list below is based on ideas of the AAP along with those of other authorities (Coghlan, King, & Wake, 2003; Mathews & Burns, 1992; Meltzer, Levine, Palfrey, Aufseeser, & Oberklaid, 1981; Office of Innovation and Improvement, 2007).

What Parents Should Look for at a Child Care Center or Preschool

Staffing

- How large are groups of children? Refer to Table 13.2.
- How many adult caregivers are always available to children?
- Are there enough adult caregivers to meet needs of children?
- How long have caregivers and teachers been employed by the center or preschool?

Indoor Environment

- Is the environment safe, bright, cheerful, and well ventilated?
- Does the classroom indoor space equal or exceed 50 square feet for each child in the room?
- During nap-time, is there enough space for the separation of children by a minimum of 3 feet?
- Does the school meet all requirements for access by children with disabilities (wheelchair ramps, wide doors and halls, accessible bathrooms)?
- Do bathrooms provide children with disposable paper towels and liquid soap?
- Are there easily accessible bathrooms with one toilet and sink for every eight children? Are bathroom fixtures sized to children?
- Are there child appropriate drinking fountains with fresh water available for all children?
- Is the center or school completely protected with fire extinguishers and a sprinkler system?
- Do all doors opening to the outside have self closing and locking systems? Are the doors equipped with panic-bolts for emergency egress?
- Does each child have a storage area (cubby) with at least 10 cubic feet of space?
- Is the room kept at a comfortable temperature throughout the year?
- Are there an adequate number and variety of toys, and are they disinfected and cleaned on a regular basis?
- Is the center or school completely accessable for children with disabilities?
- Is the school or center (including outside areas) completely free of tobacco smoke? Is the no smoking policy posted?
- Does the school or center have a posted rule banning firearms in the building and on the grounds?

Outdoor Environment

- Does the play yard provide a minimum of 35 square feet per child?
- Is the play yard covered with a low-impact ground covering (e.g., grass, wood chips, neoprene mats, or artificial turf) and is it clean and free of signs of animal intrusion?
- Is the play yard enclosed by tall fences that children cannot climb or reach through?
- Is there extra padding under and around all climbing frames and tall equipment?
- Is the play yard equipment well maintained, stable, free of dangerous sharp points and edges, and appropriate for the developmental level of the child.

Operations

- Are licenses and accreditations updated and posted in a public area?
- Are bulletin boards for parent information notices updated daily?
- Are the school's menus posted for parents to review?
- Is the curriculum plan posted and available for parents to review?
- Do caregivers wash their hands frequently as they move from activity to activity and child to child?
- Are there separate staff bathrooms (minimum of 2) with a ratio of one toilet and sink for each 20 adults?
- Do children appear to be happy and engaged?
- When a child cries or acts-out do caregivers respond?
- Do children talk and interact with each other?

Food Service

- Does the food service match the posted menu?
- Is the food sized correctly, nutritious, served at the correct temperature, and appetizing?
- Is there a separate kitchen area providing refrigeration, cooking, and cleaning and preparation work stations?

Summary

The central reason for this chapter is to address the question of how we know if an early childhood education program is providing quality experiences for young learners.

The infusion of money into American education in the 1960s brought with it the need to carefully account for its expenditure. One important innovation of Lyndon Johnson's presidency was the Head Start program.

Each state has developed standards for early childhood education that should mesh with standards for learning established for public schools of the states. Head Start and other funded early childhood programs are now evaluated through the use of those standards.

Over 40 states provide financial support for early childhood education programs. These states are now putting evaluation systems in place to guarantee the efficacy of both private and public preschools and day care centers. There is a movement underway to provide a seamless transition from preschool onward through a four-year college education at a state university. This is referred to as a P–16 educational program.

The evaluation of early education can also be conducted as a required part of a grant supported project. Agencies and foundations providing funds for educational programs require a systematic model for the evaluation of how the project worked, and where money was spent.

Informal evaluations of early education programs are also done by parents who are looking for a placement for a young child. Parents want a quality educational experience that is a good fit for their child's needs.

Over 10,000 early childhood programs have been through the evaluation process associated with the NAEYC accreditation system. This system is based on 10 standards covering all aspects of operating an early childhood center or preshool.

Discussion Questions

1. How much weight should funding agencies give to the quality of an evaluation that will be part of the educational program? What elements should a good evaluation model for a Title I application include?
2. What policy modifications would you initiate if you were a director of a prekindergarten program in a state that uses a high-stakes assessment of children to evaluate a funded preschool program? For example, would you limit which children could be admitted? What change would you initiate for the curriculum?
3. What role is there for private day care providers in states moving to adopt a comprehensive linkage of public education from preschool through state university graduation (P–16)? Should private early childhood centers eventually be part of a state system? Explain your reasoning.
4. Should all teachers in preschools have a bachelors degree (or an advanced degree) in an early childhood-related field? How can better educated teachers be paid reasonable salaries? What is the likelihood of your local community increasing taxes to pay early childhood teachers a livable salary?
5. Use the Internet to find your state's policy toward the support and improvement of prekindergarten programs. Is this approach adequate for meeting the challenge of assuring that the state's young children recieve a quality prekindergarten education? What needs to be done to improve early childhood programs of your state?

Related Readings

Haskins, R., & Casey, A. E. (2006). Putting education into preschools. In P. E. Peterson (Ed.), *Generational change* (pp. 47–87). Boulder, CO: Rowman & Littlefield.

Popham, W. J. (1992). *Educational evaluation* (3rd ed.). Boston: Allyn & Bacon.

Rust, F. O. (2003). Counting the cost of caring: Intended and unintended consequences of early childhood policies. In J. P. Isenberg & M. R. Jalongo (Eds.), *Major trends and issues in early childhood education* (2nd ed., pp. 153–163). New York: Teachers College Press.

Schultz, T., & Kagan, S. L. (2007). *Taking stock: Assessing and improving early childhood learning and program quality*. Philadelphia: Pew Charitable Trusts. Retrieved June 25, 2008, from http://www.policyforchildren.org/pdf/Task_Force_Report.pdf.

Notes

1. Lawrence Schweinhart is the president of the HighScope Educational Research Foundation.
2. At any time, only a third of these children are enrolled in a child care or preschool program. Most children are cared for by relatives including grandparents.
3. States without state-supported preschool education are Alaska, Hawaii, Idaho, Indiana, Mississippi, Montana, New Hampshire, North Dakota, Rhode Island, South Dakota, Utah, and Wyoming.

4. This arrangement is one that saves the state from added costs, but is unpopular among both public school administrators who dislike paying for another unfunded mandate, and by providers of prekindergarten programs (Hanson, 2006). Prekindergarten providers would rather see some form of a growth or value-added approach used to assess the quality of their programs. Florida's Early Learning Coalitions have called for pre- and posttesting children with a system that is developmentally appropriate and based on observational data such as the *Creative Curriculum Developmental Continuum Assessment* (Dodge, Colker, & Heroman, 2001).
5. A number of states have begun referring to a P–20 model that implies a seamless educational program from age 3 through earning a doctoral degree.
6. In fiscal year 2008–2009, Congress authorized the U.S. Department of Education to spend $25 billion on Title I programs. The administration of President George W. Bush held back $11 billion of that appropriation. The Second Iraq War effort required different spending priorities. Most of the lost funding was returned by President Barack Obama in 2009–2010.
7. The general principle is that the larger the database, the more "statistically powerful or sensitive" is the statistical analysis procedure. Type II error is reduced and the background "noise" is soothed by large numbers.
8. In 1929, there were only a handful of colleges in the United States that would admit women students as undergraduates. In the 1800s, most women who desired advanced education attended a seminary affiliated with a college for young men. Before the Civil War, there were only three colleges that would admit women, Antioch, Oberlin, and Hillsdale. There were no colleges open for African American women until after the Civil War when Spelman and Bennett colleges opened. In the 20th century, several states began to make their institutions coeducational. Leaders in this included University of Iowa, University of Utah, Douglass College (a part of Rutgers University in New Jersey), Texas Woman's University, and the Mississippi University for Women. The "sister seven" highly selective colleges were founded in the 19th century, and by 1960 there were 200 colleges for women only.
9. In the era before modern immunizations and antibiotics, childhood illnesses could have devastating and/or deadly effects. Diseases such as chicken pox, measles, scarlet fever, and polio were common and frightening for all parents and early childhood teachers.
10. There are also 2,500 home child care centers enrolling a minimum of three children and operating at least 15 hours per week that are accredited by the National Association of Family Childcare.
11. The education standards are being phased in over a 14-year period between 2006 and 2020.

Glossary

academic growth: Measured change in the amount and depth of learning and/or new skill development over a specified period of time.

academic redshirting: Describes when parents of a young child elect not to enroll that child in school until he or she is a year older than the normal cohort of kindergarten children. This is done to provide the child with a developmental advantage over his/her peers.

accommodations: Modifications in the testing or evaluation environment made to compensate for a child's disabling condition that make the test more fair and inferences made on the basis of its scores more accurate.

accountability: Being held to account for both the expenditure of educational funds, and for the achievement outcomes for students.

achievement gap: Mean (average) group differences between identifiable subgroups of the population on standardized achievement test scores.

achievement test: A test measuring an individual's knowledge of specific facts and his/her proficiency in completing cognitive processes such as problem solving.

adequate yearly progress (AYP): AYP specifies the proportion of a school's students who achieve at a proficient or better level each year, as well as the attendance rates for the mandated tests, and the eventual graduation rates for the schools.

alpha coefficient: An expression of reliability (internal consistency) of a test or other measurement. Lee J. Cronbach of Stanford University originally developed the coefficient alpha.

American nativism: Belief that new immigrants to America are somehow inferior or dangerous.

analytical intelligence: One of the three types of intelligence that is part of Sternberg's proposed triarchic model of mental ability.

analytical rubric: When a rubric assesses multiple aspects or dimensions of a performance by employing several ordinal scales elaborated as separate scoring rubrics. These can also be summed into a total overall score.

anecdotal data collection: Elements of a true-to-life, factual anecdote that was observed and recorded.

anecdotal observation: Factual reporting of detailed behavior(s) as witnessed and written as a case study.

anecdotal record: Ongoing liner report of an occurrence or incident. A written description of observations, devoid of judgments or evaluation.

Angoff committees: Committee of experts brought together to set the minimum level for cut-off scores on a high-stakes test. Named for William H. Angoff of ETS.

anschauung: Mental framework for learning established through interactions with the physical world. Pestalozzi proposed that play was a method used by children to develop their personal anschauung or sensory intuition.

A.P.G.A.R.: In 1952, Dr. Virginia Apgar used her name as an acronym for the five subtests of her new measure of the status of newborn babies: A = appearance, P = pulse, G = grimace, A = activity, R = respiration.

appropriateness: Component of validity referring to the application that the test is given. A particular test may be valid in one arena, but inappropriate when used for another measurement task.

Asperger's disorder: A mental disorder that appears during early childhood characterized by severe impairment in social interaction skills and the development of repetitive actions and behavioral patterns.

assessment: The measurement of one or more variables related to the current condition, ability, status, or knowledge of an individual.

assessment battery: Two or more tests designed to measure aspects of achievement or ability for children.

at risk: Children endangered by environmental, congenital, or health-related problems for developmental and/or educational problems.

attention deficit disorder (ADD): Developmentally inappropriate lack of attention and focus on tasks and activities.

attention deficit/hyperactivity disorder (AD/HD): Disorder of a child's ability to attend and focus on learning that may appear prior to school age and be manifested by impulsivity; high, randomly directed activity; and inattention to tasks and directions.

attitudinal grades: Report card grades assigned by teachers in nonacademic areas related to children's perceived attitudes and work habits.

attitudinal measurement: Measurement of the opinion or attitude toward a topic or person by the respondent to a questionnaire or interviewer.

authentic assessment: Performance assessment task based on a "real world" problem or task that is based on issues encountered in the world beyond the school.

autistic disorder: Mental disorder that first appears in early childhood involving sustained inability to engage in social behaviors or use nonverbal communication behaviors, slow development of language, and repetitive use of stereotyped behaviors.

autistic savant disorder: A cognitive disorder experienced by people with autism who also have extraordinary skills, talents, or abilities not exhibited by most people.

autistic spectrum disorders (ASD): Related group of pervasive developmental disorders including early infantile autism, autism, childhood autism, Kanners disorder, and Asperger's disorder.

average: Generic term for one or all of the following ways of defining the central tendency of a data set: mean, median, or mode.

basal level: That item on a test (arranged from easy to hard items) where it is assumed that a child would get all the preceding items correct.

Basic Interpersonal Communication Skill (BICS): The everyday level of language used in social settings. The language used by children on the playground and in the lunchroom or in sports.

bell curve: Also known as the Gaussian normal curve. This symmetric curve represents the distribution of error around the average of a large set of independent observations.

below proficient: Score on an achievement test that falls below the minimum score (set by an Angoff committee) required to have met a prescribed standard for learning.

benchmarks: A point of reference based on a standard for learning, including illustrative examples of successful completion or achievement.

best products: Selected materials including only the highest-quality products and other artifacts for inclusion in a child's portfolio, especially in preparation for a portfolio assessment.

biannual review: The elements of an Individual Family Service Plan must be reviewed every six months and modified as needed.

bias: Test bias occurs whenever a nonrandom group of individuals (e.g., ethnic or racial group) are systematically mismeasured (too high or too low) and cannot perform as the test indicated.

Bloom's taxonomy: Taxonomy for categorizing the level of abstraction required to answer questions that commonly occur in educational settings. It is a useful structure for categorizing test questions according to the cognitive skill level required to answer them correctly.

bubble youngsters: Description of children who scored just slightly below the level of proficient on a high-stakes test. These children are most likely to receive the most support and help from the school.

case law: Decisions made in response to a suit of law by a federal or state court establishing new procedures or social policy, and having the full enforcement power of a law.

Cattell-Horn-Carroll (C-H-C): A structural model of the contents of human intellect including 3 stratum, 10 major factors, and 70 cognitive skills.

ceiling level: Item on a test (arranged with increasing levels of difficulty) above which it is assumed the child will not answer any questions correctly.

central tendency: A measure of the "average" performance of individuals. It includes the mean, median, and mode.

checklist: One form of rating scale that has items to check or mark indicating the presence of an item or behavior being observed.

Child Find: Mandate of IDEIA for states to locate and evaluate all children (birth to age 21) who need early intervention or special education.

children with disabilities: Any person between birth and age 21 with an impairment preventing the full attainment of a developmentally appropriate goal or acquiring an appropriate level of education.

child study movement: This era began in the 19th century when the methods associated with modern science were applied to the systematic study of human infancy and childhood.

code-switching: A stage in learning a second language when the syntax and vocabulary of the primary and second languages become entwined, causing errors to occur in the production of both languages.

cognitive ability: A synonym for traditionally defined mental ability that emphasizes verbal, spatial, and mathematical reasoning ability.

Cognitive Academic Language Proficiency (CALP): The level of language required for formal academic learning in content-based subject fields.

cohort: A group of individuals having a statistical factor (age or background) in common.

communication: The ethical use of a test requires that those taking the test (or their parents) are aware of the assessment, know why it is being given, and understand what it measures.

composite scores: A combined score from a battery of tests that provides a generalized assessment score covering several subtests.

computer adaptive testing (CAT): Testing that employs software that can estimate the ability and background knowledge of each test taker and guide the appropriate selection of test items from a computerized item bank.

concordance: A statistical statement of the degree to which two variables produce similar findings when used with the same subjects, and expressed in the form of a nonparametric correlation.

concurrent validity: The correlation between a known test, outcome, or measure and the scores on another measure of the same dimension.

confidence interval: A parameter linked to a normal curve of probability. It provides two points representing the limits of what obtained scores would have been randomly drawn from a normal population.

confidentiality: Not revealing the source or findings of data collected about individuals. Also keeping test materials secured and never revealed to others not commissioned to use them.

construct validity: A validation technique used with variables of hypothetical traits or abilities lacking an operational (observable) definition. This involves demonstrating both the legitimacy of the variable and the measure of it.

content validity: The fidelity of the test items to the topic that was taught and/or the goals of the curriculum area being measured.

control group: One of two or more randomly assigned groups in an experiment. The control group does not receive the experimental treatment and provides a point of comparison for the other groups.

correlation: A measure of the degree to which two variables are statistically related.

correlation coefficient: Any of a series of mathematical ratios (e.g., Pearson product–moment correlation coefficient) that demonstrate the amount of variance shared by two variables. The numerical value is on a range of ±1.00 as the maximum and 0.00 as the minimum.

covariance: The amount of common variance shared by two different measures. It is reported as a coefficient of correlation.

creative intelligence: One of the three types of intelligence that makes up the triarchic model for intelligence proposed by Robert Sternberg.

creativity: The ability to use the imagination to organize ideas and make, design, or write unusual or highly productive products.

criterion measures: Tests using an absolute level of correctness as the standard for passing or being proficient.

criterion-referenced measure: Tests designed to measure how well an individual has learned a specific skill or acquired a specified knowledge. The reference is absolute and not dependent on a comparison to other test takers.

criterion–referenced–scores: Scores presented in terms of reaching or failing to reach an absolute standard for correctness on the measure.

critical–theoretical: Critical–theoretical evaluations are based on a large view of our society, examining how educational programs fit within the larger social system.

Cronbach alpha: A statistical estimation of test reliability or consistency that can be used with scaled and/or binary measures of a single dimension. This reliability is equivalent to the average of all possible permutations of split-halves that can be made with a set of test item data from a sample of subjects.

cross-sectional evaluation: The collection and analysis of data from different age groups in order to evaluate multilevels of an educational system.

cross-sectional model: Data collection conducted at one point in time covering several variables.

cross-sectional model of evaluation: Evaluation model based on testing each subject only once, and seeing trends by examining individuals in other age cohorts, grade levels, or groups.

crystallized intelligence factor: That part of mental ability that is the product of what is learned, experienced, or absorbed from the culture.

cultural prejudice: The belief that identifiable groups of people are from an inferior culture and are less moral or able than members of the "better" groups.

curriculum-based assessment (CBA): The combination of curriculum-based measurements with standardized achievement tests into a single assessment.

curriculum-embedded performance assessment: Integration of assessment into the ongoing teaching–learning process so that students are not aware when they are being taught and when they are being assessed.

curriculum map: A publicly available document that captures the scope and sequence (the school's master plan) of the learning objectives, activities, and assessments in each subject and in each grade.

curriculum probe: Brief tests (5 to 10 minutes) that are administered on a regular basis and are part of a curriculum-based measurement.

cut scores: The raw score on a standards-based test that denotes a break between two ordinal levels of success (e.g., proficient vs. highly proficient).

decenter: Establishment of new norms for a standardized test.

decontextualized: Assessment that does not involve tasks related to the perceived needs and/or interests of the individual. Most select format questions are of this type, while authentic assessments are not.

demographic variable: Variable measuring characteristics of a population, for example, age, disability status, socioeconomic status, ethnicity, and gender.

developmental age: An age-normed measurement scale score used for various dimensions of human growth and development.

developmental assessments: Measurement instrument used to determine the developmental status of a child across a number of dimensions.

developmental delay: A significant departure from the normal pattern of growth and development in terms of cognitive and/or physical growth.

developmental inventories: Large-scale measuring device used to determine the developmental status of a child across multiple dimensions of growth and development.

developmental screening assessments: Brief measurement of the developmental status of a child.

developmental test: A measurement of multiple aspects of child growth including both the physical and cognitive domains.

developmental validity: An expression of the age and status appropriateness of the measurement tasks included on a test.

deviation IQ scores (DIQ): See IQ score.

dialectic: Tool used to explore "true meaning" through rhetorical reasoning and disputation.

differential item functioning (DIF): This analytical method is used to test the appropriateness of individual test items for identified subgroups of the population taking the test (e.g., ethnic minorities).

differentiated instruction: An approach to teaching emphasizing the individualization of learning by matching the needs and optimal learning modalities of each child.

discrete visual analog scales: A form of Likert scale using emotionally expressive cartoons as responses to the initial stimulus statement.

distribution: An array of scores from the measurement of a variable aligned from low to high that can depict the frequency of occurrence for each of the possible scores.

due process: A right granted to all citizens by the U.S. Constitution providing protection from governmental agencies taking property or changing educational opportunities without an open, impartial hearing where all parties are able to present their positions.

Early Childhood Special Education: Part B of the IDEIA mandates that states provide special education services for identified children between the ages of 3 and 5 years old.

Early Intervention (EI): Part C of the IDEIA mandates that states locate, evaluate, and provide intervention services for children from birth through the age of 3 years.

e-assessments: Online educational assessments that employ a computer-adapted testing format.

EDGAR: Acronym for the U.S. Education Department General Administrative Regulations.

emotional strength: Confidence and self-assurance within the child. A sense of sangfroid and an even temper prevail when the child faces new challenges.

empirical: Derived from experience and direct observation.

empirical–analytical: Application of scientific methods for analysis to data that is empirically derived.

engagement: An attitude of close cooperation between parents and educators of children enrolled in school.

English language learners (ELL): Children for whom English is not the native language and who are in the process of learning to achieve English at a cognitive academic level of proficiency.

entitlement conference: Conference including educators, educational specialists, and parents of a child being evaluated for a possible placement in special education.

entitlement decision: Decision involving the provision of services or other assistance needed to "level the playing field" for children who have special needs.

equal protection: Statement included in the 14th Amendment to the U. S. Constitution that has been used to argue for the inclusion of special education students in all aspects of public school programs.

evaluation: Designed and facilitated to assess the strengths and weaknesses of programs, policies, personnel, products, and organizations.

evaluation standards: Guidelines and appropriate procedures for educational evaluations first delineated by Daniel Stufflebeam in 1981.

evaluative portfolio: A well-planned portfolio of the best products and artifacts demonstrating a child's growth and acquisition of new skills and learning (used for evaluation).

event sampling: Observations carried out during a defined and limited time frame (e.g., lunchtime) and focused on the activities and behaviors of one child.

executive function: Cognitive process that controls and manages other mental processes and operations.

experimental study: Use of scientific method including randomly assigned experimental and control groups to determine the efficaciousness of a program or procedure.

expressive language: The use of spoken language to represent thoughts and ideas when communicating with others.

extended school year services (ESY): Special education services that extend throughout the summer vacation period. This is offered if a child with special needs is in danger of losing ground when away from the special education program.

factors: Latent structures that are mathematically identified within test data and that share common internal measurement outcomes.

factor structure: When mathematically analyzed, test data may be divided into several factors, each of which shares common internal measurement characteristics while being independent of the other factors of the structure.

fadeout effect: Impact of an enervating primary grade school experience on the academic skills of a child who was ready and able to learn.

fairness: Fairness implies that all children who are being tested have had an equal opportunity to learn the material.

fair test: A measure that is not impacted by a priori differences between identifiable groups of test takers. Therefore, background and socioeconomic advantage have little impact on the scores from a fair test.

fluency: Facile in use of language (oral and written) including a wide vocabulary.

fluid intelligence: An inherited type of intelligence needed to solve nonverbal problems that is independent of what is learned and is not linked to experiences.

formative evaluations: Ongoing monitoring of the learners (e.g., integrating questions) during the teaching process. Measures or assessments that inform the ongoing instructional process.

free and appropriate educational program: Educational mandate for all children including those with a disability. Expressed in Public Law 94-142.

free or reduced cost lunch: Subsidized and free lunches for children of families that are too poor to pay for them. In 2008–2009, a child of a single parent earning less than $25,900/year would qualify.

frequency sampling: Observational method involving counting the occurrences of an observed behavior during a particular time frame.

frequency scales: Hierarchical measurement scale involving a simple count during a defined period of time.

full-scale IQ: Single score expressing an individual's measured total mental ability. Usually reported with a mean of 100 and a standard deviation of 15.

gamesmanship: Practice of educational and political leaders of finding and exploiting loopholes in the reporting requirements under the No Child Left Behind Act.

genetically given factor (Gf): Fluid intelligence as defined in the C-H-C model of mental ability.

genetic epistemology: The study of the origins of human intelligence through analysis of its operations and development within children. Term coined by Jean Piaget.

"g" factor: Core of mental energy inborn within an individual from which other mental ability factors and talents draw for elaboration.

gifted: Educators consider gifted children to have special talents and high levels of academic aptitude (e.g., IQ ≥ 130).

Good Start, Grow Smart: A standards-based system for learning and assessment developed during George W. Bush's administration and including high-stakes tests for Head Start students.

grade retention: Grade retention occurs when a child is required to remain in the same grade for another school year while his/her peers move ahead to the next grade level.

grading: The use of symbols, letters, or ordinal numbers to represent the teacher's evaluation of the quality of a student's work.

Great Society: Part of a goal statement made by President Lyndon B. Johnson during the state of the union address on January 4, 1965, which outlined the "War on Poverty."

Guttman scale: Hierarchical measurement scale where each category assumes all categories below it have been achieved.

Haemophilus influenzae: A dangerous bacterium that can attack children and lead to many illnesses including influenza.

Head Start: Program started by President Lyndon B. Johnson in 1965. It was originally a summer program for children of poverty. It is now part of the Department of Health and Human Services, providing educational, nutritional, and developmental assistance to 925,000 preschool children from impoverished families a year.

heavy metals: Metallic chemical elements found in nature and included in many household items including lead, arsenic, mercury, and copper. They can cause brain damage and death if ingested by children.

hierarchical scales: Ordinal scale of measurement on which each step on the scale assumes the satisfaction of all lower steps before it.

higher-order thinking: Mental skill set including an ability to apply, analyze, synthesize, and evaluate information.

highly proficient: Standards-based score on an achievement test indicating a student achieved significantly more than was required.

HighScope approach: Early childhood education model emphasizing active learning and a hands-on curriculum presented by teachers well educated in child development.

high-stakes testing: Tests for which failing scores carry serious consequences and sanctions for children and/or educators.

holistic assessment: A "big picture" approach to evaluation that provides one ordinal score for the whole performance.

holistic rubric: Scoring rubric that provides one "big picture" score for a performance assessment. It is used for evaluation by testing companies and with state assessments involving essay-writing tasks.

identification: First step in the process of providing help for a child at risk. It involves sensing a problem and using informal and published screening measures to make a tentative identification of the problem.

Inclusion classes: Classes of students, some with special education needs and others without. These classes are often taught by a combination of regular education and special education teachers.

Individual Educational Plan (IEP): Plan required by law (IDEIA) for all children with a disability that includes goals, services, accommodations, and description of how progress toward the goals will be measured.

Individual Educational Plan Committee (IEP Committee): Committee of educators, specialists, and a child's parents working together to make an entitlement decision and then create an individual educational plan for the child.

Individual Family Service Plan (IFSP): Family-oriented plan that addresses the abilities and limitations of the child, and provides a plan of action to remediate those areas of developmental delay.

informal screening: First step in the process of special education identification, usually carried out by teachers and counselors, involving observation, a review of records, collection of work samples, and parent conferencing.

Instructional Support Team (IST): A committee made up of the child's parents and all school personnel responsible for the child being referred for intervention. Formed in order to share information and address educational problems the child is having, to map out strategies for the teacher and parent.

intensity scales: Hierarchical scale that can explore the extent or depth of feelings and attitudes held by a person.

internal consistency: A reliability estimation based on one administration of a measure involving the intercorrelations of the individual items of the measure.

internal consistency reliability: An expression of statistical reliability based on the measurement consistency of the questions on a scale. Expressed as a correlational statistic.

interpretative: Latent factor within the pattern of answers given by respondents to Likert-type scaled questions involving deduction and interpretation.

interrater reliability coefficient: Statistical statement of the degree to which two or more raters (evaluators) agree when rating the same items.

interval data: An ordered dataset with each unit of measurement for the variable being equal, and the distribution of scores scaled by reference to a standard score system.

interval sampling: Observational method for data collection involving the timing of behavioral occurrences, for example, temper tantrums.

interval scale: Measurement scale composed of steps having the same mathematical unit size and based on a standardized data distribution.

IQ score: Abbreviation for intelligence quotient. A score representing mental ability reported in a standardized form where the average is 100. Subscores of verbal IQ and mathematical IQ may be provided. Sometimes expressed statistically as a deviation IQ or DIQ.

Kanners disorder: Mental disorder identifiable in young children, first described by Leo Kanner in 1943, that presents as a serious form of childhood autism.

kindergarten: Literally a "child's garden." The term was first used by Friedrich Wilhelm August Froebel in the 1830s to describe a preschool for children that was based on active learning.

kindergarten readiness: Having the prerequisite cognitive and social skills needed for entering a kindergarten program.

kindergarten roundup: The process of bringing together and enrolling children in a public school kindergarten program.

knowledge: Term used by Bloom's committee to describe the most basic units of learning and thinking. This is composed of basic facts and rote learning.

Kuder-Richardson 20 (K-R 20): The statistical measure of reliability for tests scored using a binary (right-wrong) system. It is equivalent to a compilation of all possible permutations of split-half consistency (reliability) calculations.

language centers in the brain: Language abilities are housed in the left hemisphere of the human brain. Expressive language in Wernicke's area and reading in the Broca's area.

L2: The second (nonnative) language learned by a person.

learning standards: Specified levels of accomplishment to be achieved by learners.

least restrictive educational environment: Mandate of Public Law 94-142 requiring children with special needs be provided extra service and education along with their nondisabled peers, or in environments as close to the quotidian norm as possible.

level of precision: The exactness of data. There are four broad categories used to designate the precision of data: nominal, ordinal, interval, and ratio (NOIR).

Lexile measures: Lexile measures provide a numerical evaluation level for the reading difficulty level of books (levels range from 200 to 1700+ for advanced readers).

Likert-type scales: Opinion-measuring scales composed of one or several simple declarative sentences about the topic being measured and statements (usually 5 or 7 in number) expressing a degree of agreement with the statements.

limited English proficient (LEP): Description used to identify children who have insufficient skill with the English language to succeed in an English-only classroom. A synonym is English language learner (ELL).

longitudinal data: Data that are collected from a group of subjects over a long time frame. Multiple tests or observations are made on the same group of subjects and analyzed for trends.

lower schools: Private elementary and preschools, usually associated with upper schools (preparatory schools).

mandated assessments: Measurements of knowledge or skill development of students required by state regulation or law.

marginal notes: Notes written in the margins of a questionnaire indicating the researchers' hunches, insights, or unexpected observations.

math screening: Any of a class of brief measures of a child's readiness for learning mathematical concepts, and/or present status of previous mathematics learning.

maturation: The process of growth leading to maturity or adult status in terms of the physical, cognitive, psychological, and learned aspects of human development.

mCLASS software: Proprietary computer software designed to assist teachers in assessing student achievement and abilities.

mean: A measure of central tendency referred to as an arithmetic average of a set of scores.

measurement: A procedure used to determine and document a student's current status on a variable.

measurement error: A standard (normal curve) distribution of differences that can be expected to occur above and below an observed test score on retesting the same subject.

median: The score equal to the center of a rank ordered data set. The 50th percentile.

mental ability: Inferred amount of cognitive strength, as assessed by a test, that is available to an individual for problem solving and interpreting the environment.

mental age: A measure of the difficulty level of problems that a person can solve expressed as a comparison to a reference sample of subjects of a particular age.

meritocracy: The organization of a system where rewards are provided to those shown through competition to be deserving of merit. Meritocracies are designed to reward talent, competence, and effort, not connections and social standing.

merit pay: Extra compensation above and beyond the common pay scale in the form of a bonus awarded to teachers viewed as being highly effective.

mobility: Extent to which children and their families move to different homes. The average American family moves once every five years.

mode: The most frequently occurring score or outcome in a distribution of scores.

morphemes: The smallest unit of a language that has its own linguistic (spoken) meaning, for example, a syllable.

motor tics: Mental disorder presenting with uncontrolled, repetitive, stereotyped motor movement, and/or verbal outbursts.

multidisciplinary team: Committee of educators, specialists, and a child's parents working to design appropriate educational activities and instructional approaches to help the child learn.

multiple intelligences model (MI): Howard Gardner's model, which focuses on eight unique human intelligences or evolutionary products that make interaction with the environment possible.

narrative reports: Report cards written out by teachers in narrative form describing the child's various achievements and problems during the school term.

National Assessment of Educational Progress (NAEP): The NAEP is the only nationally representative test given continually since 1969.

National Association for the Education of Young Children (NAEYC): The professional association of teachers, professors, and researchers involved with the welfare and education of young children.

nativist: Person who believes that newly immigrating people are somehow inferior, dangerous, or unworthy.

negative skew(ness): This occurs in data that have an excess of low scores causing the mean to be lower than the median of the data.

New Deal: Economic recovery program initiated by President Franklin D. Roosevelt between March 1933 and the start of World War II.

NOIR: Mnemonic device, based on the French word for the color black, representing the levels of data precision: nominal, ordinal, interval, ratio.

nominal data: Data from a variable that are expressed as a series of names or descriptors that are devoid of a mathematical measurement scale.

nominal scale: A scale composed of mutually exclusive categories that are given names and are not able to be ordered or sequenced.

normal curve: Mathematically defined natural distribution of the occurrence of data. This assumes a "bell shape" and implies most cases occur in the center and few in the high or low fringe areas.

normal curve equivalent (NCE): A standardized transformation of normally distributed raw score data having a distribution with a mean of 50 and a standard deviation of 21.06.

normal distribution: See normal curve.

normative or norm group: A distribution of measurement scores from a group of subjects with known characteristics (age, sex, grade in school, etc.) to whom a person's performance may be compared.

norm group: Sample of subjects selected to represent the range of typical performances on a measure.

norm referenced score: The interpretation of the meaning of a test score is based on how a sample of other people performs on the same measure. An individual's score is then expressed in terms of a relative standing as compared with others.

norms: Tables or other devices used to convert an individual's test score to a norm-referenced test score.

numeracy An understanding of the concept of number and an awareness of counting and the consistent nature of numbers.

numeracy problem: Specific learning problem for the construct of number and/or the operations of arithmetic.

observational data: Data gained through the use of one's senses (e.g., vision) of the physical status, activity, or productivity of who or what is observed.

online report cards: Internet-based system for reporting student academic progress interfaced with a comprehensive system for teacher–parent online communication.

opinionnaire: Semantic scale questionnaire designed to elicit the opinions of respondents to issues of topics.

oral prompt: A verbally read writing prompt to guide children being assessed for their writing skills.

ordinal scale: A scale of mutually exclusive categories in an ordered sequence. The categories have differing dimensions and the scale is not mathematical.

ordinal type II: Ordinal data that are mathematically treated as though the data were truly interval with equal interval size (e.g., grade point average).

overachievement: Achievement of a child that is significantly better than that which tests of ability predict.

P–16 model: Standards-based model for education within a state that is set out for children in preschools, K–12 public schools, and four-year state colleges.

parent conferences: Meetings (scheduled or informal) between a child's parent(s) and teacher, focusing on the child's successes, skills, and problem areas.

Pearson correlation coefficient: A statistical expression of the degree to which two variables covary. The minimum correlation is 0.00 and the maximum is ±1.00.

percentile: Part out of one hundred. A hundredth part of any group or set of data or objects.

personal digital assistant (PDA): Handheld communications and computer device.

performance-based assessment: Assessments that measure both skills and knowledge acquired by students and require students to demonstrate critical thinking and complex problem-solving skills.

performance level: Student outcomes presented on a 4- or 5-point scale ranging from the performance level "below proficient" to the highest performance level "advanced proficiency."

performance test: A measure involving the learner in creative tasks or problems requiring the application of learned skills and acquired knowledge.

pervasive developmental disorder (PDD): Psychiatric diagnostic classification for children involving stereotyped behavior, interests, and activities. Often paired with low IQ and poor communication skills.

phonemes: Minimum unit of sound that is part of a spoken word, an element of a morpheme.

phonemic awareness: Having knowledge of the link between small units of speech and the corresponding sounds represented by the letters of the alphabet.

phonics: The connection between the sounds that result from the blending of phonemes (letters) together into word units. Also called the sound-spelling correspondence.

plasticity: The ability of the growing human brain to overcome physical insults to the brain matter and/or overcome environmentally induced developmental problems.

play-based assessment: Formal assessment system for the evaluation of a child through the use of structured play and careful, highly nuanced observation.

portfolios: A compendium of data sources documenting the growth of a student's skills and knowledge over time in an area.

positive skew(ness): This occurs in data that have an excess of high scores causing the mean to be higher than the median of the data.

practical intelligence: One of three mental abilities that makes up Sternberg's proposed triarchic model of mental ability.

pre-assessment conference: Parent conference including a school counselor, teacher, and parents to discuss the plan being developed to assess a child.

precision of the scale: Variables can be measured with different levels of precision loosely described as nominal, ordinal, interval, and ratio.

procedural due process: The elements and procedures required for providing due process are included in the operations and policies of the school. No child or parent's interest will be damaged or modified without a fair and open hearing.

processes: The human endeavors that go into a project designed to provide a product.

products: Outcomes of a project including tangible or material items, and/or measured changes among participants, for example, improved achievement.

proficiency levels: The several levels (ordinals) of tested achievement a child can score on a high-stakes test. The Angoff committee of the state's education department defines the minimum score for each level.

proficient: A level of academic achievement equivalent to the minimum requirement set in the state's standards for learning.

progress reports: Term for teacher to parent communication replaced in education jargon by the term "report card."

qualifying terms: Part of a scoring rubric describing the level of success or achievement required for each ordinal level of a scale.

qualitative: Pertaining to the general quality of an aspect of a person or object.

questionnaire: Data collection instrument designed to learn about characteristics, attitudes, opinions, or status of respondents.

rater drift: Tendency for the evaluation scores assigned by a rater to become higher after evaluating many performance assessments.

rating scales: Measurement device designed to evaluate and rate the quality of a product or individual.

ratio data: A mathematical method for scaling data that employs real numbers of equal unit size. It includes the value 0 and can also include negative numbers.

ratio scale: Mathematically appropriate scale of measurement based on physically observable and consistent real numbers.

raw score: The number of questions answered correctly on a test or assessment. This number may be corrected for guessing, but no other statistical transformation will have occurred with raw score data.

readiness: Mentally and/or physically prepared for a learning experience. Usually refers to readiness to enter school.

readiness tests: Measuring device used to determine a child's level of school readiness.

real time: Experiences that are happening in the moment they are considered. Right now.

receptive language: The comprehension of spoken language.

referral: The process of initiating a request for the further evaluation of a child in school. Can be initiated by teachers, administrators, and educational specialists.

reinforcement: An object or procedure that is satisfying to an individual and can serve as a motivator for continued effort.

relational concepts: Words in the language linked to concepts of placement, temporal sequences, and direction, for example, up, last, under, and so on.

reliability: A statement of the stability and/or consistency of the test scores from the administration of a measure.

reliability coefficient: Any of a series of correlation-based mathematical expressions describing either the stability or internal consistency of a measurement.

respondent: Person who completes a measurement or questionnaire and provides data for consideration.

response to intervention (RTI): Approach to assisting children with learning problems including provision of needed, research-based instructional assistance, and the close monitoring of the intervention's success and problems.

reversibility: Mental operation, central to learning mathematics, that makes it possible to mentally rearrange misleading visual arrays and return to their original configuration. Described by Jean Piaget.

rubber ruler: Using gamesmanship to make average test scores appear better than they would be if examined by an independent party (e.g., lowering the bar with a state's proficiency standards).

rubric: An ordinal sequence of qualitative ranks with definitions and examples for each level that can be used to evaluate performance assessments.

running record: Assessment of reading performance by having a child read a 100 to 150-word passage from a benchmark book and transcribing his/her reading skills, strategies, and errors.

sample of convenience: A nonstatistical sample drawn from subjects available to the researcher, and not representative of a larger population.

sampling adequacy: Sampling adequacy is achieved when the items of a measure represent an appropriate collection of what is being measured. It can also be used to refer to a statistical assumption needed to create subsets within a large set of data.

school psychologist: Educational professional who is certified by a state education department to provide for the mental health of school students.

school report card: One mandate of the No Child Left Behind Act requires each school building to create and publish a report card showing the average achievement levels, attendance, and graduation rate for students.

score gap: Significant mean differences found between groups when scores are disaggregated.

scoring rubric: Written criteria, organized as an ordinal scale used for evaluating the quality of extended-response (essay) questions and performance tasks.

screening assessment: Brief measure of an aspect of a child's ability, skills, or achievement.

Section 504: Section of the Rehabilitation Act of 1973 requiring public schools provide the support services needed to make public education available to all children with disabilities.

self-concept: The internalized picture an individual has of him/herself.

self-esteem: The evaluation made by an individual of his or her self-concept.

semantic differential scale: Method for construction of questionnaires with a stem question followed by a series of polar-opposite choices for expressing an attitude or feeling about the question's topic.

semantic scales: Questionnaires constructed to elicit the attitudes, feelings, or opinions of respondents. They include Likert-type and semantic differential scales.

semilingualism: Awkward phase when a person is learning a second language and has trouble clearly expressing thoughts in either language.

sensitivity review: An ethical step taken by test publishers prior to the publication of a new measure or evaluation. The step involves using a panel of experts representing various identifiable groups and subdivisions within the general population to evaluate individual test items for possible item fairness or bias problems.

settlement house: Centers where private philanthropy supports a range of social services for those in need.

skew: Asymmetry in a distribution of scores. Distribution is negatively skewed when most scores fall on the low end of the distribution and positively skewed when most scores fall on the high end of the distribution.

social promotion: Decision to promote a child to the next grade level even though he/she is not achieving up to the standard for entering the next grade.

Spearman-Brown prophesy: Mathematical coefficient for expressing split-half reliability (internal consistency) of data from a test or measurement.

Spearman correlation coefficient: A method for expressing the amount of concordance shared by two ordinal measures on a group of subjects.

special education: Educational programs designed to meet the specific learning needs of children with disabilities. Programs are mandated under the Individuals With Disabilities Educational Improvement Act of 2004 (P.L. 108-446).

special needs children: Children who have been identified as having a specific disability in one or more of the following areas: cognitive, physical, or sensory.

split-half reliability: Measure of the internal consistency (reliability) of a test by correlating half of the questions with the other half.

stability: The reliability that demonstrates that the scores obtained on a measure by a group of subjects will be correlated with a retest using the same measure and subjects at a later time.

stakeholders: People within an organization who perceive themselves as possibly being impacted by a study or evaluation of that organization.

standard deviation: The square root of variance. The square root of the squared individual variations of scores from the mean score.

standard error of measurement: A statistic used to estimate the probable range within which a person's true score on a test falls. The standard deviation of scores obtained around an individual's true score.

standardized achievement test: Measure of the breadth and depth of understanding of curriculum areas developed by an individual. Scores based on comparisons with like age group normative samples.

standards-based assessments: High-stakes tests with close links to both the curriculum and the approved standards for learning. These tests are scored showing the extent to which the student reached the standard for achievement.

standards-based grades: An evaluation of student performance based on a measure of an approved standard for learning.

standards-based report cards: Report cards describing a child's academic progress in terms of the achievement of enumerated standards for learning and the rubric for making grading decisions.

standards-for-learning: Statewide, approved, and highly specified goals for student learning in every grade and for all subject areas.

standard score: A derived test score expressed in deviation units indicating how far the score is from the mean score of the group.

standardized test: Any measure where individual scores are derived by comparing an individual's performance to that of a representative sample of the performances of others.

stanine: A score system that divides the area under the Gaussian normal curve into nine parts. Each of the seven center parts is one half of a standard deviation in width. From *sta*ndard *nine (stanine).*

summative assessment: Measurement of student achievement after an instructional process.

table of specifications: Two-dimensional blueprint for a test. Dimensions are the content and level of cognition the test items will require. This approach ensures the measure will have content validity.

teaching to the test: Unethical instruction designed to improve student's test scores by teaching the actual test items to children.

technical manual: A publication included with the administration information for a standardized test. It provides data on reliability, validity, normative sampling, and standard error.

test battery: Test battery refers to a series of subtests that make up a larger measurement device. For example the Armed Services Test Battery is composed of five separate subtests: Math Skills Test, Reading Skills Test, Mechanical Comprehension Test, Spatial Apperception Test, and the Aviation and Nautical Information Test.

test–retest reliability: The correlation between the scores from two sequential administrations of a test to one group of subjects providing an estimation of test stability.

time sampling: Observational system involving making periodic observations after the precise duration of a preselected unit of time.

Tourette syndrome: An inherited neurological disorder involving transient but chronic tics involving both uncontrollable motor movement and verbal outbursts.

It can also present as the painful facial neuralgia of "tic douloueux." The disorder normally presents for the first time during the elementary school years.

transitions: The periods in the life of a child when he/she moves to another educational setting (e.g., preschool to kindergarten).

traumatic head injuries: Internal damage and/or external wound to the head causing significant injury and loss.

triarchic model of intelligence: Sternberg's conceptualization of mental ability as being composed of three elements: analytical, creative, and practical intelligences.

true score: An observed score plus or minus some amount of error.

tuition driven: Educational program that is neither privately endowed nor publicly supported, and must earn all expenses through tuition payments.

typical products: Everyday products and quotidian examples of a child's work added to his/her portfolio as a demonstration of what is typical for the child.

underachievement: Pattern of achievement below that which is expected based on ability test scores and/or previous work.

valance: Positive or negative wording of a question, commonly employed with Likert-type items on a questionnaire.

validity: A statement of both the appropriateness of the test and its components, and of the veracity of the test scores and their interpretations.

value added: An assessment approach that focuses on the change that has occurred for each individual over a period of time. Seen as a method of evaluating growth and change within individuals.

value-added assessments: A longitudinal approach to assessment involving following the same children for several years to see the pattern of achievement growth.

value-added evaluation: A data-driven longitudinal evaluation of schools, educators, and students accomplished by charting the growth of individuals in the educational context of the school.

variability: A statistical measure of the amount that individual scores on a measurement will spread out from the mean of the data.

variable: A factor, conceptual entity, characteristic, or attribute that is likely to vary between individuals and/or within individuals over time.

variance: The average of the sum of the squared deviations of individual scores from the mean.

verbal contagion: Verbal repeating, singing, rhyming, or chanting games played with an infant anytime throughout the day.

verbal tics: Symptom of a mental disorder characterized by repetitive, stereotyped, inappropriate, brief verbal outbursts.

War on Poverty: Sobriquet used by the administration of President Lyndon B. Johnson to describe his domestic policy initiatives. One of these initiatives was the ESEA (1965).

work sampling system: A type of curriculum-embedded assessment system employing probes to measure academic achievement, skills, behavior, and problem solving.

Works Progress Administration (WPA): Federal agency established by President Franklin D. Roosevelt in 1933 to put people, including teachers, back to work and earning a living.

References

Abbott, M. L., Joireman, J., & Stroh, H. R. (2002). *The influence of district size, school size and socioeconomic status on achievement in Washington: A replication study using hierarchical linear modeling* (Technical Report No. 3). Lynnwood: Seattle Pacific University, Washington School Research Center. (ERIC Document Reproduction Service No. ED470668)

Ackerman, D. J., Barnett, W. S., & Robin, K. B. (2005). *Making the most of kindergarten: Present trends and future issues in the provision of full-day programs.* New Brunswick, NJ: National Institute for Early Education Research.

Adams, G. R., & Ryan, B. A. (2000, June). *A longitudinal analysis of family relationships and children's school achievement in one- and two-parent families.* Quebec: Human Resources and Skills Development Canada. Retrieved June 25, 2009, from http://www.hrsdc.gc.ca/eng/cs/sp/sdc/pkrf/publications/research/2000-000180/page08 .shtml.

Ainsworth, L. B., & Viegut, D. J. (2006). *Common formative assessment: How to connect standards-based instruction and assessment.* Thousand Oaks, CA: Corwin Press.

Alexander, K. L., Entwisle, D. R., & Olson, L. S. (2007). Lasting consequences of the summer learning gap. *American Sociological Review, 72*(2): 167–180.

Allen, F. L. (1931). *An informal history of the 1920's.* New York: Harper & Row.

Allen, J. A. (1985). Understanding the family: A central concern in child welfare. In J. Laird and A Hartman (Eds.), *A handbook of child welfare: Context, knowledge, and practice* (pp. 149-177). New York: Free Press.

Alliance for Healthy Homes. (2006). *Healthy homes equals healthy families and communities.* Retrieved February 25, 2008, from http://www.afhh.org.

Alvarado, M. (2006, December 10). Swimming upstream in the mainstream. *The Record* [North Jersey]. Retrieved February 27, 2007, from http://www.northjersey.com/.

American Academy of Pediatrics. (2002). *What's the best way to choose the right childcare center for my child?* Retrieved December 6, 2007, from http://www.aap.org/publiced/BR_ChildCare.htm.

American Council for the Teaching of Foreign Languages. (1985). *ACTFL proficiency guidelines.* Hastings-on-Hudson, NY: ACTFL Materials Center. Retrieved May 20, 2009, from http://www.sil.org/lingualinks/language learning/OtherResources/ACTFLProficiencyGuidelines/contents.htm.

American Psychiatric Association. (1994). *Diagnostic and statistical manual of mental disorders* (4th ed.). Washington, DC: Author.

Amrein-Beardsley, A. (2008). Methodological concerns about the education value added assessment system. *Educational Researcher, 37*(2), 65–75.

Arias, M. B., & Morillo-Campbell, M. (2008). *Promoting ELL parental involvement: Challenges in contested times.* Tempe: Arizona State University, Education Policy Research Unit. Retrieved June 18, 2009, from http://epsl.asu.edu/epru/documents/EPSL-0801-250-EPRU.pdf.

Armbruster, B. B., Lehr, F., & Osborn, J. (2003). *Put reading first: The research building blocks for teaching children to read.* Washington, DC: National Reading Panel, Office of Educational Research and Improvement. Retrieved July 2, 2005, from http://www.nationalreadingpanel.org.

Armour, S. A. (2008, May 15). Mortgage crisis leading to mental health crisis. *USA Today.* Retrieved May 29, 2009, from http://www.wbir.com/news/health/story.aspx?storyid=58049.

Athanasiou, M. (2007). Battelle developmental inventory, 2nd ed. [Review]. In K. E. Geisinger, R. A. Spies, J. F. Carlson, & B. S. Plake (Eds.), *The seventeenth mental measurements yearbook* [Electronic version]. Retrieved December 13, 2007, from the Buros Institute's Test Reviews Online Web site: http://www.unl.edu/buros/.

Barkley, R. A. (1998). Attention-deficit hyperactivity disorder. In E. J. Mash & R. A. Barkley (Eds.), *Attention-deficit hyperactivity disorder: A handbook for diagnosis and treatment* (2nd ed., pp. 63–112). New York: Guilford.

Barnett, W. S., Hustedt, J. T., Friedman, A. H., Boyd, J. S., & Ainsworth, P. (2007). *The state of preschool 2007: State preschool yearbook.* New Brunswick, NJ: Rutgers University, Graduate School of Education, National Institute for Early Education Research.

Barton, P. E., & Coley, R. J. (2007). *The family: America's smallest school.* Princeton, NJ: Educational Testing Service.

Bassuk, E. L., & Friedman, S. M. (2005). *Facts on trauma and homeless children.* Retrieved June 8, 2009, from the National Child Traumatic Stress Network Web site: http://www.nctsnet.org/nctsn_assets/pdfs/promising_practices/Facts_on_Trauma_and_Home less_ Children.pdf.

Bassuk, E. L., Konnath, K., & Volk, K. T. (2006). *Understanding traumatic stress in children.* Newton, MA: National

Center on Family Homelessness. Retrieved June 25, 2009, from http://www.nctsnet.org/nccts/nav.do?pid=faq_under.

Bateson, D. (1994). Psychometric and philosophic problems in "authentic" assessment: Performance tasks and portfolios. *Alberta Journal of Educational Research, 40*(2), 233–245.

Bayley, N. (2006). *Bayley scales of infant and toddler development, 3rd ed., Screening test.* San Antonio, TX: Pearson Education.

Beach, J. (1995). *Literacy development among low achieving kindergarten students.* Unpublished master's thesis, St. Xavier University, Chicago, IL. Retrieved August 22, 2008, from http://eric.ed.gov/ERICDocs/data/ericdocs 2sql/content_storage_01/0000019b/80/14/27/35.pdf.

Beatty, B. (2004, November 1). Past, present, and future: What we can learn from the history of preschool education. *The American Prospect.* Retrieved January 3, 2008, from http://www.prospect.ogr/cs/articles?articleID= 8770.

Behavioral Diagnostics. (2008). *The Quotient ADHD system patient report.* Retrieved August 18, 2008, from http:// www.biobdx.com/reliable_data_the_patient_report.html.

Belluck, P. (2006, February 5). And for perfect attendance, Johnny gets . . . a car. *New York Times.* Retrieved September 15, 2007, from http://www.nytimes.com.

Benes, K. M., & Rogers, B. G. (1992). Peabody individual achievement test, revised [Review]. In J. J. Kramer & J. C. Conoley (Eds.), *The eleventh mental measurements yearbook* (pp. 649–652). Lincoln, NE: Buros Institute of Mental Measurements.

Bennett, S., & Kalish, N. (2006, June 19). No more teachers, lots of books. *New York Times.* Retrieved June 20, 2006, from http://www.nytimes.com/2006/06/19/opinion/19 bennett.html.

Bergen, D., & Coscia, J. (2000). Brain research and child education. Olney, MD: Association for Childhood Education International.

Berninger, V. W. (2007). *Process assessment of the learner, 2nd ed.* San Antonio, TX: Pearson Assessment.

Bettelheim, B. (1987). The importance of play. *The Atlantic.* Retrieved April 17, 2008, from http://www .theatlantic.com/doc/print/198703/importance-play.

Bhattacharjee, Y. (2008, February, 24). Idea lab: Baby talk show. *New York Times Magazine,* p. 20.

Black, P., & William, D. (1998). Inside the black box: Raising standards through classroom assessment. *Phi Delta Kappan, 80*(2), 139–148.

Blank, B. T. (1998). Settlement houses: Old idea in new form builds communities. *The New Social Worker Online, 5*(3). Retrieved January 3, 2008, from http://www.social worker.com/settleme.htm.

Bloom, B. S., et al. (Ed.). (1956). *Taxonomy of educational objectives: The classification of educational goals: Handbook I. Cognitive domain.* New York: David McKay.

Bodden, M. (2005, December 8). *Testimony of Michelle Bodden, elementary school vice president before education committee of the NYS legislature.* Retrieved July 5, 2008, from http://www.uft.org/news/issues/ testimony/testimony_earlychildhood/.

Boehm, A. E. (2001). *Boehm test of basic concepts* (3rd ed.). San Antonio, TX: Pearson Education.

Booher-Jennings, J. (2005). "Below the bubble": Educational triage and the Texas accountability system. *American Educational Research Journal, 42*(2), 231–268.

Booth, W. (1998, February 22). One nation, indivisible: Is it history? *The Washington Post,* p. A1. Retrieved July 3, 2008, from http://www.washingtonpost.com/wpsrv/national/ longterm/meltingpot/melt0222.htm.

Borja, R. R. (2005, October 10). Growing niche for tutoring chains: Prekindergartners' academic prep. *Education Week, 25*(8), 10.

Borman, G. D., & Dowling, N. M. (2006). The longitudinal achievement effects of multi-year summer school: Evidence from the Teach Baltimore randomized field trial. *Educational Evaluation and Policy Analysis, 28,* 25–48.

Borzekowski, D. L. G., & Robinson, T. N. (2005). The remote, the mouse, and the no. 2 pencil. *Archives of Pediatrics and Adolescent Medicine, 159*(7), 607–613.

Bowe, F. G. (2004). *Birth to eight: Early childhood special education* (3rd ed.). Clifton Park, NY: Delmar-Thomson Learning.

Boyce, B. A., & Poteat, G. M. (2005). ASQ, the ages and stages questionnaires: A parent-completed, child-monitoring system, 2nd ed. [Review]. In R. A. Spies & B. S. Plake (Eds.), *The sixteenth mental measurements yearbook* [Electronic version]. Retrieved July 2, 2005, from the Buros Institute's Test Reviews Online Web site: http://www.unl .edu/buros.

Boyd, R. D., Welge, P., Sexton, D., & Miller, J. H. (1989). Concurrent validity of the Battelle developmental inventory: Relationship with the Bayley scales in young children with known and suspected disabilities. *Journal of Early Intervention, 13*(1), 14–23.

Bracey, G. W. (1989). Moving around and dropping out. *Phi Delta Kappan, 70*(5), 407–410.

Bracey, G. W. (2004). The perfect law. *Dissent.* Retrieved June 23, 2008, from http://www.dissentmagazine .org/article?article=318.

Braden, J. P., & Thorndike, R. M. (2005). Kaufman assessment battery for children, 2nd ed. [Review]. In R. A. Spies & B. S. Plake (Eds.), *The sixteenth mental measurements yearbook* [Electronic version]. Retrieved July 2, 2008, from the Buros Institute's Test Reviews Online Web site: http://www.unl.edu/buros.

Braun, H., & Wainer, H. (2007). Value-added modeling. In *Handbook of statistics, 26,* 867–892. Amsterdam: Elsevier.

Braun, S. J., & Edwards, E. P. (1972). *History and theory of early childhood.* Worthington, OH: Charles A. Jones.

Brazelton, T. B., & Nugent, J. K. (1995). *The neonatal behavioral assessment scale, 3rd ed.* Port Chester, NY: Cambridge University Press.

Bricker, D., Capt, B., & Pretti-Frontczak, K. (1993). *The assessment, evaluation, and programming system: Birth to age three.* Baltimore: Paul H. Brookes.

Bricker, D., Clifford, J., Yovanoff, P., Waddell, M., Allen, D., Pretti-Frontczak, K., & Hoselton, R. (2007). *Determining and corroborating eligibility decisions, revised.* Baltimore: Paul H. Brookes.

Bricker, D., & Cripe, J. J. W. (1992). *An activity-based approach to early intervention.* Baltimore: Paul H. Brookes.

Bricker, D., Squires, J., Mounts, L., Potter, L., Nickel, R., Twombly, E., & Farrell, J. (1999). *Ages & stages questionnaires: A parent-completed, child-monitoring system, 2nd ed.* Baltimore: Paul H. Brookes.

Bricker, D. Yovanoff, P., Capt, B., & Allen, D. (2003). Use of a curriculum-based measure to corroborate eligibility decisions. *Journal of Early Interventions, 26*(1), 20–30.

Brigance, A. H., & Glascoe, F. P. (2004). *Brigance diagnostic inventory of early development, 2nd ed.* North Billerica, MA: Curriculum Associates.

Brody, J. E. (2009, January 20). Trying anything and everything for autism. *New York Times, 156*(54,561), p. D7.

Brookhart, S. M. (1991). Grading practices and validity. *Educational Measurement: Issues and Practice, 10*(1), 35–36.

Brown, R. (1974). *First language, the early stages.* Cambridge, MA: Harvard University Press.

Brown, R. T., Perwien, A., Faries, D. E., Kratochvil, C. J., & Vaughn, B. S. (2006). Atomoxetine in the management of children with ADHD: Effects on quality of life and school functioning. *Clinical Pediatrics, 45*(9), 819–827.

Brown, T. E. (2001). *Brown-attention-deficit-disorder scales for children and adolescents.* San Antonio, TX: Harcourt Assessment Division, Psychological Corporation.

Brown, T. E. (2005). *Attention deficit disorder: The unfocused mind in children and adults.* New Haven, CT: Yale University Press.

Browning, R., Salvia, J., & Ysseldyke, J. E. (1979). Technical characteristics of the Peabody individual achievement test as a function of item arrangement and basal and ceiling rules. *Psychology in the Schools, 16*(1), 4–7.

Bruder, M. B. (2003/2004). The Individual Family Service Plan (IFSP). *ERIC Digest.* Retrieved June 17, 2009, from http://www.ericdigests.org/2001-4/ifsp.html.

Brumbaugh, E. (2008, Summer). DAP in ECE: Respect. *Kappa Delta Pi Record, 44*(4), 170–175.

Brunsman, B. A. (2005). *DIBELS: Dynamic indicators of early literacy skills, sixth edition* [Review]. In R. A. Spies & B. S. Plake (Eds.), *The sixteenth mental measurements yearbook* [Electronic version]. Retrieved July 2, 2005, from the Buros Institute's Test Reviews Online Web site: http://www.unl.edu/buros.

Burrell, J. (2007, October 28). Strong academic pressure seeps down to preschools. *Oakland Tribune.* Retrieved December 12, 2008, from http://findarticles.com/p/articles/mi_qn4176/is_20071028/ai_n21076875/print?tag=artBody;col1.

Bush, G. W. (2002). *Good Start, Smart Start: The Bush administration's early childhood initiative* [Press release]. Washington, DC: White House Press Office. Retrieved December 12, 2007, from http://www.eric.ed.gov/ERICDocs/data/ericdocs2sql/content_storage_01/0000019b/80/1a/1b/37.pdf.

Byrne, J. M., Backman, J. E., & Bawden, H. N. (1995). Minnesota child development inventory: A normative study. *Canadian Psychology.* Retrieved February 19, 2008, from http://findarticles.com/p/articles/mi_qa3711/is_199505/ai_n8726839/print.

Camilli, G., & Monfils, L. F. (2004). Test scores and equity. In W. A. Firestone, R. Y. Schorr & L. F. Monfils (Eds.), *The ambiguity of teaching to the test: Standards, assessment, and educational reform* (pp. 143–157). Mahwah, NJ: Erlbaum.

Cannon, J. S., & Karoly, L. A. (2007). *Who is ahead and who is behind? Gaps in school readiness and student achievement in the early grades for California's children* (Labor and Population Division Report). Santa Monica, CA: RAND.

Case, B. J. (2004, January). *It's about time: Stanford achievement test series, 10th ed.* (Assessment Report). San Antonio, TX: Harcourt Assessment.

Castelli, R. A. (1994). *Critical thinking instruction in liberal arts curricula.* Unpublished doctoral dissertation, Widener University, Chester, PA. (ProQuest No. AAT 9617432)

Cattell, R. (1963). Theory of fluid and crystallized intelligence: A critical experiment. *Journal of Educational Psychology, 1*(54), 1–22.

Cech, S. J. (2007, July 16). Much of learning gap blamed on summer. *Education Week.* Retrieved August 3, 2007, from http://www.edweek.org/ew/articles/2007/07/18/43summer.h26.html?print=1.

Chae, S. E. (2008, March). *Effects of individual and collective parent involvement on kindergarten children's reading achievement.* Paper presented at the annual meeting of the American Educational Research Association, New York.

Chamberlin, M., & Plucker, J. (2008). P–16 education: Where are we going? Where have we been? *Phi Delta Kappan, 89*(7), 472–479.

Chang, K. D. (2005, June 20). Attention-deficit/hyperactivity disorder. *E-Medicine.* Retrieved June 30, 2005, from http://www.emedicine.com/med/topic3103.htm.

Chittooran, M. M., & Kessler, C. E. (2001). *Mullen scales of early learning: AGS ed.* [Review]. In B. S. Plake & J. C. Impara (Eds.), *The fourteenth mental measurements yearbook* (pp. 792–795). Lincoln, NE: Buros Institute of Mental Measurements.

Chomsky, N. (1972). *Language and mind.* Boston: Houghton Mifflin Harcourt.

Christakis, D. I., Zimmerman, F. J., DiGiuseppe, D. L., & McCarty, C. A. (2004). Early television exposure and subsequent attention problems in children. *Pediatrics, 113*(4), 708–713.

Christina, R., & Nicholson-Goodman, J. (2005). *Going to scale with high-quality early education.* Santa Monica, CA: RAND. Retrieved November 5, 2007, from http://www.rand.org.

Cizek, G. J., & Fairbank, D. W. (2001). Developmental indicators for the assessment of learning, 3rd ed. [Review].

In B. S. Plake & J. C. Impara (Eds.), *The fourteenth mental measurements yearbook* (pp. 394–403). Lincoln, NE: Buros Institute of Mental Measurements.

Cizek, G. J., Johnson, R. L., & Mazzie, D. (2005). TerraNova [Review]. In R. A. Spies & B. S. Plake (Eds.), *The sixteenth mental measurements yearbook* [Electronic version]. Retrieved November 8, 2006, from the Buros Institute's Test Reviews Online Web site: http://www.unl.edu/buros.

Cizek, G. J., & Sandoval J. (2003). Woodcock-Johnson, 3rd ed. [Review]. In B. S. Plake, J. C. Impara, & R. A. Spies (Eds.), *The fifteenth mental measurements yearbook* (pp. 1019–1028). Lincoln, NE: Buros Institute of Mental Measurements.

Clarridge, P. B., & Whitaker, E. M. (1997). *Rolling the elephant over: How to effect large scale change in the reporting process.* Portsmouth, NH: Heinemann.

Clinton, W. J. (1999a, January 14). *State of the union address* [Transcript]. Retrieved August 8, 2008, from http://www.cnn.com/ALLPOLITICS/stories/1999/01/19/sotu.transcript/.

Clinton, W. J. (1999b). *Taking responsibility for ending social promotion: A guide for educators and state and local leaders* [Archived presidential document]. Retrieved May 23, 2008, from http://www.ed.gov/pubs/socialpromotion/execsum.html.

Coghlan, D., King, J. S. H., & Wake, M. (2003). Parents' evaluation of developmental status in the Australian day-care setting: Developmental concerns of parents and carers. *Journal of Paediatrics and Child Health, 39*(1), 49–54.

Cohen, J. (1988). *Statistical power analysis for the behavioral sciences, 2nd ed.* Hillsdale, NJ: Erlbaum.

Cohen, L. G. (2001). Early childhood attention deficit disorders evaluation scale [Review]. In B. S. Plake & J. C. Impara (Eds.), *The fourteenth mental measurements yearbook* (pp. 442–446). Lincoln, NE: Buros Institute of Mental Measurements.

Collins, A., & Dana, T. M. (1993). Using portfolios with middle grade students. *Middle School Journal, 25*(2), 14–19.

Colton, D., & Covert R. W. (2007). *Designing and constructing instruments for social research and evaluation.* San Francisco: Jossey-Bass.

Committee on Quality Improvement and Subcommittee on Attention-Deficit/Hyperactivity Disorder. (2001). Clinical practice guideline: Treatment of the school-aged child with attention-deficit/hyperactivity disorder. *Pediatrics, 108*(4), 1033–1044.

Conners, K. (1997/2000). *Conners' rating scales–Revised.* Toronto, Canada: Multi-Health Systems.

Connolly, A. J. (2007). *Key math, 3rd ed.* Upper Saddle River, NJ: Pearson Education.

Cook, V. (2008). *Second language learning and teaching.* New York: Oxford University Press.

Cooper, H., Robinson, J. C., & Patall, E. A. (2006). Does homework improve academic achievement? A synthesis of research. *Review of Educational Research*, 76, 1–62.

Coopersmith, S. (1967). *The antecedents of self-esteem.* San Francisco: W. H. Freeman.

Crain, W. (2003). *Reclaiming childhood: Letting children be children in our achievement oriented society.* New York: Henry Holt.

Crehan, K. D., & Monsaas, J. A. (2005). Test of early mathematics ability, 3rd ed. [Review]. In R. A. Spies & B. S. Plake (Eds.), *The sixteenth mental measurements yearbook* (pp. 1035–1040). Lincoln, NE: Buros Institute of Mental Measurements.

Crocker, L. (2003). Teaching for the test: Validity, fairness, and moral action [2003 NCME presidential address]. *Educational Measurement: Issues and Practice, 22*(3), 5–11.

Cross, L. J., & Fager, J. J. (2001). Peabody individual achievement test, 2nd ed. [Review]. In B. S. Plake & J. C. Impara (Eds.), *The fourteenth mental measurements yearbook* (pp. 904–908). Lincoln, NE: Buros Institute of Mental Measurements.

Czadnowski, C. M., & Goldenberg, D. S. (2001). *Developmental indicators for the assessment of learning, 3rd ed.* Circle Pines, MN: Pearson Assessment.

D'Amato, R. C., Johnson, J. A., & Kush, J. C. (2007). Stanford-Binet intelligence scales, 5th ed. [Review]. In K. E. Geisinger, R. A. Spies, J. F. Carlson, & B. S. Plake (Eds.), *The seventeenth mental measurements yearbook* [Electronic version]. Retrieved December 13, 2007, from the Buros Institute's Test Reviews Online Web site: http://www.unl.edu/buros/.

Darwin, C. R. (1877). A biographical sketch of an infant. *Mind: A Quarterly Review of Psychology and Philosophy, 2*(7), 285–294.

Datar, A. (2003). *The impact of changes in kindergarten entrance age policies on children's academic achievement and the child care needs of families* (Report No. RGSD-177). Santa Monica, CA: Pardee Rand Graduate School.

Davis, A. S., & Holmes, F. W. (2007). Brigance diagnostic inventory of early development, 2nd ed. [Review]. In K. E. Geisinger, R. A. Spies, J. F. Carlson, & B. S. Plake (Eds.), *The seventeenth mental measurements yearbook* [Electronic version]. Retrieved December 13, 2007, from the Buros Institute's Test Reviews Online Web site: http://www.unl.edu/buros/.

Davis, K. F., Parker, J., Montgomery, G. (2004). Sleep in infants and young children: Part one: Normal sleep. *Journal of Pediatric Health Care, 18*(2), 65–71.

Dawes, J. (2008). Do data characteristics change according to the number of scale points used? An experiment using 5-point, 7-point and 10-point scales. *International Journal of Market Research, 50*(1), 61–77.

Dawson, D. (2003). *Listening to music and increasing reading achievement scores in vocabulary and comprehension and total reading ability.* Unpublished doctoral dissertation, Widener University, Chester, PA. (AAT 3116329).

Dawson, D. A. (1991). Family structure and children's health and well-being: Data from the National Health Interview Survey on Child Health. *Journal of Marriage and the Family, 53*, 573–584.

DeBruin Parecki, A. (2005). *Early literacy skills assessment.* Ypsilanti, MI: HighScope Educational Research Foundation.

deFur, S. H. (2003). Test of early reading ability, 3rd ed. [Review]. In B. S. Plake, J. C. Impara, & R. A. Spies (Eds.), *The fifteenth mental measurements yearbook* (pp. 1239–1242). Lincoln, NE: Buros Institute of Mental Measurements.

DeGregory, L. (2008, August 9). The feral child. *Naples Daily News,* pp. D1, D3.

della Cava, M. R. (2005, September 21). Out-of-line preschoolers increasingly face expulsion. *USA Today*. Retrieved September 27, 2005, from http://www.usatoday.com/news/education/2005-09-20-expelledpreschoolers_x.htm.

Dessoff, A. (2008). Action teams. *District Administration, 43*(6), 41–44.

de Vise, D. (2007a, March 4). A concentrated approach to exams. *The Washington Post.* Retrieved March 8, 2007, from http://www.washingtonpost.com/.

de Vise, D. (2007b, May 23). More work, less play in kindergarten. *The Washington Post.* Retrieved May 25, 2007, from http://www.washingtonpost.com/wpdyn/content/article/2007/05/22/AR200705220166.html.

Dillon, S. (2006, March 26). Schools cut back subjects to push reading and math. *New York Times.* Retrieved June 25, 2009, from http://www.nytimes.com/2006/03/26/education/26child.html?_r=1&pagewanted=2.

Dillon, S. (2007, February 7). Advanced placement tests are leaving some behind. *New York Times, 156*(53,848), p. A17.

Dillon, S. (2008a, December 17). In early education Obama stirs great hope. *New York Times, 158*(54,527), pp. A1, A3.

Dillon, S. (2008b, May 2). An initiative on reading is rated ineffective. *New York Times, 157*(54,298), p. A11.

DiRanna, K., Osmundson, E., Topps, J., Barakos, L., Gearhart, M., Cerwin, K., et al. (2008). *Assessment centered teaching: A reflective practice.* Thousand Oaks, CA: Corwin Press.

Dodge, D. T., Colker, L., Heroman, C. (2001). *A teachers guide to using the creative curriculum developmental continuum assessment system*. Washington, DC: Teaching Strategies.

Doggett, A., & Johnson-Gros, N. (2007). Bayley scales of infant and toddler development, 3rd ed. [Review]. In K. E. Geisinger, R. A. Spies, J. F. Carlson, & B. S. Plake (Eds.), *The seventeenth mental measurements yearbook* [Electronic version]. Retrieved July 13, 2008, from the Buros Institute's Test Reviews Online Web site: http://www.unl.edu/buros/.

Doherty, K. M. (2004, August 11). Assessment. *Education Week*. Retrieved August 22, 2004, from http://www.edweek.org/context/topics/issuespage.cfm?id=41.

Dong, Y. R. (2007, Summer). Learning to think in English. *Educational Leadership, 64,* 22–26.

Du Bois, P. H. (1970). *A history of psychological testing.* Boston: Allyn & Bacon.

Duncan, G. J., & Gibson-Davis, C. M. (2006). Connecting child care quality to child outcomes: Drawing policy lessons from nonexperimental data. *Evaluation Review, 30*(5), 611–630.

Dunn, D. M., & Dunn, L. M. (2007). *Peabody picture vocabulary test, 3rd ed.* Upper Saddle River, NJ: Pearson Education.

Early Childhood Measurement and Evaluation Resource Center. (2008). *Tools review.* Alberta, Canada: Community-University Partnership for the Study of Children, Youth, and Families. Retrieved February 29, 2008, from the University of Alberta Web site: http://www.cup.ualberta.ca/tool-reviews/view-category.

Eckholm, E. (2008, June 24). To avoid student turnover, parents get help with rent. *New York Times, 157*(54,351), pp. A1, A19.

Elder, T. E., & Lubotsky, D. H. (in press). Kindergarten entrance age and children's achievement: Impacts of state policies, family background and peers. *Journal of Human Resources.* Retrieved August 20, 2008, from http://www.ilir.uiuc.edu/lubotsky/Elder%20Lubotsky%20June%202008.pdf.

Elementary and Secondary Education Act (ESEA). Pub. L. No. 89-10, § 201 (1965).

Elementary and Secondary Education Act (ESEA). Improving America's Schools Act, Pub. L. No. 103-382 (1994).

Elementary and Secondary Education Act (ESEA). No Child Left Behind Act, Pub. L. No. 107-110 (2002).

Elkind, D. (2007). *The power of play: Learning what comes naturally.* Philadelphia: Da Capo.

Elliott, A. (2008, June 23). Daewoo's "Lukid" low cost UMPC shown in Korea: Classmate-based budget offering. *Gadget News and Reviews.* Retrieved June 25, 2008, from http://www.pocket-lint.co.uk/.

Elliott, S. (2007, December 6). Straight A's with a burger as a prize. *New York Times, 157*(54,150), p. C4.

El Nasser, H., & Overberg, P. (2007, November 30). Millions more Americans move to new states. *USA Today.* Retrieved May 27, 2008, from the reporter index at http://usatoday.com.

Epstein, J. L., Coates, L., Salinas, K. C., Sanders, M. G., & Simon, B. S. (1997). *School, family, and community partnerships: Your handbook for action.* Thousand Oaks, CA: Corwin Press.

Epstein, J. L., Sanders, M. G., Salinas, C., Jansom, N. R., & Voorhis, F. L. (2002). *School, family, and community partnerships: Your handbook for action* (2nd ed.). Thousand Oaks, CA: Corwin Press.

Epstein, J. L., & Sheldon, S. B. (2006). Moving forward: Ideas for research on school, family, and community partnerships. In C. F. Conrad & R. Stein (Eds.), *Sage handbook for research in education. Engaging ideas and enriching inquiry* (pp. 117–138). Thousand Oaks, CA: Sage.

Erford, B. T., & Pauletta, D. (2005, October). Psychometric analysis of young children's responses to the Slosson intelligence test–Primary. *Measurement and Evaluation in Counseling and Development, 38,* 130–140.

Erford, B. T., Vitali, G., & Slosson, S. W. (1999). *Manual for the Slosson intelligence test–Primary.* Los Angeles, CA: Western Psychological Services.

Evans, D. W., King, R. A., & Leckman, J. F. (1996). Tic disorders. In E. J. Mash & R. A. Barkley (Eds.), *Child psychopathology* (pp. 436–454). New York: Guilford.

Fair Test. (2007). *First, do no harm: A response to the proposed New York City third grade retention policy.* Cambridge, MA: Fair Test E-Newsletter. Retrieved August 8, 2008, from http://www.fairtest.org/first-do-no-harm-response-proposed-new-york-city-t.

Family Educational Rights and Privacy Act. U.S. Code: Title 20, C 31 (SC 3), § 1232h (1974).

Farah, M. J., Noble, K. G., & Hurt, H. (2005). *Poverty, privilege, and brain development: Empirical findings and ethical implications.* Unpublished manuscript, University of Pennsylvania. Retrieved March 10, 2008, from www.psych.upenn.edu/~mfarah/farah_SES_05.pdf.

Fein, G. (1981). Pretend play in childhood: An integrative review. *Child Development, 52*(4), 1095–1118.

Feingold, B. (1975). *Why your child is hyperactive.* New York: Random House.

Finger, D. (2006, May 31). Does it pay to reward students for success? *The Gainesville Sun.* Retrieved June 23, 2008, from http://www.gainesville.com/apps/pbcs.dll/article?AID=/20060531/LOCAL/205310337/1078.

Finley, M. T. (1995). *Critical thinking skills as articulated in the instructional practices, objectives, and examination items of higher level secondary school courses.* Unpublished doctoral dissertation, Widener University, Chester, PA. (ProQuest No. AAT 9605418)

Finn, C. E., Jr. (1991). *We must take charge: Our schools and our future.* New York: Free Press.

Fox News 29 (Saint Lucie, FL). (2008, May 28). *Florida teacher allegedly lets kindergarteners kick autistic boy out of class in "Survivor"-like vote* [Television broadcast]. Video news clip available at http://www.foxnews.com/story/0,2933,358956,00.html.

Francis, R. (2006). Report cards: Do they make the grade? *Education World.* Retrieved August 11, 2008, from http://www.educationworld.com/a_admin/admin/admin195.shtml.

Frankenburg, W. K. (1974). Selection of diseases and the tests in pediatric screening. *Pediatrics, 54*(5), 612–618.

Frankenburg, W. K., Dodds, J., Archer, P., Bresnick, B., Maschka, P., Edelman, N., & Shapiro, H. (1990). *Denver II.* Denver, CO: Denver Developmental Materials.

Franklin, B. (1751). *Observations concerning the increase of mankind, peopling of countries, etc.* Retrieved April 10, 2008, from http://bc.barnard.columbia.edu/~lgordis/earlyAC/documents/observations.html.

Froebel, F. W. A. (1948). The education of man. In R. Ulich (Ed.), *Three thousand years of educational wisdom* (pp. 523–576). Cambridge, MA: Harvard University Press.

Fuchs, L. S., & Fuchs, D. (2004). Determining adequate yearly progress from kindergarten through grade six with curriculum-based measurement. *Assessment for Effective Instruction, 29*(4), 25–38.

Gadbury-Amyot, C. C., Kim, J., Palm, R. L., Mills, G. E., Noble, E., & Overman, P. R. (2003). Validity and reliability of portfolio assessments of competency in a baccalaureate dental hygiene program. *Journal of Dental Education, 67*(9), 991–1002.

Gadsden, V., & Ray, A. (2003). *Father's role in children's academic achievement and early literacy.* Champaign, IL: ERIC Clearinghouse on Early Education and Parenting. (ERIC Document Reproduction Service No. ED482051)

Gaetano, C. (2006, August 31). General education teachers face special education realities. *East Brunswick Sentinel.* Retrieved February 27, 2007, from http://ebs.gmnews.com/news/2006/0831/Schools/043.html%20.

Gamoran, A. (Ed.). (2007). *Standards-based reform and the poverty gap: Lessons for No Child Left Behind.* Washington, DC: Brookings Institution.

Gao, H. (2005, April 11). Kindergarten or "kindergrind"? School getting tougher for kids. *San Diego Union Tribune.* Retrieved April 13, 2005, from http://www.signonsandiego.com/uniontrib/20050411/news_1n11kinder.html.

Gardner, H. (1995). *An unschooled mind: How children think and how schools should teach.* New York: Basic Books.

Gardner, H. (1998) A reply to Perry D. Klein's "Multiplying the problems of intelligence by eight." *Canadian Journal of Education, 23*(1), 96–102.

Gardner, H. (1999). *Intelligence reframed: Multiple intelligence for the 21st century.* New York: Basic Books.

Gardner, R., Jr. (2005). Failing at four. *New York Magazine.* Retrieved August 19, 2004, from http://www.newyorkmetro.com/nymetro/urban/education/features/1508/index.html.

Garner, R. (2007, June 5). Short summer break leads to higher grades. *The Independent.* Retrieved June 5, 2007, from http://education.independent.co.uk/news/article2611741.ece.

Georgia Association of School Psychologists (GASP). (2003). *Position statement: The use of high-stakes testing.* Stone Mountain, GA: Author. Retrieved July 7, 2005, from http://www.gaspnet.org.

German, D. J., & Newman, R. S. (2007). Oral reading skills of children with oral language (word finding) difficulties. *Reading Psychology, 28*(5), 397–442.

Gesell, A. (1940). *The first five years of life: A guide to the study of the preschool child.* New York: Harper Brothers.

Gierl, M. J., Tan, X., & Olivarez, A., Jr. (2005). Early math diagnostic assessment [Review]. In R. A. Spies & B. S. Plake (Eds.), *The sixteenth mental measurements yearbook* [Electronic version]. Retrieved July 2, 2005, from the Buros Institute's Test Reviews Online Web site: http://www.unl.edu/buros.

Gifford, S. (2007, November 19). *Follow-up to Reading at Risk links declines in reading with poorer academic and social outcomes.* Washington, DC: National Endowment for the Arts. Retrieved May 5, 2008, from http://www.nea.gov/news/news07/TRNR.html.

Gillberg, C. (2006). Autism spectrum disorders. In C. Gillberg, R. Harrington, & H. C. Steinhausen (Eds.), *A clinician's handbook of child and adolescent psychiatry* (pp. 447–488). New York: Cambridge University Press.

Gilliam, W. S. (2005, May). *Prekindergartners left behind: Expulsion rates in state prekindergarten programs* [Policy

Brief No. 3]. New York: Foundation for Child Development. Retrieved July 14, 2008, from http://www.fcd-us.org/usr_doc/ExpulsionPolicyBrief.pdf.

Ginsberg, H. (2007). *mCLASS: Math.* Brooklyn, NY: Wireless Generation. Retrieved August 1, 2008, from http://www.wirelessgeneration.com/solutions/mclass-math.html.

Ginsburg, H. P., & Baroody, A. J. (2003). *Test of early mathematical ability, 3rd ed.* Lutz, FL: Psychological Assessment Resources.

Ginsberg, M. R. (2008). *Our history.* Washington, DC: National Association for the Education of Young Children. Retrieved June 18, 2009, from http://www.naeyc.org/about/history.

Glickman-Bond, J., & Rose, K. (2006). *Creating and using rubrics in today's classrooms: A practical guide.* Norwood, MA: Christopher-Gordon.

Glod, M. (2006, October 27). Closing the gap, child by child. *The Washington Post.* Retrieved March 10, 2007, from http://www.washingtonpost.com/wp-dyn/content/article/2006/10/26/AR2006102601600_pf.html.

Glod, M., (2008, July 17). Coping with their parent's war: Multiple deployments compound strain for children. *The Washington Post.* Retrieved July 18, 2008, from http://www.washingtonpost.com/wp-dyn/content/article/2008/07/16/AR2008071602878_pf.html.

Goddard, H. H. (1920). *Human efficiency and levels of intelligence* [Lewis Clark Vanuxem Memorial Foundation annual lecture]. Princeton, NJ: Princeton University Press.

Goldsmith, S., & Meyer, R. (2006). *Pre-K: Shaping the system that shapes children* (Civic Bulletin No. 42). New York: Manhattan Institute. Retrieved April 14, 2008, from http://www.manhattan-institute.org/html/cb_42.htm.

Gonzalez, J. (2008, May 21). Bronx 8th-graders boycott practice exam but teacher may get ax. *New York Daily News.* Retrieved May 6, 2009, from http://www.nydailynews.com/ny_local/education/2008/05/21/2008-05-21_bronx_8thgraders_boycott_practice_exam_b-1.html.

Good, R. H., III, Cummings, K. D., & Baker, D. L. (2004). *Indicadores dinámicos del éxito en la lectura (IDEL)* [mCLASS]. Brooklyn, NY: Wireless Generation. Retrieved August 1, 2008, from http://www.wirelessgeneration .com/solutions/mclass-dibels.html.

Good, R. H., III, Kaminski, R. A., Moats, L. C., Smith, D., & Dill, S. (2002). *Dynamic indicators of basic early literacy skills, 6th ed.* (DIBELS). Longmont, CO: Sopris West.

Gordon, M. (2007, August 19). Iowa's rigid rule keeps kids from kindergarten. *The Des Moines Register.* Retrieved August 22, 2007, from http://www.desmoinsregister.com.

Gould, S. J. (1996). *The mismeasure of man.* New York: Norton.

Government Accountability Office (GAO). (2005, May). *Head Start: Further development could allow results of new test to be used for decision making* (Congressional Report GAO-05-343). Washington, DC: Author. Retrieved August 15, 2005, from http://www.gao.gov/.

Graham, P. A. (1966). Joseph Mayer Rice as a founder of the progressive education movement. *Journal of Educational Measurement, 3*(2), 129–133.

Graham, T., & Kutsick, K. (2005). Boehm test of basic concepts-Preschool, 3rd ed. [Review]. In R. A. Spies & B. S. Plake (Eds.), *The sixteenth mental measurements yearbook* [Electronic version]. Retrieved February 13, 2008, from the Buros Institute's Test Reviews Online Web site: http://www.unl.edu/buros/.

Graham, T., & Ward, S. B. (2005). STAR early literacy(r) [Review]. In R. A. Spies & B. S. Plake (Eds.), *The sixteenth mental measurements yearbook* [Electronic version]. Retrieved February 13, 2008, from the Buros Institute's Test Reviews Online Web site: http://www.unl.edu/buros/.

Graue, M. E., Kroeger, J., & Brown, C. (2003). The gift of time: Enactments of developmental thought in early childhood practice. *Early Childhood Research & Practice, 5*(1). Retrieved May 20, 2009, from http://ecrp.uiuc.edu/v5n1/graue.html.

Green, J. P. (2008, July 13). Pro-con on social promotion: No holding back: All we need to do is follow the law. *The Atlanta Journal-Constitution.* Retrieved August 7, 2008, from http://www.ajc.com/search/content/opinion/stories/2008/07/13/retention.html.

Gross et al. v. Lopez et al., 419, U.S. § 565 (1975). Ch. 11

Grossman, K. N. (2006, July 26). Law opens free preschool to middle class. *Chicago Sun-Times.* Retrieved July 28, 2006, from http://www.highbeam.com/doc/1P2-1631603.html.

Guber, P. (Producer), & Levinson, B. (Director). (1988). *Rain man* [Motion picture]. United States: Metro-Goldwyn-Mayer.

Gulliksen, H. (1950). *Theory of mental tests.* New York: John Wiley.

Guskey, T. R. (2002). *How's my kid doing? A parent's guide to grades, marks, and report cards.* San Francisco: Jossey-Bass.

Guttman, L. (1944). A basis for scaling qualitative data. *American Sociological Review, 9,* 139–150.

Hall, G. S. (1904). *Adolescence: Its psychology, anthropology, sociology, sex, crime, religion, and education.* New York: Appleton.

Halpern, D. F. (2006). Assessing gender gaps in learning and academic achievement. In P. A. Alexander & P. H. Winne (Eds.), *Handbook of educational psychology* (pp. 635–654). London:Routledge.

Ham, B. D. (2003). The effects of divorce on the academic achievement of high school seniors. *Journal of Divorce & Remarriage, 38*(3), 167–185.

Hamre, B. K., & Pianta, R. C. (2005). Can instructional and emotional support in the first-grade classroom make a difference for children at risk for school failure? *Child Development, 76*(5), 949–967.

Haney, W. M. (2006, September). *Evidence on education under NCLB (and how Florida boosted NAEP scores and reduced the race gap).* Paper presented at the Hechinger Institute "Broad Seminar for K–12 Reporters." New York: Teachers College Press.

Hanson, T. (2006, August 16). Preschoolers will be judged by kids' tests. *Naples Daily News,* pp. B1–B2.

Hardman, M. L., Drew, C. J., & Egan, M. W. (2008). *Human exceptionality* (9th ed.). Boston: Allyn & Bacon.

Harms, T., Clifford, R. M., & Cryer, D. (1998). *Early childhood environment rating scale, Revised* New York: Teachers College Press.

Harrison, S. (2005, June 28). Midyear promotions: Half flunk FCAT again. *The Miami Herald.* Retrieved June 29, 2005, from http://www.susanohanian.org/atrocity_fetch.php?id=4419.

Hart, B., & Risley, T. R. (1995). *Meaningful differences in the everyday experience of young American children.* Baltimore: Paul H. Brookes

Hart, B., & Risley, T. R. (1999). *The social world of children learning to talk.* Baltimore: Paul H. Brookes.

Hauser, R. M. (2001). Should we end social promotion? Truth and consequences. In G. Orfield & M. Kornhaber (Eds.), *Raising standards or raising barriers? Inequality and high-stakes testing in public education* (pp. 151–178). New York: Century Foundation Press.

Hayden, S. (2008, October 16). Why is learning English so difficult? *Suite 101.* Retrieved May 20, 2009, from http://esllanguageschools.suite101.com/article.cfm/why_is_learning_english_so_difficult.

Heise, D. R. (1970). The semantic differential and attitude research. In G. F. Summers (Ed.), *Attitude measurement* (pp. 235–253). Chicago: Rand McNally.

Hemphill, C. (2006). In kindergarten playtime, a new meaning for "play." *New York Times, 155*(53,652), p. A16.

Henig, R. M. (2008, February 17). Taking play seriously. *New York Times Magazine,* pp. 38-45, 60, 75.

Herrnstein, R. J., & Murray, C. (1994). *The bell curve: Intelligence and class structure in American life.* New York: Simon & Schuster.

Hess, A. K. (2001). Conners' rating scales, Revised [Review]. In B. S. Plake & J. C. Impara (Eds.), *The fourteenth mental measurements yearbook* (pp. 331–337). Lincoln, NE: Buros Institute of Mental Measurements.

Hoff, D. J. (2008, December 19). More schools facing sanctions under NCLB. *Education Week.* Retrieved December 22, 2008, from http://www.edweek.org/login.html?source=http://www.edweek.org/ew/articles/2008/12/18/16ayp.h28.html&destination=http://www.edweek.org/ew/articles/2008/12/18/16ayp.h28.html&levelId=2100

Holbrook, R. G., & Wright, R. J. (2004, February). *Non-curricular factors related to success on high stakes tests.* Paper presented at the annual meeting of the Eastern Educational Research Association, Clearwater, FL.

Holmes, C. T. (2006, Winter). Low test scores and high retention rates: More dropouts. *Kappa Delta Pi Record, 42*(2), 56–58.

Holzman, M. (2005, January 19). Preschoool's effects at 40: The news from Ypsilanti. *Education Week, 24*(19), p. 33.

Horvath, W. J. (2004). *Selected factors related to the success of transfer students into a rural school district from grades six through twelve.* Unpublished doctoral dissertation, Widener University, Chester, PA.

Hu, W. (2007, July 6). Schools move toward following student's yearly progress on tests. *New York Times, 156*(53,997), p. C10.

Hughes, S., & Mirenda, P. (1995). *Denver II* [Review]. In J. C. Conoley & J. C. Impara (Eds.), *The twelfth mental measurements yearbook* (pp. 263–266). Lincoln, NE: Buros Institute of Mental Measurements.

Hulse, C. (2006, May 18). Senate votes to set English as national language. *New York Times.* Retrieved July 7, 2008, from http://www.nytimes.com/2006/05/19/washington/19immig.html?_r=1&oref=slogin.

Hurst, M. D. (2004). Groups link preschool education, economic growth. *Education Week, 24*(10), p. 6.

Illinois Association of Directors of Title I. (2006). *2006 accountability workbook changes.* Springfield, IL: Author. Retrieved March 20, 2007, from http://www.isbe.state.IL.us/nclb/powerpoint/accountability_work06.PPT#302,31.

Information Technology Services. (2007). *Psychomotor domain taxonomy.* University Park: Pennsylvania State University. Retrieved May 3, 2008, from http://tlt.psu.edu/suggestions/research/Psychomotor_Taxonomy.shtml.

Ireton, H. (1992). *Child development inventory.* Minneapolis, MN: Behavior Science Systems.

Jacobson, L. (2004, November 24). Research updates lives of Perry preschoolers. *Education Week, 24*(4), p. 5.

Jacobson, L. (2008a, November 17). Children's lack of playtime seen as troubling health, school issue. *Education Week.* Retrieved December 23, 2008, from http://www.edweek.org/ew/articles/2008/11/17/14play.h28.html?print=1.

Jacobson, L. (2008b, February 13). Full-day kindergarten fees draw critics, legal concerns. *Education Week, 27*(3), pp. 20–21.

Jacobson, L. (2008c, April 30). Parent's role in schools earns fresh respect. *Education Week, 27*(35), p. 16.

Jehlen, A. (2007, April). Testing: How the sausage is made. NEA Today. Retrieved April 15, 2007, from http://www.edweek.org/login.html?source=http://www.edweek.org/ew/articles/2008/04/30/35parent.h27.html&destination=http://www.edweek.org/ew/articles/2008/04/30/35parent.h27.html&levelId=2100.

Jencks, C., & Phillips, M. (1998). *The Black-White test score gap.* Washington, DC: Brookings Institution.

Jennings, K. E. (2003). Test review of the Brown attention-deficit disorder scales for children and adolescents. In B. S. Plake & J. C. Impara (Eds.), *The fifteenth mental measurements yearbook* [Electronic version]. Retrieved June 29, 2005, from the Buros Institute's Test Reviews Online Web site: http://www.unl.edu/buros/.

Jennings, K. E. (2005). Test review of the Process Assessment of the Learner, 2nd ed. [Review]. In R. A. Spies & B. S. Plake (Eds.), *The sixteenth mental measurements yearbook* [Electronic version]. Retrieved July 2, 2005, from the Buros Institute's Test Reviews Online Web site: http://www.unl.edu/buros/.

Jensen, A. R. (1998). The g factor: The science of mental ability. (Human evolution, behavior, and intelligence). Santa Barbara, CA: Praeger.

Jeynes, W. H. (2006). Standardized tests and Froebel's original kindergarten model. *Teachers College Record, 108*(10), 1937–1959.

Johnson, L. B. (1966). *Public papers of the presidents of the United States: Book 1. 1965.* Washington, DC: U.S. Government Printing Office.

Joint Committee on Testing Practices. (2005). Code of fair testing practices in education. *Educational Measurement: Issues and Practice, 24*(1), 23–27.

Jones, E., & Cooper, R. M. (2006). *Playing to get smart.* New York: Teachers College Press.

Jones, E., & Reynolds, G. (1992). *The play's the thing.* New York: Teachers College Press.

Jowers, K. (2008, June 27). Elmo and friends to visit children at bases. *Navy Times.* Retrieved July 22, 2008, from http://www.navytimes.com/news/2008/06/military_sesamestreet_tour_062608w/.

Kaase, K., & Dulaney, C. (2005, May). *The impact of mobility on educational achievement: A review of the literature.* Raleigh, NC: Wake County Public Schools, Research Watch. Retrieved November 29, 2006, from http://www.wcpss.net/evaluation-research/reports/2005/0439mobility_review.pdf.

Kaczor, B. (2008, April 7). State disciplines teachers who cheat on FCATs. *South Florida Sun-Sentinel.* Retrieved April 10, 2008, from http://www.usatoday.com/travel/cruises/item.aspx?type=quote"e_id=01gI4dbe1M1ZL&tid=01G16hCfSCaFM&pn=1&aid=07Ux9xobrC3lT.

Kamerman, S. B. (2005). Early childhood education and care in advanced industrial countries: Current policy and program trends. *Phi Delta Kappan, 87*(3), 193–195.

Katsiyannis, A., & Herbst, M. (2004). Punitive damages in special education. *Journal of Disability Studies, 15*(1), 9–11.

Kaufman, A. S., & Kaufman, N. L. (2004a). *Kaufman assessment battery for children, 2nd ed.* Bloomington, MN: Pearson Assessment.

Kaufman, A. S., & Kaufman, N. L. (2004b). *Kaufman brief intelligence test, 2nd ed.* Bloomington, MN: Pearson Assessment.

Katz, L. G. (2000). *Academic redshirting and young children.* Champaign, IL: ERIC Clearinghouse on Elementary and Early Childhood Education. Retrieved September 7, 2006, from http://www.kidsource.com/education/red.shirting.html.

Keen, C. (1998). UF study: Delinquency risk no greater in families with stepparents. *University of Florida News.* Retrieved June 17, 2009, from http://news.ufl.edu/1998/11/04/steps/.

Keller, H. R. (2001). Early childhood attention deficit disorders evaluation scale [Review]. In B. S. Plake & J. C. Impara (Eds.), *The fourteenth mental measurements yearbook* (pp. 442–446). Lincoln, NE: Buros Institute of Mental Measurements.

Keller, M. (2006, July 5). Academic redshirting is getting a mixed report card. *Los Angles Times,* p. B3.

Kelly, K. (1999, January/February). Retention vs. social promotion: Schools search for alternatives. *Harvard Education Letter.* Retrieved August 7, 2008, from http://www.edletter.org/past/issues/1999-jf/retention.shtml.

Kilpatrick, J., Swafford, J., & Findell, B. (2001). *Adding it up: Helping children learn mathematics.* Washington, DC: National Academy Press.

Kimmel, E., & Paget, K. D. (2001). Early screening inventory, Revised [Review]. In B. S. Plake & J. C. Impara (Eds.), *The fourteenth mental measurements yearbook* (pp. 450–453). Lincoln, NE: Buros Institute of Mental Measurements.

Kindergarten Readiness Issues Group, Partners in Research Forum. (2003). *North Carolina early grade retention in the age of accountability.* Chapel Hill: The University of North Carolina, FPG Child Development Institute.

Kingore, B. (2008). *Developing portfolios for authentic assessment, preK–3: Guiding potential in young learners.* Thousand Oaks, CA: Corwin Press.

Kingston, D. (2005, May). Teaching matters straight across the board. *Teaching Matters: Newsletter,* St. John, Canada: University of New Brunswick.

Kirnan, J. P., & Crespo, D. (1998). Child development inventory [Review]. In J. C. Impara & B. S. Plake (Eds.), *The thirteenth mental measurements yearbook* (pp. 224–228). Lincoln, NE: Buros Institute of Mental Measurements.

Klein, A. (2007, December 19). Bush signs Head Start with qualms. *Education Week, 27*(16), p. 18.

Klin, A., McPartland, J., & Volkmar, F. R. (2005). Asperger's syndrome. In F. R. Volkmar, R. Paul, A. Klin, & D. J. Cohen (Eds.), *Handbook of autism and pervasive developmental disorders: Vol. 1. Diagnosis, development, neurobiology, and behavior* (3rd ed., pp. 88–126). Hoboken, NJ: John Wiley.

Knight, H. (2005, December 12). Offering incentives boosts attendance and test scores. *San Francisco Chronicle.* Retrieved December 15, 2005, from http://www.sfgate.com.

Knobloch, H., Stevens, F., Malone, A. F., Ellison, P., & Risemburg, H. (1979). The validity of parental reporting of infant development. *Pediatrics, 63*(6), 872–879.

Kranzler, J. (1997). Educational and policy issues related to the use and interpretation of intelligence tests in the schools. *School Psychology Review, 26*(2), 150–166.

Krathwohl, D. R., Bloom, B. S., & Masia, B. B. (1964). *Taxonomy of educational objectives: Handbook II. Affective domain.* New York: David McKay.

Kronholz, J. (2005, June 12). Prep courses ready kids for kindergarten. *Pittsburgh Post-Gazette.* Retrieved August 19, 2005, from http://www.post-gazatte.com/pg/pp/05193/536696.stm.

Laczko-Kerr, I., & Berliner, D. C. (2002).The effectiveness of "Teach for America" and other under-certified teachers on student academic achievement: A case of harmful public policy. *Education Policy Archives, 10*(37). Retrieved July 9, 2005, from http://epaa.asu.edu/epaa/v10n37/.

Lamb, M. E. (Ed.). (2003). *The role of the father in child development* (4th ed.). Hoboken, NJ: John Wiley.

Larsson, H. J., Eaton, W. W., Madsen, K. M., Vestergaard, M., Olsen, A. V., Agerbo, E., et al. (2005). Risk factors for autism: Perinatal factors, parental psychiatric history, and socioeconomic status. *American Journal of Epidemiology, 161*(10), 916–925.

Law, J. G., Jr. (2001). Scales for diagnosing attention-deficit-hyperactivity disorder [Review]. In B. S. Plake & J. C. Impara (Eds.), *The fifteenth mental measurements yearbook* [Electronic version]. Retrieved June 29, 2005, from the Buros Institute's Test Reviews Online Web site: http://www.unl.edu/buros/.

Lee, V. E., Burkam, D. T., Ready, D. D., Honigman, J., & Meisels, S. J. (2006). Full-day versus half-day kindergarten: In which program do children learn more? *American Journal of Education, 112*(2), 163–208.

Leland, J. (2008, November 2). Coming full circle. *New York Times,* pp. EL32, EL33.

Lenneberg, E. H. (1967). *Biological foundations of language.* New York: John Wiley.

Lesisko, L, J., & Wright, R. J. (2009, February 24–27). *An analysis of a rural school district's Pennsylvania System of School Assessment (PSSA): Test data for a consecutive three year period.* Paper presented at the annual meeting of the Eastern Educational Research Association, Sarasota, FL.

Leslie, M. (2000, July/August). The vexing legacy of Lewis Terman. *Stanford Magazine.* Retrieved January 30, 2005, from http://www.stanfordalumni.org/news/magazine/2000/julaug/articles/terman.html.

Levitt, S. D., & Dubner, S. J. (2005). *Freakonomics.* New York: HarperCollins.

Lichtenstein, R. (2002). Learning disabilities criteria: Recommendations for change in IDEA reauthorization. *NASP Communiqué, 30*(6). Retrieved July 15, 2004, from http://www.nasponline.org/advocacy/NASP_IDEA.aspx.

Lin, W. V. (2001). *Parenting beliefs regarding young children perceived as having or not having inattention and/or hyperactivity-impulsivity behaviors.* Unpublished doctoral dissertation, University of South Dakota, Vermillion. (ProQuest No. AAT 3007070)

Linder, T. W. (1993). *Transdisciplinary play-based assessment.* Baltimore: Paul H. Brooks.

Linn, R. L. (2007, April). *Approaches to educational accountability.* Paper presented at the annual meeting of the National Council on Measurement in Education, Chicago, IL.

Linn, R. L., & Gronlund, N. (2000). *Measurement and assessment in teaching* (8th ed.). San Francisco: Prentice Hall.

Linn, R. L., & Miller, M. D. (2005). *Measurement and assessment in teaching* (9th ed.). Upper Saddle River, NJ: Prentice Hall.

Lipton, E. S., & Barboza, D. (2007, June 19). As more toys are recalled, trail ends in China. *New York Times.* Retrieved February 25, 2008, from http://www.nytimes.com/2007/06/19/business/worldbusiness/19toys.html?_r=1&oref=slogin.

Lloyd, C. (2005, March 27). How much is a school worth? Parents add test scores into home-purchase equations. *San Francisco Chronicle.* Retrieved July 15, 2005, from http://sfgate.com.

LoCasale-Crouch, J., Mashburn, A. J., Downer, J. T., & Pianta, R. C. (2008). Pre-kindergarten teachers' use of transition practices and children's adjustment to kindergarten. *Early Childhood Research Quarterly, 23*(1), 124–139.

Lockwood, J. R., McCaffrey, D. F., Hamilton, L. S., Stecher, B., Vi-Nhuan, L., & Martinez, J. F. (2007). The sensitivity of value-added teacher effect estimates to different mathematics achievement tests. *Journal of Educational Measurement, 44*(1), 47–67.

Lopez, E. J., & Flores, J. P. (2005). Hispanic preschool children: What about assessment and intervention? *Young Children, 60*(6), 48–54.

Lou, L. (2007, March 28). District considers "grade bump" incentives for students who do well on state tests. *San Diego Union Tribune.* Retrieved June 26, 2007, from http://www.signonsandiego.com/uniontrib/20070328/news_1mi28smgrade.html.

Louvouezo, C. (2008). *As schools spend more time on reading and math, magnitude of curriculum-narrowing effect revealed.* Washington, DC: Center on Educational Policy. Retrieved August 4, 2008, from http://www.cep-dc.org/document/docWindow.cfm?fuseaction=document.viewDocument&documentid=234&documentFormatId=3714.

Lowrey, G. H. (1974). *Growth and development of children.* Chicago: Year Book Medical Publishers.

Lucadamo, K. (2007, September 12). Poor families line up for Bloomberg cash-for-school plan. *New York Daily News.* Retrieved May 8, 2008, from http://www.nydailynews.com/news/2007/09/13/2007-09-13_poor_families_line_up_for_bloomberg_cash-1.html.

Lukin, L. E., & McCabe, P. P. (2005). Wide range achievement test, 4th ed., Early reading assessment [Review]. In R. A. Spies & B. S. Plake (Eds.), *The sixteenth mental measurements yearbook* [Electronic version]. Retrieved July 2, 2005, from the Buros Institute's Test Reviews Online Web site: http://www.unl.edu/buros/.

Lukin, L. E., & McGregor, C. M. (2005). *Metropolitan achievement test, 8th ed.* [Review]. In R. A. Spies & B. S. Plake (Eds.), *The sixteenth mental measurements yearbook* [Electronic version]. Retrieved July 2, 2008, from the Buros Institute's Test Reviews Online Web site: http://www.unl.edu/buros/.

Lynn, D. B. (1997). *Father: His role in child development* (2nd ed.). Monterey, CA: Thomson/Brooks Cole.

Lynn, R. (1994). Sex differences in intelligence and brain size. *Personality and Individual Differences, 17*(2) 257–271.

Lyon, R. L. (1998, April 28). *Overview of reading and literacy initiatives of the Child Development and Behavior branch of the National Institute of Child Health and Human Development, National Institutes of Health* [Report to the House of Representatives, Committee on Labor and Human Resources]. Washington, DC. Retrieved July 1, 2005, from http://www.readbygrade3.com/lyon.htm.

Lyons, K. S. (2007, August 31). Raleigh takes up a global movement to involve fathers more, especially at school. *Christian Science Monitor*. Retrieved September 1, 2007, from http://www.csmonitor.com/2007/0831/p02s01-usgn.htm.

Madle, R. A., & Meikamp, J. (2005). Wechsler intelligence scale for children, 4th ed. [Review]. In R. A. Spies & B. S. Plake (Eds.), *The sixteenth mental measurements yearbook* [Electronic version]. Retrieved December 13, 2007, from the Buros Institute's Test Reviews Online Web site: http://www.unl.edu/buros/.

Manzo, K. K. (2005a, September 28). National clout of DIBELS test draws scrutiny. *Education Week, 25*(5), pp. 1–12.

Manzo, K. K. (2005b, March 16). Social studies losing out to reading, math. *Education Week, 24*(27), pp. 1, 16.

Manzo, K. K., & Klein, A. (2008, July 15). "Reading First" funds headed for extinction. *Education Week*. Retrieved July 24, 2008, from http://www.edweek.org/ew/articles/2008/07/16/43read.h27.html?print=1.

Marchant, G. J., Ordonez-Morales, O., & Paulson, S. E. (2008, August). *Contributions of race, income, and cognitive ability to school level achievement*. Paper presented at the conference of the American Psychological Association, Boston, MA.

Margolis, H., & Free, J. (2001). The consultant's corner: Computerized IEP programs: A guide for educational consultants. *Journal of Educational and Psychological Consultation, 12*(2), 171–178.

Markow, D., & Martin, S. (2005).*The MetLife survey of the American teacher: Transitions and the role of supportive relationships*. New York: Harris Interactive.

Marks, R. (1974). Lewis M. Terman: Individual differences and the construction of social reality. *Educational Theory, 24*(4), 336–355.

Marshall, H. H. (2003, September). Opportunity deferred or opportunity taken? An updated look at delaying kindergarten entry. *Young Children* on the web, beyond the journal. Retrieved February 6, 2008, from http://www.journal.naeyc.org/btj/200309/DelayingKEntry.pdf.

Marshall, T. (2007, February 22). FCAT blessing raises a ruckus. *St. Petersburg Times*. Retrieved May 5, 2007, from http://www.sptimes.com/2007/02/22/Hernando/FCAT_blessing_raises_.shtml.

Marzano, R. J. (2000). *Transforming classroom grading*. Alexandria, VA: Association for Supervision and Curriculum Development.

Mash, E. J., & Dozois, D. J. A. (1996). Child psychopathology: A developmental-systems perspective. In E. J. Mash & R. A. Barkley (Eds.), *Child psychopathology* (pp. 3–62). New York: Guilford.

Mashburn, A. J. (2008). Measures of classroom quality in prekindergarten and children's development of academic, language, and social skills. *Child Development, 79*(3), 732–749.

Massachusetts Department of Education. (2005, April). *Grade retention in Massachusetts public schools 2003–2004*. Malden, MA: Author.

Mather, N., & Woodcock, R. J. (2001). *Examiner's manual: Woodcock-Johnson III tests of achievement*. Rolling Meadows, IL: Riverside Publishing.

Mathews, F. N., & Burns, J. M. (1992). Parent evaluation of a public preschool gifted program. *Roper Review, 15*(2c), 69–72.

Mathis, W. J., Fleming, K., & Lecker, W. C. (2005, March 18). *The NCLB rebellion: Money, politics and student learning*. Paper presented at the annual meeting of the American Education Finance Association, Louisville, KY. Retrieved May 26, 2005, from http://www.rnesu.k12.vt.us/superpub/bill_papers/nclb/The%20NCLB%20Rebellion_%20Money%20Politics%20and%20Student%20Learning05.pdf.

Matus, R. (2007, June 3). FCAT tests us: So what? *St. Petersburg Times*. Retrieved June 2, 2008, from http://www.sptimes.com.

Mawdsley, H. P., & Hauser-Cram, P. (2008, August 14–17). *From early intervention to preschool: Parent's views and children's behaviors*. Paper presented at the annual meeting of the American Psychological Association, Boston, MA.

Maxwell, L. (2008, April 30). Test scores in big-city schools seen to be on upswing. *Education Week, 27*(5), 5.

McAfee, O., & Leong, D. (1994). *Assisting and guiding young children's development and learning*. Boston: Allyn & Bacon.

McCann, D., Barrett, A., Cooper, A., Crumpler, D., Dalen, L., Grimshaw, K., et al. (2007). Food additives and hyperactive behaviour in 3-year-old and 8/9-year-old children in the community: A randomised, double-blinded, placebo-controlled trial. *The Lancet*. Retrieved September 7, 2007, from http://www.ncbi.nlm.nih.gov/pubmed/17825405.

McCarney, S. B., & Johnson, N. W. (1995). *Early childhood attention deficit disorder evaluation scale*. Columbia, MO: Hawthorn Educational Services.

McCarter, R. (1999). *Frank Lloyd Wright: Architect*. London: Phaidon.

McGregor, C. M. (2001). *Neonatal behavioral assessment scale, 3rd ed.* [Review]. In B. S. Plake & J. C. Impara (Eds.), *The fourteenth mental measurements yearbook* (pp. 831–833). Lincoln, NE: Buros Institute of Mental Measurements.

McGrew, K. S. (2003, November 28). *Cattell-Horn-Carroll definition project.*. Retrieved March 7, 2005, from the Institute of Applied Psychometrics at http://www.iapsych.com/chcdef.htm.

McGroder, S. M. (1990, March 29). *Head Start: What do we know about what works?* [Report for the U.S. Department of Health and Human Services]. Retrieved April 27, 2008, from http://aspe.hhs.gov.

McLanahan, S., & Bumpass, L. (1988). Intergenerational consequences of family disruption. *American Journal of Sociology, 94*(1), 130–137.

McLaughlin, B., Blanchard, A. G., Osanai, Y. (1995). *Assessing language development in bilingual preschool children* (Program Information Guide Series No. 22).

Washington, DC: George Washington University, School of Education and Human Development, National Clearinghouse for Bilingual Education.

McLean, M. (1996). Assessment and its importance in early intervention–early childhood special education. In M. McLean, D. B. Bailey, & M. Wolery (Eds.), *Assessing infants and preschoolers with special needs* (2nd ed., pp. 1–22). Englewood Cliffs, NJ: Merrill.

McLean, M., McCormick, K., Bruder, M. B., & Burdg, N. B. (1987). An investigation of the validity and reliability of the Battelle developmental inventory with a population of children younger than 30 months with identified handicapping conditions. *Journal of the Division of Early Childhood, 11*(3), 238–245.

McLean, M., Worley, M., & Bailey, D. B. (2003) *Assessing infants and preschoolers with special needs* (3rd ed.). Upper Saddle River, NJ: Prentice Hall.

McMurray, B. (2007). Defusing the childhood vocabulary explosion. *Science, 3*, 631.

McMurrer, J. (2008). *Instructional time in elementary schools: A closer look at changes for specific subjects.* Washington, DC: Center on Educational Policy. Retrieved August 4, 2008, from http://www.ecs.org/html/Document.asp? chouseid= 7757.

Mechelli, A., Crinion, J. T., Noppeney, U., O'Doherty, J., Ashburner, J., Frackowiak, R. S., & Price, C. J. (2004, October 14). Neurolinguistics: Structural plasticity in the bilingual brain. *Nature, 431*(7010), 757.

Medina, J. (2008, May 5). Next question: Can students be paid to excel? *New York Times.* Retrieved May 8, 2008, from http://www.nytimes.com/2008/03/05/nyregion/05incentive.html.

Meek, L. H. (1929). Foreword. In M. D. Davis, J. Johnson, & A. E. Richardson, *Minimum essentials for nursery school education.* Washington, DC: National Committee on Nursery Schools, Standards Subcommittee.

Meisels, S. J. (2000). On the side of the child: Personal reflections on testing, and early childhood education. *Young Children, 55*, 16-19.

Meisels, S. J. (2007, March 13). *Risk and success in early childhood.* Paper presented at the Kindergarten Transition Summit, Duluth, MN. Retrieved July 2, 2008, from http://www.northlandfdn.org.

Meisels, S. J., & Atkins-Burnett, S. (2004, January). The Head Start National Reporting System: A critique. *Young Children.* Retrieved September 27, 2004, from http://www.journal.naeyc.org/btj/200401/meisels.asp.

Meisels, S. J., Atkins-Burnett, S., Xue, Y., Bickel, D. D., & Son, S. (2003). Creating a system of accountability: The impact of instructional assessment on elementary children's achievement test scores. *Education Policy Analysis Archives, 11*(9). Retrieved July 2, 2008, from http://epaa.asu.edu/epaa/v11n9/.

Meisels, S. J., Marsden, D. B., Wiske, M. S., & Henderson, L. W. (1997). *Early screening inventory-Revised.* Ann Arbor, MI: Rebus.

Meltzer, L. J., Levine, M. D., Palfrey, J. S., Aufseeser, C., & Oberklaid, F. (1981). Evaluation of a multidimensional assessment procedure for preschool children. *Developmental and Behavioral Pediatrics, 2*(3), 67–73.

Mendler, A. N. (2006). *Handling difficult parents: Successful strategies for educators.* Rochester, NY: Discipline Associates.

Menninger, K. (1992). *Number words and number symbols: A cultural history of numbers* (P. Broneer, Trans.). New York: Dover.

Michigan Department of Education. (2001). *What research says about involvement in children's education in relation to academic achievement* [Decision Making Yardstick Report]. Lansing, MI. Retrieved June 12, 2008, from http://www.michigan.gov/documents/Final_Parent_Involvement_Fact_Sheet_14732_7.pdf.

Michigan Department of Education (2008). *Helping children learn to read.* Retrieved August 4, 2008, from http://www.michigan.gov/printerFriendly/0,1687,7-140-5233-23207—,00.html.

Minnesota Parent Teacher Association. (2008). *Our history.* Chicago: Author. Retrieved June 17, 2008, from http://www.mnpta.org/History.html.

Mokken, R. J. (1971). *A theory and procedure of scale analysis with applications in political research.* The Hague: Mouton.

Monastersky, R. (2008). Researchers probe how poverty harms children's brains. *The Chronicle of Higher Education, 54*(25), p. A8.

Monteiro, M. (2008). *Monteiro interview guidelines for diagnosing Asperger's syndrome (MIGDAS): A team-based approach.* Los Angeles: Western Psychological Services.

Montessori, M. (1949). *The absorbent mind.* New York: Dell.

Montgomery, K. K., & Wiley, D. A. (2008). *Building e-portfolios using PowerPoint: A guide for educators* (2nd ed.). Thousand Oaks, CA, Sage.

Moreno, R. (2008). *Description and analysis of the Florida kindergarten readiness screener (FLKRS)* [Report on the accountability measures for the Voluntary Prekindergarten Program in the State of Florida]. West Palm Beach, FL: Palm Beach Community College, Institute for Excellence in Early Care and Education.

Morris, T. (2006). *Social work research methods: Four alternative paradigms.* Thousand Oaks, CA: Sage.

Morrow, E. M., Yoo, S. Y., Flavell, S. W., Kim, T. K., Lin, Y., Hill, R. S., et al. (2008). Identifying Autism loci and genes by tracing recent shared ancestry. *Science, 321*(5886), 218–223.

Mott, S. E. (1987). Concurrent validity of the Battelle developmental inventory for speech and language disordered children. *Psychology in the Schools, 24*, 215–221.

Moyer, L. (2007, September 19). Education costs: The most expensive preschools. *Forbes.* Retrieved December 16, 2007, from http://forbes.com/2007/09/18/education-preschool-kindergarden-biz-cx_lm_0919preschool.html.

Mullen, E. M. (1995). *Mullen scales of early learning: AGS ed.* San Antonio, TX: Pearson Education.

Murphy, G., & Likert, R. (1938). *Public opinion and the individual: A psychological study of student attitudes on public questions with a retest five years later*. New York: Harper.

National Assessment of Educational Progress (NAEP). (2004). *The nation's report card*. Washington, DC: National Center for Education Statistics. Retrieved July 7, 2005, from http://nces.ed.gov/nationsreportcard.

National Association for the Education of Young Children (NAEYC). (2001). *History of NAEYC*. Retrieved January 3, 2008, from http://www.naeyc.org/positionstatements.

National Association for the Education of Young Children (NAEYC). (2002). *Early childhood mathematics: Promoting good beginnings* [Joint position statement with the National Council of Teachers of Mathematics]. Retrieved June 13, 2009, from http://www.naeyc.org/positionstatements.

National Association for the Education of Young Children (NAEYC). (2004). *Where we stand on school readiness*. Retrieved May 20, 2009, from http://www.naeyc.org/positionstatements.

National Association for the Education of Young Children (NAEYC). (2005a). *Where we stand on curriculum, assessment, and program evaluation*. Retrieved February 8, 2008, from http://www.naeyc.org/positionstatements.

National Association for the Education of Young Children (NAEYC). (2005b). *Where we stand on the screening and assessment of young English-language learners*. Retrieved February 8, 2008, from http://www.naeyc.org/positionstatements.

National Association for the Education of Young Children (NAEYC). (2006). *Early childhood workforce: Critical facts in ECE*. Retrieved June 25, 2008, from http://www.naeyc.org/positionstatements.

National Association for the Education of Young Children (NAEYC). (2007). *10 signs of a great preschool*. Retrieved February 6, 2008, from http://208.118.177.216/academy/pdf/IntroducingTORCH.pdf.

National Association for Sick Child Daycare (NASCD). (2000). *About the National Association for Sick Child Daycare*. Retrieved July 18, 2008, from http://www.nascd.com/index.htm.

National Association of Early Childhood Specialists in State Departments of Education (NAEC/SED). (2000). *STILL! Unacceptable trends in kindergarten entry and placement*. Retrieved February 7, 2008, from http://www.eric.ed.gov/ERICDocs/data/ericdocs2sql/content_storage_01/0000019b/80/16/85/d3.pdf.

National Association of School Psychologists. (2003, April 12). *Position statement on student grade retention and social promotion*. Retrieved May 28, 2008, from http://www.nasponline.org/about_nasp/pospaper_graderetent.aspx.

National Center for Educational Statistics. (1998). *Parent involvement in children's education: Efforts by public elementary schools* (NCES Report No. 98032). Retrieved June 10, 2008, from http://nces.ed.gov/surveys/frss/publications/98032/index.asp?sectionID=4.

National Center for Educational Statistics. (2005). *Children's skills and proficiency in reading and mathematics through grade 3* (Table 8-1a). Retrieved June 10, 2008, from http://nces.ed.gov/programs/coe/2005/section2/table.asp?tableID=239.

National Center for Educational Statistics. (2006). *The condition of education 2006* (Indicator No. 25, Grade Retention, NCES No. 2006-071). Washington, DC: Author. Retrieved June 17, 2009, from http://nces.ed.gov/pubs2006/2006071.pdf.

National Center for Educational Statistics. (2007a). *Digest of educational statistics* (Table 47). Washington, DC: Author. Retrieved June 24, 2009, from http://nces.ed.gov/programs/digest/d07/tables/dt07_047.asp.

National Center for Educational Statistics. (2007b). *Preschool: First findings from the third follow-up of the early childhood longitudinal study, birth cohort (ECLS-B)* (NCES No. 2008-025]). Retrieved June 10, 2008, from http://nces.ed.gov/pubs2008/2008025.pdf.

National Center for Educational Statistics. (2008, July 29). *Data file: Common core of data, School district financial survey FY 2006 final*. Retrieved August 8, 2008, from http://nces.ed.gov/pubsearch/pubsinfo.asp?pubid=2008341.

National Center for Health Statistics. (2008). Births, marriages, divorces, and deaths: Provisional data for 2007. *National Vital Statistics Reports, 56*(21). Retrieved July 18, 2008, from http://www.cdc.gov/nchs/data/nvsr/nvsr56/nvsr56_21.htm.

National Governors Association. (2005). *Final report of the NGA task force on school readiness*. Washington, DC: Author. Retrieved January 28, 2005, from http://www.nga.org/cda/files/0501TaskForceReadiness.pdf.

National Institute of Child Health and Human Development, Early Child Care Research Network, & Duncan, G. J. (2003). Modeling the impacts of child care quality on children's preschool cognitive development. *Child Development, 74*, 1454–1475.

National Institute of Mental Health (NIMH). (2007). *Autism spectrum disorders (pervasive developmental disorders)*. Retrieved June 6, 2008, from http://www.nimh.nih.gov/health/publications/autism/index.shtml.

Neal, D., & Schanzenbach, D. W. (2007). *Left behind by design: Proficiency counts and test-based accountability*. Unpublished manuscript, University of Chicago, National Bureau of Economic Research.

Neisworth, J. T., & Bagnato, S. J. (2004). The mismeasure of young children: The authentic assessment alternative. *Infants and Young Children, 17*(3), 198–212.

Newborg, J. (2005). *Battelle developmental inventory, 2nd ed.* Rolling Meadows, IL: Riverside Publishing.

Nichols, S. L., Glass, G. V., & Berliner, D. C. (2006). High-stakes testing and student achievement: Does accountability pressure increase student learning? *Educational Policy Analysis Archives, 14*(1). Retrieved May 26, 2008, from http://epaa.asu.edu/epaa/v14n1/v14n1.pdf.

Northwest Regional Educational Laboratory. (2005). *Focus on effectiveness: Differentiated instruction*. Retrieved July 28, 2008, from http://www.netc.org/focus/challenges/instruction.php.

Office of Innovation and Improvement. (2007). *Choosing a school for your child*. Washington, DC: U.S. Department of Education.

Ohio State Board of Education. (2009, June). *Report on the first year assessment of kindergarten readiness, literacy*. Retrieved May 10, 2006, from http://www.ode.state.oh.us/GD/Templates/Pages?ode/OdeDetail.aspx? page=3&TopicRelationID=778&ContentID=3930&Content=69005

Olsen, D., & Snell, L. (2009, June). *Assessing proposals for preschool and kindergarten: Essential information for parents, taxpayers and policymakers*. [Heritage Foundation Policy Study 344]. Retrieved November 20, 2007, from http://www.ode.state .oh.us/GD/Templates/Pages/ODE/ ODEDetail.aspx?Page=3&TopicRelationID=778& Content=69005.

Osborne, L. (2002). *American normal: The hidden world of Asperger's syndrome*. New York: Copernicus Books.

Osgood, R. L. (2005). *The history of inclusion in the United States*. Washington, DC: Gallaudet University Press.

Pakkala, T. (2006, May 31). Does it pay to reward students for success? *Gainesville Sun*. Retrieved June 5, 2006, from http://www.gainsville.com.

Pardini, P. (2002). The history of special education. *Rethinking Schools Online, 16*(3). Retrieved June 2, 2008, from http://www.rethinkschools.org/archive/16_03/H ist163.shtml.

Parents as Teachers National Center. (2005). *National & international Born to Learn training*. Retrieved June 24, 2009, from http://www.parentsasteachers.org/site/pp.asp?c=ekIRLcMZJxE&b=345885.

Park, K. M., & Leung, F. K. S. (2003). Factors contributing to East Asian students' high achievement in mathematics: The case in Korea. In *TIMSS and comparative studies in mathematics education* (pp. 7–19) [Proceedings of the Second East Asia Regional Conference on Mathematics Education]. Singapore: Association of Mathematics Education.

Patrick, K., & Eichel, L. (2006, June 25). Education tests: Who's minding the scores? *The Philadelphia Inquirer*. Retrieved June 26, 2006, from http://www.accessmylibrary.com/coms2/summary_0286-15732778_ITM.

Paul, P. (2007, November 17). Tutors for toddlers. *Time*. Retrieved November 26, 2007, from http://www.time.com/time/magazine/article/0,9171,1686826,00.html.

Paulson, C. M. (2007). *Half-day vs. full-day kindergarten: Which is the best choice for your child?* Retrieved May, 26, 2009, from the Associated Content Society at http://www.associatedcontent.com/article/138339/halfday_vs_fullday_kindergarten_which.html?singlepage=true&cat=4.

Peisner-Feinberg, E. S., & Maris, C. L. (2005). *Evaluation of the North Carolina More at Four Prekindergarten Program: Year 3 report (July 1, 2003 to June 30, 2004)*. Chapel Hill: University of North Carolina, FPG Child Development Institute.

Pemberton, E. (1933). A technique for measuring the optimum rating scale for opinion measure. *Sociology and Social Research, 17*, 470–472.

Pemberton-Butler, L. (1999). Letter grades are returning to students' report cards. *The Seattle Times*. Retrieved August 11, 2008, from http://community.seattletimes.nwsource.com/archive/?date=19990810&slug=2976514.

Pennsylvania Department of Education. (2007). *Early childhood resources and research*. Retrieved June 30, 2008, from http://www.pde.state.pa.us/early_childhood/cwp/view.asp?q=101706&a=179.

Perez, M., & Ines, Y. (2004). *Validation of the Spanish version of the behavior assessment system for children: Parent rating scale for children (6–11) in Puerto Rico*. Unpublished doctoral dissertation, Temple University, Philadelphia.

Pestalozzi, J. H. (1973). *How Gertrude teaches her children: An attempt to help mothers to teach their own children and an account of the method* (L. E. Holland & F. C. Turner, Trans.). New York: Gordon Press. (Original work published 1894)

Peters, M. (1995). Does brain size matter?: A reply to Rushton and Ankney. *Canadian Journal of Experimental Psychology, 49*(4), 570–576.

Pew Hispanic Center. (2006). *Statistical portrait of Hispanics in the United States, 2006*. Washington, DC: Author. Available at http://pewhispanic.org/factsheets/factsheet.php?FactsheetID=35.

Pew Hispanic Center. (2008). Latinos account for half of U.S. population growth since 2000 [Interactive report]. Retrieved May 20, 2009, from http://pewhispanic.org/states/.

Phye, G. D. (Ed.). (1996). *Handbook of classroom assessment: Learning, achievement, and adjustment*. Burlington, MA: Academic Press.

Piaget, J. (1932). *The moral judgment of the child*. London: Kegan Paul.

Piaget, J. (1952). *The child's conception of number*. London: Routledge and Kegan Paul.

Piaget, J. (1955). *The language and thought of the child*. (M. Gabain, Trans.). New York: Meridian Books.

Piaget, J. (1960). *The child's conception of the world*. (J. Tomlinson & A. Tomlinson, Trans.). Totowa, NJ: Littlefield, Adams.

Piaget, J. (1962). *Play, dreams, and imitation in childhood*. New York: Norton.

Piaget, J. (1965). *The child's conception of number*. London: Routledge.

Piaget, J. (1967). Foreword. In *John Amos Comenius on education*. New York: Teachers College Press.

Piaget, J., & Inhelder, B. (1956). *The child's conception of space*. London: Routledge and Kegan Paul.

Piaget, J., Inhelder, B., & Szeminska, A. (1960). *The child's conception of geometry* (E. A. Lunzer, Trans.). London: Kegan Paul.

Pierangelo, R. (2004). *Special educator's survival guide* (2nd ed.). San Francisco: Josey-Bass.

Pomerantz, E. M., Moorman, E. A., & Litwack, S. D. (2007). The how, whom, and why of parent's involvement in children's academic lives: More is not always better. *Review of Educational Research, 77*(3), 373–410.

Poole, C., Miller, S. A., & Church, E. B. (2004, September). Ages and stages: How children develop self-concept. *Early Childhood Today*. Retrieved May 23, 2008, from http://content.scholastic.com.

Pope, M. L. (2008, May 14). Left behind? None of Alexandria's schools met federal standards for students with disabilities. *Alexandria Gazette Packet*. Retrieved May 19, 2008, from http://www.connectionnewspapers.com/article.asp?article=314842&paper=59&cat=104.

Popham, W. J. (1999). *Classroom assessment: What teachers need to know* (2nd ed.). Boston: Allyn & Bacon.

Popham, W. J. (2000, December). The mismeasurement of educational quality. *The School Administrator* [Web edition]. Retrieved September 21, 2004, from http://www.thefreelibrary.com/The+Mismeasurement+of+Educational+Quality-a077236964.

Preschool Curriculum Evaluation Research Consortium. (2008, July). *Effects of preschool programs on school readiness* Washington, DC: U.S. Department of Education. National Center for Education Research, Institute of Education Sciences.

Pressey, S. L., & Pressey, L. C. (1923). *Introduction to the use of standard tests*. Yonkers-on-Hudson, NY: World Book Co.

Putman, E. (2007, July 11). Penmanship takes a back seat in many elementary schools. *San Diego Union Tribune*. Retrieved July 12, 2007, from http://www.signonsandiego.com/news/education/20070711-1010-spe-backtoschool-cursive.html.

Psychological Corporation. (2002). *Early math diagnostic assessment*. San Antonio, TX: Pearson Assessment.

Psychological Corporation. (2003). *Early reading diagnostic assessment, 2nd ed.* San Antonio, TX: Pearson Assessment.

Qualls, A. L., Hoover, H. D., Dunbar, S. B., & Frisbie, D. A. (2003). *Qualls early learning inventory*. Itasca, IL: Riverside Publishing.

Quintanar, A. P., & Warren, S. R. (2008). Listening to the voices of Latino parent volunteers. *Kappa Delta Pi Record, 44*(3), 119–123.

Raber, S. M., & Frechtling, J. A. (1985). *Special education placement and longitudinal outcomes of preschool and kindergarten-identified handicapped children* (Final report). Rockville, MD: Montgomery County Public Schools, Office of Special Education and Rehabilitative Services. (ERIC Document Reproduction Service No. ED278191)

Reckase, M. D. (1995). Portfolio assessment: A theoretical estimate of score reliability. *Educational Measurement: Issues and Practice, 14*(1), 12–14, 21.

Reeve, J., Deci, E. L., Ryan, R. M. (2004). Self-determination theory: A dialectical framework for understanding sociocultural understanding of student motivation and learning. In T. M. McInerney & S. Van Etten (Eds.), *Big theories revisited* (pp. 31–60). Greenwich, CT: Information Age.

Repp, A. C., Roberts, D. M., Slack, D. J., Repp, C. F., & Berkler, M. S. (1976). A comparison of frequency, interval, and time-sampling methods of data collecting. *Journal of Applied Behavior Analysis, 9*(4), 501–508.

Resnick, L. B. (Ed.). (2004). Teachers matter: Evidence from value-added assessments. *Research Points: Essential Information for Educational Policy, 2*(4) 1–4.

Reynolds, C., & Kamphaus, R. (2004). *Behavior assessment system for children, 2nd ed.* Circle Pines, MN: Pearson Education, American Guidance Service.

Rice, Joseph M. (1893). *The public-school system of the United States*. New York: Century.

Robinson, G. J. (2005). Wide range achievement test, Expanded early reading assessment (WRAT-ERA) [Review]. In R. A. Spies & B. S. Plake (Eds.), *The sixteenth mental measurements yearbook* [Electronic version]. Retrieved July 2, 2005, from the Buros Institute's Test Reviews Online Web site: http://www.unl.edu/buros.

Roderick, M., & Nagaoka, J. (2005). Retention under Chicago's high-stakes testing program: Helpful, harmful, or harmless? *Educational Evaluation and Policy Analysis, 27*(4), 309–340.

Roid, G. H. (2003). *Stanford-Binet intelligence scales, 5th ed.* Rolling Meadows, IL: Riverside Publishing.

Roll-Hansen, N. (2008). Wishful science: The persistence of T. D. Lysenko's agrobiology in the politics of science. *Osiris, 23*(1), 166–188.

Rose, E. (2003). *A mother's job: The history of day care 1890–1960*. New York: Oxford University Press.

Roseberry-McKibbin, C., & Brice, A. (2005). *Acquiring English as a second language: What's "normal," what's not*. Rockville, MD: American Speech-Language-Hearing Association. Retrieved March 30, 2006, from http://www.asha.org/public/speech/development/easl.htm.

Rumberger, R. W., Gándara, P., & Merino, B. (2006, Winter). Where California's English learners attend school and why it matters. *University of California Linguistic Minority Research Institute Newsletter, 15*(2), pp. 1–3.

Rust, F. O. (2003). Counting the cost of caring: Intended and unintended consequences of early childhood policies. In J. P. Isenberg & M. R. Jalongo (Eds.), *Major trends and issues in early childhood education* (2nd ed., pp. 153–163). New York: Teachers College Press.

Ryan, A. G. (1988). Program evaluation within the paradigms. *Science Communication, 10*(1), 25–47.

Ryser, G., & McConnell, K. (2002). *Scales for diagnosing attention deficit/hyperactivity disorder*. Austin, TX: PRO-ED.

Sadker, D., & Zittleman, K. (2004). Test anxiety: Are students failing tests—or are tests failing students? *Phi Delta Kappan, 85*(10), 740–744, 751.

Salvia, J., Yesseldyke, J. E., & Bolt, S. (2007) *Assessment in special and inclusive education*. New York: Houghton Mifflin.

Samuels, C. A. (2008, January 23). "Response to intervention" sparks interest, questions. *Education Week, 22*(20), pp. 1, 13.

Sanders, W. L. (1998). Value-added assessment. *The School Administrator, 11*(3), 24-27.

Sanders, W. L., & Rivers, J. C. (1996). *Cumulative and residual effects of teachers on future student academic achievement* [Research progress report]. Knoxville: University of Tennessee, Value Added Assessment Center.

Sanders, W. L., Saxton, A. M., & Horn, S. P. (1997). The Tennessee value-added assessment system, a quantitative, outcomes-based approach to educational measurement. In J. Millman (Ed.), *Grading teachers, grading schools: Is student achievement a valid evaluation measure?* (pp. 137–162). Thousand Oaks, CA: Corwin Press.

Sattler, J. M., & Dumont, R. (2004). *Assessment of children: WISC-IV and WPPSI-III supplement.* San Diego, CA: Jerome M. Sattler.

Saulny, S. (2006, March 3). In baby boomlet, preschool derby is the fiercest yet. *New York Times.* Retrieved May 4, 2006, from http://www.nytimes.com/2006/03/03/education/03preschool.html.

Save the Children. (2004). *Child poverty in our own backyard.* Westport, CT: Author. Retrieved June 8, 2009, from http://www.savethechildren.org/programs/us-literacy-and-nutrition/facts-and-figures.html.

Scarborough, A. A., Spiker, D., Mallik, S., Hebbeler, K. M., Bailey, D. B., & Simeonsson, R. J. (2004). A national look at children and families entering early intervention. *Exceptional Children, 70*(4), 469–483.

Schendel, D., & Bhasin, T. K. (2008). Birth weight and gestational age characteristics of children with autism, including a comparison with other developmental disabilities. *Pediatrics, 121*(6), 1155–1164.

Schulting, A. (2008, Spring). Promoting parent-school relationships during the transition to kindergarten. *Evaluation Exchange, 14*(1 & 2). Retrieved June 6, 2008, from http://www.gse.harvard.edu/hfrp.

Schultz, T., & Kagan, S. L. (2007). *Taking stock: Assessing and improving early childhood learning and program quality* (Report of the National Early Childhood Accountability Task Force). Philadelphia: Pew Charitable Trusts, Foundation for Child Development. Retrieved June 25, 2008, from http://www.policyforchildren.org/pdf/Task_Force_Report.pdf.

Schumacker, R. E. (2005). *Measuring with a rubber ruler.* Unpublished manuscript, Southern Illinois University, Carbondale.

Schweinhart, L. J. (2008, March 19). Creating the best prekindergartens: Five ingredients for long-term effects and returns on investment. *Education Week, 27*(28), pp. 36, 27.

Schweinhart, L. J., Montie, J., Xiang, Z., Barnett, W. S., Belfield, C. R., & Nores, M. (2005). *Lifetime effects: The HighScope Perry preschool study through age 40.* (Monographs of the HighScope Educational Research Foundation No. 14). Ypsilanti, MI: HighScope Press.

Scriven, M. (2007). The logic and methodologies of checklists. Unpublished manuscript, Western Michigan University, Kalamazoo. Retrieved April 24, 2008, from http://www.wmich.edu/evalctr/checklists/papers/logic_methodology.htm.

Shaw, L. (2008, April 22). Seattle teacher, suspended for refusing to give WASL, calls test "bad for kids." *The Seattle Times,* Retrieved May 6, 2009, from http://seattletimes.nwsource.com/html/education/2004364815_wasl22m.html.

Shellenbarger, 2005, August 18). "No child left behind" poses preschool problems. *Pittsburgh Post-Gazette.* Retrieved August 14, 2006, from http://www.post-gazette.com/pg/05230/555980-298.stm.

Shurkin, J. N. (1992). *Terman's kids: The groundbreaking study of how the gifted grow up.* Boston: Little, Brown.

Siegler, R. S. (1992). The other Alfred Binet. *Developmental Psychology, 28*(2), 179–190.

Sink, C. A., Eppler, C., & Vacca, J. J. (2007). Stanford-Binet intelligence scales for early childhood, 5th ed. [Review]. In K. E. Geisinger, R. A. Spies, J. F. Carlson, & B. S. Plake (Eds.), *The seventeenth mental measurements yearbook* [Electronic version]. Retrieved December 13, 2007, from the Buros Institute's Test Reviews Online Web site: http://www.unl.edu/buros/.

Smallwood, L. M. (1935). *An historical study of examinations and grading systems in early American universities.* New York: Cambridge, University Press.

Smith, L. (2007, August 20). Kindergarten parents shed tears at Boo Hoo breakfast. *Naples Daily News.* Retrieved August 20, 2008, from http://www.naplesnews.com/news/2007/aug/20/kindergarten_parents_shed_tears_bonita_boo_hoo_bre/.

Smith-Arrants, G. (2006, May 1). No more naps in kindergarten. *Charlotte Observer.* Retrieved May 6, 2006, from http://community.learnnc.org/dpi/ee/archives/2006/05/rest_time_in_ki_1.php.

Smrekar, C. E., & Owens, D. E. (2003). It's a way of life for us: High mobility and high achievement in department of defense schools. *Journal of Negro Education.* Retrieved May 27, 2008, from http://findarticles.com/p/articles/mi_qa3626/is_200301/ai_n9186199/print.

Solano-Flores, G. (2008). Who is given tests in what language by whom, when, and where? The need for probabilistic views of language in the testing of English language learners. *Educational Researcher, 37*(4), 189–199.

Spinelli, C. G. (2008). Addressing the issues of cultural and linguistic diversity and assessment: Informal evaluation measures for English language learners. *Reading and Writing Quarterly, 24*(1), 101–118.

Spock, B. (1957). *Baby and child care.* New York: Pocket Books.

Sprenger, M. B. (2008). *Differentiation through learning styles and memory.* Thousand Oaks, CA: Corwin Press.

Stein, O. C. (1972). The comprehensive child development bill and its veto. *American Journal of Pediatric Health, 62*(4), 463–464.

Steinberg, L. (1996). *Beyond the classroom: Why school reform has failed and what parents need to do.* New York: Touchstone.

Steinberg, S., & Kincheloe, J. (2004). *Kinderculture: The corporate construction on childhood.* Boulder, CO: Westview.

Stephens, S. (2006, May 7). Exam proves what teachers know—affluent districts, ready kindergarteners. *Cleveland Plain Dealer*. Retrieved August 22, 2008, from http://oh.aft.org/index.cfm?action=article&articleID=cc3931af-2aa8-4fa2-ba7b-94af5f6e63d4.

Sternberg, R. J. (1999). Intelligence as developing expertise. *Contemporary Educational Psychology, 24*, 359–375.

Sternberg, R. J. (2008). Assessing what matters. *Educational Leadership, 65*(4), 20–26.

Sternberg, R. J., Grigorenko, E. L., & Kidd, K. K. (2005). Intelligence race and genetics. *American Psychologist, 60*(1), 46–59.

Sternberg, R. J., Wagner, R. K., Williams, W. M., & Horvath, J. A. (1995). Testing common sense. *American Psychologist, 50*(11), 912–927.

Stevens, S. S. (1946). On a theory of scales of measurement. *Science, 103*, 677–680.

Stiggins, R. J. (2002). Assessment crisis: The absence of assessment for learning. *Phi Delta Kappan, 83*(10), 758–765.

Stiggins, R. (2007). *Introduction to student-involved assessment for learning* (5th ed.). Upper Saddle River, NJ: Prentice Hall.

Stiggins, R. J., & Bridgeford, N. J. (1985). The ecology of classroom assessment. *Journal of Educational Measurement, 22*(4), 271–286.

Stipek, D. (2005, August). Early childhood education at a crossroads. *Harvard Education Letter*. Retrieved August 13, 2005, from http://www.edletter.org/current/crossroads.shtml.

Stipek, D. (2006, June). Accountability comes to preschool: Can we make it work for young children? *Phi Delta Kappan, 87*(10), 740–747.

Strauss, V. (2006, October 10). The rise of the testing culture: As exam-takers get younger, some say value is overblown. *The Washington Post*, p. A9.

Strauss, V. (2007, May 3). House votes to end test central to GOP's shift on Head Start. *The Washington Post*. Retrieved June 3, 2007, from http://www.washingtonpost.com/wp-dyn/content/article/2007/05/02/AR2007050202650.html?nav=rss_politics.

Stufflebeam, D. L. (1981). A brief introduction to standards for evaluations of educational programs, projects, and materials. *Evaluation News, 2*(2), 141–145.

Sunderman, G. L., & Kim, J. (2005, May 5). *Teacher quality: Equalizing educational opportunities and outcomes*. Cambridge, MA: Harvard University, Civil Rights Project. Retrieved July 12, 2005, from http://www.civilrightsproject.harvard.edu/research/archive.php.

Suzuki, T., & Swuz, D. (Producers), & Sheetz, C. (Director). (2001). *Recess: School's out*. [Motion picture]. United States: Disney.

Terman, L. M. (1916). *The measurement of intelligence: An explanation of and a complete guide for the use of the Stanford revision and extension of the Binet-Simon intelligence scale*. Boston: Houghton Mifflin.

Texas Education Agency. (2006). *Sequences for TPRI assessment*. Retrieved August 5, 2008, from http://www.tpri.org/About/.

Texas Education Agency. (2009). *Technical digest 2007–2008: Appendix B. 2008 scale distributions and statistics by subject area and grade*. Retrieved May 26, 2009, from http://ritter.tea.state.tx.us/student.assessment/resources/techdigest/2008/appendix_b.pdf.

Thies, K. M., & Travers, J. F. (2000). *Human growth and development through the lifespan*. Boston: Jones & Bartlett.

Thompson, C. L., & Cunningham, E. K. (2000). *Retention and social promotion: Research and implications for policy*. Retrieved August 7, 2008, from http://www.eric.ed.gov/ERICDocs/data/ericdocs2sql/content_storage_01/0000019b/80/29/c8/b6.pdf. (ERIC Document Reproduction Service No. ED449241)

Thurstone, L. L. (1927). A law of comparative judgment. *Psychological Review, 3*, 273–286.

Thurstone, L. L. (1938). Primary mental abilities (Psychometric Monograph No. 1). Chicago: University of Chicago Press.

Thurstone, L. L. (1947). Multiple-factor analysis: A development and expansion of the vectors of the mind. Chicago: University of Chicago Press.

Tierney, J. (2004, November 21). When every child is good enough. *New York Times*. Retrieved November 22, 2004, from http://www.nytimes.com/2004/11/21/weekinreview/21tier.html?_r=1&scp=4&sq=&st=nyt.

Tobin, R. M., Hoff, K. E., & Venn, J. (2007). Bayley scales of infant and toddler development, 3rd ed. [Review]. In K. E. Geisinger, R. A. Spies, J. F. Carlson, & B. S. Plake (Eds.), *The seventeenth mental measurements yearbook* [Electronic version]. Retrieved December 13, 2007, from the Buros Institute's Test Reviews Online Web site: http://www.unl.edu/buros/.

Tomlinson, C. A. (2008). Learning to love assessment. *Educational Leadership, 65*(4), 8–13.

Toppo, G. (2007, July 1). How Bush education law has changed our schools. *USA Today*. Retrieved May 5, 2008, from http://www.usatoday.com/news/education/2007-01-07-no-child_x.htm.

Torulf, P. (2008). Performance assessment and authentic assessment: A conceptual analysis of the literature. *Practical Assessment, Research and Evaluation, 13*(4). Retrieved April 22, 2008, from http://pareonline.net/pdf/v13n4.pdf.

Tupper, D. E. (1999). Introduction: Neuropsychological assessment après Luria. *Neuropsychology Review, 9*(2), 1–7.

Uebersax, J. S. (2006). *Likert scales: Dispelling the confusion*. Retrieved April 24, 2008, from http://ourworld.compuserve.com/homepages/jsuebersax/likert.htm.

University of Texas, Health Science Center. (2005). *Tejas LEE*. Houston: Author. Retrieved August 5, 2008, from http://www.tejaslee.org.

U.S. Census Bureau. (2003, October 28). *Speakers of languages other than English at home and English ability by language group: 2000*. Washington, DC: U.S. Department of Commerce. Retrieved May 16, 2009, from http://www.census.gov/prod/2003pubs/c2kbr-29.pdf.

U.S. Census Bureau. (2007a, August 28). *Household income rises, poverty rate declines, number of uninsured up* [Press release]. Washington, DC: U.S. Department of Commerce. Retrieved December 11, 2007, from http://www.census .gov/Press-Release/www/releases/archives/income_ wealth/010583.html.

U.S. Census Bureau, Housing and Household Economic Statistics Division. (2007b). *Three-year-average median household income by state: 2004–2006*. Retrieved May 26, 2009, from http://www.census .gov/hhes/www/income/income06/statemhi3.html.

U.S. Census Bureau. (2008, February 28). *Who's minding the kids? Child care arrangements: Spring 2005, detailed tables*. Washington, DC: U.S. Department of Commerce. Retrieved June 25, 2008, from http://www.census.gov/ population/www/socdemo/child/ppl-2005.html.

U.S. Department of Education, Office of Special Education Programs. (2007). *Data analysis system (DANS)*. Washington, DC: Author. Retrieved June 17, 2009, from https://www.ideadata.org/default.asp.

U.S. Department of Health and Human Services. (2005). *Child maltreatment*. Washington, DC: Administration for Children and Families. Retrieved February 19, 2008, from http://www.childwelfare.gov.

U.S. Department of Health and Human Services. (2007a). Enhancing Head Start communications. *Head Start Bulletin*. Retrieved December 12, 2007, from http:// www.headstartinfo.org/publications/bullet.htm.

U.S. Department of Health and Human Services. (2007b). *Lead toxicity: Where is it found?* Retrieved July 29, 2008, from http://www.atsdr.cdc.gov/csem/lead/pbwhere_found 2.html.

U.S. Department of Health and Human Services, National Child Care Information Center (2006). *Selected state early learning guidelines on the Web*. Washington, DC: Administration for Children and Families. Available at http://www.nccic.org/pubs/goodstart/elgwebsites.html.

Van de Walle, J. A., & Lovin, L. A. (2005). *Teaching student-centered mathematics: Grades K–3*. Needham Heights, MA: Allyn & Bacon.

Van Moorlehem, T. (1998). Home sales, custody fights hinge on exam. *Detroit Free Press*. Retrieved July 15, 2005, from http://nl.newsbank.com/nl-search/we/Archives?s_ site=freep&p_product=FP&p_theme=gannett&p_action= keyword.

Viadero, D. (2006, June 21). Race report's influence felt 40 years later: Legacy of Coleman study was a new view of equity. *Education Week*. Retrieved May 16, 2009, from http://www.coveringeducation.org/docs/keyDocs/EdWeek %202006%20Article%20on%20the%20Coleman%20 Report%20and%20its%20legacy.doc.

Viadero, D. (2007, November 8). No quick fixes to "poverty gap" under NCLB. *Education Week*. Retrieved November 9, 2007, from http://www.edweek.org.

Viadero, D. (2008a, May 7). Scrutiny heightens for "value-added" research methods. *Education Week, 27*(36), pp. 1, 12, 13.

Viadero, D. (2008b, February 27). Students in cash-incentives study score higher in math. *Education Week, 21*(25), p. 6.

Viadero, D. (2009, July 15). 'Value added' gauge of teaching probed. Education Week, 28(36), pp. 1, 13.

Vygotsky, L. S. (1929). The problem of the cultural development of the child. *Journal of Genetic Psychology, 36*, 415–432.

Vygotsky, L. S. (1998). *The collected works of L. S. Vygotsky: Vol. 5. Child psychology* (R. W. Rieber, Ed., & M. J. Hall, Trans.). New York: Springer. (Original work published 1934)

Walkup, J. T. (2006). *Questions and answers about Tourette syndrome*. Bayside, NY: Tourette Syndrome Association.

Wallis, C. (2008, June 20). *No Child Left Behind: Doomed to fail?* Retrieved June 20, 2008, from http:// www.time.com/time/nation/article/0,8599,1812758, 00.html.

Waltman, K. K., & Frisbie, D. A. (1994). Understanding their children's report card grades. *Applied Measurement in Education, 7*(3), 223–240.

Wang, J., & Lin, E. (2005). Comparative studies on U.S. and Chinese mathematics learning and the implications for standards-based mathematics teaching reform. *Educational Researcher, 34*(5), 3–13.

Warner, R. M. (2008). *Applied statistics from bivariate through multivariate techniques*. Thousand Oaks, CA: Sage.

Way, W. D. (2005). *Practical questions in introducing computerized adaptive testing for K12 assessments* (Report No. 05-03). San Antonio, TX: Pearson Assessment. Retrieved August 5, 2008, from http://www .pearsoned.com/RESRPTS_FOR_POSTING/ ASSESSMENT_RESEARCH/AR6.%20PEM%20 Prac%20Questions%20in%20Introl%20Computer% 20Test05_03.pdf.

Wechsler, D. (2002). *Wechsler preschool and primary scale of intelligence, 3rd ed.: Administration and scoring manual*. San Antonio, TX: Psychological Corporation.

Wechsler, D. (2009). *Wechsler individual achievement test, 3rd ed*. San Antonio, TX: Pearson Assessment.

Wechsler, D., Kaplan, E., Fein, D., Kramer, J., Morris, R., & Delis, D. (2003). *Wechsler intelligence scale for children, 4th ed.: Technical and interpretative manual*. San Antonio, TX: Psychological Corporation.

West, J., Meek, A., & Hurst, D. (2000). *Children who enter kindergarten late or repeat kindergarten: Their characteristics and later school performance*, [Report No. 2000-039). Washington, DC: National Center for Educational Statistics.

White, R. W. (1959). Motivation reconsidered: The concept of competence. *Psychological Review, 66*, 297–333.

Whitehead, M. M., & Shaw, S. R. (2005). Early reading diagnostic assessment, 2nd ed. [Review]. In R. A. Spies & B. S. Plake (Eds.), *The sixteenth mental measurements yearbook* [Electronic version]. Retrieved July 2, 2005, from the Buros Institute's Test Reviews Online Web site: http://www.unl.edu/buros.

Wilens, T. E., Faraone, S. V., Biederman, J., Gunawardene, S. (2003). Does stimulant therapy of attention-deficit/hyperactivity disorder beget later substance abuse? A meta-analytic review of the literature. *Pediatrics, 111,* 179–185.

Williams, K. T. (2007). *Expressive vocabulary test, 2nd ed.* Circle Pines, MN: Pearson Assessment.

Wilson, A. (2008, May 14). Teacher refuses to give NC end-of-grade tests: Jackson County educator suspended for protest. *Asheville Citizen-Times.* Retrieved May 6, 2009, from http://www.democraticunderground.com/discuss/duboard.php?az=view_all&address=103x359459.

Winerip, M. (2004, May 28). On education: The changes unwelcome, a model teacher moves on. *New York Times, 154,* p. B7.

Witelson, S. F., Beresh, H., & Kigar, D. L. (2006). Intelligence and brain size in 100 postmortem brains: Sex, laterization and age factors. *Brain, 129,* 386–398.

Wolery, M. (1994). Assessing children with special needs. In M. Worley & J. S. Wilbers (Eds.), *Including children with special needs in early childhood programs* (Research Monograph Vol. 6, pp. 71–96). Washington, DC: National Association for the Education of Young Children.

Wong, D. L., Hockenberry-Eaton, M., Wilson, D., Winkelstein, M. L., & Schwartz, P. (2001). *Wong's essentials of pediatric nursing* (6th ed.). St. Louis, MO: Mosby.

Woodcock, R. W., McGrew, K. S., Mather, N., & Schrank, F. A. (2001). *Woodcock-Johnson tests of cognitive abilities, 3rd ed.* Rolling Meadows, IL: Riverside Publishing.

Woods, M. (2007, March 4). Hey kids, lets make an FCAT deal. *Florida Times-Union.* Retrieved March 21, 2007, from http://www.jacksonville.com/tuonline/stories/030407/woo_8371517.shtml.

Wortham, S. C. (2008). *Assessment in early childhood education, 5th ed.* Upper Saddle River, NJ: Prentice Hall.

Wright, F. L. (1943). *Frank Lloyd Wright: An autobiography.* New York: Duell, Sloan and Pearce.

Wright, J. B. (1979). *The measured academic achievement of two groups of first grade students matched along five variables when one group has been retained.* Unpublished doctoral dissertation, Temple University, Philadelphia.

Wright, R. J. (1975). The affective and cognitive consequences of open education upon middle class elementary students. *American Educational Research Journal, 12*(4), 449–468.

Wright, R. J. (2008). *Educational assessment: Tests and measurement in the age of accountability.* Thousand Oaks, CA: Sage.

Wright, R. J., Martland, J., & Stafford, A. K. (2006). *Early numeracy: Assessment for teaching and intervention.* Thousand Oaks, CA: Paul Chapman.

Wybranski, N. A. M. (1996). *An efficacy study: The influence of early intervention on the subsequent school placements of children with Down syndrome.* Unpublished doctoral dissertation, Widener University, Chester, PA. (ProQuest No. AAT9701172)

Xie, Y., & Goyette, K. (1998, January). *Social mobility and the educational choices of Asian Americans.* Paper presented at the meeting of the International Sociological Association, Taipei, Taiwan.

Zigler, E. F., Marsland, K., & Lord, H. (2009). *The tragedy of childcare in America.* New Haven, CT: Yale University Press.

Zigler, E., & Muenchow, S. (1994). *Head Start: The inside story of America's most successful educational experiment.* New York: Basic Books.

Index

About the Author

Robert J. Wright is a professor of educational psychology who specializes in the study of measurement and assessment of children. This new textbook is drawn from his 30-plus-year career as a teacher, researcher, and mentor. He earned his doctorate in child development and educational psychology from Temple University and went on to further study in school psychology at Lehigh University. As a doctoral student, he also completed an advanced fellowship training program in clinical and rehabilitation psychology at Moss Hospital of the Albert Einstein Medical Center in Philadelphia.

Professor Wright's dissertation was an experimental study of the impact of a humanistic education model. Later in the 1970s he studied Montessori teaching methods and introduced a graduate level educational program in Montessori's methods at Widener University. The St. Nicholas Montessori Society of London certified graduates of this program. In 1980 he was the founder and first director of the University's Child Development Center. Under his leadership the Child Development Center obtained its first state licenses as both a childcare facility and as a private academic preschool and nursery. He hired the first full-time director and served as a board member with the center for ten years. During that time he also served as the resident psychologist for the center. The University's Child Development Center has flourished and has a new building (2008) and now enrolls approximately 75 children between the age of 3 and 6 years.

Professor Wright has also served on test development committees responsible for the writing of new state-mandated teacher licensing examinations, and he has been a reader for the new SAT II Writing Test.

For much of Professor Wright's career, he has mentored doctoral students in the development of their research programs. His scholarship has been focused on testing and assessment and state standards based testing programs. Many of the 100-plus doctoral dissertations he chaired over his career have focused on the impact of instructional methods on the achievement outcome as measured by high-stakes testing.